Digitalizing Talent Management Strategy for Higher Education

Sapheya Aftimos
https://orcid.org/0000-0002-5810-9856
Australian University, Kuwait

IGI Global
Scientific Publishing
Publishing Tomorrow's Research Today

Vice President of Editorial	Melissa Wagner
Director of Acquisitions	Mikaela Felty
Director of Book Development	Jocelynn Hessler
Production Manager	Mike Brehm
Cover Design	Jose Rosado

Published in the United States of America by
IGI Global Scientific Publishing
701 East Chocolate Avenue
Hershey, PA, 17033, USA
Tel: 717-533-8845 | Fax: 717-533-7115
Website: https://www.igi-global.com E-mail: cust@igi-global.com

Library of Congress Cataloging-in-Publication Data

Names: Aftimos, Sapheya, 1991- editor
Title: Digitalizing talent management strategy for higher education / [edited by] Sapheya Aftimos.
Description: Hershey, PA : IGI Global Scientific Publishing, [2027] | Includes bibliographical references and index. | Summary: "This book advances current research by positioning talent management as a strategic pillar of digital transformation in higher education, addressing a gap where digitalization and human capital are often examined separately. By integrating theoretical perspectives, empirical evidence, and applied frameworks, it will deepen understanding of how digital technologies, artificial intelligence, and data-driven systems reshape talent practices, academic roles, and institutional capabilities across diverse contexts"-- Provided by publisher.
Identifiers: LCCN 2026011970 (print) | LCCN 2026011971 (ebook) | ISBN 9798337389592 hardcover | ISBN 9798337389608 paperback | ISBN 9798337389615 ebook
Subjects: LCSH: College personnel management | Universities and colleges--Faculty | College teachers
Classification: LCC LB2331.66 .D55 2026 (print) | LCC LB2331.66 (ebook)
LC record available at https://lccn.loc.gov/2026011970
LC ebook record available at https://lccn.loc.gov/2026011971

British Cataloguing in Publication Data
A Cataloguing in Publication record for this book is available from the British Library.

Table of Contents

Detailed Table of Contents

human-centered management techniques which will lead to the development of both strong, sustainable ecosystems of talent.

Artificial intelligence and data analytics are transforming how higher education institutions attract, develop, and retain talent. HEIs are entering a digital era that extends beyond operational change to encompass deeper cultural and strategic transformation. This chapter proposes a six-pillar framework: strategic alignment, continuous learning, adaptive culture, data capability, ethical governance, and human-centered design. The framework examines transformation across four levels: institutional, HR, academic unit, and individual. It also addresses emerging ethical and governance challenges linked to the increasing reliance on algorithmic decision-making in academia. To achieve sustainability, innovation, and global competitiveness, universities must align technological capabilities with core academic values. The chapter concludes that the future of academic work lies in the productive coexistence of human expertise and intelligent systems, where data-driven insights enhance, rather than replace, the scholarly process.

This chapter examines the transformative role of artificial intelligence (AI) in reshaping higher education through the integration of academic learning and vocational training. It explores how AI supports industry-aligned curricula, adaptive learning environments, and skills-based education that enhance graduate employability and workforce readiness. The chapter also highlights the emergence of intelligent governance systems in higher education institutions, where data-driven decision-making and human–AI collaboration improve institutional performance and talent management. Drawing on governance, socio-technical, and human capital theories, the chapter proposes a comprehensive framework for understanding AI-enabled educational transformation. In addition, it addresses critical challenges related to ethics, algorithmic bias, data privacy, and the need for responsible and sustainable AI governance in higher education

Preface

INTRODUCTION

Higher education is experiencing one of the most significant periods of transformation in its history. Rapid advances in digital technologies, artificial intelligence, automation, analytics, and data-driven decision-making have fundamentally reshaped the ways universities operate, teach, conduct research, and engage with society. While much attention has been devoted to the technological dimensions of this transformation, the long-term success of digital initiatives ultimately depends on an institution's ability to attract, develop, support, and retain talented individuals who can lead and sustain meaningful change. Talent management has therefore emerged as a strategic imperative, serving as the foundation upon which digitally mature and future-ready higher education institutions are built.

Digitalizing Talent Management Strategy for Higher Education has been developed to examine where talent management and digital transformation meet in universities today. Rather than viewing technology and human capital as separate organizational priorities, this volume presents them as complementary forces that together shape institutional resilience, innovation, and sustainable growth. The chapters included in this collection demonstrate that digital transformation extends far beyond technological implementation; it requires strategic investment in people, competencies, leadership, and organizational culture.

The contributions assembled in this volume explore how digital technologies are redefining talent management across multiple dimensions of higher education. Authors examine emerging approaches to digital recruitment, faculty and staff development, competency assessment, leadership, organizational change, academic career pathways, student success, and institutional governance. Collectively, these chapters provide valuable insights into how universities can leverage artificial intelligence, digital platforms, analytics, and innovative learning environments to strengthen workforce capabilities while fostering more agile, inclusive, and future-oriented institutions.

A defining strength of this book is its interdisciplinary perspective. Drawing upon research in higher education, human resource management, educational technology, organizational development, digital innovation, and public policy, the contributors offer both theoretical foundations and evidence-based applications that address the evolving demands placed upon higher education institutions worldwide. The volume presents a balance of conceptual discussions, empirical investigations, systematic reviews, and practical frameworks that together provide a comprehensive understanding of digital talent management strategies across diverse institutional and cultural contexts.

The chapters further highlight the importance of developing digital competencies among faculty, administrators, and students while recognizing that technological advancement must be accompanied by organizational readiness, continuous professional development, ethical leadership, and inclusive institutional policies. As universities respond to evolving labor markets, changing student expectations, and increasing global competition, talent management becomes central to maintaining academic excellence, fostering innovation, and ensuring institutional sustainability.

This volume also contributes to the growing scholarly conversation surrounding digital transformation by addressing an important gap in the literature. Although extensive research has examined digitalization and higher education independently, comparatively fewer studies have explored how talent management functions as a strategic enabler of successful digital transformation. By integrating perspectives from human capital development, digital innovation, leadership, and organizational strategy, the chapters advance new frameworks that encourage researchers and practitioners to view institutional transformation through both technological and human-centered lenses.

The intended audience for this book includes researchers, faculty members, graduate students, university leaders, human resource professionals, educational administrators, policymakers, and institutional planners seeking to better understand the strategic relationship between talent management and digital transformation. Undergraduate and postgraduate students will also find the volume valuable as it provides contemporary perspectives on how digital technologies influence academic careers, institutional effectiveness, learning environments, and workforce development within higher education.

As Editor, I extend my sincere appreciation to all contributing authors whose expertise, dedication, and scholarly rigor have made this volume possible. Their diverse perspectives reflect the global nature of higher education and demonstrate the many innovative approaches institutions are adopting to prepare their workforces for an increasingly digital future. I also express my gratitude to the reviewers for their thoughtful evaluations and constructive recommendations, which have significantly strengthened the quality and impact of the chapters presented in this collection.

It is my hope that *Digitalizing Talent Management Strategy for Higher Education* will serve as both a valuable scholarly resource and a practical guide for advancing research, informing institutional strategy, and supporting evidence-based decision-making. As higher education continues to evolve in response to technological innovation and societal change, placing talent at the center of digital transformation will remain essential for building resilient, inclusive, and sustainable institutions capable of meeting the challenges and opportunities of the future.

ORGANIZATION OF THE BOOK

The opening chapter establishes the foundation for this volume by critically examining the disconnect between higher education institutions' digital transformation ambitions and their actual recruitment practices. Through large-scale analysis of academic job advertisements, the chapter reveals a significant "Hollow Digital" paradox in which institutions promote the vision of the digital university while continuing to recruit talent using frameworks that emphasize traditional academic expectations rather than innovative digital capabilities. This timely contribution challenges institutional leaders to reconsider how recruitment strategies can better reflect authentic digital transformation and align talent acquisition with long-term strategic goals.

If the opening chapter is about identifying talent, Chapter 2 turns to developing it, examining digital information competence as a core element of that work within higher education. Using the DigComp 3.0 framework, the chapter evaluates undergraduate business students' self-perceived digital capabilities and uncovers important disparities between digital confidence and conceptual understanding. The findings reinforce the need for universities to integrate structured digital competency development into institutional talent management strategies, ensuring that future graduates possess not only technical skills but also the knowledge required to thrive in increasingly digital academic and professional environments.

Chapter 3 shifts the discussion toward the changing nature of academic careers in digitally transforming universities. Recognizing that traditional linear career models no longer adequately support emerging academic roles, the authors propose a comprehensive talent management framework designed to accommodate evolving responsibilities in digital pedagogy, research data management, and technology-enabled scholarship. The chapter emphasizes strategic alignment, continuous professional development, and flexible career pathways as essential components of sustainable workforce development within modern higher education institutions.

Chapter 4 widens the lens to the institutional level, examining how digital technologies are reshaping talent management practices across universities. The chapter illustrates how artificial intelligence, human resource information systems, and advanced analytics are enabling universities to adopt more proactive and evidence-based approaches to recruitment, development, and retention. Importantly, it advocates for balancing technological innovation with human-centered management practices to cultivate resilient institutional cultures capable of supporting long-term academic excellence and organizational sustainability.

Chapter 5 stays with artificial intelligence and data analytics, proposing a six-pillar framework for their role in academic talent management. The discussion extends beyond technological implementation to address organizational culture, continuous learning, ethical governance, and strategic alignment across multiple institutional levels. By emphasizing the complementary relationship between human expertise and intelligent systems, this chapter demonstrates how universities can harness data-driven decision-making while preserving the core values that define academic institutions.

Chapter 6 extends the discussion of Artificial Intelligence outward, examining its influence across governance, teaching, and professional training systems. The chapter highlights how intelligent technologies can support adaptive learning, industry-responsive curricula, institutional decision-making, and workforce development while simultaneously addressing important ethical considerations such as algorithmic fairness, privacy, and responsible governance. The through-line is that technological advancement and institutional accountability must be pursued together, not traded off against each other.

Leadership development becomes the central focus of Chapter 7, which positions postgraduate education as a critical environment for cultivating digital leadership competencies. The chapter demonstrates how future organizational leaders must possess the vision and capabilities necessary to guide digital transformation initiatives while fostering innovation, organizational agility, and sustainable technology adoption. Leadership development, on this account, is not separate from talent management but one of its most consequential investments.

Chapter 8 contributes a practical decision-making perspective by presenting a multi-criteria framework for prioritizing digital talent initiatives within universities. Drawing upon evidence from higher education institutions in Türkiye, the authors identify digital infrastructure, learning management systems, faculty development, and competency enhancement as key priorities for successful digital transformation. The framework offers institutional leaders a transparent methodology for aligning strategic investments with organizational needs while recognizing differences in institutional scale and capacity.

Recognizing that faculty members remain central to institutional transformation, Chapter 9 introduces a Digital Competency and Career-Stage Development Model that positions faculty upskilling as a strategic component of talent management. The chapter demonstrates how continuous professional development should extend beyond isolated training initiatives and become fully integrated into recruitment, promotion, performance evaluation, and career progression systems. In doing so, it presents faculty development as a cornerstone of sustainable digital transformation within higher education.

Chapter 10 examines the organizational dimensions of digital transformation by highlighting the interconnected roles of change management and institutional culture. The chapter illustrates how leadership, effective communication, stakeholder engagement, and continuous learning contribute to successful technology adoption while reducing resistance to change. By emphasizing collaborative and innovation-oriented organizational cultures, the authors underscore the importance of creating environments where digital transformation can flourish over the long term.

Chapter 11 introduces a postdigital university maturity framework, reframing digital transformation as a process of capability reconfiguration rather than mere technological expansion. Integrating perspectives from organizational theory, talent analytics, and AI-enabled human resource management, the chapter emphasizes governance, institutional trust, ethical decision-making, and workforce well-being as critical determinants of sustainable transformation. This sophisticated framework highlights the growing importance of balancing technological capability with human-centered institutional design.

The volume concludes with Chapter 12, which provides a practical roadmap for implementing artificial intelligence and big data solutions in talent acquisition. Moving beyond theoretical discussions, the chapter addresses the organizational, technological, and ethical challenges associated with deploying AI-powered recruitment systems. By examining data infrastructure, algorithmic transparency, change management, and integration with existing HR systems, the authors offer valuable guidance for institutions seeking to modernize recruitment practices while maintaining fairness, accountability, and strategic alignment with broader talent management objectives.

Collectively, these chapters demonstrate that successful digital transformation in higher education depends not solely on technological innovation but on the strategic development, management, and empowerment of institutional talent. Together, they provide an integrated body of scholarship that equips researchers, practitioners, and institutional leaders with the conceptual frameworks, empirical evidence, and practical strategies necessary to build agile, digitally capable, and sustainable higher education institutions prepared for the evolving demands of the future.

CONCLUDING REMARKS

The chapters presented in *Digitalizing Talent Management Strategy for Higher Education* collectively demonstrate that the future of higher education depends not only on technological advancement but also on the strategic cultivation of human talent. As universities navigate an increasingly digital landscape, the integration of talent management with digital transformation emerges as a defining factor in achieving institutional resilience, academic excellence, and sustainable innovation. Throughout this volume, the contributors illustrate that successful digital transformation is ultimately a people-centered endeavor—one that requires visionary leadership, adaptive organizational cultures, continuous professional development, ethical governance, and inclusive institutional strategies.

Taken together, the chapters provide a comprehensive examination of how digital technologies, artificial intelligence, data analytics, and emerging digital competencies are reshaping recruitment, faculty development, leadership, academic careers, organizational culture, governance, and institutional decision-making. They demonstrate that technology alone cannot transform higher education; rather, meaningful transformation occurs when institutions intentionally align digital capabilities with strategic talent management practices that empower faculty, staff, administrators, and students alike. By presenting diverse theoretical perspectives, empirical investigations, conceptual frameworks, and practical applications, this volume contributes to a richer understanding of how human capital serves as the catalyst for successful digital transformation.

An important contribution of this collection lies in its recognition that higher education institutions operate within increasingly complex and rapidly evolving environments. The challenges of demographic change, technological disruption, shifting workforce expectations, and global competition require universities to rethink traditional approaches to talent acquisition, career development, performance evaluation, leadership, and organizational learning. The chapters encourage institutional leaders to move beyond reactive approaches toward proactive, evidence-informed talent strategies that foster agility, collaboration, innovation, and lifelong learning across the academic enterprise.

Equally significant is the emphasis placed on responsible digital transformation. Several chapters highlight the ethical considerations surrounding artificial intelligence, algorithmic decision-making, data privacy, transparency, and institutional accountability. These discussions remind readers that technological innovation must always remain grounded in the core values of higher education, ensuring that digital systems enhance rather than diminish academic integrity, equity, trust, and human judgment.

It is my hope that this book will inspire continued scholarship and practical innovation at the intersection of digital transformation and talent management. The ideas presented throughout these chapters offer valuable guidance for researchers seeking new avenues of inquiry, university leaders developing institutional strategies, human resource professionals designing future-ready workforce initiatives, and policymakers shaping the next generation of higher education systems. By placing talent at the center of digital transformation, institutions can better prepare themselves to respond to emerging challenges while creating inclusive, resilient, and globally competitive learning environments.

As the digital evolution of higher education continues, the conversations initiated within this book will remain highly relevant. The future will undoubtedly introduce new technologies, new organizational models, and new expectations for academic institutions. Yet one principle will remain constant: sustainable transformation is achieved not simply through digital innovation, but through investing in the people who drive that innovation. It is my sincere hope that this volume serves as both a scholarly resource and a catalyst for advancing strategic, ethical, and human-centered approaches to talent management that will shape the future of higher education for years to come.

Chapter 1
Topic Modelling the Talent Gap:
Deconstructing the "Digital University" Recruitment Narrative

Richard Nathan Rutter
http://orcid.org/0000-0002-6080-783X
Australian University, Kuwait

Sara Al Shihab
http://orcid.org/0009-0002-0905-0816
Australian University, Kuwait

ABSTRACT

The convergence of demographic decline, financial austerity and technological disruption – known as the 'triple crunch' – has resulted in the emergence of the "Digital University" as the primary strategic response by Higher Education Institutions. This study analyses 9,148 academic job advertisements from US universities (91.5%), and Canada, Australia, New Zealand and the UK to explore four skills dimensions comprised within each job posting: Computational Fluency, Digital Pedagogy, Traditional Scholarship, and Student-Centric Practice, employing Keyword Assisted Topic Models (KeyATM). The results of this study are suggestive of a recruitment paradox described as 'Hollow Digital' in which Computational Fluency appears to exist predominantly within short-term, STEM-focused research posts; in contrast, Digital Pedagogy appears to be defined in terms of administrative competence and not pedagogical innovation. Unless the operational language of hiring reflects the strategic language of transformation, the Digital University will remain a brand rather than an actual entity.

DOI: 10.4018/979-8-3373-8959-2.ch001

1. INTRODUCTION

This chapter will argue that there is a disconnect between the strategic rhetoric and operational reality when it comes to digital transformation at universities. As digital transformation at universities is often defined when considering policy (James et al., 2025; Miao & Holmes, 2023), the data are drawn from the intended, not actual hiring practices of universities.Are universities hiring the Digital Scholars needed to drive digital transformation, or are they hiring for traditional skills while expecting current staff to upskill? While individual job postings may offer a fragmented glimpse of reality, an aggregate computational analysis of the connections between digital skills in the wider higher education sector can decode the intended systemic signals within the labour market. This chapter draws on the Resource-Based View (RBV) of organisations (Barney, 1991) as its theoretical lens, operationalised through a computational topic modelling analysis of academic job postings drawn from five Anglophone countries: the United States, United Kingdom, Canada, Australia and New Zealand.

Higher Education Institutions (HEIs) sit at the intersection of a "perfect storm" of demographic, financial and technological change (Clark et al., 2025; Madgavkar et al., 2025), placing them in a challenging geopolitical environment (Brøgger et al., 2025). In terms of demographic change, a population decrease in developed countries (Grawe, 2018; Madgavkar et al., 2025) combines with decreasing public funding (Pew Charitable Trusts, 2025) and a changing business model for teaching and research. Finally, and perhaps most disruptively, the rapid growth of technologies such as MOOCs, AI, VR and Big Data represents an acceleration of technological change (Chui et al., 2018).

The digital university should be defined not as a sometimes rushed attempt to move the physical classroom into the virtual one, but as a holistic, integrated institution using digital technology to improve its core operations, including data-driven research, automated administration and enhanced physical pedagogy (Johnston et al., 2019). However, strategy is only as good as the people hired to implement it (Wright & McMahan, 1992). Extracting the essence of the University brand, the job advert is an operational proxy of the mission. It is the process of converting a university's priorities into revenue by committing funds to develop and acquire specific skills (Backhaus & Tikoo, 2004; Barney, 1991). If a university is indeed transforming into a Digital University, then that transformation should be detectable in the job descriptions it writes.

The analysis proceeds as follows: Section 2 reviews the literature on digital transformation in HEIs and the academic skills gap; Section 3 presents the RBV theoretical framework; Section 4 details the computational methodology; Sections 5 and 6 present findings and discussion; and Section 7 concludes with recommendations and limitations. Specifically, it addresses the gap in the literature by answering four research questions: *(1) What is the current balance between digital and traditional academic skills in university advertising practices? (2) Are there differential levels of demand for these skills across the academic labour hierarchy, with some roles or grades requiring more digital expertise than others? (3) Does the demand for digital skills vary across academic disciplines, or is digital fluency becoming a transversal requirement? (4) Are there global standards for academic job advertisements, or does demand for skills vary between different national labour markets?*

2. LITERATURE REVIEW

The literature review is organized around the causal chain that motivates this study. Section 2.1 examines the external demographic, financial and geopolitical pressures reshaping the sector. Section 2.2 reviews the strategic response of HEIs through digital transformation. Section 2.3 addresses the academic skills gap that complicates that response, and Section 2.4 considers the role of credential inflation. Section 2.5 establishes the theoretical and empirical case for using job postings as strategic signals, before Section 2.6 identifies the research gap this study addresses.

2.1. Shifting Tide of Higher Education

Universities are facing a 'triple crunch' comprising demographic decline, financial austerity, and technological disruption, compounded by an emerging geopolitical fragmentation of international higher education (Brøgger et al., 2025). Enrolments in colleges and universities in the U.S. reached a maximum of 18 million students in 2010, and have been declining ever since, with a total decline of 15% in the ensuing years (NCES, 2023). Examining demographic trends, Grawe (2018) identified declines in traditional age students to accelerate following 2025, a conclusion confirmed by Clark et al. (2025), as the so-called “demographic cliff” looms (Figure 1.)

Figure 1. The "Melting Glacier": Total US undergraduate enrolment (2010–2025.)
Note: Combined data from National Student Clearinghouse (2024); NCES (2023).

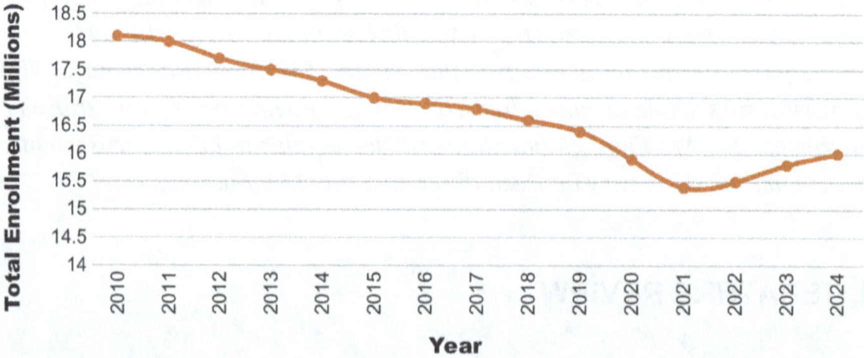

Financially, many HEIs face fiscal uncertainty, as state appropriations continue to decrease (Pew Charitable Trusts, 2019; SHEEO, 2024), while the costs of maintaining their massive physical infrastructure keep increasing, and new investments in digital systems are non-stop. This pattern of structural deficit is evident worldwide (OECD, 2025b). Figure 2 highlights these divergences.

de Wit et al. (2025) and Brøgger et al. (2025) explain that we are reaching the end of the era of seamless internationalisation that the higher education sector has undergone over the past few decades. Given the rising tide of global protectionism, universities are increasingly seen as national assets and the era of internationally mobile students will be increasingly confined to regional blocs (see Figure 3), with the "Big Four" countries having much less market share, a rise of educational hubs in countries not previously thought of as higher educational powerhouses and greater inequality, with a divide between students with and students without access to technology.

Figure 2. The financial scissors: Diverging revenue and cost trajectories in US higher education (2015–2024) (Commonfund Institute, 2025; OECD, 2025b; SHEEO, 2025). Note: Data were normalised to a 2015 baseline (Index = 100) to compare relative growth rates

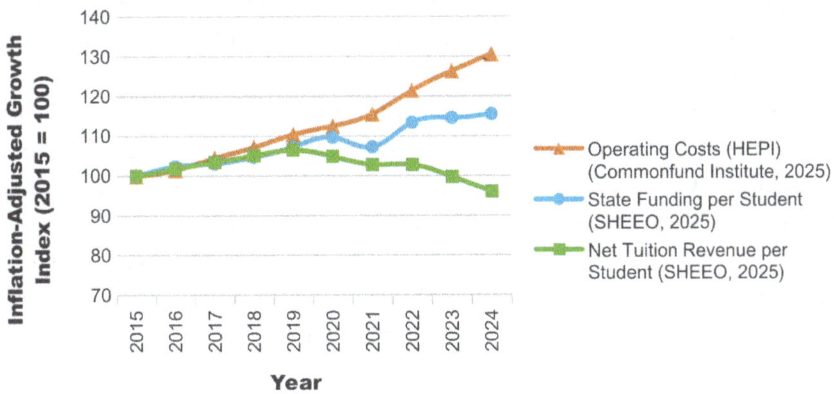

Figure 3. Market share divergence (2000–2030) (IIE, 2025; OECD, 2025a; UNESCO, 2025). Note: Projected numbers for 2030 derived from ICEF Monitor (2025)

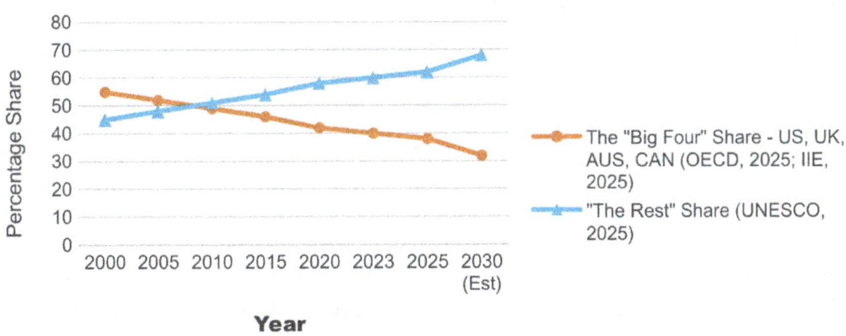

2.2. Digital Transformation Strategies in HEIs

Carmo et al. (2025) argue Digital University is a vital tool which enables universities to withstand external pressures, particularly in highly politically driven and resource restricted HE environments. The Digital University requires universities to disassociate from traditional ways of working and fundamentally change operations throughout all parts of the organisation (Miao & Holmes, 2023), as digitalisation interacts with academic, administrative and strategic functions in a more all-encompassing way than ever before. This has led to further debate around the nature and extent of digitalisation within the HE sector, with Marin (2021) questioning how far and feasibly digitally recreating traditional core pedagogies can be pursued. On the other side, Education 4.0 standards envision universities as intelligent ecosystems where AI, big data and cloud computing will become the norm (Elhussein et al., 2023).

Taking a closer look at educational institutions, a risk exists that the institutions acquire new and familiar technology, for instance AI licenses, cloud systems and high-speed networks, but continue using them in largely the same ways as before. Robert et al. (2025) argue that the "Smart University" vision often leaves behind the faculty members, which might not play the role of data managers and digital curator, but are faced with an immutable condition of digitalisation, perceived as an imposition, not as a professional evolution, which results in a productivity paradox, between declining student enrolments and funds and a significant increase in fixed costs, as investments in digital infrastructure for HEIs have been significant (Carmo et al., 2025).

2.3. The Academic Skills Gap

The clear link between digitalisation and strategic success relies on human capacity to extract maximum advantage, thus there is interplay between the digital and human capital perspectives. In this respect, digitalisation is a tool to reduce marginal costs when processes are automated (Csernoch, 2025) and to combine existing capacities into new revenue recombination (e.g., micro-credentials and lifelong learning) (Salama & Hinton, 2023). This depends on the successful acquisition of human capital, without which a strategy will not succeed (Carmo et al., 2025; Csernoch, 2025).

Faculty members therefore face a 'double disruption' (WEF, 2023). On the one hand, they have to produce and develop computational fluency (e.g. the use of Python as well as artificial intelligence applications for research purposes) and, on the other, they are required to navigate hybrid physical and virtual spaces where the classroom itself is augmented with digital components. The reality is that faculty members often lack the digital competence required to work in this type of learning environment (Redecker & Punie, 2017). This gap in digital competence does not only include lack of AI literacy, but also pedagogical agility in order to use the full capability of AI tools and navigate ethical considerations while creating new assessments that over-rely on traditional modes of assessment (Miao & Holmes, 2023). Figure 4 demonstrates that faculty must integrate digital fluency into both their research activities as well as their teaching activities.

Figure 4. The "double disruption" facing faculty, requiring the integration of Computational Fluency in research and Digital Pedagogy in teaching alongside deep subject matter expertise (Adapted from WEF, 2023)

A gap has formed between how people perceive particular literacy constructs compared to what they actually achieve. The workforce must be prepared for working in Industry 4.0 and 5.0 (coding, data analytics, ethical behaviour, and Human/AI teams); however, faculty hiring and promotion continue to favour the past literacies relevant to academia (i.e., research publications and grants) delaying the inclusion of digital literacy into both curricula and research (HolonIQ, 2024). The moving target nature of digital literacy only serves to complicate matters since the requirement is for ongoing learning and there is currently no formal process in place to reward faculty members for achieving this knowledge as part of their tenure/promotion process (Robert et al., 2025).

2.4 Skills & Credential Inflation

Global demand is rising for professionals with a strong technical background (e.g., a degree in data science or engineering) combined with strong domain expertise (e.g., a degree in medicine, education or business). Fuller and Raman (2017) explain that many jobs require qualifications that are not needed, representing a skill mismatch. Qualifications are also used as a stratification tool (Bone et al., 2025) such as BSc in Data Science, MSc in AI, and PhD in Computational X. This becomes common for roles that are not traditionally recognised as technology dependent, including senior-level teaching positions. Applicants to teaching positions must provide evidence of using technology in their practice alongside their research or pedagogical qualifications (Miao & Holmes, 2023; Robert et al., 2025). Some job advertisements include requirements for higher qualifications compared to previous job postings of the same position, even though the responsibilities remained unchanged, again representing a skill mismatch. Older professionals who did not upskill digitally may find themselves at a disadvantage compared to recent graduates.

This inequality is compounded by uneven access to professional development. Research-intensive universities can recruit staff with strong digital track records, but less-resourced HEIs often face a choice between leaving posts vacant and hiring less-qualified applicants (Robertson et al., 2024). Even where staff are hired with the necessary qualifications, heavy teaching loads and minimal administrative support leave little time or incentive to retrain (HolonIQ, 2024; Robert et al., 2025). Faculty with the resources to engage in lifelong learning develop significant digital capabilities; others struggle to access even basic upskilling. This inequality in digital capability is subsequently reproduced in the labour market, where job advertisements increasingly require competencies that many experienced faculty have never had the opportunity to develop.

2.5. Job Postings as Strategic Signals

To study how organisations actually value their investment in human capital compared to digital technology and skill gaps, researchers need to bypass the institutional rhetoric. From a RBV perspective, job postings represent the more administrative functions of the organisation and should be viewed as a "litmus test" for understanding how well resources are allocated to support the strategic priorities of an organisation (Backhaus & Tikoo, 2004; Barney, 1991).

Figure 5 interprets the job advertisements as an essential "Resource-allocating filter" between strategic intentions and outcomes. For example, a University which has a "Digital First" policy but which continues to advertise positions for which no digital skills are required will produce a very different realised strategy (Mintzberg & Waters, 1985). This can be related to the issue of administrative inertia (Simon, 2013), it might be that HR departments within universities are simply rolling out variations of the same job advertisements they have always used and not taking account of the universities' strategic plans. This filter mechanism is operationalised in the present study through computational analysis of job posting language, as described in Section 4.

Figure 5. A conceptual framework illustrating how the job advertisement acts

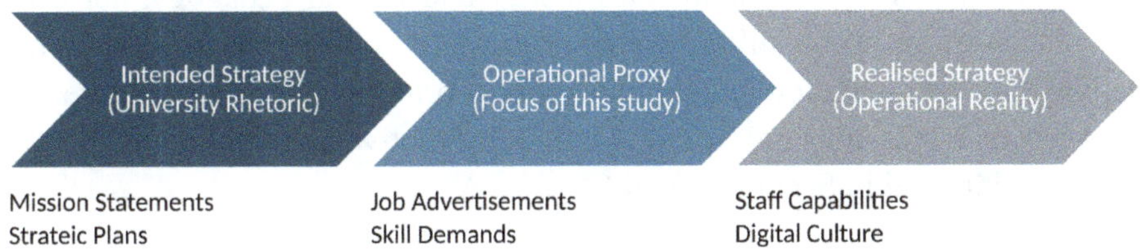

as a resource allocation filter (Adapted from Mintzberg & Waters, 1985; Backhaus & Tikoo, 2004)

Text mining of job advertisements has been established as a surrogate measure of desirable skills and can indicate changes in demand for occupations that precede a lagging reflection in formal classifications or labour markets themselves (Börner et al., 2018). Text mining has been instrumental in the development of skill taxonomies in the IT field, however few applications for academic labour markets exist. This research uses linguistic and semantic content analysis to track the evolving nature of skills and to identify hybrid occupations in the academic labour market that blend traditional academic skills with those of the digital age (Bone et al., 2025). In addition to identifying these new hybrid traits and skill sets, a more nuanced approach must be taken to separate 'Computational Fluency', related to proficiency with computers, computational systems, and the application of analytical techniques, from 'Digital Pedagogy', related to the methods of teaching and learning using digital technology, as well as the continued demands placed upon practitioners of traditional forms of scholarship.

2.6. Summary & Research Gap

The multi-layered crisis affecting higher education (depicted in Figure 6) results from demographic decline and financial austerity (Section 2.1) driving towards Digital University strategies (Section 2.2) while the faculty required to implement those strategies lack many of the digital skills needed (Section 2.3). In addition to the skills gap caused by the digital-economy transition, credential inflation (Section 2.4) is a barrier for experienced faculty who possess the required level of subject field competency but may not possess the required digital competencies.

While digital transformation is stated as a key strategy by universities, it is not clear whether hiring practices within the higher education sector reflect this stated priority. The Resource-Based View (RBV) of organisations explains that, regardless of stated priorities, organisations demonstrate their true priorities through their resource allocation decisions (see Section 2.5). Yet, there have been no systematic analyses of whether and in what ways academic job postings specify dual competency requirements in Computational Fluency and Digital Pedagogy, nor do we know if such requirements differ by type of institution, discipline, or geographical location. This study, therefore, addresses this gap in the research literature. This convergence of pressures provides the empirical motivation for the four research questions addressed in Sections 5 and 6.

Figure 6. Conceptual framework: From multi-layered crisis to research gap

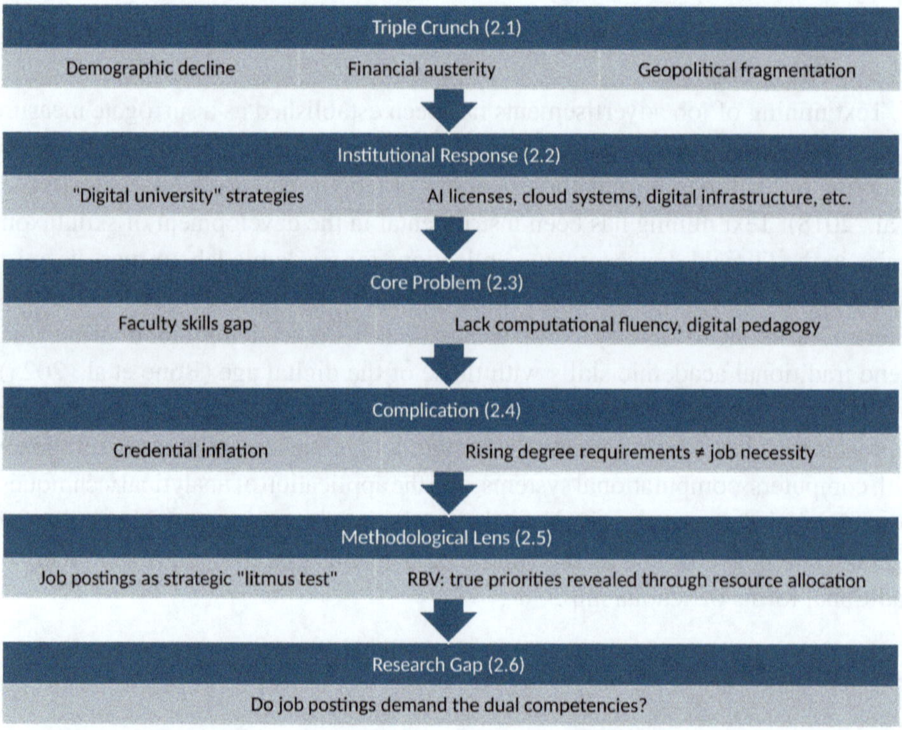

3. THEORETICAL FRAMEWORK

This section establishes the conceptual foundations of the study. Section 3.1 defines the unit of analysis, skills rather than competencies, and Section 3.2 presents the four-dimensional Digital Skills Framework that directly informs the computational methodology in Section 4.

3.1. Unit of Analysis: Competencies vs. Skills

In both the HRM and Education literature, the similar terms of 'ability', 'competence', 'capability', and 'skill' have frequently been utilised to indicate interchangeable rather than distinct constructs (OECD, 2018). However, there are distinct differences.

Capabilities are the assessment of potential future performance whereas abilities are characteristics that have little to no change through training and development, such as the speed at which someone processes cognitive information. Competencies refer to the mobilisation of knowledge, attitude, and skill to manage complex situations (OECD, 2018). For example, the DigCompEdu framework provides a set of competencies to holistically assess educators' digital competence (Redecker & Punie, 2017). Competency, unlike behaviour, is an internal attribute, and so not readily observable. Skills are concrete and are focused on specific activities (Attewell, 1990) -the 'atomic' components of human capital. Employers have an obligation to transform their company's internal need into an external sign of the workforce through a job posting (Backhaus & Tikoo, 2004). It is likely easier and more reliable to communicate specific skills needed in a job posting than abstract competencies. Therefore, it is assumed that skills are a more reliable proxy in this study. Finally, considering the RBV framework used in this research, faculty skill sets represent a tangible organisational resource which can impact university competitiveness.

The diagram presented in Figure 7 represents a hierarchical structure from initial skills to strategic capabilities. Skills, as the observable atomic units of the labour market, therefore form the methodological unit of analysis in this study.

Figure 7. The pyramid of expertise. Progression from innate Ability to strategic Capability. Definitions adapted from: Ability (Armstrong & Taylor, 2023); Skills (Attewell, 1990); Competency (Redecker & Punie, 2017); Capability (Hase & Davis, 1999)

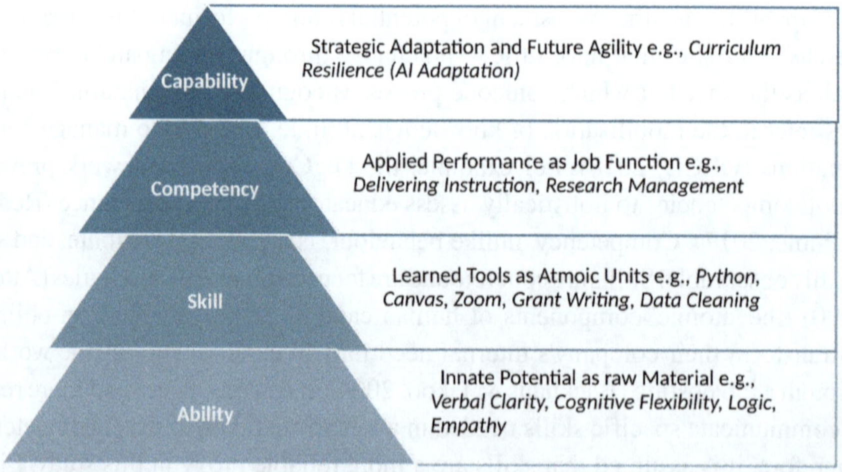

3.2. Digital Skills Framework

To respond to increasing global demand for mobile technology literacy and 'data' literacy, often referred to as (1) 'computational fluency'(WEF, 2023), it is not uncommon for data scientists to be employed by academic faculty to manipulate datasets via programming (HolonIQ, 2024). This is distinct from the (2) 'digital pedagogical' competence adjacent to technical coding. The digital aspect of 'pedagogical competence', as defined by the European Framework for Digital Competence of Educators (DigCompEdu), is related to curating digital resources in a way that empowers students to study in a hybrid learning environment (Redecker & Punie, 2017). Traditional scholarship, such as Boyer's (1990) "Scholarship of Discovery", will remain, and there is still a need for original academic merit through peer-reviewed publication and grants (WEF, 2023) as (3) 'traditional scholarship'. Universities need to increasingly focus on non-automated work, since automation takes over routine cognitive work, other non-routine human work and output become more valued (WEF, 2023). This includes more (4) 'student centric' practices such as socio-emotional mentoring, equitable access and supporting all types of learning styles (Redecker & Punie, 2017). Table 1 operationalises these dimensions through keyword indicators.

These four skill dimensions and their associated keyword indicators form the direct bridge between the theoretical framework and the computational methodology described in Section 4.

Table 1. Theoretical alignment of topic models and seed keywords

Topic	Operational Indicators	Operational Description	Sources
Topic 1: Computational Fluency	python, sql, data, analytics, ai, programming, statistics, modeling, computational, quantitative, machine, algorithm	According to the Future of Jobs Report, the fastest-growing skill will be "AI and Big Data", and it states that the two skills which will drive the core competitiveness of the workforce until 2027 will be "Technological Literacy" and "Analytical Thinking", as determined by the World Economic Forum (WEF, 2023). The manifestation of this is through the technical hard skill of manipulating large datasets and algorithmic models (Python, SQL) for academic research. It also demonstrates the requirement for faculty trained in computational methods to support industry 4.0 in areas such as FinTech or Bioinformatics, which is consistent with the higher education development council (HEDC) framework's definition of high level ICT Proficiency (HolonIQ, 2024).	HolonIQ (2024); WEF (2023)
Topic 2: Digital Pedagogy	lms, canvas, blackboard, moodle, elearning, online, hybrid, zoom, instructional_design, gamification, visualization, multimedia, technology, literacy	According to the European Framework for the Digital Competence of Educators (DigCompEdu), the predominant understanding of digital competence for most faculty does not involve coding but instead is reflected in an educator's ability to take advantage of digital resources to improve their instruction (Redecker & Punie, 2017). This is specifically referencing DigCompEdu Area 2 (Digital Resources) and Area 5 (Empowering Learners). The distinction that HEDC makes between the advanced ICT skills versus the practical competencies needed for the "Course Design" and the "Digital Learning Environments" is further supported by the Higher Education Digital Capability (HEDC) framework (HolonIQ, 2024).	HolonIQ (2024); Redecker and Punie (2017)
Topic 3: Traditional Scholarship	publication, publishing, grant, writing, editing, review, proposal, methodology, dissertation, peer-reviewed, monograph, fellowship	The academic hiring process is still heavily based on the "Scholarship of Discovery," according to Ernest Boyer's definition. In his work, Boyer (1990) described the academic profession as having four functions: discovery, integration, application and teaching, but he pointed out that historically there has been too much emphasis on "Discovery" (that is, the output of research) as an indicator of merit. The concept of "Institutional Isomorphism" has been developed in the contemporary academic literature and suggests that universities continue to place an emphasis on the traditional indicators of legitimacy and prestige (tenure, peer-review publishing and grant funding) when hiring academics (DiMaggio & Powell, 1983). Therefore, Traditional Scholarship serves as a baseline variable for assessing the continuing influence of the "Publish or Perish" paradigm in academic hiring.	Boyer (1990); DiMaggio and Powell (1983)
Topic 4: Student-Centric Practice	mentoring, advising, counselling, facilitation, collaboration, equity, inclusion, diversity, engagement, outreach, leadership, student_success	With more creative jobs becoming automated by machines, human skill sets are gaining higher levels of importance than their automation counterparts. According to the WEF (2023), two of these critical human-centric competencies are "Leadership and Social Influence," as well as "Empathy," which both require a level of cognition that machines cannot replicate. To support this shift toward higher regard for these two skill sets in academia, higher education will already be able to provide evidence through the DigCompEdu competency associated with Area 5 ("Empowering Learners") that is focused on equity, inclusion and mentoring (Redecker & Punie, 2017), as well as Boyer's (1990) notion of "Scholarship of Application," wherein he promoted this change in terms of service, the engaged or community-based aspect of academic labour and the impact that this service and engagement would have on the broader society.	Boyer (1990); Redecker and Punie (2017); WEF (2023)

4. METHODOLOGY

This study utilised a cross-sectional computational content analysis of university job postings to infer how Higher Education Institutions are communicating a need for "Digital University" skill sets. Since those employed must meet the specifications of a job announcement, subsequent job postings can be used as evidence of demand for these capabilities. Rather than indicating (perhaps idealised) priorities, job postings were an observable set of "revealed preference" data from HEIs. The limitations of job postings as proxies for institutional priorities are discussed in the concluding section.

4.1. Data Collection and Curation

We collected electronic university job postings in early January 2026, from the U.S.A., U.K., Canada, Australia and New Zealand. The initial number of job postings included 9,621.

We filtered these job postings to include only faculty, postdocs, researchers, and academic staff. Non-academic job postings (e.g., maintenance, security, food service) as well as administrative jobs incorrectly categorised (e.g., assistant dean or student worker) were removed via automated rule-based filtering. After filtering, the final dataset included 9,148 job postings. The differences among sample sizes (U.S. = 8,371; New Zealand = 10; Australia = 123) reflect the differences in the size of the respective higher education markets. The U.S. has thousands of degree-granting institutions, while the U.K. has about 160; Australia has approximately 43; and New Zealand has approximately 8. This study is best described as an exploration of the US market, with comparative data from four other Anglophone markets, rather than a globally representative sample (91.5% of sample is American).

4.2. Academic Position Classification

Job titles do not have a standardised title across nations; therefore, we placed all jobs into six functional buckets so that we could compare each country. For example, a US Lecturer is an instructor but a UK Lecturer is equivalent to a US Assistant Professor. Therefore, the UK job would be placed as Tenure Track while the US job would be classified as Instructor. In some cases, titles are ambiguous (e.g., Visiting Assistant Professor). A hierarchy of title priorities included: Leadership > Research Post > Tenure > Instructor > Other Faculty > Admin. A full explanation is available in Table 2.

Table 2. Role classification buckets

Bucket	Functional Description	Examples & Keywords
Tenure Track	Continuing, research-active faculty	*Assistant/Associate/Full Professor; UK/AU Lecturer/ Senior Lecturer/Reader.*
Instructors	Teaching-focused, often contingent	*Instructor, Adjunct, Sessional; US Lecturer; Visiting Lecturer.*
Leadership	Academic administration and strategy	*Dean, Provost, Vice-Chancellor, Department Chair, Head of School.*
Research-Post	Early-career research focus	*Postdoc, Research Fellow, Research Associate, Research Scientist.*
Other Faculty	Non-ranked or clinical academic roles	*Professor of Practice, Clinical Faculty, Artist-in-Residence, Visiting Scholar.*
Administrative	Professional staff and support	*Instructional Designer, Learning Technologist, Program Manager, Registrar.*

To establish the classification, 457 advertisements (~5% of corpus) were selected for a stratified random sample for manual review which was done in all job buckets and major disciplines. Both coders independently compared the classification done by text comparing it to the functional descriptions. Agreement between raters: 94.3% (Cohen's $\kappa = 0.92$), which indicates that reliability is high. Some disagreements occurred; the final error rate was 2.8% (13 ads). Most of the errors were due to very specific cases, e.g., Visiting Assistant Professor roles were classified as Instructors when they should have been classified as Tenure Track. Any misclassified job postings were manually corrected prior to analysis. Table 3 provides an overview of job postings by country and category.

Table 3. Distribution of job postings by country and category

Country	Ten	Inst	Leader	Res	Oth (Fac)	Staff/ Admin	Total Jobs
USA	3,804 (45.4%)	2,706 (32.3%)	181 (2.2%)	49 (0.6%)	1,345 (16.1%)	286 (3.4%)	**8,371**
Canada	147 (37.6%)	129 (33.0%)	28 (7.2%)	10 (2.6%)	48 (12.3%)	29 (7.4%)	**391**
UK	133 (52.6%)	96 (37.9%)	2 (0.8%)	5 (2.0%)	7 (2.8%)	10 (4.0%)	**253**
Australia	54 (43.9%)	47 (38.2%)	1 (0.8%)	9 (7.3%)	6 (4.9%)	6 (4.9%)	**123**
NZ	9 (90.0%)	1 (10.0%)	0 (0.0%)	0 (0.0%)	0 (0.0%)	0 (0.0%)	**10**
Total	**4,147 (45.3%)**	**2,979 (32.6%)**	**212 (2.3%)**	**73 (0.8%)**	**1,406 (15.4%)**	**331 (3.6%)**	**9,148**

The proportion of Tenure Track + Instructors (core faculty) makes up approximately 70-90% of total vacancies across the US, UK, Canada and Australia. The proportion of teaching-focused Instructor positions amongst total vacancies between the United States (32.3%) and Australia (38.2%) are relatively consistent. The UK has the highest percentage of Tenure Track (52.6%) based on a classification decision that UK Lecturers (permanent and research active) will be considered as Tenure Track for the total number of Tenure Track within the respective countries.

4.3. Disciplinary Classification

To investigate differences in demand for digital skills based on area of study, we classified all job postings by their disciplinary domain. Due to limited precision of marketplace metadata (e.g., "Computer Science" is often classified as General Science), we used a keywords-based rule-based dictionary classification of job titles and department listings to categorise the corpus into the 16 different academic disciplines.

Table 4 has an evident bias to professional/vocational areas of education - the percentages for Education (33.8%) and Medicine & Health (30.4%) clearly show that these two fields constitute the major portion of all positions posted - due to many adjunct faculty and clinical faculty. In contrast, there are few job postings in relation to traditional humanities or hard sciences.

Table 4. Distribution of job postings by discipline

Discipline	Count (*n*)	Share (%)
Education	3,096	33.8%
Medicine & Health	2,777	30.4%
Business & Management	1,023	11.2%
Computer Science & AI	640	7.0%
Biology & Life Sciences	346	3.8%
Environmental & Earth Sciences	313	3.4%
Mathematics & Statistics	270	3.0%
Engineering	215	2.4%
Chemistry & Materials	76	0.8%
Humanities	70	0.8%
Physics	51	0.6%
Law & Policy	50	0.5%
Communication & Media	46	0.5%
Social Sciences	44	0.5%
Arts & Music	36	0.4%

continued on following page

Table 4. Continued

Discipline	Count (*n*)	Share (%)
Other / Unspecified	95	1.0%
Total	**9,148**	**100.0%**

Validation of the rule-based dictionary approach occurred with the same 457 advertisement sample, with a manual review indicating that 91.7% of discipline assignments matched the stated departmental affiliation. The 8.3% discrepancy was mainly due to legitimate interdisciplinary postings (for example, "Biostatistics position in School of Public Health" had both Medicine and Health and Mathematics and Statistics keywords). For these cases, we reported the classification assigned to the advertisement's primary academic unit based on advertisement metadata.

4.4. Text Pre-processing

Data was cleaned so that both noise and sparsity were minimised before topic modelling was conducted. Initially, the text was transformed to lowercase and different non-alphabetic characters such as punctuation and special characters were removed. The next step involved elimination of English stop words (e.g., and, the) and specific HR terms (e.g., "equal opportunity", "apply", or "curriculum vitae"). Next, we broke down the text to word level tokens and retained most frequently occurring bigrams for domain-wise interpretation yet applying single word processing at other places (e.g., "machine learning," "artificial intelligence," higher education"). Stemming and lemmatisation are not performed with a purpose to differentiate job-specific skills which require precise wording from linguistic style variations and keep enough detail in order to represent digital skills.

4.5. Topic Modelling Strategy

We have developed a probabilistic model with two steps for predicting the skill requirements of employees. The first step was to use LDA to investigate underlying topic structures in an unsupervised fashion (Blei et al., 2003). A model of five topics was fitted, and we analysed relationships between the most common words occurring in each topic to classify them based on teaching, research, and technical skills. Unfortunately, most of the content in those five topics consisted of academic/research-based words and general academic teaching words, which were not helpful for identifying adequate digital literacy competence.

The second step was Keyword Assisted Topic Models (KeyATM) as the foundation of the main analysis, to overcome the LDA challenges mentioned (Eshima et al., 2024). KeyATM uses a semi-supervised process allowing researchers to include pre-determined seed keywords or topics into the model prior to analysis. This allows researchers to leverage both their knowledge of the theoretical concepts (i.e., what were the relevant things to study) and the ability of KeyATM to work at scale through computational means. The current research provided four supervised topics based on the initial theoretical model: Student-Centric, Traditional Academic, Digital Pedagogy and Computational Fluency (see Table 5 for example seed words). The model also provided two unsupervised (or latent) topics to account for the noise of the data. Once the model was fitted, we then explored the relative prevalence of each of the six topics (four supervised, two unsupervised) across the entire corpus. Finding that all four of the pre-determined or strategic supervised topics were the only topics that accounted for 78.9% of the content of the entire corpus (see Section 5.2.1); therefore we renormalised the four supervised topics to be equivalent to a 100% within the document (thus eliminating "Other" from all the calculations) allowing for a comparison of the relative proportions of the digital versus the traditional competencies, while minimising the effect of administrative/general terminology.

Table 5. KeyATM topic definitions and seed keywords

Topic	Seed Keywords (Examples)
Student-Centric	teaching, mentoring, student, engagement, pedagogy, advising, inclusion
Traditional Academic	research, publication, scholarship, discipline, peer-reviewed, grant, monograph
Digital Pedagogy	online, e-learning, instructional design, technology, digital, lms, canvas, hybrid
Computational Fluency	data, programming, computational, quantitative, analytics, python, sql, ai

4.6. Comparative Analysis

In order to determine whether the demand for different skills changes depending on the occupation or field, as well as the country the advertisement is in, we completed two different types of analyses. First, we looked at the average proportion of each of the topics across the different job buckets to get an overall idea of the importance of each of the different groups of skills. Secondly, we ran Kruskal-Wallis H tests (Kruskal & Wallis, 1952) to test whether there were statistically significant differences between the different groups for each of the supervised topics. This non-parametric rank-based method (Dunn, 1961) can be used because it does not assume a normal distribution, and remains robust with unequal sample sizes across disciplinary groupings (Table 4). In addition, we reported Bonferroni-adjusted p-values (Dunn, 1961) and η^2 effect sizes (Cohen, 2013). Once we found statistically significant differences, specific pairs of groups that were statistically significantly different were checked using Dunn's post-hoc tests. Finally, to verify results based on the compositional nature of reading proportions (i.e., if one topic increases in proportion to the others decreasing in proportion) we fitted Dirichlet regression models (Maier, 2014). For comparisons between disciplines, we used job bucket as a covariate; for comparisons between countries, we used both discipline and job bucket as covariates when fitting the models. Multivariate analysis ensures that differences observed (i.e., high proportion of computational score achieved in Physics) can be statistically attributed to the discipline itself and not to artifacts created by differences in composition of the roles (i.e., higher number of research only roles in science).

5. ANALYSIS AND FINDINGS

This section presents the results of topic modelling and statistical inferences by job type, country and discipline of skill dimensions.

5.1. Methodological Validation: LDA vs. KeyATM

First, exploratory analysis used LDA to examine the semantic structure of a natural corpus, Table 6. However, the unsupervised results were largely dominated by general academic language that was ubiquitous and cross-loaded on multiple topics (for example, teaching, research, and communication). Strategic competences could not be identified by LDA (e.g., "Digital Pedagogy" vs. "Traditional Scholarship") which instead primarily grouped documents based on general application requirements (letter, curriculum, statement).

Table 6. LDA unsupervised topics and keywords

Topic 1	Topic 2	Topic 3	Topic 4	Topic 5
teaching	teaching	teaching	research	teaching
curriculum	research	research	design	research
management	statement	communication	communication	development
writing	letter	curriculum	management	management
program	development	collaboration	service	learning
diversity	professional	professional	science	diversity
learning	diversity	learning	diversity	program
strong	phd	development	student	cover

continued on following page

Table 6. Continued

Topic 1	Topic 2	Topic 3	Topic 4	Topic 5
masters	communication	supervision	inclusion	communication
leadership	data	leadership	engineering	mentoring

Second, we employed a semi-supervised technique known as KeyATM (Eshima et al., 2024) using our predefined topics and seed words. The results are shown in Table 7. KeyATM is able to separate HR (e.g., insurance, benefits) and clinical language into the "Noise" topics (2 unsupervised topics), ensuring semantic purity of four (supervised) strategic topics: Computational Fluency, Digital Pedagogy, Traditional Academic, and Student-Centric.

Table 7. KeyATM semi-supervised topics and keywords

Computational Fluency	Digital Pedagogy	Traditional Scholarship	Student-Centric Practice	Other 1 (Niche/ Clinical)	Other 2 (HR/ Benefits)
data	microsoft	certification	diversity	certification	insurance
design	leadership	fellowship	curriculum	theatre	benefits
systems	data	writing	inclusion	dentistry	retirement
analysis	time	grant	equity	safety	professional
computer	teamwork	center	professional	instructor	leave
software	problem	equal	social	professional	tuition
analytics	thinking	diversity	studies	bls	paid
machine	solving	services	psychology	interpersonal	vision
information	analysis	internal	collaboration	dds	employee
programming	technology	leadership	leadership	dmd	plans

Third, we calculated mean topic proportions across all 9,148 advertisements to judge strategic dimension dominance. Altogether four strategic topics represent 78.9% of semantic content: Student-Centric Practice (41.4%), Digital Pedagogy (18.8%), Computational Fluency (11.6%), and Traditional Scholarship (7.1%). Two unsupervised Other topics consist of 21.1%: clinical/professional jargon (5.2%) and HR/benefits language (15.8%). The results pre-renormalisation are shown in Table 8 below. High standard deviations reflect that topics are very specialised and not all equally distributed. An example of this would be a posting from a physics department allocating 40% of its effort to Computational Fluency and 0% to Digital Pedagogy while at the same time an instructional designer would assign the opposite in their efforts. This diversity supports that there are dimensions of distinctiveness and job bucket (categories) and discipline are predictive. Additionally, the HR/benefits language (15.8%) is close to Digital Pedagogy (18.8%) and higher than Traditional Research (7.1%) which highlights another point of concern about bureaucratic drift in the signals within organisations (Simon, 2013).

Table 8. Mean topic proportions across all job advertisements (n=9,148) before renormalisation. Standard deviations reflect substantial heterogeneity across job types and disciplines

Topic	Mean %	SD
Computational Fluency	11.6	24.8
Digital Pedagogy	18.8	29.4
Traditional Scholarship	7.1	17.3
Student-Centric	41.4	36.9
Other 1 (Clinical/Niche)	5.2	16.1
Other 2 (HR/Benefits)	15.8	30.9
TOTAL	**99.9**	

Figure 8 presents the model convergence diagnostics, confirming that the KeyATM model reached stability before analysis proceeded. The KeyATM diagnostic indicates the model has stabilised convergence after 1500 iterations. From iteration 1 to 1500, there was an improvement of the Log-Likelihood from -28,882,883 to -24,023,356 and improvement in Perplexity from 8678 to 1887 (78.3% reduction). The curves for both log-likelihood and perplexity increased fast in early iterations and then began to flatten, suggesting model stabilisation. Further iterations will not likely change the fit of the model (see Figure 8).

Figure 8. KeyATM model perplexity and log-likelihood

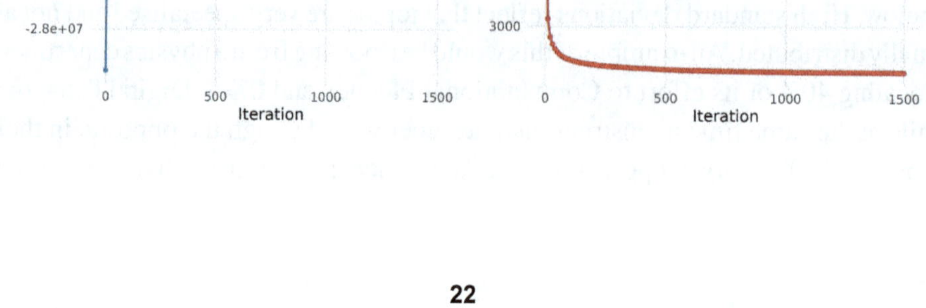

Finally, in order to conduct the comparative analysis of the four strategic topics, we re-normalised all four topics to sum to 100% for each document. In other words, we removed the 21.1% for 'Other' topics - to provide a side-by-side comparison, whilst retaining approximately three-quarters of the overall semantic content.

5.2. Descriptive Analysis of Skill Dimensions

In the second stage, we then ranked the skill frequency of topics, as per topic frequency (see Figure 10). Computational Fluency keywords performed as expected, with Python, data, analytics and AI dominating the topic. Digital Pedagogy, however, the highest ranked terms relate to administration and not to pedagogy. Although baseline administrative competency in being able to navigate a Learning Management System (decentralised), administer digital work flows, and use Microsoft Office are necessary competencies for teaching with technology today; our concern is not simply the presence of these skills but more specifically their prominence over pedagogically innovative skills such as gamification, instructional design, and multimedia storytelling. Our findings indicated that universities continued to emphasise hiring for digital management rather than hiring to aid in digital transformation. While we did seed the model with gamification and instructional design, our model predominantly identified Microsoft, teamwork, time, and leadership as indicators of that competency. This dynamic is the basis for what we refer to as the "Hollow Digital" recruitment paradox.

Figure 9. The "hollow digital" recruitment model

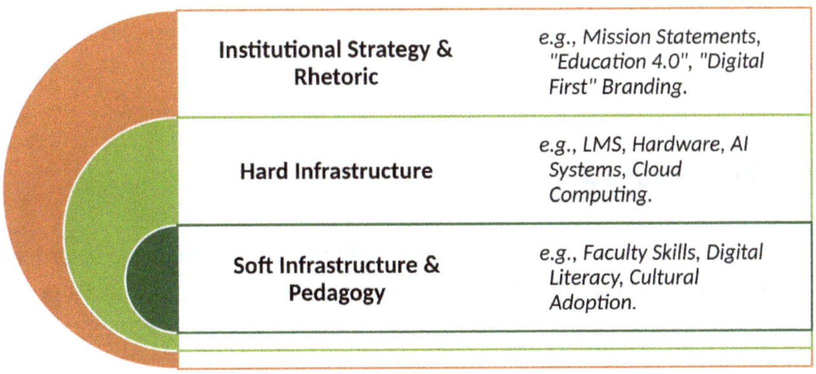

Figure 9 presents a conceptual framework to derive from the research findings; the outer layers (i.e. strategy and hard infrastructure) are well-developed whilst the centre of the framework (i.e. pedagogy and skills) are relatively less developed.

The uppermost layer of the hierarchy has been affected by the time taken to create a plan, as "Digital Learning" has rapidly progressed into being included in the general description of "Workflow Management." Workflow management and Digital Learning are just two of the many examples of a bureaucratic drift away from what was originally intended within Education. At the middle of the hierarchy, due to the absence of Next Generation Technologies (VR, Simulation, and AI Literacy) would be indicative of an innovation gap. The combined data indicates a divergence between the Computational Research wing, which has become specialised in a narrow area, while the Pedagogical wing has hired generalist administrative personnel to assist in the administration of the mechanics of the digital campus instead of providing innovation within that space.

Figure 10. Ranked topic skill frequency per topic (top 1-10)

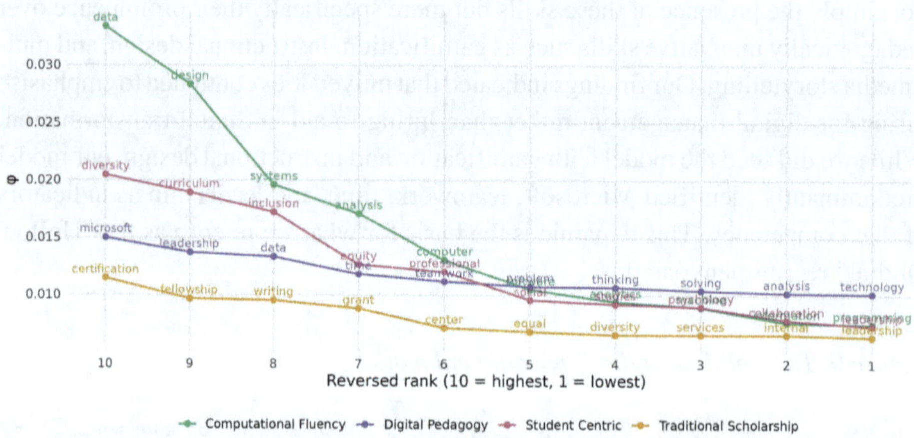

5.3 Labour Classifications

In the third stage, we analysed the postings by position type in order to highlight any division within academic work as per the job advertisement postings (see Figure 11):

1. **Digital Pedagogy:** The average proportion of administrative positions that contained digital pedagogy content was significantly greater ($M=0.506$) than that of research-post positions ($M=0.160$; $H=340.95$, $df=5$, $p<.001$; $\eta^2=0.037$). Thus, it can be concluded that a significantly greater proportion of administrative type postings (i.e., instructional designers, learning technologists) contain content

related to digital teaching infrastructure compared to research type postings. This finding supports the previous interpretation of a "Hollow Digital".

2. **Computational Fluency:** The Research-Post bucket has the highest mean proportion (M=0.281); the Administrative bucket has the lowest mean proportion (M=0.059) and there is a significant difference across the buckets (H=130.390, df=5, $p<.001$, $\eta^2=0.014$). This indicates that there are more computational skills found in the Research Bucket (Data Analysis and Programming) than in the Other Administrative role.
3. **Traditional Academic Skills:** Positions in research had higher means (M=0.236), while positions in administration had much lower means (M=0.054). There was a statistically significant difference between the two types of position (H=102.26, df=5; $p<.001$; $\eta^2=0.011$). This supports the idea that conventional academic skills and publishing output are the most important factor when looking for candidates in research-track positions.
4. **Student-Centric Skills:** The mean ranking of student-centered skills for the tenure-track is significantly greater (M=0.555) than for post-doctoral researcher positions (M=0.324), (H=110.26, df=5, $p<.001$, $\eta^2=0.012$). The language associated with student-centered teaching, advising, and inclusion continues to dominate the tenure-track category, while post-doctoral researchers emphasise technical outcomes over interaction with students.

The dominance of Student-Centric activities (41.4% overall; 55.5% Tenure Track) is notable. This demonstrates that faculty are not replacing traditional forms of scholarship with digital equivalents, but rather maintaining the usual commitments to pastoral and mentoring responsibilities which have characterised the professoriate over time. Although Student-Centric competencies (e.g., advising, empathy, or inclusion) are separate from those associated with Digital Pedagogy (e.g., managing an LMS, creating hybrid course designs), and Traditional Scholarship (e.g., research output), the significant prevalence of Student-Centric activities suggests that universities define faculty work through the lens of relational/ humanistic competencies almost entirely unrelated to the emergence of digital technologies.

Figure 11. KeyATM mean differences by skill topic between each job type

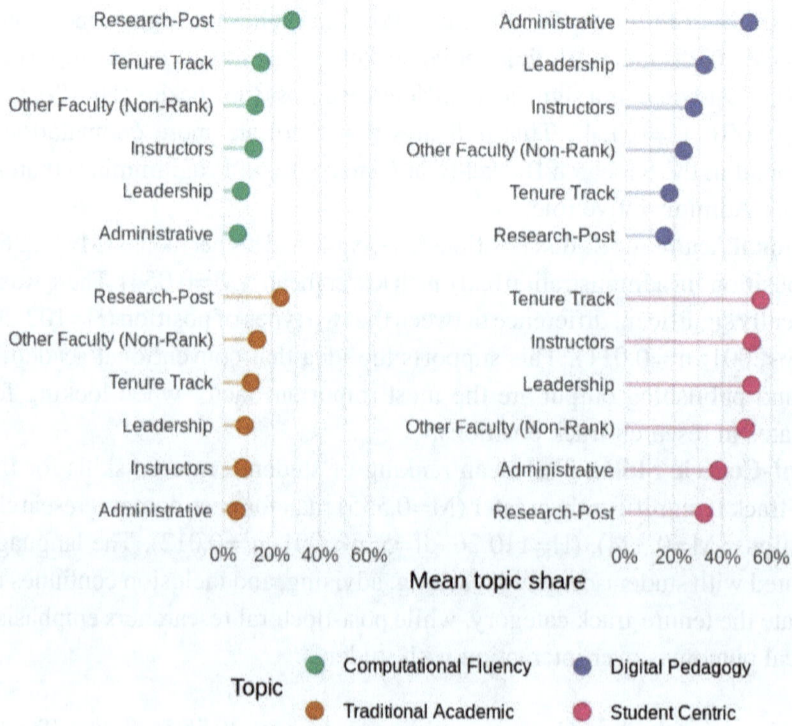

These two modes of decoupling, computational fluency within short-term research posts and digital pedagogy delegated to administrative staff, provide an empirical basis through which we could outline a third phenomenon: the 'Hollow Digital' recruitment paradox.

5.4 Discipline Classifications

In the fourth stage, we investigated how the emphasis placed on skill and/or topic differs by discipline. This was by assigning a dominant topic (the one with the highest probability) to each advertisement and using Pearson's chi-square test for association. By looking at the standardised residuals, we identified what discipline/ topic combinations were causing this association (Figure 12).

Physics, Engineering, and Computer Science & AI have the highest rates of Computational Fluency (37.8%, 33.5%, and 30.9%, respectively), while Humanities and Education have the lowest (9.5% and 10.5%). The multinomial model also showed a substantial difference in computation dominance in both Computer Science and AI (odds of approximately 3.75 times) and Engineering (odds of approximately 3.76 times), with Digital Pedagogy being the only sector where the dominance due to digital pedagogy had an approximate value of 2.49 in Business and Management ($p < .001$ - Bonferroni adjustment).

In order to support the validity of our findings, we used a second method by creating a multinomial logistic regression with discipline as the variable predicting where to fall within a grade against dominant topic (base = Student-Centric Skills) as the dependent variable. There was a significant association between discipline and topic emphasis, $\chi^2(27) = 846.97$, $p < .001$. Using standardised residuals, we see that the Computational Fluency variable had very high and positive standardised residuals within Computer Science & Artificial Intelligence (AI) ($z = +16.99$), as well as large and positive standardised residual in terms of Engineering ($z = +9.46$). The Digital Pedagogy variable also had high positive residuals, but in relation to Business & Management ($z = +11.49$). The variable Student-Centric has a large and positive association with education ($z = +8.70$), however, it had a large negative Standardized Residual in comparison to Traditional Academic ($s = 8.44$).

The prominence of Digital Pedagogy in Business & Management should be investigated as a potential empirical counter-argument to the "hollow digital" notion. For decades, business schools have been leaders in the implementation of educational technology based on their adherence to the professional accreditation standards set forth by the AACSB, which encourage both innovation and partnerships with industry. However, the skill composition from the job advertisements indicates that what these represent administrative infrastructure of business schools (i.e. LMS management, Microsoft Office) rather than actual digital pedagogical innovation. To determine if business schools are leading in digital pedagogy, a qualitative follow-up is necessary to look at actual practices of instruction related to the discourse surrounding actual recruitment processes.

Figure 12. KeyATM mean differences by skill topic between each discipline

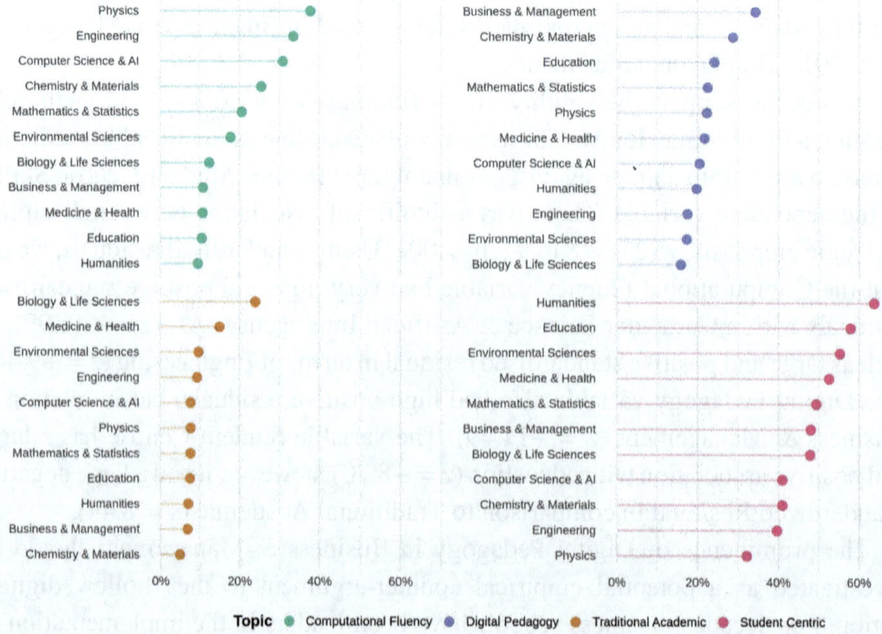

Figure 13. Mean Topic Proportions by Country (n=9,148; US=8,371 [91.5%], Canada=391 [4.3%], UK=253 [2.8%], Australia=123 [1.3%], NZ=10 [0.1%]). Note: Cross-national comparisons are presented as robustness checks given the marked US dominance in the sample. After controlling for discipline and job type via Dirichlet regression, no statistically significant country effects remain (all p > .10), indicating homogeneity across Anglophone markets

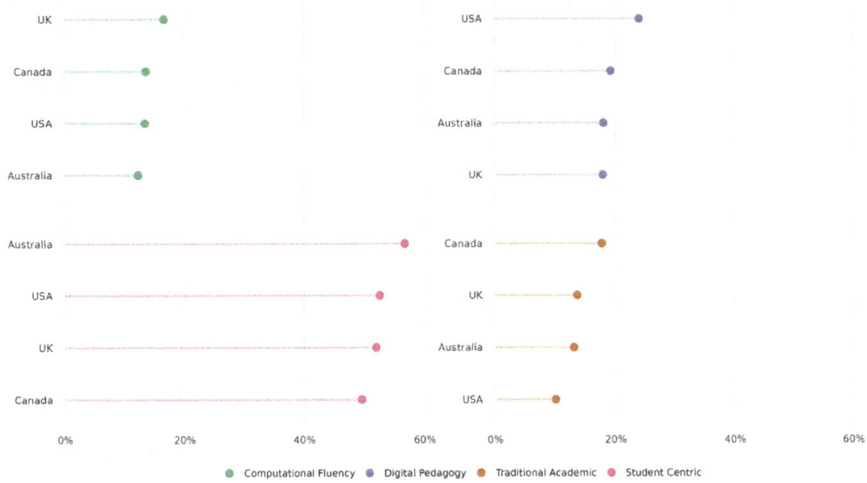

5.5. Anglophone Market Homogeneity: A Cross-National Validation Check

Fifth, our objective was to find out if the pattern of topics was an American phenomenon, or did it exist in other English-speaking countries? A cross-national validation compared the topics written across the five countries (US: 91.5%; Canada: 4.3%; UK: 2.8%; Australia: 1.3%; NZ: 0.1%). Given NZ had such a small proportion of the sample, this comparison should not be taken as a final judgment, and generalisations need further exploration. The results can be seen in Figure 13 above: Computational Fluency ranges from ~12% (Australia) to 18% (UK); Digital Pedagogy from 18% (UK) to 26% (USA); Traditional Academic from 14% (USA) to 24% (Canada); Student-Centric from 48% (Canada) to 53% (Australia).

The cross-country differences for each of the four topics are statistically significant according to Kruskal-Wallis tests ($p < .05$), yet all effect sizes were small ($\eta2<0.01$) indicating that the countries explained very little of the variance in their respective results. Therefore, we also performed Dirichlet regression using discipline and job bucket as covariates (Maier, 2014) to examine whether there would still be differences between the countries after controlling for these covariates and it was determined that there did not remain any statistically significant country-level effects (all $p > .10$). Examples are: USA as compared to Australia on Digital Pedagogy (0.154, $z = 1.63$, $p = .103$), UK on Computational Fluency (0.087, $z = 0.77$, $p = .442$), and Canada on Traditional Academic (0.066, $z = 0.62$, $p = .537$).

Taken together, the results imply that the slight differences in bivariate analyses between countries are due to distinctions in the make-up of the profession and the type of work being performed by employees rather than true differences in national skill signifiers. For example, an Engineering professor in the UK would have a similar job profile as one working in the United States or Australia. Discipline and job category define what is included in the topic composition for each job instead of which country the job is based in.

The current study demonstrates that topic modelling can elicit differences between an organisation's stated priorities and what they subsequently emphasise within job postings. In contrast, our findings highlight a remarkable degree of Global Isomorphism between HEIs in the US, UK, Canada and Australia. Once discipline and position were controlled for, the description of academic positions was strikingly similar across these countries. Our findings lend weight to previous theoretical work that describes the academic community as a 'normative tribe' and indicates that the reproduction of the academic profession is now highly standardised at a global level, at least in terms of labour market posting structure (Becher & Trowler, 2001). This finding is explored theoretically in Section 6.1.

5.6. Summary of Findings

Table 9 combines the findings of the various computational and statistical analyses to provide an overview of the evidence collected. Empirical findings from the research relate to four research questions and reveal the disparity between how "Digital University" is portrayed in strategy and the operational reality of labour market demand.

Table 9. Overview of the research findings

Research Question	Key Finding
RQ1: Definition of "Digital"	"Hollow Digital" recruitment paradox: while Computational Fluency signals a high degree of technical ability (AI, Python), Digital Pedagogy defines itself in terms of administrative knowledge (LMS administration, Microsoft Office), as opposed to pedagogical innovation.
RQ2: Labour Market Demand	Strategic disconnect: Digital skills are not transversal. Digital Pedagogy is needed mainly in administrative and support positions whilst Computational Fluency predominantly exists in research-based positions. Tenure-track positions remain classified as Traditional Academic Qualification and Student-Centered (pastoral care) competencies.
RQ3: Disciplinary Variation	Competencies in isolation: The demand for Computational Fluency skills are mostly concentrated within STEM (Computer Science, Engineering, and Physics). There is minimal evidence that "digital fluency" is an increasingly generalised expectation within the Humanities or Social Sciences.
RQ4: National Differences	Anglophone similarity: There is very little variance between national systems across the five Anglophone systems (US, UK, Canada, Australia, NZ). When controlling for both discipline and role type, there are no significant country effects suggesting a common normative framework within the Anglophone higher education system. Further research is needed to determine if there is an extension of this phenomenon to non-Anglophone systems.

This study finds that whilst the language of digital transformation now forms a part of the strategic vocabulary of HEIs and their position within an increasingly competitive marketplace, it has yet to permeate or influence the operational logic of hiring practices. These findings are interpreted through theoretical lenses of institutional isomorphism, competency definition and disciplinary stratification.

6. DISCUSSION & INTERPRETATION

The analysis demonstrates a substantial differentiation between the kind of strategic language that HEIs use in trying to recruit employees (Clark et al., 2025; Madgavkar et al., 2025) and what is actually happening in practice.

6.1. "Digital" vs "Hollow Digital" & Institutional Isomorphism

One plausible explanation for our findings is the existence of institutional isomorphism, as theorised by DiMaggio and Powell (1983). The authors explain that there are three different forms that isomorphic pressure can take: coercive, which can be thought of as rules or expectations which bind organisations (for example, those regarding digital competences); mimetic, which can be thought of as a form of imitation in situations of uncertainty; and normative, which can be thought of as conformity to social expectations (for example, those regarding accreditation and ranks). Consistent with the cross-national homogeneity observed in Section 5.5,

Universities, as other organisations, often face regulative, mimetic and normative demands from their environments (i.e. regulators, competitors and university ranking organisations). For instance, regulative demands are imposed by accreditation bodies and ministries, mimetic demands arise for using the AI-Enabled Campus slogan and normative demands for directing expenditure towards digitalisation. Universities often react to these institutional pressures by adopting the Service Model, by imposing on other organisational members digitalisation policies, by recruiting administrative staff to manage the digital infrastructure and sometimes by putting up a façade of digitalisation without actually being digital. The latter, has been referred to as 'ceremonial adoption', whereby goals can be unconnected with the daily practice (Meyer & Rowan, 1977).

Our findings reveal a two-mode decoupling: Computational Fluency is concentrated in short-term research posts, while Digital Pedagogy is delegated to administrative staff. This "hollow digital" hiring dilemma is reflected in concerns raised in different research strands. Marin (2021) points to the duplication of academically based work in electronic forms without any fundamental change to its content. DiMaggio and Powell's (1983) research on institutional isomorphism highlight the danger of merely replicating existing institutional processes during a digital transformation. Carmo et al. (2025) go further, asserting that intellectual capital rather than digital capital is the driving force in transformation. As Barney (1991) explains, in a resource-based view of organisations, it is not the possession of scarce resources alone that leads to competitive advantage, but their effective use. Thus, rather than consider a radical transformation of the HEI, the "hollow digital" hiring dilemma appears to resolve the productivity paradox by hiring digitally competent personnel on a contract basis, thus addressing the transactional aspects of digital transformation, while core faculty positions remain defined by the traditional traits of scholarship and pastoral care.

6.2. The "Definition Gap": Administrative vs. Pedagogical Competence

Through topic modelling, this research reveals a large disconnect between the theoretical and labour market definitions of digital pedagogical competencies. The Digital Competence Framework for Educators (DigCompEdu) (Redecker & Punie, 2017) is specifically developed to assess digital competence in education and defines digital competence as the ability to use digital technologies to empower the learner and facilitate development through innovation. However, employers in this study are defining digital competence through use of technology for administrative purposes, such as Microsoft Office and LMS. Further, Nyale et al. (2025) report a disconnect between the advanced digital pedagogical competence of faculty required by academia and the much lower-level administrative digital requirements by employers in the labour market. Specifically, while there is demand for faculty who can easily navigate higher education's new AI driven university campus (Robert et al., 2025), the findings of the current study and Nyale's study show that higher education institutions are looking at bureaucratic operational efficiency over the development of a digitally fluent pedagogy. The critical competency gap is the preference for Administrative Digital Literacy over Pedagogical Digital Fluency. The amount of benefits language in job adverts is more than double that of Traditional Scholarship (7.1%), although slightly less than Digital Pedagogy (18.8%) language. In other words, the job recruitment discourse equates insurance plans and equal opportunity statements with pedagogical competencies. It appears that academic jobs are increasingly presented as benefit packages, while digital competencies are not adequately specified.

6.3. Siloed Modernisation & Transversal Myth

This study provided empirical evidence that contradicts existing economic studies that suggest digital skills translate universally into the labour market. The findings also contradict predictions from the World Economic Forum (2023) as the results show that the demand for digital skills on the labour market is not universal, nor are the skills interchangeable across academic disciplines. Instead, "Silos of Modernisation" have materialised where the need for computational fluency is rewarded only in the STEM disciplines, while no tangible link is detected in the Humanities and Education fields.

Bone et al. (2025) argue that the rigidity of degree classification versus verifiable transversal skill sets results in structural inefficiencies and the data show that these inefficiencies manifest within universities' own recruiting processes.

7. CONCLUSIONS, RECOMMENDATIONS, LIMITATIONS & FUTURE RESEARCH

This chapter examines the 'Digital University' within the context of the academic labour market and finds that while Higher Education Institutions communicate strategic digital transformation in their public agendas, this is not reflected in the hiring practices. Computational fluency is only required in the short-term research contract job market while digital pedagogy is conflated with administrative competence. Tenure-track hiring is business as usual, with an emphasis on traditional scholarship and pastoral care. We conclude that unless hiring practices reflect strategic transformation, the Digital University will remain a brand rather than an actual entity.

7.1. Practical Recommendations

This research yields several useful practical recommendations for HEIs:

First, conduct annual Rhetoric-Reality Audits using the following process: compare what is committed to in the institution's strategic plan with what has been accomplished in hiring practices by taking the following three steps: *(1) extract all instances from the institution's strategic plan where digital competencies are referenced; (2) for all job postings from the past 12 months, identify in a coding system and record the same competencies referenced in the strategic plan; (3) calculate the percentage of tenure-track hires made in the previous 12 months by competency referenced in both the strategic plan and in job postings.* An example would be if an institution's strategic plan committed to AI enhanced learning but < 10% of its teaching hires reflected a requirement for AI Literacy, there would be an observable decoupling of strategy from operations.

Second, update job description templates (written before 2020) to digital competency matrices that are specific to the individual role within an organisation. For those on research-oriented roles, showing proficiency in at least one type of programming language (e.g. Python, R, MATLAB) is expected. For those in teaching-oriented roles: provide evidence of experience designing and delivering hybrid courses through a Learning Management System (Canvas, Blackboard, Moodle); developing and using multimedia content and interpreting student learning analytics. These must be treated as equal to qualifications with respect to digital fluency being achieved e.g., the same amount of text for describing the digital qualifications/competencies as for more traditional qualifications (e.g., publications/grants).

Third, establish digital transparency standards, by recognising digital competencies in permanent job classification systems. For instance, hybrid course redesign, AI-enhanced teaching and learning analytics should all be recognised as credited workload components. Otherwise, digital transformation runs the risk of exploiting contingent labour that is not acknowledged with these components.

Fourth, reintegrate digital pedagogy into faculty roles. Do not allocate the bulk of digital pedagogical responsibilities exclusively to instructional designers and learning technologists. Rather than differentiate between competencies that are uniquely the province of instructional designers versus faculty, institutions should insist that digital pedagogy be a competency shared across today's tenure-track job descriptions. Instead of asking faculty to tell students to 'check Blackboard for their latest grades', we should require evidence of hybrid course design, use of learning analytics, and pedagogical innovation in the faculty appointment process. As well, contributions to digital pedagogy should be recognised in promotion and tenure criteria.

7.2. Limitations and Future Research

This research has several limitations which provide useful avenues for future research.

First, the sample limitations. Data are US-based (approximately 91.5%) meaning the results cannot be generalised globally. New Zealand's contribution to the sample is minimal (n=10). We currently only have evidence of global isomorphism from five Anglophone countries. In order to determine if these hiring behaviours represent a true global academic shift rather than an English-language phenomenon, additional studies should examine other areas of the world. Furthermore, because we used a cross-sectional design, we cannot monitor how exactly digital hiring demand will change over time. Academic job markets in continental Europe, East Asia, and the Global South operate within entirely different systems from those in the Anglophone countries and may not have undergone the same types of changes. Future research could examine longitudinal changes; to assess whether the patterns we observe are stabilising and represent an equilibrium state, or whether they are transitional.

Second, the validity of job advertisements as a proxy for the entire hiring process. They may contain aspirational statements although may not contain all possible selection criteria (that would be considered by the selection committee.) Future research could include interviews with members of hiring committees to assist in validating how 'what is stated' in job advertisements translates into the hiring decisions. Further, research which explores the hiring outcome to validate the relationship between the competencies specified in advertisements and the candidates that are hired.

Third, the seed keyword dependency of KeyATM. Although the seed keywords were derived from well-known and established frameworks (DigCompEdu, WEF, and Boyer), topic compositions are always sensitive to specific keywords provided. Future research should test the robustness of our finding regarding "Hollow Digital" by replicating the analysis with alternative keyword specifications or by using fully unsupervised methods as a type of cross-validation.

REFERENCES

Armstrong, M., & Taylor, S. (2023). *Armstrong's handbook of human resource management practice: A guide to the theory and practice of people management*. Kogan Page Publishers.

Attewell, P. (1990). What is Skill? *Work and Occupations*, *17*(4), 422–448. DOI: 10.1177/0730888490017004003

Backhaus, K., & Tikoo, S. (2004). Conceptualizing and researching employer branding. *Career Development International*, *9*(5), 501–517. DOI: 10.1108/13620430410550754

Barney, J. (1991). Firm resources and sustained competitive advantage. *Journal of Management*, *17*(1), 99–120. DOI: 10.1177/014920639101700108

Becher, T., & Trowler, P. (2001). *Academic tribes and territories* (2nd ed.). McGraw-Hill/Open University Press.

Blei, D. M., Ng, A. Y., & Jordan, M. I. (2003). Latent dirichlet allocation. *Journal of Machine Learning Research*, *3*(Jan), 993–1022.

Bone, M., Ehlinger, E. G., & Stephany, F. (2025). Skills or degree? The rise of skill-based hiring for AI and green jobs. *Technological Forecasting and Social Change*, *214*, 124042. DOI: 10.1016/j.techfore.2025.124042

Börner, K., Scrivner, O., Gallant, M., Ma, S., Liu, X., Chewning, K., Wu, L., & Evans, J. A. (2018). Skill discrepancies between research, education, and jobs reveal the critical need to supply soft skills for the data economy. *Proceedings of the National Academy of Sciences of the United States of America*, *115*(50), 12630–12637. DOI: 10.1073/pnas.1804247115 PMID: 30530667

Boyer, E. L. (1990). *Scholarship reconsidered: Priorities of the professoriate*. Carnegie Foundation for the Advancement of Teaching.

Brøgger, K., Moscovitz, H., Robertson, S. L., & Lee, J. J. (2025). *World Yearbook of Education 2026: The Shifting Geopolitics of Higher Education: Knowledge, Power, Protest*. Taylor & Francis., DOI: 10.4324/9781003442264

Carmo, J. E. S., Lacerda, D. P., Klingenberg, C. O., & Piran, F. A. S. (2025). Digital transformation in the management of higher education institutions. *Sustainable Futures : An Applied Journal of Technology, Environment and Society*, *9*, 100692. DOI: 10.1016/j.sftr.2025.100692

Chui, M., Manyika, J., Miremadi, M., Henke, N., Chung, R., Nel, P., & Malhotra, S. (2018). *Notes from the AI frontier: Insights from hundreds of use cases*. M. G. Institute. https://www.mckinsey.com/featured-insights/artificial-intelligence/notes-from-the-ai-frontier-applications-and-value-of-deep-learning

Clark, C., Cluver, M., Fishman, T., & Kunkel, D. (2025). *2025 higher education trends*. https://www.deloitte.com/us/en/insights/industry/articles-on-higher-education/2025-us-higher-education-trends.html

Cohen, J. (2013). *Statistical power analysis for the behavioral sciences*. Routledge. DOI: 10.4324/9780203771587

Commonfund Institute. (2025). *2025 Higher Education Price Index (HEPI) Report*. https://www.commonfund.org/research-center/press-releases/2025-higher-education-price-index-hepi-report-released

Csernoch, M. (2025). Lean digital education to resolve the paradox of the illusion of digital prosperity. *Journal of Innovation & Knowledge*, *10*(1), 100676. DOI: 10.1016/j.jik.2025.100676

de Wit, H., Altbach, P., & Glass, C. (2025). Global Higher Education Transformation: The 2025 International Crisis. *International Higher Education*, (123), 1–2. DOI: 10.6017/895b9e0d.789fabbc

DiMaggio, P., & Powell, W. (1983). The iron cage revisited: Institutional isomorphism and collective rationality in organizational fields. *American Sociological Review*, *48*(2), 147–160. DOI: 10.2307/2095101

Dunn, O. J. (1961). Multiple comparisons among means. *Journal of the American Statistical Association*, *56*(293), 52–64. DOI: 10.1080/01621459.1961.10482090

Elhussein, G., Leopold, T., Silva, A., & Zahidi, S. (2023). *Defining education 4.0: A taxonomy for the future of learning*. https://www3.weforum.org/docs/WEF_Defining_Education_4.0_2023.pdf

Eshima, S., Imai, K., & Sasaki, T. (2024). Keyword-assisted topic models. *American Journal of Political Science*, *68*(2), 730–750. DOI: 10.1111/ajps.12779

Fuller, J. B., & Raman, M. (2017). *Dismissed by degrees: How degree inflation is undermining US competitiveness and hurting America's middle class. Published by Accenture, Grads of Life*. Harvard Business School.

Grawe, N. D. (2018). *Demographics and the demand for higher education*. JHU Press.

Hase, S., & Davis, L. (1999). *From competence to capability: The implications for human resource development and management* Association of Management and International Association of Management 17th Annual Conference, San Diego, CA.

Holon, I. Q. (2024). *Higher Education Digital Capability (HEDC) Framework*. https://www.holoniq.com/higher-education-digital-capability-framework

IIE. (2025). *Open Doors 2025: Report on International Educational Exchange*. https://opendoorsdata.org/wp-content/uploads/2025/11/OpenDoors25_PresentationPDF.pdf

James, J., Malkin, T., & Nusche, D. (2025). *Trends Shaping Education 2025*. OECD Publishing., DOI: 10.1787/6ae408c1-

Johnston, B., MacNeill, S., & Smyth, K. (2019). *Conceptualising the digital university: The intersection of policy, pedagogy and practice*. Springer.

Kruskal, W. H., & Wallis, W. A. (1952). Use of ranks in one-criterion variance analysis. *Journal of the American Statistical Association*, *47*(260), 583–621. DOI: 10.1080/01621459.1952.10483441

Madgavkar, A., Canal Noguer, M., Bradley, C., White, O., Smit, S., & Radigan, T. (2025). *Dependency and Depopulation? Confronting the Consequences of a New Demographic Reality*. M. G. Institute. https://www.mckinsey.com/~/media/mckinsey/mckinsey%20global%20institute/our%20research/dependency%20and%20depopulation%20confronting%20the%20consequences%20of%20a%20new%20demographic%20reality/dependency-and-depopulation-confronting-the-consequences-of-a-new-demographic-reality.pdf

Maier, M. (2014). *DirichletReg: Dirichlet Regression for Compositional Data in R*. https://doi.org/DOI: 10.57938/ad3142d3-2fcd-4c37-aec6-8e0bd7d077e1

Marin, L. (2021). The Digital University. In *On the Possibility of a Digital University: Thinking and Mediatic Displacement at the University* (pp. 57–77). Springer International Publishing. https://doi.org/DOI: 10.1007/978-3-030-65976-9_4

Meyer, J. W., & Rowan, B. (1977). Institutionalized organizations: Formal structure as myth and ceremony. *AJS; American Journal of Sociology*, *83*(2), 340–363. DOI: 10.1086/226550

Miao, F., & Holmes, W. (2023). *Guidance for generative AI in education and research*. https://www.unesco.org/en/articles/guidance-generative-ai-education-and-research

Mintzberg, H., & Waters, J. A. (1985). Of strategies, deliberate and emergent. *Strategic Management Journal*, *6*(3), 257–272. DOI: 10.1002/smj.4250060306

Monitor, I. C. E. F. (2025). *New analysis forecasts international student mobility through 2030: Regulated Regionalism.* https://monitor.icef.com/2025/07/new-analysis-forecasts-international-student-mobility-through-2030/

National Student Clearinghouse. (2024). *Current term enrollment estimates: Fall 2024.* https://nscresearchcenter.org/current-term-enrollment-estimates/

NCES. (2023). *Undergraduate enrollment (Condition of Education).* https://nces.ed.gov/programs/coe/indicator/cha

Nyale, D., Karume, S., Kipkebut, A., & Mukudi, F. (2025). Digital skills landscape: A systematic review of current academic programs, industry demands, and the digital divide's impact on graduate competencies. *Industry and Higher Education, 0*(0), 09504222251370105. DOI: 10.1177/09504222251370105

OECD. (2018). *The future of education and skills 2030: The future we want.* https://www.oecd.org/content/dam/oecd/en/publications/reports/2018/06/the-future-of-education-and-skills_5424dd26/54ac7020-en.pdf

OECD. (2025a). *Education at a Glance 2025: OECD Indicators.* https://doi.org/ DOI: 10.1787/1c0d9c79-en

OECD. (2025b). *The Financial Sustainability of Higher Education: Insights from Policy in OECD Countries* (Vol. P). OECD Publishing., DOI: 10.1787/f544ccfe-

Pew Charitable Trusts. (2019). *Two Decades of Change in Federal and State Higher Education Funding.* https://www.pew.org/-/media/assets/2019/10/fedstatefundinghigheredu_chartbook_v1.pdf

Pew Charitable Trusts. (2025). *Higher Education's Uncertain Fiscal Future* https://www.pew.org/en/research-and-analysis/articles/2025/11/12/higher-educations-uncertain-fiscal-future

Redecker, C., & Punie, Y. (2017). European framework for the digital competence of educators. *DigCompEdu*, (927973718X). Advance online publication. DOI: 10.2760/159770

Robert, J., Muscanell, N., McCormack, M., Pelletier, K., Arnold, K., Arbino, N., Young, K., & Reeves, J. (2025). 2025 EDUCAUSE Horizon Report: teaching and learning edition. *Horizon Report.*

Robertson, J., Johnson, R. B., & McGhee, J. (2024). Significant challenges facing small institutions in America. *New Directions for Student Services, 2024*(188), 11–22. DOI: 10.1002/ss.20533

Salama, R., & Hinton, T. (2023). Online higher education: Current landscape and future trends. *Journal of Further and Higher Education*, *47*(7), 913–924. DOI: 10.1080/0309877X.2023.2200136

SHEEO. (2024). *State higher education finance (SHEF): FY 2023*. State Higher Education Executive Officers Association.

SHEEO. (2025). *State Higher Education Finance: FY 2024*. https://shef.sheeo.org/wp-content/uploads/2025/05/SHEEO_SHEF_FY24_Report.pdf

Simon, H. A. (2013). *Administrative behavior* (4th ed.). Simon and Schuster.

UNESCO. (2025). *UIS Data Browser: Global flow of tertiary-level students*. https://uis.unesco.org/en/uis-student-flow

WEF. (2023). *The future of jobs report*. https://www.weforum.org/publications/the-future-of-jobs-report-2023/

Wright, P. M., & McMahan, G. C. (1992). Theoretical perspectives for strategic human resource management. *Journal of Management*, *18*(2), 295–320. DOI: 10.1177/014920639201800205

Chapter 2

Assessing Digital Information Competence as a Talent Development Priority: A DigComp 3.0 Pilot Study of Business Students in Higher Education

Bodour H. AlShakhss
http://orcid.org/0000-0002-6001-8347
Australian University, Kuwait

Nevena Veselinovic
http://orcid.org/0000-0001-8283-265X
Institute of Economic Sciences, Serbia

Vladimir Simovic
http://orcid.org/0000-0002-6441-833X
Australian University, Kuwait & Institute of Economic Sciences, Serbia

ABSTRACT

This chapter presents a pilot study assessing self-perceived digital information competence among undergraduate business students using the DigComp 3.0 framework, focusing on Area 1 competences of browsing, searching, filtering, evaluating, and managing digital information. Data collected from 23 students reveal three key findings. First, self-assessed competence scores are moderate and statistically uniform across the three information literacy domains. Second, a steep and consistent

DOI: 10.4018/979-8-3373-8959-2.ch002

decline in perceived competence occurs as DigComp proficiency levels increase from Basic to Highly Advanced, with the gradient reaching statistical significance across all domains. Third, Knowledge scores are significantly lower than Attitude and Skill scores, indicating a conceptual understanding deficit despite positive digital orientations. The findings are discussed in relation to their implications for digitalizing talent management strategy in higher education

1. INTRODUCTION

Digital competence has become a vital challenge in university education because of the use of digital technologies in almost every stage of the students' academic life. Teaching is delivered through learning platforms, reading materials are read online, communication with instructors happens through digital channels, and research depends on electronic resources rather than printed material (Wang, Ma, Zhang, & Miao, 2025). In this environment, digital competence is no longer an option but a basic academic necessity. Carretero, Vuorikari, and Punie (2017) define digital competence as the critical and responsible use of digital technologies for learning, communication, and problem-solving. This description is important in universities because it moves the conversation beyond technical skills and toward the quality of students' judgment when they engage with information.

The need for digital competence has grown a lot and the need for training is required. As the volume of digital information available to students has expanded dramatically, the challenge is no longer simple access but navigating abundance (Tafesse, Aguilar, Sayed, & Tariq, 2024). Search engines, academic databases, digital libraries, online reports, and AI-supported tools all propose multiple entry points to information. Although these entry points are beneficial, it often produces information overload. Students may struggle to decide where to search, which results to trust, and how to narrow their findings to a controllable set of sources. The task is therefore not simply to find information but to find the right information. In undergraduate and graduate schools, the academic value of browsing and searching depends on strategy and critical judgment rather than speed alone (Leeder & Shah, 2016).

Browsing is often considered a casual activity, yet it plays a serious role in academic work. Through browsing, students define a topic, identify repeating ideas, notice disciplinary language, and determine which sources dominate a field. Searching is more targeted and requires students to translate their information into useful terms and keywords. Filtering follows these two stages and requires students to reduce results into smaller, higher-quality set of sources. These processes are interrelated. Weakness in the beginning stage often affect the next. Students who search randomly cannot filter effectively, while students who browse superficially may misunderstand the scope of a topic before they begin the actual searching (ACRL, 2015; Kuhlthau, 2004) .

The growing availability of artificial intelligence has changed this process again. Instead of providing a list of sources to review, many AI systems provide direct answers, summaries, or reorganized content. This can save time, but it also modifies how students process knowledge. When answers are presented in a confident style, students may assume accuracy without checking origin, authorship, or evidence (Tzirides et al., 2024). As a result, digital competence now includes the ability to question synthesized outputs, trace claims back to initial sources, and distinguish between assistance and authority. The rise of AI has therefore made browsing, searching, and filtering more important because students must verify what has been generated for them.

The issue is relevant for business students. Business education depends heavily on the use of market reports, financial statements, business research documents, management industry findings, journal articles, and feasibility study materials. Students in this field often need to compare information from scholarly sources and to judge both academic credibility and practical usefulness. Weak digital competence may lead them to rely on blog posts, promotional reports, or insignificant summaries instead of peer-reviewed research. Effective competence, by contrast, allows them to make better differences between source types and to support their academic arguments with credible and current evidence.

Another reason this topic matters is the repeated gap between what students think they can do and what they actually do. Many students are confident users of digital devices and social platforms, yet this confidence does not always extend to academic information tasks (Zhao, Sánchez Gómez, Pinto Llorente, & Zhao, 2021; Getenet, Cantle, Redmond, & Albion, 2024). Being active online is not the same as being digitally competent in information search. A student may be an expert in navigating apps and websites while still lacking the skills to refine database searches or assess AI-generated content. This distinction is crucial because it explains why universities cannot assume that technologically active students automatically possess strong academic information literacy.

Digital transformation has expanded rapidly across education. Universities have adopted e-learning systems, expanded access to online journals, and encouraged use of digital tools in teaching and assessment (Wang et al., 2025; Zhao, Pinto Llorente, & Sánchez Gómez, 2021). These updates create new opportunities for faculty and students, but they also reveal challenges in skill development. Students may enjoy access to various devices while still needing help in evaluating information, searching through databases, and filtering findings. Examining digital competence is important because it helps identify whether students are genuinely advancing in their use of information through digital access, or whether access is outpacing critical competence. This topic therefore reviews literature on digital competence with a focus on browsing, searching, and filtering information through the use of academic resources properly.

2. LITERATURE REVIEW

Digital competence frameworks provide the theoretical basis for research in this field. The European Digital Competence Framework for Citizens, DigComp, first released in 2013 and most recently updated as DigComp 3.0, divides digital competence into five areas: information and data literacy, communication and collaboration, digital content creation, safety, and problem-solving (Carretero et al., 2017). The framework's key contribution lies in its recognition that information literacy is not a peripheral skill but a prerequisite for all other digital activities. Before students can communicate, create, or apply knowledge digitally, they must first be able to locate and evaluate information. In the higher education context, this means that information work must be treated as an intellectual process rather than a routine technical function, a perspective that positions DigComp as a theoretically appropriate lens for studying student digital behavior (Zhao et al., 2021).

The evolution toward DigComp 3.0 reflects the changing nature of digital environments. The updated framework gives substantially greater attention to emerging challenges such as algorithmic content curation, misinformation, data privacy, and artificial intelligence (Cosgrove & Cachia, 2025). Search results are now shaped by algorithms, recommendations are personalized, and AI systems increasingly determine how information appears to users. DigComp 3.0 therefore extends the argument that browsing and searching require not only keyword strategy but an awareness of how digital systems themselves shape knowledge access. This is particularly relevant in light of the rapid mainstreaming of generative AI tools, which Chiu et al. (2024) argue have redefined what it means to be an information-literate student, requiring competence not only in retrieval but in the critical appraisal of AI-generated content.

Research on students' browsing behavior reveals that many learners approach digital information superficially. Rather than exploring a topic broadly before narrowing their focus, students frequently move directly from a search prompt to a small number of visible results, relying on the organization of search engine rankings as a proxy for credibility (Dahlen & Hanson, 2023). This reliance on easily accessible, non-scholarly sources with limited depth of exploration has been empirically documented in undergraduate economics and business students (Watson et al., 2025). The consequences are academically significant: when browsing is reduced to scanning the first page of results, students enter the searching stage with weak topic understanding, vague questions, poor keyword selection, and scattered source choices.

Searching behavior among university students shows consistent limitations. Lund et al. (2026) report that students commonly use traditional search engines and generative AI tools side by side, guided primarily by convenience and perceived usefulness rather than by any principled understanding of each tool's strengths or limitations. Students do not necessarily substitute one tool for another; instead, they combine them in ways that may or may not serve academic quality. Search engines are used for quick discovery while AI tools are used for explanation or summarization, but without critical oversight the information-seeking process becomes unreliable even when it appears efficient. If students accept AI-generated summaries without returning to original sources, their research lacks the traceability that academic work requires (Tzirides et al., 2024). Information-seeking behavior of university students shows that students routinely overestimate their ability to locate high-quality academic material using general search strategies, often selecting sources based on surface features such as presentation quality and position in search results rather than on scholarly criteria (Georgopoulou et al., 2025).

Filtering is one of the most demanding components of digital information literacy because it requires evaluative judgment under conditions of information abundance. Urenda et al. (2022) connect filtering directly to content curation competence, arguing that academic information work requires not merely encountering sources but actively selecting, organizing, and evaluating them according to disciplinary criteria. Students who cannot filter effectively tend to accumulate large numbers of weak sources, feel overwhelmed, or rely on the most immediately available material rather than the most credible. This is consistent with the broader finding of Kamela (2024), who argues that conventional source evaluation instruction often fails because it teaches students to apply checklists mechanically rather than developing the contextual judgment needed to assess credibility in dynamic digital environments.

Sahid and Ridzuan (2025) provide evidence that students with stronger information literacy skills are significantly more likely to use institutional library resources and databases, as they possess the practical competencies needed to navigate academic information environments. This supports the argument that digital competence shapes not only what students know about information but also where they seek it: digitally competent students are more likely to transition from informal web searching toward more scholarly resource use. Alenezi (2025), studying students in Kuwait, confirms that access to digital library resources does not automatically translate into the ability to use those resources effectively, particularly at higher levels of information complexity.

The implications of digital information competence are particularly pronounced in business education. O'Callaghan et al. (2021), writing about accounting students, demonstrate that digital literacy has direct consequences for both academic performance and professional preparation. In disciplines such as accounting and business management, information must be interpreted in professional context, compared across source types (peer-reviewed research, industry reports, regulatory documents), and evaluated for both scholarly credibility and practical relevance. Students who lack advanced filtering and evaluation skills risk relying on blog posts, promotional summaries, or unverified reports, which undermine the quality of their analysis and decision-making. O'Callaghan et al. (2021) make a strong case for discipline-embedded digital competence training rather than generic stand-alone skills workshops, a recommendation that aligns with Cabero-Almenara, Gutiérrez-Castillo, Guillén-Gámez, and Gaete-Bravo (2022), who demonstrated that digital competence is a statistically significant predictor of academic success in a large-scale study of Chilean university students. Simovic et al. (2023) extend the relevance of digital information competence into the domain of entrepreneurship education. Their work demonstrates that browsing and filtering are not exclusively academic competencies but are foundational to entrepreneurial opportunity recognition, market analysis, and evidence-based decision-making. Students who can efficiently locate, compare, and critically assess digital information are better positioned to identify market trends, evaluate competitive landscapes, and construct well-evidenced business arguments. This finding reinforces the case that digital information competence reaches beyond classroom performance into future professional practice and innovation, and that its development in business education serves both academic and career goals simultaneously.

The rise of generative artificial intelligence has fundamentally altered the information landscape in which students operate. Unlike traditional search engines, which direct users to content created by identifiable authors and organizations, AI systems frequently synthesize and summarize information directly, removing the visible trail between the user's query and the original sources that underlie the generated response. This represents a substantial challenge for academic information literacy because the ability to identify original authors, compare evidence, and evaluate competing claims is a defining standard of scholarly work. Tzirides et al. (2024) argue that AI tools can only support learning responsibly when students treat AI-generated content as a prompt for further investigation rather than as final evidence, a habit that requires explicit instruction and deliberate cultivation.A further consequence of AI integration is that it can reduce the visible effort of research. When students receive a prepared response to an academic query, the stages of topic exploration, source comparison, and evaluative judgment that would ordinarily occur during browsing and searching are bypassed or hidden. These stages are precisely where conceptual understanding develops: a student who examines multiple sources, encounters conflicting evidence, and refines their question learns substantially more than one who accepts a single synthesized summary. Chiu et al. (2024) and Cosgrove and Cachia (2025) both argue that AI literacy must therefore be treated as an integral component of digital competence frameworks rather than as a separate topic, because AI fundamentally changes what it means to locate, evaluate, and manage information. This argument is directly reflected in DigComp 3.0's integration of AI-related competences across all five framework areas.

Taken together, the literature establishes that digital information competence is both essential and unevenly developed. Students are active digital users, but digital activity does not guarantee academic quality. Browsing tends to remain superficial, searching tends to favor convenience over rigor, and filtering tends to rely on heuristics of presentation quality rather than scholarly criteria. The availability of AI tools intensifies these challenges by making information easier to access but harder to evaluate. The literature also demonstrates consistently that access to technology does not automatically produce competence: what is required is deliberate, curriculum-embedded educational provision that develops the evaluative judgment, conceptual knowledge, and strategic skill that effective digital information work demands.

The research gap is clear. More rigorous work is needed specifically on business students' information practices, differentiating between confidence and demonstrated skill, on the impact of AI tools on academic source evaluation, and on how institutional curriculum design shapes digital competence development. Studies that combine self-report measures with performance-based evidence would be especially valuable, as would research that connects information-seeking behavior with actual academic outcomes. Against this backdrop, the present pilot study assesses undergraduate business students' self-perceived digital competence under domain Information and data literacy, using DigComp 3.0.

3. METHODS

3.1. Research Design

This study employed a quantitative, cross-sectional pilot design aimed at examining the self-assessed digital information competences of business students within the framework of the European Digital Competence Framework for Citizens (DigComp 3.0). Pilot studies are particularly useful for the preliminary examination of measurement instruments and for identifying response patterns that may inform subsequent large-scale research. The present analysis focused exclusively on Area 1 of the DigComp framework, which encompasses competences related to information and data literacy. Given the exploratory character of the study and the modest sample size, the analysis emphasized internal consistency, descriptive profiling, and within-subject comparisons rather than broad population-level generalizations.

3.2. Participants

The sample comprised 23 undergraduate business students enrolled in a single higher education institution (Australian University, Kuwait). Of these, 18 (78.3%) were female and 5 (21.7%) were male. Participants were drawn from six study programs: Marketing (n = 7; 30.4%), Management (n = 5; 21.7%), Human Resources (n = 4; 17.4%), Finance and Accounting (n = 3; 13.0%), Events Marketing (n = 2; 8.7%), and Management Information Systems (n = 2; 8.7%). All participants completed the questionnaire voluntarily after being informed of the study's purpose, the anonymity of their responses, and their right to withdraw at any stage without consequence. No personally identifiable information was collected, and the data were stored and processed in accordance with institutional ethical guidelines. Sample characteristics are summarised in Table 1.

Table 1. Sample characteristics (N = 23)

Characteristic	*n*	%
Gender		
Female	18	78.3
Male	5	21.7
Study program		
Marketing	7	30.4
Management	5	21.7
Human Resources	4	17.4
Finance and Accounting	3	13.0
Events Marketing	2	8.7
Management Information Systems	2	8.7

Note. Percentages may not sum to 100 due to rounding.
Source: *Authors' calculation*

3.3. Instrument

The instrument used in this study was a self-assessment questionnaire designed in accordance with DigComp 3.0 Area 1 framework. It comprised 58 competence statements, organised into three competence domains: Competence 1.1, Browsing, Searching and Filtering Information (15 items); Competence 1.2, Evaluating Information (21 items); and Competence 1.3, Managing Information (22 items). Each statement was further classified along two dimensions defined within the DigComp 3.0 framework. The first dimension was proficiency level, with statements distributed across four levels of complexity: Basic (15 items), Intermediate (17 items), Advanced (14 items), and Highly Advanced (12 items). The second dimension was construct type, distinguishing between Knowledge items (n = 26), which capture conceptual understanding of digital tools, processes, and phenomena; Skill items (n = 22), which refer to the practical ability to perform digital tasks; and Attitude items (n = 10), which reflect dispositions and values toward digital information practices.

Each item was rated on a four-point self-assessment scale: 1, no competence (no skills, knowledge, or disposition in this area); 2, basic awareness, indicating limited ability to apply the competence independently; 3, can apply with support or in familiar contexts; and 4, fully competent, indicating the ability to apply the competence independently and confidently across contexts. Higher scores therefore reflect stronger self-assessed digital competence. The questionnaire also collected basic demographic information on gender and study program. The instrument was administered in English and using Google Forms.

3.4. Data Analysis

All statistical analyses were conducted using Stata version 14. Prior to analysis, the dataset was screened for missing values and inconsistencies. No missing responses were identified, and the full sample of 23 participants was retained for all analyses. Item-level scores were used to compute mean composite scores for each respondent across several aggregations: by competence domain (1.1, 1.2, 1.3), by proficiency level (Basic, Intermediate, Advanced, Highly Advanced), by item type (Attitude, Knowledge, Skill), and by twelve cross-classified competence-by-level cells. A total mean score across all 58 items was also calculated for each respondent.

Internal consistency was assessed using Cronbach's alpha for each competence domain and for the full instrument. Descriptive statistics included means, standard deviations, medians, minimum and maximum values, and, where relevant, interquartile ranges. Given the small sample size, the ordinal response format, and the repeated-measures structure of the data, non-parametric procedures were used for inferential analyses.

To assess differences across the three competence domains, the four proficiency levels, and the three item types, the Friedman test for related samples was applied. Where the omnibus test indicated significant differences, post-hoc pairwise comparisons were conducted using the Wilcoxon signed-rank test, with Bonferroni correction applied to the significance threshold to account for multiple comparisons ($\alpha = 0.05/k$, where k is the number of pairwise tests). The same Friedman procedure was also applied within each competence domain separately to test whether the gradient across proficiency levels was consistent across the three domains.

To examine the convergent structure of the instrument, Spearman's rank-order correlation coefficient was computed between the three competence composite scores. Spearman's rho was preferred over Pearson's correlation due to the ordinal nature of the underlying items and the modest sample size. Finally, exploratory comparisons of self-assessment scores by gender were conducted using the Mann-Whitney U test (Wilcoxon rank-sum test), applied to the overall score and to each of the three competence domains. These comparisons were undertaken with the explicit recognition that the substantial gender imbalance in the sample (18 female versus 5 male respondents) limited statistical power and constrained any inferences to a strictly exploratory level. Statistical significance was set at $p < 0.05$ for omnibus tests, with Bonferroni-adjusted thresholds for post-hoc comparisons. All effect sizes and confidence statements were interpreted in light of the sample size and the pilot nature of the study.

4. RESULTS

Before proceeding to comparative analyses, the internal consistency and descriptive properties of the DigComp 3.0 Area 1 self-assessment instrument were examined (Table 2). Cronbach's alpha coefficients indicated satisfactory to very good reliability across the three competence domains, ranging from 0.74 for Competence 1.1 (Browsing, Searching and Filtering Information) to 0.84 for Competence 1.3 (Managing Information). Competence 1.2 (Evaluating Information) also demonstrated good internal consistency ($\alpha = 0.82$). For the full 58-item instrument, Cronbach's alpha reached 0.93, indicating excellent overall reliability. These findings suggest that the instrument performed consistently in the present pilot sample and provided a stable basis for subsequent analyses.

Descriptive statistics further showed a highly uniform pattern across the three competence domains. Mean self-assessment scores were nearly identical: 1.1 Browsing, Searching and Filtering Information (M = 2.51, SD = 0.24, Mdn = 2.47), 1.2 Evaluating Information (M = 2.51, SD = 0.26, Mdn = 2.52), and 1.3 Managing Information (M = 2.50, SD = 0.26, Mdn = 2.59). The total instrument mean was also 2.50 (SD = 0.23, Mdn = 2.55), indicating a generally moderate level of self-assessed digital information competence. In addition, the competence scores were strongly and positively correlated, with Spearman's ρ ranging from 0.69 to 0.79 (all $p < 0.001$). The strongest association was observed between Competence 1.1 and Competence 1.2 ($\rho = 0.79$), followed by the relationship between Competence 1.2 and Competence 1.3 ($\rho = 0.74$), while the correlation between Competence 1.1 and Competence 1.3 was slightly lower but still substantial ($\rho = 0.69$). Overall, these results indicate that the three competence domains are closely related, while still capturing non-identical aspects of digital information literacy.

Table 2. Descriptive statistics, internal consistency, and inter-competence correlations

Competence	*k*	*M*	*SD*	*Mdn*	α	**1.1**	**1.2**
1.1 Browsing, Searching and Filtering	15	2.51	0.24	2.47	0.74	-	
1.2 Evaluating Information	21	2.51	0.26	2.52	0.82	0.79***	-
1.3 Managing Information	22	2.50	0.26	2.59	0.84	0.69***	0.74***
Total instrument	**58**	**2.50**	**0.23**	**2.55**	**0.93**		

Note. k = number of items; α = Cronbach's alpha; values in the rightmost columns are Spearman's ρ correlations between competence scores. *** p <0.001.

Source: *Authors' calculation*

To determine whether the small numerical differences between competence domains were statistically meaningful, a Friedman test was conducted. The test revealed no significant difference among the three competence scores, $\chi^2(2) = 1.24$, $p = 0.538$. This suggests that respondents did not differentiate strongly between browsing, evaluating, and managing information in their self-assessments. Rather than showing a pronounced profile of strengths and weaknesses across domains, the students reported a relatively uniform level of competence across all three.

A more differentiated pattern emerged when self-assessment scores were examined across proficiency levels and construct types (Table 3). A clear gradient emerged across proficiency levels, with mean scores decreasing monotonically from Basic (M = 3.35, SD = 0.23, Mdn = 3.33) to Intermediate (M = 2.74, SD = 0.27, Mdn = 2.77), Advanced (M = 2.05, SD = 0.25, Mdn = 2.07), and Highly Advanced levels (M = 1.65, SD = 0.31, Mdn = 1.67). A Friedman test confirmed that these differences were highly significant, $\chi^2(3) = 69.00$, $p < 0.001$. Importantly, this value corresponds to the theoretical maximum for the given sample size, indicating complete consistency in the rank ordering of proficiency levels across participants. Post-hoc Wilcoxon signed-rank tests with Bonferroni correction further showed that all six pairwise comparisons between proficiency levels were statistically significant (all z = 4.20, all $p < 0.001$). These findings indicate that students felt substantially more confident in performing basic digital information tasks than in handling tasks requiring more advanced and highly advanced competences.

A complementary pattern emerged across construct types. Knowledge items received the lowest scores (M = 2.40, SD = 0.24, Mdn = 2.46), compared with Attitude items (M = 2.60, SD = 0.21, Mdn = 2.60) and Skill items (M = 2.59, SD = 0.26, Mdn = 2.59). The Friedman test again indicated statistically significant differences, $\chi^2(2) = 23.74$, $p < 0.001$. Post-hoc Wilcoxon tests showed that Knowledge scores were significantly lower than both Attitude scores ($z = 3.99$, $p < 0.001$) and Skill scores ($z = -4.02$, $p < 0.001$), whereas no statistically significant difference was observed between Attitude and Skill scores ($z = 0.30$, $p = 0.761$). Overall, this pattern suggests that students reported relatively similar levels of positive attitudes and self-assessed skills, while evaluating their conceptual knowledge somewhat lower.

Table 3. Self-assessment scores by proficiency level and item type

Grouping	k	M	SD	Mdn	Range
Proficiency level					
Basic	15	3.35	0.23	3.33	2.80-3.67
Intermediate	17	2.74	0.27	2.77	2.35-3.24
Advanced	14	2.05	0.25	2.07	1.57-2.36
Highly advanced	12	1.65	0.31	1.67	1.00-2.25
Item type					
Attitude	10	2.60	0.21	2.60	2.20-3.00
Knowledge	26	2.40	0.24	2.46	1.96-2.73
Skill	22	2.59	0.26	2.59	2.14-3.00

Note. k = number of items; scale range 1-4. Friedman test for proficiency level: $\chi^2(3) = 69.00$, $p < 0.001$; all six post-hoc Wilcoxon signed-rank comparisons significant after Bonferroni correction (all $z = 4.20$, all $p < 0.001$). Friedman test for item type: $\chi^2(2) = 23.74$, $p < 0.001$; post-hoc tests indicated Knowledge significantly lower than both Attitude ($z = 3.99$, $p < 0.001$) and Skill ($z = -4.02$, $p < 0.001$), while Attitude and Skill did not differ ($z = 0.30$, $p = 0.761$). Source: *Authors' calculation*

To further examine whether the decline in self-assessment scores with increasing task complexity was consistent across the three competence domains, mean scores were also analyzed by competence and proficiency level (Table 4). In Competence 1.1 (Browsing, Searching and Filtering Information), mean scores declined from 3.26 (SD = 0.26) at the Basic level to 2.84 (SD = 0.34) at the Intermediate level, 2.10 (SD = 0.29) at the Advanced level, and 1.73 (SD = 0.35) at the Highly Advanced level. A similar pattern emerged for Competence 1.2 (Evaluating Information), with means decreasing from 3.33 (SD = 0.28) to 2.63 (SD = 0.32), 1.90 (SD = 0.33), and 1.59 (SD = 0.40), respectively. Competence 1.3 (Managing Information) showed the same monotonic decline, from 3.44 (SD = 0.33) at the Basic level to 2.82 (SD = 0.32) at the Intermediate level, 2.14 (SD = 0.28) at the Advanced level, and 1.61 (SD = 0.33) at the Highly Advanced level. Friedman tests confirmed that the differences across proficiency levels were statistically significant within each competence domain (1.1: $\chi^2(3) = 61.47$, $p < 0.001$; 1.2: $\chi^2(3) = 64.66$, $p < 0.001$; 1.3: $\chi^2(3) = 69.00$, $p < 0.001$). Overall, these results indicate that the downward gradient across proficiency levels was not limited to the aggregate scale, but was consistently observed within each of the three DigComp Area 1 competence domains.

Table 4. Mean self-assessment scores by competence and proficiency level

Competence	Basic	Intermediate	Advanced	Highly adv.	$\chi^2(3)$
1.1 Browsing	3.26 (0.26)	2.84 (0.34)	2.10 (0.29)	1.73 (0.35)	61.47***
1.2 Evaluating	3.33 (0.28)	2.63 (0.32)	1.90 (0.33)	1.59 (0.40)	64.66***
1.3 Managing	3.44 (0.33)	2.82 (0.32)	2.14 (0.28)	1.61 (0.33)	69.00***

Note. Cell values are M (SD); N = 23 for all cells. The rightmost column reports the Friedman test statistic for the four-level comparison within each competence; the value of $\chi^2 = 69.00$ represents the theoretical maximum, indicating that every participant ranked the four levels in the same descending order. *** $p < 0.001$.

Source: *Authors' calculation*

Finally, exploratory analyses were conducted to examine possible gender differences in self-assessed digital competence. Mann-Whitney U tests revealed no statistically significant differences between female and male students in the overall DigComp Area 1 score ($z = 1.38$, $p = 0.168$), nor in any of the three competence domains: 1.1 Browsing, Searching and Filtering Information ($z = 1.31$, $p = 0.189$), 1.2 Evaluating Information ($z = 1.35$, $p = 0.179$), and 1.3 Managing Information ($z = 0.49$, $p = 0.627$). Given the substantial gender imbalance in the sample, these findings should be interpreted with caution and treated as exploratory rather than confirmatory.

5. DISCUSSION AND CONCLUSIONS

The findings of this pilot study offer several theoretically and practically relevant insights into the self-assessed digital information competence of undergraduate business students, examined through the lens of the DigComp 3.0 framework. Taken together, the results reveal a pattern of moderate but undifferentiated competence across domains, a consistent and steep decline with increasing task complexity, and a notable gap between students' conceptual knowledge and their attitudes and perceived skills. Each of these findings warrants careful interpretation in light of the existing literature and the broader context of digitalizing talent management strategy in higher education.

5.1. Uniform Self-Assessment Across Competence Domains

The absence of statistically significant differences across the three DigComp 3.0 Area 1 competence domains, browsing, searching and filtering information (1.1), evaluating information (1.2), and managing information (1.3), with nearly identical mean scores of M = 2.51, 2.51, and 2.50 respectively (Friedman $\chi^2(2) = 1.24$, $p = .538$), reflects a pattern documented across the broader literature on digital competence self-assessment in higher education. Zhao et al. (2021), in a systematic review of digital competence research in higher education covering both Scopus and Web of Science, found that the majority of studies report moderate and relatively undifferentiated levels of self-assessed digital competence among university students, particularly when measured using DigComp-based instruments. The convergence of domain scores in the present study is consistent with this global picture. Similarly, Draganac et al. (2022), examining digital competencies across European university students from the University of Belgrade and University of Zagreb, reported that students demonstrated notably uniform self-perceptions across distinct competence areas, especially in information literacy and communication domains, suggesting that students tend to generalize their digital experience rather than differentiate among competence types.

This interpretation is reinforced by the strong inter-domain correlations observed in the present study (Spearman's $\rho = .69–.79$), which mirror findings reported in other DigComp-based studies. The high correlations indicate that the three domains are measuring a common underlying self-perception of digital competence rather than genuinely distinct skill profiles. Sillat et al.(2021) highlighted precisely this risk in their systematic review of digital competence assessment methods in higher education: self-report instruments tend to produce inflated and non-discriminating scores because students rely on general impressions of digital familiarity rather than targeted reflection on specific competence behaviors. In this sense, the present results do not reflect a genuinely well-balanced competence profile, but rather a central tendency response pattern that conceals real within-person variation across information literacy tasks.

Georgopoulou et al. (2025), in a study of university students' online information practices grounded in DigComp 2.2, found that students were often able to articulate the criteria for good source evaluation without consistently applying them in practice, a pattern they described as a discrepancy between stated and enacted competence. This distinction between declarative and procedural knowledge is directly relevant to the uniform domain scores observed in this study: students may be responding to questionnaire items based on their conceptual familiarity with what good information practice looks like, rather than on the basis of accurate self-knowledge about their actual performance. This concern is particularly salient in the context of the present instrument's reliance on a four-point self-assessment scale, which, as Schaal et al. (2025) demonstrated in a cross-national DigComp 2.2 study of health students, can produce self-reported scores that diverge substantially from performance-based assessments of the same competences.

From a talent management perspective in higher education, the undifferentiated self-assessment profile has a direct practical implication: institutions that rely on self-report competence inventories to identify student development needs cannot use such instruments to distinguish among the three information literacy competences in targeting their interventions. A digitalizing talent management strategy requires granular, accurate competence data. As Safi et al. (2024) argued in the context of workforce digital readiness, digital competence is not a single dimension but a complex ecosystem of capabilities that must be mapped and selectively developed. The uniform scores observed in this study suggest that instruments sensitive enough to produce reliable domain differentiation may require a performance-based component alongside the self-report questionnaire, a methodological direction that several authors in the field have independently endorsed (Sillat et al., 2021; Schaal et al., 2025; Mejías-Acosta et al., 2024).

5.2. The Proficiency-Level Gradient: Confidence Declines as Complexity Rises

The most striking finding of this study is the sharp and consistent decline in self-assessed competence as proficiency levels increase. Mean scores fell from M = 3.35 at the Basic level to M = 2.74 at Intermediate, M = 2.05 at Advanced, and M = 1.65 at the Highly Advanced level. The Friedman test statistic of $\chi^2(3) = 69.00$ represented the theoretical maximum for this sample size, indicating that every participant ranked the four proficiency levels in exactly the same descending order. All six pairwise post-hoc Wilcoxon comparisons were statistically significant after Bonferroni correction (all $z = 4.20$, $p < .001$), and the gradient was replicated within each of the three DigComp competence domains (1.1: $\chi^2(3) = 61.47$; 1.2: $\chi^2(3) = 64.66$; 1.3: $\chi^2(3) = 69.00$; all $p < .001$).

This proficiency-level gradient has substantial support in the international literature, though the present study provides unusually clear evidence of its uniformity. Kuluşaklı (2024), in a study of 243 distance learners at Turkish higher education institutions assessed using DigComp-aligned instruments, found that basic digital competence was comparatively high in communication but significantly lower in information literacy and problem-solving domains, a pattern that aligns with the present finding that basic-level tasks are rated far more confidently than advanced ones. The distinction Kuluşaklı (2024) makes between communicative and analytical digital tasks is mirrored in the gradient observed here: DigComp tasks at the Basic level tend to involve familiar, communicative activities, while Advanced and Highly Advanced tasks involve the kind of analytical, critical, and strategic information work that students find considerably more challenging to self-assess as competent.

The gradient is also consistent with findings from a cross-national DigComp validation study by Mejías-Acosta et al. (2024), who developed and validated a digital competence measurement scale for higher education students and found that self-assessment scores were systematically lower for competencies involving higher-order cognitive processing, such as critical evaluation and problem-solving, compared to basic operational and communicative competences. Similarly, Cabero-Almenara et al. (2022), in a large-scale study of 17,301 university students in Chile, demonstrated that digital competence levels are significantly lower in domains requiring complex information processing and that students who had not repeated an academic year showed higher competence scores overall — suggesting a direct link between advanced digital information skills and academic success, which further contextualizes the significance of the gaps found at the Advanced and Highly Advanced levels in the present study.

The steep drop between Intermediate (M = 2.74) and Advanced (M = 2.05) levels is particularly noteworthy. Advanced DigComp 3.0 competences in the domain of information literacy include tasks such as systematically evaluating the reliability of complex and conflicting information sources, developing refined search strategies across multiple databases, and critically appraising algorithm-mediated and AI-generated content. These represent the competencies most directly relevant to higher academic work and to the information judgment demands of professional practice in business. Sahid & Ridzuan (2025) found an analogous pattern in their study of Generation Z students in Malaysian higher education: despite reporting moderate to high digital proficiency overall (M = 3.47), students' engagement with institutional digital library resources remained limited (M = 2.96), confirming that the gap between basic digital familiarity and advanced information practice is not unique to the present sample but reflects a global higher education challenge. O'Callaghan et al. (2021), specifically studying accounting students, showed that this gap has direct professional implications: in business disciplines, the inability to apply advanced information evaluation and filtering skills impairs students' capacity to interpret financial reports, assess industry evidence, and support professional arguments with credible sources.

It is worth comparing the present results to the European Commission's own data on digital competence levels among EU citizens. According to the Joint Research Centre (2025), as of 2023, only 56% of EU adults possessed above-basic digital skills, while 43% of secondary school students failed to reach even basic digital skill levels. Among workers, 42% reported significant AI skills gaps in 2024–2025. While these aggregate statistics are not directly comparable to the present study's

DigComp 3.0 proficiency-level findings, they provide a policy context within which the Advanced and Highly Advanced level gaps identified here take on additional significance: if even basic and intermediate digital competence remains unevenly distributed across European populations, the near-floor-level scores ($M = 1.65$) at the Highly Advanced level in the present sample represent a critical upstream challenge for talent management strategies that aspire to produce digitally capable business graduates.

5.3. The Knowledge Deficit

The pattern across construct types, with Knowledge items receiving significantly lower scores ($M = 2.40$) than both Attitude ($M = 2.60$) and Skill items ($M = 2.59$), is a substantively meaningful finding with clear implications for how digital competence development is designed and delivered. The Friedman test confirmed the significance of these differences ($\chi^2(2) = 23.74$, $p < .001$), and post-hoc Wilcoxon tests showed that Knowledge was significantly lower than Attitude ($z = 3.99$, $p < .001$) and Skill ($z = -4.02$, $p < .001$), while Attitude and Skill did not differ ($z = 0.30$, $p = .761$). This asymmetry reveals a student cohort that feels positively disposed toward digital information work and reasonably confident in performing familiar tasks, but possesses weaker theoretical and conceptual understanding of the processes, systems, and phenomena that underlie effective digital information practice.

The knowledge-attitude-skill asymmetry identified here is well-established in the digital competence literature, though its specific dimensionality within a DigComp 3.0 instrument has not previously been reported. Getenet et al. (2024), studying first-year university students in Australia, showed that positive attitudes toward digital technology and self-assessed digital literacy contributed significantly to self-efficacy, which in turn predicted online engagement. However, their study also demonstrated that attitude and engagement do not guarantee accuracy in information judgment, a distinction that maps closely onto the knowledge gap observed in the present study. Students who feel positive about digital tools and confident in using them are not necessarily equipped with the conceptual framework needed to evaluate those tools critically. Zhao et al. (2021) similarly found in their systematic review that, across the higher education literature, students' perceptions of digital competence tended to be more positive in communication and collaboration domains than in information literacy and critical evaluation, domains that are inherently more knowledge-dependent.

The knowledge deficit has particular relevance to the role of artificial intelligence in academic information practice. Cosgrove & Cachia (2025), in DigComp 3.0, explicitly integrate AI competence across all five areas of the framework, including Area 1, on the grounds that understanding how AI systems curate, generate, and present information is now a basic requirement of digital information literacy. The knowledge-level competences at stake here, understanding how search algorithms prioritize results, how AI-generated text is produced, and what limitations affect the reliability of AI outputs, are precisely the competences where the present sample reported the lowest self-assessed proficiency. Lund et al. (2026) demonstrated that university students in the United States use traditional search engines and generative AI tools side-by-side, guided primarily by convenience and perceived usefulness rather than by principled understanding of each tool's informational properties. This behavioral pattern is consistent with a knowledge gap: students with positive attitudes toward digital tools and reasonable practical familiarity with them, but without conceptual grounding in how those tools work, are likely to make tool selection decisions based on habit and surface features rather than on the basis of academically informed judgment.

The relative strength of Attitude scores (M = 2.60) compared to Knowledge scores (M = 2.40) is consistent with findings across different national and disciplinary contexts. Mejías-Acosta et al. (2024), in their validation study of digital competence among university students in Ecuador, reported that attitudinal dimensions of digital competence were systematically rated more highly than knowledge-based dimensions, a pattern they attributed to students' extensive informal digital experience generating a sense of comfort and positive orientation toward technology without generating parallel conceptual depth. Draganac et al. (2022), examining business and economics students in Serbia and Croatia, populations directly comparable to the present study's business student sample, found that digital competence in information literacy and programming was rated significantly lower than in communication and social media use, with knowledge-level deficits proving especially pronounced. This comparative evidence places the present study's knowledge gap squarely within a regional and disciplinary pattern rather than treating it as a sample-specific anomaly.

Urenda et al. (2022), in their work on digital competencies for content curation, argue that effective information filtering involves not just the practical act of selecting sources but the conceptual ability to organize, compare, and evaluate them according to scholarly criteria. Filtering, like searching, is ultimately a knowledge-dependent activity: it requires students to know what peer review means, why publication context matters, how to recognize algorithmic influence on search results, and what distinguishes scholarly evidence from informal or promotional content. The consistently lower Knowledge scores in the present study suggest that students may be performing filtering tasks based on heuristics of convenience and presentation quality, as documented by Georgopoulou et al. (2025), rather than on the conceptually grounded evaluation criteria that DigComp 3.0 envisages at the Advanced and Highly Advanced levels.

5.4. Gender Differences

The exploratory Mann-Whitney U tests revealed no statistically significant gender differences in overall DigComp Area 1 scores or in any of the three competence domains (all $p > .10$). While these results must be interpreted with extreme caution given the substantial gender imbalance in the sample (18 female vs. 5 male participants), they are not inconsistent with patterns reported in the broader literature. The evidence on gender and digital competence is mixed internationally. Draganac et al. (2022) found that male students in their European sample reported slightly higher digital competence scores overall, particularly in programming-related competences, but these differences were not pronounced in information literacy domains. Mejías-Acosta et al. (2024) found that gender had a less consistent effect on digital competence than other variables such as prior training and study program. Zhao et al. (2021) noted in their systematic review that gender effects in higher education digital competence research are inconsistent across national contexts, with some studies reporting male advantages and others reporting female advantages, and still others finding no significant differences, a pattern that makes the null gender finding in the present study impossible to interpret without larger and more balanced samples. Future studies in the present institutional context should ensure gender-balanced sampling to provide a meaningful test of possible gender effects.

5.5. Implications for Digitalizing Talent Management in Higher Education

The results of this study, considered alongside the broader literature, carry important implications for how higher education institutions design and implement digital talent management strategies. The moderate, undifferentiated, and knowledge-deficient competence profile identified here is not a sample-specific curiosity but a reflection of patterns documented across multiple national and disciplinary contexts. What distinguishes this study is the application of DigComp 3.0's full proficiency-level and construct-type structure to a business student population, which reveals exactly where the most critical gaps lie, namely at the Advanced and Highly Advanced levels, and specifically in the knowledge dimension of information literacy.

Alenezi (2025), examining the relationship between digital library use, digital competence, and AI literacy among students in Kuwait, found that access to institutional digital resources does not automatically translate into the ability to use those resources effectively at higher levels of sophistication. This finding is directly applicable to the talent development challenge facing the institution studied here: investment in digital infrastructure, database subscriptions, AI tools, e-learning platforms, does not substitute for structured competence development that targets the Advanced and Highly Advanced levels of DigComp. Similarly,

Cabero-Almenara et al. (2022) demonstrated that digital competence is a statistically significant predictor of academic success in higher education, with students who have not repeated an academic year showing substantially higher digital competence scores. This finding implies that the Advanced and Highly Advanced level gaps observed in the present study are not merely an abstract measurement concern but a concrete academic risk factor: students who cannot confidently evaluate, filter, and manage complex digital information at higher proficiency levels are likely to produce lower-quality academic work, depend on weaker sources, and struggle to meet the evidence standards required by their programmes. For business education specifically, where academic performance is closely linked to information quality, in market analysis, feasibility studies, financial assessments, and management research, the proficiency gaps identified here carry direct implications for learning outcomes. Simovic et al. (2023) extended this argument to entrepreneurship: information browsing and filtering skills are not exclusively academic competencies but are foundational to entrepreneurial opportunity recognition, market analysis, and evidence-based decision-making, reinforcing the case that closing the Advanced-level gap serves both academic and career-development goals.

The knowledge deficit finding has particular implications for how digital competence development is positioned within the curriculum. Ahmad et al. (2023) found that distance learners who engaged with digital platforms primarily through self-directed, informal use, rather than through structured, concept-focused instruction, developed practical tool familiarity while remaining conceptually underprepared to critically evaluate the outputs of those tools. This dynamic is especially pronounced in business education, where the informal use of search engines, AI tools, and social media is pervasive but rarely academically supervised. Sahid & Ridzuan (2025) similarly found that information literacy emerged as the strongest predictor of academic library engagement ($\beta = .48$, $p < .001$) among Malaysian Generation Z students, well above problem-solving and critical thinking, a finding that underlines the foundational role of knowledge-level competence in driving effective information behavior. Together, these studies support the argument that digital talent management in higher education must move beyond digital exposure and towards the systematic development of conceptual knowledge about information systems, source evaluation, and AI-mediated content.

The internal consistency of the instrument provides a firm methodological basis for these interpretations. Cronbach's alpha coefficients of 0.74 for Competence 1.1, 0.82 for Competence 1.2, and 0.84 for Competence 1.3, with a total instrument alpha of 0.93, indicate satisfactory to excellent reliability across all components. These values are consistent with those reported in other DigComp-based self-assessment studies. Getenet et al. (2024) reported alpha values in the range of .78–.93 for digital literacy and self-efficacy subscales in their Australian study, and Mejías-Acosta et al. (2024) reported similarly strong reliability indices for their digital competence measurement scale. The psychometric quality of the present instrument therefore supports confidence in the substantive findings, while the pilot nature of the study and the small sample size continue to limit the generalizability of those findings beyond the specific institutional context.

5.6. Limitations and Directions for Future Research

Several limitations must be acknowledged. The sample of 23 undergraduate business students from a single institution is small and cannot support generalizations to broader student populations. All findings are strictly exploratory and hypothesis-generating. The gender imbalance (18 female vs. 5 male) severely constrains the gender comparisons. As a self-report instrument, the questionnaire captures subjective perception rather than demonstrated performance. The literature consistently cautions that self-assessed and objectively measured digital competence can diverge substantially (Sillat et al., 2021; Schaal et al., 2025; Georgopoulou et al., 2025). Future studies should complement self-assessment data with performance-based measures such as observed search tasks, source evaluation exercises, or assessment-embedded information tasks.

The cross-sectional design does not permit causal inference or conclusions about how digital competence develops over the academic career. Longitudinal designs that track students across years and across curriculum-embedded interventions would be particularly valuable. Several comparable studies have demonstrated the utility of this approach: Mejías-Acosta et al. (2024) in Ecuador and Draganac et al. (2022) in the European context both demonstrated that academic experience, prior training, and disciplinary context are significant moderators of digital competence development, moderators that longitudinal research would be better positioned to examine. This study focused exclusively on DigComp 3.0 Area 1. Future research should examine the relationships between Area 1 competences and other DigComp areas, particularly Area 2 (Communication and Collaboration) and Area 5 (Problem-Solving), as well as the moderating role of AI literacy in the relationship between self-assessed competence and academic performance.

DISCLOSURE OF DELEGATION TO GENERATIVE AI

The authors declare the use of generative AI in the research and writing process. According to the GAIDeT taxonomy (2025), the following tasks were delegated to GAI tools under full human supervision:

- Defining the research objective
- Writing the literature review
- Text generation
- Proofreading and editing
- Formulation of conclusions

The GAI tool used was: Claude Sonnet 4.6.

Responsibility for the final manuscript lies entirely with the authors.

GAI tools are not listed as authors and do not bear responsibility for the final outcomes.

Declaration submitted by: Collective responsibility

REFERENCES

Ahmad, R., Mehmood, S. T., & Ijaz, S. (2023). Digital literacy competencies: A study of distance learners of Higher Education Regulatory Authority Khyber Pakhtunkhwa. *Pakistan Journal of Distance & Online Learning*, *9*(1). https://eric.ed.gov/?id=EJ1401028

Alenezi, F. (2025). The use of digital libraries and its relationship to digital competence and AI literacy among students of the College of Basic Education in Kuwait. *Education for Information*. Advance online publication. DOI: 10.3233/EFI-240078

Association of College and Research Libraries (ACRL). (2015). *Framework for information literacy for higher education.* American Library Association. https://www.ala.org/acrl/standards/ilframework

Cabero-Almenara, J., Gutiérrez-Castillo, J. J., Guillén-Gámez, F. D., & Gaete-Bravo, A. F. (2022). Digital competence of higher education students as a predictor of academic success. *Technology. Knowledge and Learning*, *28*(2), 683–702. DOI: 10.1007/s10758-022-09624-8

Carretero, S., Vuorikari, R., & Punie, Y. (2017). *DigComp 2.1: The digital competence framework for citizens with eight proficiency levels and examples of use.* Publications Office of the European Union., DOI: 10.2760/38842

Chiu, T. K. F., Ahmad, Z., Ismail, M., & Sanusi, I. T. (2024). What are artificial intelligence literacy and competency? A comprehensive framework to support them. *Computers and Education Open*, *6*, 100171. Advance online publication. DOI: 10.1016/j.caeo.2024.100171

Cosgrove, J., & Cachia, R. (2025). *DigComp 3.0: European Digital Competence Framework* (5th ed.). Publications Office of the European Union., DOI: 10.2760/0001149

Dahlen, S. P., & Hanson, K. (2023). In their words: Student reflections on information-seeking behaviors. *Journal of Academic Librarianship*, *49*(4), 102713. DOI: 10.1016/j.acalib.2023.102713

Draganac, D., Jović, D., & Novak, A. (2022). Digital competencies in selected European countries among university and high-school students: Programming is lagging behind. Business Systems Research: International journal of the Society for Advancing Innovation and Research in Economy, 13(2), 135-154. DOI: 10.2478/bsrj-2022-0019

Georgopoulou, M. S., Troussas, C., Krouska, A., & Sgouropoulou, C. (2025). Digital literacy in higher education: Examining university students' competence in online information practices. *Computers*, *14*(12), 528. DOI: 10.3390/computers14120528

Getenet, S., Cantle, R., Redmond, P., & Albion, P. (2024). Students' digital technology attitude, literacy and self-efficacy and their effect on online learning engagement. *International Journal of Educational Technology in Higher Education*, *21*(1), 3. Advance online publication. DOI: 10.1186/s41239-023-00437-y

Joint Research Centre. European Commission. (2025). *Digital Competence Framework for Citizens (DigComp)*. Publications Office of the European Union. https://joint-research-centre.ec.europa.eu/digcomp_en

Kamela, M. (2024). Cut the CRAAP: Replacing vertical evaluation with lateral reading. *New Directions for Teaching and Learning*, *2024*(178), 71–80. DOI: 10.1002/tl.20608

Kuhlthau, C. C. (2004). Seeking meaning: A process approach to library and information services. *Information Research*, *9*(3).

Kuluşaklı, E. (2024). Distance learners' basic digital competence in higher education. *Yükseköğretim ve Bilim Dergisi*, *14*(2), 358–365. DOI: 10.5961/higheredusci.1455479

Leeder, C., & Shah, C. (2016). Practicing critical evaluation of online sources improves student search behavior. *Journal of Academic Librarianship*, *42*(4), 459–468. DOI: 10.1016/j.acalib.2016.04.001

Lund, B. D., Warren, S. J., & Teel, Z. A. (2026). Measuring university students' satisfaction with traditional search engines and generative AI tools as information sources. *arXiv preprint* arXiv:2601.00493. https://arxiv.org/abs/2601.00493 [Preprint; under review]

Mejías-Acosta, A., D'Armas Regnault, M., Vargas-Cano, E., Cárdenas-Cobo, J., & Vidal-Silva, C. (2024). Assessment of digital competencies in higher education students: Development and validation of a measurement scale. *Frontiers in Education*, *9*, 1497376. Advance online publication. DOI: 10.3389/feduc.2024.1497376

O'Callaghan, S., Calloway, L. J., Walker, J. P., Elson, R. J., Dwyer, C., & Boumediene, S. (2021). Digital literacy and accounting students: Implications for the profession. *Global Journal of Accounting and Finance*, *5*(1), 45–63. DOI: 10.47177/GJAF.05.01.2021.045

Safi, M., Abdallah, F., Erturk, A., & Alkhayyat, R. (2024). Digital readiness of the workforce for successful digital transformation: Exploring new digital competencies. *Proceedings*, *101*, 21. DOI: 10.3390/proceedings2024101021

Sahid, N. Z., & Ridzuan, N. B. (2025). Digital literacy skills and academic-library engagement among Generation Z students in Malaysian higher education. *International Journal of Research and Innovation in Social Science*, *9*(10), 7643–7656. Advance online publication. DOI: 10.47772/IJRISS.2025.910000623

Schaal, T., Tischendorf, T., Sydorenko, O., Karagulova, M., Chettykbayev, R., & Brauweiler, H.-C. (2025). Self-assessed vs. reported digital competence among health students in Germany, Sillat, L. H., Tammets, K., & Laanpere, M. (2021). Digital competence assessment methods in higher education: A systematic literature review. *Education Sciences*, *11*(8), 402.

Simovic, V., Safi, M., Bradić-Martinović, A., Sarhan, H., Bhagat, R., & Ivanovic, D. (2023). How competent are our students in digital entrepreneurship? *Proceedings*, *85*(1), 18. DOI: 10.3390/proceedings2023085018

Tafesse, W., Aguilar, M. P., Sayed, S., & Tariq, U. (2024). Digital overload, coping mechanisms, and student engagement: An empirical investigation based on the S-O-R framework. *SAGE Open*, *14*(1), 21582440241236087. Advance online publication. DOI: 10.1177/21582440241236087

Tzirides, A. O., Zapata, G., Kastania, N. P., Saini, A. K., Castro, V., Ismael, S. A., You, Y., Santos, T. A. D., Searsmith, D., O'Brien, C., Cope, B., & Kalantzis, M. (2024). Combining human and artificial intelligence for enhanced AI literacy in higher education. *Computers and Education Open*, *6*, 100184. Advance online publication. DOI: 10.1016/j.caeo.2024.100184

Urenda, S. D. R., Yparrea, N. G., Moreira, E. L., Uicab, M. C., & Grez, A. G. (2022, September). Digital Competencies for Content Curation in the Open Education Framework. In *2022 XII International Conference on Virtual Campus (JICV)* (pp. 1-4). IEEE. DOI: 10.1109/JICV56113.2022.9934776

Wang, Q., Ma, Z., Zhang, G., & Miao, Q. (2025). Digital transformation driving educational reforms in higher education: A paradigm shift in teaching and learning. *SAGE Open*, *15*(1), 254–272. Advance online publication. DOI: 10.1177/25902547251395880

Watson, D., Webb, R., Cook, S., & Grant, K. (2025). Does the internet lead to surface searching and a deficiency of discovery in student learning? *Education and Information Technologies*, *30*(14), 19853–19878. DOI: 10.1007/s10639-025-13498-5

Zhao, Y., Pinto Llorente, A. M., & Sánchez Gómez, M. C. (2021). Digital competence in higher education research: A systematic literature review. *Computers & Education*, *168*, 104212. Advance online publication. DOI: 10.1016/j.compedu.2021.104212 PMID: 36568577

Zhao, Y., Sánchez Gómez, M. C., Pinto Llorente, A. M., & Zhao, L. (2021). Digital competence in higher education: Students' perception and personal factors. *Sustainability (Basel)*, *13*(21), 12184. DOI: 10.3390/su132112184

Chapter 3
Digital Transformation and the Future of Academic Careers: A Talent Management Framework for Higher Education

Sapheya Aftimos
http://orcid.org/0000-0002-5810-9856
Australian University, Kuwait

Randa Diab-Bahman
American International University, Kuwait

Dunya Hassoun
Australian University, Kuwait

ABSTRACT

This chapter examines how digital transformation is reshaping academic careers in higher education and why universities must rethink talent management to support emerging roles. As teaching, research, and administration become digitally enabled, career models based on linear pathways are becoming less suitable. Drawing on strategic talent management, digital transformation, and boundaryless career perspectives, the chapter explores roles such as digital pedagogy specialists, data-intensive researchers, research data stewards, and scholarship leaders. It highlights the limits of systems for recruitment, development, evaluation, and promotion. In response, the chapter proposes a conceptual framework built around strategic

DOI: 10.4018/979-8-3373-8959-2.ch003

alignment, flexible career pathways, inclusive performance systems, continuous capability development, and human-centered talent practices. It concludes that universities must align digital ambitions with adaptive, inclusive career structures.

1. INTRODUCTION

The world of higher education is evolving very rapidly. In today's digitally disrupted, globally mobile, resource-scarce, society-impact and innovation-driven landscape, the university environment has become extremely competitive (Lei et al., 2023). Institutions are expected to adopt innovative approaches to teaching and learning, be strong in research, and contribute directly to economic and social development.

This transformation is at the heart of digital technologies. Artificial Intelligence, learning analytics, digital platforms, and data-intensive research infrastructures are transforming how higher education institutions operate (Kharchenko et al., 2024). Online systems and digital learning environments increasingly support teaching and learning, and research increasingly draws on large datasets, computational processes, and collaborative platforms. Administrative and academic decision-making is also increasingly becoming data-driven.

Technology is not the only thing that has changed. There are many changes in the way academic work is done. Traditionally, academic jobs have been more predictable, with scholars progressing from lecturer to researcher to administrator. These roles were reflected in promotion systems, evaluation criteria, and professional development opportunities. Success criteria were generally considered to include teaching performance, research publications, and institutional service (Pham, 2021).

This is the model that the digital university is revolutionizing. Academic tasks now demand more skills and abilities, and academics are now using their disciplinary knowledge alongside digital, analytical, and collaborative skills. Digital environments are used for teaching, complex data analysis, and new technologies in research, and collaboration is increasingly multi-disciplinary and cross-institutional.

As such needs increase, new academic positions are emerging in universities. Digital pedagogy experts support technology-enhanced learning; digital pedagogy designers assist faculty in designing engaging digital courses; digital pedagogy researchers utilize sophisticated computational tools; digital pedagogy research data stewards oversee complex datasets; and digital pedagogy leaders and interdisciplinary knowledge brokers bridge expertise across disciplines (Sejdiu & Sejdiu, 2025).

Many systems are not fully adapted within their universities. Recruitment, promotion, and development processes may still be based on the traditional academic career model. New digital roles are not always explicitly defined in institutional structures, and digitally enabled teaching and research capacities may be of minor relevance to career progression systems.

This leaves an increasing gap. While universities invest heavily in digital transformation, their talent processes may still be stuck in the academic model. If this imbalance becomes a habit, institutions risk missing emerging knowledge and digital innovation, thus failing to have the desired ripple effects.

This chapter fills this gap by taking a multi-disciplinary approach that incorporates three areas of research: digital transformation in higher education, strategic talent management, and future-of-work studies. It brings these views together and explores what this means for academic roles and for universities' responses. This chapter also develops a conceptual framework for understanding the potential to re-imagine talent strategies to accommodate new academic positions while maintaining academic values, including autonomy, scholarly creativity, and intellectual diversity.

2. CHAPTER OBJECTIVES

I. To examine how digital transformation is reshaping academic work and career structures in higher education institutions.
II. To identify emerging academic roles and competencies required in the digital university.
III. To analyze challenges faced by traditional academic career systems in adapting to digital transformation.
IV. To explore talent management strategies that support flexible and hybrid academic career pathways.
V. To develop a conceptual framework that guides universities in redesigning academic careers in the digital university.

3. THEORY AND CONCEPTUAL PRINCIPLES

This chapter is grounded in an interdisciplinary theoretical foundation that brings together strategic talent management, digital transformation theory, and perspectives from higher education research. These bodies of knowledge provide a lens through which to understand how academic work is changing and how institutions can respond. Their integration is important because a single factor does not drive the transformation of academic careers; rather, it is the interaction among technology, institutional strategy, and workforce systems that drives it. Together, these perspectives support a more nuanced understanding of how universities can redesign academic careers in a digitally evolving landscape.

3.1 Strategic Talent Management Theory

The strategic talent management theory provides a key foundation for this chapter. It highlights a connection between the HR policies and the business strategy. The theory proposes that institutions that can recruit, train, and retain individuals whose skills and capabilities are congruent with their strategic goals achieve sustainable performance (Collings & Mellahi, 2009; Aftimos & Khafash, 2026). Talent, then, is not managed in isolation, but directly linked to the direction and priorities of the organization.

This view is relevant for higher education. Universities do not operate in a stable environment with predictable demands. They are confronted with digital disruption, global talent mobility, and pressure to innovate and make a difference (Blankesteijn & Ghorbani, 2025). Consequently, the prevalence of digital education, transdisciplinary research, and greater interaction with external actors has been increasingly discussed in institutional strategies. These shifts call for new forms of expertise and new modes of organizing academic work.

The theory points out the need to adapt academic career systems to these changing priorities. The workforce planning process needs to be forward-looking and flexible. Recruit people with a mix of discipline and digital skills. Professional development systems should provide access to continuing learning and skills development. There should also be emerging ways of making contributions, such as digital teaching innovations and team-based research (Kelley, 2022; Aftimos & Diab-Bahman, 2025), which should be recognized in promotion and assessment systems.

One of the main lessons learned from this theory is that talent systems become enablers of strategy. They help enhance performance and innovation when they align with institutional objectives, but can become a limitation when they do not. There is still a gap between digital transformation strategies and the current academic career systems at many universities (Abhari, 2025). Institutions can invest in digital technologies, but their recruitment, development, and promotion structures can still be based on traditional models. This incongruity can reduce the impact of digital transformation efforts.

Understanding that differentiation should be at the heart of strategic talent management is another good part of it. Not every job is created equal. Certain roles are critical to creating competitive advantage (Collings & Mellahi, 2009). These are roles in the digital university, such as digital pedagogy specialists, data-intensive scholars, and interdisciplinary knowledge brokers. In this regard, strategic talent management implies that such positions should be well-defined, supported, and institutionalized to foster and retain critical skills.

The theory also highlights the importance of talent development. Aside from hiring the right people, institutions need to invest in workforce development in dynamic environments continually. This is particularly true in the digital university, where technologies and practices are constantly changing. Academics need regular opportunities to stay up to date with their skills to be effective in teaching and research, as well as in collaborating with others (Haque et al., 2024). Structured professional development and learning opportunities are then vital elements of talent strategy.

Another key consideration is retention, as international competition among universities for the highly skilled academic and professional workforce intensifies. Highly capable employees are more likely to stay when institutions provide opportunities to develop and grow their careers, make a difference, and be recognized for their efforts (Gandy et al., 2018). Institutions can lose key talent when emerging roles are not recognized or supported. The focus of strategic talent management is on providing integrated, flexible career structures that enable diverse roles and career paths.

This aligns with the boundaryless careers perspective. Academic careers today are not limited to a single institution or discipline (Gerli et al., 2015). Researchers are conducting research at various institutions, with industry, and in international research networks. Strategic talent management must facilitate mobility, flexibility, and collaboration. These demands move from static to more flexible systems.

Meanwhile, strategic talent management in higher education must be conducted in a manner sensitive to the unique character of academic jobs. Universities are not exclusively business entities. Their core values are academic freedom, intellectual autonomy, and scholarly integrity. Talent strategies will thus need to be developed in a way that is both strategic and maintains these values (Howaniec et al., 2022). This balance is crucial to safeguarding the identity and mission of higher education institutions.

The chapter is based on strategic talent management theory to guide the understanding of how academic career systems can be redesigned. It highlights the need for strategy and talent to "align" and the dangers of "misalignment" such as role ambiguity, capability gaps, and the effectiveness of digital transformation efforts.

The chapter moves beyond the technological understanding of digital transformation by adopting this perspective. It highlights how people are managed within institutions as an important factor of the digital university. Talent systems need to adapt to technology to embrace new roles, skills, and working methods. This insight is an important element in the framework built in this chapter.

3.2 Digital Transformation in Higher Education

Digital transformation theory refers to how new technologies are changing how things work, the jobs people do, and the organizations they belong to. In universities, digital technologies are impacting teaching and learning, research methods, knowledge sharing, and university administration. Recent literature shows that digital transformation is not merely about adopting new technologies; it also involves changes in how universities operate and generate value.

The digital transformation in universities is seen as a multidimensional process encompassing organizational, pedagogical, and technological dimensions. Recent scholarship suggests that transformation occurs through the interplay of institutional logic, technological infrastructure, implementation tools, and leadership, reshaping governance structures and educational delivery (Zabalawi et al., 2024). The same holds for Teker et al. (2025) and Zhukabayeva et al. (2025), who argue that digitalization should be linked to the institution's vision and long-term objectives, and that digital transformation is more than a mere technical change.

Teaching and learning have undergone significant change, as digital transformation has profoundly impacted pedagogical approaches. AI, learning analytics, and immersive technologies such as virtual reality (VR) are increasingly shaping personalized, adaptive learning environments for students, driven by their integration into educational systems and practices (Modi & Garg, 2025). This transformation is part of a growing trend in education known as "Education 5.0," which highlights the importance of modern technology in driving innovation, collaboration, and flexible learning. Consequently, the nature of the educational role is changing, and teachers are becoming more like facilitators of learning assisted by digital tools.

Digital transformation is also reshaping institutional operations and administrative processes, leading to data-driven, more agile institutional structures that enable institutions to respond more quickly. Empirical research indicates that digital systems, such as paperless workflows and automation, can increase transparency, efficiency, and decision-making within universities (Carmo et al., 2025). Digital transformation is also transforming research.

3.3 Boundaryless and Hybrid Career Theory

The literature on the future of work points to a more fluid, interdisciplinary, and collaborative nature of professional careers. The academic career is transforming in the digital university, shifting toward a hybrid model that integrates teaching, research, technology expertise, and innovation-focused activities.

Recent studies indicate that academic careers in higher education are becoming more open-ended, collaborative, and interdisciplinary rather than linear. This is consistent with the growing importance of boundaryless and hybrid careers, in which people operate across multiple fields and continually adapt to new institutional and technological settings. In the context of digital transformation in universities, the roles of teachers and researchers are becoming increasingly blurred and interconnected through the integration of teaching and research, innovation and technology expertise, and technological innovation (Singun, 2025; Zhukabayeva et al., 2025).

Academics working across functional and disciplinary boundaries and across institutions is a result of digital transformation and is opening the way for boundaryless career paths. The expanding application of artificial intelligence, collaborative technologies, and digital platforms facilitates learning activities that are not constrained by geographical and organizational boundaries (Tang et al., 2025). Academic jobs are becoming more fluid than ever before.

However, research also indicates that issues arise during this transition. Ambiguity, complexity, and increased workloads can result from expanding and changing roles, particularly if institutional policies are not explicitly stated or have not evolved to accommodate hybrid roles. There can also be conflicts between traditional academic systems and new digital careers (Singun, 2025). Furthermore, the lack of digital skills can hinder academics' capacity to fully engage with these new roles, especially if resources, training, and institutional support are lacking. This can lead to a differential opportunity for career advancement.

Digital transformation is a key factor enabling boundaryless and hybrid career models and is rapidly changing academic careers in higher education. Academic life is increasingly flexible and technology-oriented, and demands constant learning, constant development of digital skills, and the capacity to cross boundaries. Such shifts, generally, represent the reorientation of academics towards future-of-work patterns and a view of them as flexible providers in the increasingly multi-layered, digitalized higher education industry.

There is a coherence to these three theoretical perspectives on academic career transition in the digital university. Digital Transformation Theory is a concept that helps to understand the technology and organizational forces transforming higher education. Strategic talent management theory focuses on the institutional arrangements needed to attract, develop, and retain the capacity to support this transformation. The Boundaryless and Hybrid Career Theory explains how these changes manifest in academic careers, career mobility, and interdisciplinary working patterns. Combining these views indicates that an academic career shift is not just a result of technological change but also of the interaction between digital innovations, institutions' talent systems, and new career models. This holistic view is the basis for the conceptual framework outlined in the chapter.

4. EMERGING ACADEMIC ROLES

4.1. Digital Pedagogy Roles

Education has always been a priority for countries worldwide in the attempt to improve it. Digital learning is not a novel phenomenon in the field of learning. Information and communication technologies have become part of the strategies of many universities and schools around the world, including schools in the UAE, which have implemented online learning platforms (OLPs) or virtual learning environments (VLEs) (Alhogail & Mirza, 2011). All these platforms have been used for traditional and distance learning. The COVID-19 pandemic was declared a global emergency by the WHO in 2020, resulting in unprecedented disruption in all sectors of life, including education. This crisis led to faster adoption of digital learning technologies and greater importance in ensuring the continuity of learning.

Virtual learning environments are platforms where students and teachers can interact, share resources, and complete the learning process online, or complement in-person learning. Their primary role is to oversee, support, and improve the learning process. VLEs offer capabilities that help to develop, communicate, and assess content during the teaching-learning process, as indicated by Morais et al. (2017). Other research has also found positive impacts in various settings. For instance, some researchers in higher education, such as Dahlstrom et al. (2014), have reported that VLEs enhance the learning experience. In contrast, Morais et al. (2017) concluded that the use of VLEs can improve student performance.

The use of digital learning technologies has made learning more flexible and accessible, and improved learning effectiveness. They have come into use during the pandemic, and they have also proven their value for continuity in times of crisis. Current research has confirmed the value of VLEs in supporting student engagement and performance beyond their use as 'supplements', providing an increasing body of evidence for their positive impact. In the future, institutions should aim to improve these platforms, address issues of digital inequality and faculty preparedness, and integrate them more effectively into the pedagogical process. In this way, they can play their part in building more resilient, inclusive, and future-focused education systems.

4.2 Institutional Barriers

Online and hybrid learning are expanding rapidly, dramatically changing the face of higher education and posing numerous institutional challenges. The universities have been asked to revamp the curriculum, invest in digital infrastructure, and support faculty in adopting new teaching methods (Mishra et al., 2020). As noted earlier, developments have occurred while academic staff's expectations for teaching, research, service, and administration have grown, leading to higher workloads and professional stress (Rapanta et al., 2020).

Organizations will have priorities that can conflict with personal pedagogical choices. Teachers are often forced to incorporate new technologies and teaching methods within constrained time, staff development, and technical assistance. Barriers to online learning are categorized into four types: learner, instructor, curriculum, and university level (Muilenburg & Berge, 2005), indicating that there are multiple implementation barriers.

For the institution, challenges can include limited technological facilities, limited professional development opportunities, limited support for curriculum design, or complex curriculum approval procedures. These may be obstacles to the effective implementation of online and blended learning models and can indeed affect the quality and consistency of teaching.

While technology resources are critical, success with digital learning requires institutional readiness, leadership support, and policies that foster innovation and support faculty and students. These systemic obstacles must be overcome to maintain quality online and blended instruction.

4.3 Capability Gaps

Universities and colleges are moving away from traditional classroom-based teaching toward a flexible, blended model. New approaches, tools, and attitudes are needed for teaching today. It also requires more flexibility in both institutions and teachers. The pressure for rapid change in higher education systems has been growing due to globalization, rapid technological change, and growing competition (Diab-Bahman & Al-Enzi, 2021).

Numerous studies demonstrate the significant connection between students' and instructors' learning outcomes. Student attachment to their lecturers is associated with good performance and high levels of engagement. This relationship, sometimes referred to as rapport, fosters motivation, positive attitudes, and enhanced perceptions of learning (Wilson & Ryan, 2013). With online learning, student-teacher interaction is even more crucial for success.

Student satisfaction is also highly related to learning success. It influences the assessment of the school or college and the class. Students' satisfaction depends on their perceptions of learning effectiveness and self-confidence, particularly in digital learning environments.

There is evidence that synchronous hybrid learning is more flexible than fully online and fully face-to-face learning. It also, however, creates new challenges. These include, but are not limited to, technological disruptions and unequal opportunities for learning (Raes et al., 2020). The hybrid system can lower consistency as students and teachers often alternate between learning and teaching modes (Sharafeddine et al., 2024). This impacts the continuity of teaching and relationship building.

Measurement is another challenge. Assessing learning experiences depends on valid tools. However, there are not many valid scales to assess student–instructor rapport. A popular instrument is the Student–Instructor Relationship Scale (SIRS), which comprises 45 items (Creasey, Jarvis, & Knapcik, 2009; Wilson et al., 2010)—later shortened to the SIRS-9 to facilitate research use (Lammers & Gillaspy, 2013). Both online and physical classrooms have demonstrated a strong predictive ability for student learning experiences with this scale.

Effective student–instructor rapport often manifests as behaviors such as encouraging students, being fair, being available, and participating in classroom discussions (Benson et al., 2005). Immediacy of the teacher is also a significant factor. It refers to verbal and nonverbal actions that minimize psychological distance between students and instructors and enhance students' motivation.

Although online teaching has the above advantages, it also brings many difficulties. Building good relationships in virtual environments is a challenge for many instructors. Online interactions can sometimes be less spontaneous and more formal. Building relationships needs more intentional efforts (Murphy & Rodríguez-Manzanares, 2012). Technology management and digital communication devices also consume significant time from instructors.

Additional difficulties are the need for student identification, engagement, and timely communication. Additionally, online spaces reduce informal learning in physical classrooms. Despite these difficulties, the field of research in this area is still in its infancy and requires further enhancements (Wilson & Ryan, 2013).

The quality of learning is highly dependent on interaction and communication. It is important to plan teaching strategies for online/hybrid models. It is therefore necessary to invest in pedagogical and technological support within institutions to enhance outcomes.

4.4 Digital Learning Challenges and Student Experience

The growth of online learning has transformed the way universities develop and offer education. The teaching is now more learner-centered and tech-based. This has expanded the roles of teachers and academics (Mishra et al., 2020). Now, faculty have to manage the combination of teaching, research, administration, and digital courses. This has led to work overload and stress (Rapanta et al., 2020).

Another change in the student experience is online learning. It is difficult to keep learners engaged as they are likely to study alone. Students who lack a feeling of belonging are more likely to drop out. This risk can be minimized and success facilitated by strong interaction with instructors (Glazier, 2016).

Sometimes the expectations of the institutions do not align with the teaching preferences. Many teachers are expected to implement new technologies with limited time and training. Online learning barriers can be found on the learner level, the teacher level, the curriculum design level, and the institutional systems level (Muilenburg & Berge, 2005). Some of these barriers include access to technology, communication issues, and a lack of opportunities for interaction.

Online learning was growing even before the COVID-19 era. Very few studies have investigated whether the rapport-building strategies used in online courses are similar to those used in the hybrid courses.

Others point out the lack of emotional and social engagement that may occur in traditional classrooms in virtual learning settings (Seabolt & Arends, 2000). Students might not have time for organized discussion and networking. There is also evidence that students still prefer the traditional mode of teaching even when learning outcomes are equivalent (Piccoli et al., 2001;).

Technology can present difficulties for learners as well. Some students are more at ease with digital tools than others. Others have trouble using the online systems. Online assessments can cause more anxiety than in-class assessments. Digital forms of feedback are frequently less received by students. Second-language learners may also experience language barriers in online environments.

Teachers are not spared from these challenges. For many, using virtual learning systems for the first time can be stressful. This is particularly the case when learners are more technologically competent than teachers (Walker & White, 2013).

Digital learning is flexible and widens access to education. However, it also raises challenges in engagement, technology, and emotion. These difficulties impact not only students but also the instructor. To create effective online education, however, technology is not enough. It will take good pedagogy, support, and strategic work to enhance interaction and learning.

4.5 Digital Scholarship Leadership

The centrality of leadership in digital scholarship in higher education has become an integral part of the twenty-first century. The adoption of digital tools in research, teaching, and knowledge sharing within universities is growing. This change has altered the nature of academic leadership. Leadership is no longer about authority or control alone; it now centers on fostering collaboration, innovation, and shared knowledge-building (Scanlon, 2018).

Digital scholarship is an extension of academic scholarship. It involves data-based research, open-access publication, and online collaboration, and it requires leaders who understand both academics and digital systems. Leaders will need to facilitate flexible, networked modes of knowledge production rather than linear, hierarchical models (Scanlon, 2018).

Here, leadership is more facilitative, centered on people, ideas, and technologies; academic leaders act as enablers rather than gatekeepers. This promotes openness and broader involvement in research and education (Diab-Bahman, 2024). This is also indicative of a changing academic identity, with a focus on collaboration and shared responsibility.

An interdisciplinary effort is also essential to digital scholarship. Research today is frequently interdisciplinary, involving computing, the humanities, and the social sciences. This poses opportunities and challenges. There are distinct methods, languages, and standards within each discipline. Leaders, therefore, need to help clarify these disparities. They serve as 'boundary spanners' and facilitate communication and understanding between teams (Palmer et al., 2009).

Distributed leadership models are also essential for the successful implementation of strong digital scholarship leadership. Whereas expertise is distributed among numerous people in digital environments, it is not concentrated in a single person. Teams and networks share leadership. This enhances flexibility and aids quick, effective problem-solving. It also enhances ownership and commitment of researchers and staff (Al-Rashidi et al., 2021; Harris et al., 2013; Diab-Bahman & Bahman, 2022).

At the institutional level, leadership must be more than just a project manager. It means formulating a strategy, policy, and allocating resources. It is important to invest in digital infrastructure and support systems for universities. They also need to develop policies to foster collaboration and innovation. Digital scholarship is viable only when it becomes part of institutional structures and priorities (Boone et al., 2020).

The key to larger, more complex research teams is coordination. Digital tools enhance communication, but not collaboration. Expectations need to be managed and goals set in concert, while leaders must provide guidance on how teams can work together. They also have to manage the diversity of expertise while ensuring coherence. This has to be continuously adjusted and actively engaged (Börner et al., 2010).

Sustainability is another important issue. Long-term planning and capacity building are needed for digital scholarship. The technical and human capacities of leaders need to be developed. This includes providing staff and students with digital skills training and supporting current learning. Leadership in this sense is not a one-time effort but a continuous process of collaboration, development, and cultivation (Diab-Bahman et al., 2022).

Innovation in digital scholarship is not limited to technological aspects; it is also organizational. It depends on the integration of digital tools in day-to-day academic activities in institutions. Leaders need to foster experimentation and innovation in working practices. They are responsible for enhancing the practice of digital research and its outcomes. An ideal digital tool becomes an integral part of the academic workflow and not an additional system (Harris et al., 2013).

One of the most powerful forces for innovation is interdisciplinary collaboration. Working in a multi-disciplinary way creates new ideas and approaches. However, this process should be carefully coordinated. There can be barriers due to differences in language, methods, and criteria for assessing the work. These obstacles can be reduced through effective leadership that encourages dialogue and collaboration to pursue common goals (Palmer et al., 2009).

Innovation and collaboration are central to digital scholarship leadership. Technology needs to be tied to academics for the leaders to do their job. They need to support interdisciplinary practice, enable distributed leadership, and enhance institutional capacity. Most of all, they need to foster a context in which digital scholarship can develop sustainably and inclusively.

5. ORGANIZATIONAL AND CULTURAL CHALLENGES

While digital transformation offers numerous opportunities, universities still face challenges when redesigning academic careers and adopting hybrid career models. In higher education, governance and academic norms are generally well established and change gradually at the institutional level. Meanwhile, digital innovation is continually evolving, and the pressure on academics to take on roles beyond traditional academic work is increasing. Institutional inertia to change, inflexibility in promotion and evaluation, lack of digital skills, overload, and faculty role ambiguity are therefore important factors that limit efforts to change academic careers. When all these barriers are linked together, academic job design can become a tricky proposition in digitally transforming universities and hinder the effectiveness of digital transformation efforts.

5.1. Institutional Resistance to Change

The universities are well-grounded in disciplinary traditions, hierarchies of governance, and cultural norms that tend to prioritize continuity before disruption. These traits can have a stabilizing effect, but can also be a barrier to new technology, academic careers, and career models, leading to resistance to digital transformation. Conventional approaches to teaching and institutional norms tend to take precedence over innovation in digital instructional methods and new technologies, as well as the adoption of change in practice (Onan, 2024). A systematic review by Singun (2025) also demonstrates that faculty members may be less receptive to technological change when they are more comfortable with traditional modes and explicit forms of academic work.

In recent literature, resistance has been found to occur at institutional and individual levels. Institutions may prefer traditional bureaucratic systems to maintain control and accountability when uncertainty is present, while faculty members may see digital technologies as disruptive rather than enabling (Singun, 2025). New expectations for academics regarding the use of AI tools, digital collaboration, and the creation of digital learning environments can become burdensome if not supported, trained, and motivated to do so (Aftimos & Diab-Bahman, 2026). Institutional norms and personal comfort zones can work against the creation of new academic positions and career paths (Tang et al., 2025).

However, individual change and investment in digital infrastructure are not enough to overcome institutional resistance. It also demands a rethinking of the organizational and cultural assumptions that are rooted in academic life. To break these constraints and move toward new academic roles, universities must connect professional development programs, governance mechanisms, and incentives with digital transformation objectives.

5.2 Rigid Promotion and Evaluation Systems

One key challenge highlighted in literature is the disconnect between traditional assessment systems and the skills required for digitally enabled academic positions (Jing, 2025). Research indicates that traditional teaching methods and research findings still carry significant weight in evaluations and career advancement, whereas support for the digital transformation is sometimes underrepresented (Koseda et al., 2024). Therefore, faculty members may not be keen to invest time and effort in digital skills or to try out new teaching and learning technologies. Even the most well-designed digital strategies can fall short if the frameworks that underpin them do not complement them.

The difficulty is most stark in promotion systems that persist in using publication counts, grant acquisition, and disciplinary research results as the main measures for academic success. These are still critical, but sometimes these strategies are not able to capture the significant effort required to design online courses, create digital learning resources, incorporate artificial intelligence tools into instruction, facilitate students' participation in online classroom settings, or manage institutional digital innovation initiatives. For faculty who spend significant time on digital transformation and feel it has little impact on their career trajectory, this may lead to a lack of enthusiasm for engaging in institutional change (Jing, 2025).

Research also indicates that digital transformation is changing the nature of academic work and needs more extensive and flexible assessment criteria. Academics are now expected to be digital leaders—interdisciplinary, technologically adaptable, and able to connect with various stakeholders through virtual platforms (Tang et al., 2025). However, many universities still measure performance through traditional academic structures. This can create conflicts between the institutions' expectations and career incentives, leading to role overload, low motivation, and delayed implementation of innovative practices. Therefore, flexible academic careers require flexible promotion and evaluation systems within the university, where digital scholarship, technology-enhanced teaching, innovative activities, and institutional digital transformation are valued and considered alongside traditional academic achievements.

6. CONCEPTUAL FRAMEWORK

University transformation is underway amid profound, irreversible changes in digital technologies. E-learning is increasingly adopted, research is becoming more data-driven and collaborative, and university operations are becoming more automated and interconnected. These changes are dynamic and reinforcing, changing the central roles of higher education. It is, in consequence, profoundly changing the nature of academic work. Academic career systems have not developed in the same manner, however. They remain consistent, linear, and school-centered paths of development from a different time. This conflict is increasingly building up between institutional aspirations and labor realities.

In response to this need, the chapter proposes a conceptual framework to reimagine academic careers in the digital university. The framework is rooted in strategic talent management, digital transformation theory, and boundaryless career perspectives. It acknowledges that academic trajectories are no longer linear and predictable, but more dynamic, hybrid, and changing. Meanwhile, it reiterates that any change should be consistent with basic principles of learning, such as independence, creativity, and intellectual freedom.

The framework sees digital transformation as a key element in change in academic work. It influences the emergence of new roles, the required capabilities, and patterns of collaboration. The framework also states that talent management systems simultaneously drive the impacts of digital transformation. These systems establish roles and career pathways, and shape performance evaluation and capability development. An institution with a talent system in sync with digital transformation can better innovate, be more flexible, and be more sustainable. Otherwise, transformation initiatives can be disjointed and underdeliver.

The five dimensions of the framework are interrelated and focus on strategic alignment of talent and digital transformation, flexible and hybrid career pathways, performance evaluation and promotion, continuous professional development and digital capability building, and human-centered and inclusive talent systems. These dimensions are not independent of each other. They provide a comprehensive solution to reimagine academic careers in the context of a digitally reshaping higher education landscape.

Figure 1. Conceptual framework for reimagining academic careers in the digital university.

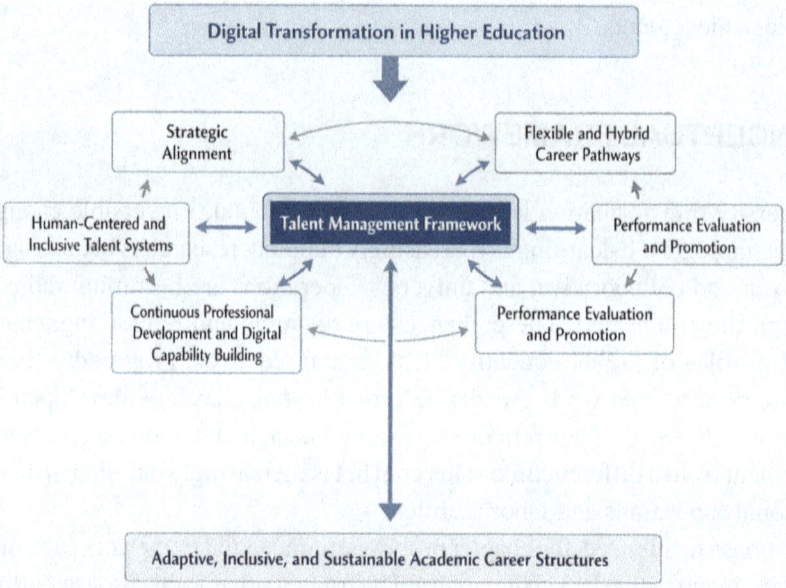

Note. This model shows digital transformation as the main driver of change, talent management as the organizing principle, five related dimensions of the framework, and the resulting academic career structures, which are adaptive, inclusive, and sustainable.

6.1 Strategic Alignment Between Talent and Digital Transformation

The first dimension is the framework's foundation: aligning institutional digital strategies with talent management processes. The journey of digital transformation starts with strategic intent, and universities use technologies to enhance their teaching and research and to make their operations more efficient. However, these aspirations will not come to fruition unless backed by the appropriate workforce competencies. This highlights the need to link strategy and talent.

Workforce planning, recruitment, and role design are aligned with institutional priorities through strategic alignment. In the case of digital learning, for instance, knowledge of online pedagogy and instructional design is required, and data-driven research demands proficiency in analytics and computational techniques. The purpose of talent strategies should be proactive and forward-looking, identifying the skills required in the future rather than merely identifying current skill gaps.

The recognition of new academic roles highlights the dimension. The digital transformation has led to the emergence of new roles, such as digital pedagogy specialists, research data stewards, and interdisciplinary knowledge brokers. Institutional innovation is dependent on such roles, but they are not necessarily built into the existing institutional career system. If there is no recognition, they can be marginalized and have undefined career pathways.

This dimension contributes significantly to the framework, influencing institutional priorities and expectations and thereby shaping the direction of the other dimensions. It affects the design of career pathways, performance measurement, and development programs. In this context, strategic alignment establishes coherence and facilitates maintaining consistency of all the elements of the framework with the common institutional objectives.

6.2 Flexible and Hybrid Career Pathways

The second dimension concerns the structure of academic careers. It represents a shift from traditional linear career structures to more flexible, adaptive ones. In the digital university, academics cannot be confined to a single domain. There is growing integration of teaching, research, and innovation, and academics are expected to perform across multiple fields.

Careers in these fields can be flexible and hybrid, enabling people to switch between them and to blend various types of expertise. For instance, an academic can design digital courses while also teaching, researching, conducting data analytics, or collaborating with industry. These overlaps should be seen as valid pathways to careers and are what students encounter in today's academic world.

Structurally, this dimension aligns strategic vision with actionable career design by developing pathways for new roles and capabilities. It also reinforces the concept of a boundaryless career, in which people cross disciplinary and institutional boundaries and adapt to shifting contexts.

This dimension is particularly important in the context of performance evaluation. Assessment systems that capture the range of ways people contribute are needed for flexible career pathways. If not, hybrid positions can be difficult to legitimate or advance successfully. Likewise, this dimension relates to individuals' professional growth, as flexible careers rely on lifelong learning and continual adaptation.

For this dimension, flexibility and responsiveness are stressed. It facilitates the development of academic careers in tandem with rapid technological and institutional transformation, ensuring academic relevance and sustainability.

6.3 Performance Evaluation and Promotion Systems

The third dimension concerns the assessment and reward of academic work. Performance evaluation systems are important tools in the university's toolbox for influencing behavior. They communicate preferences and guide academics' time and energy priorities.

There are traditional assessment models that prioritize research products, teaching duties, and administrative tasks. They are still significant, but they do not reflect the impact of digital transformation. The development of digital learning environments, research data management, and interdisciplinary collaboration are some of the less valued activities.

As the framework's incentive mechanism, this dimension can enhance or inhibit the power of the other dimensions. Flexible pathways, for instance, can only thrive if there are assessment tools that acknowledge and appreciate alternate ways of contributing to the course. Likewise, professional development is less effective when new skills are not recognized in performance measures.

This aspect is also important for strategic alignment. Criteria for evaluation should be based on institutional priorities. For those who are aiming to achieve strategic innovation through digital, contributions should be rewarded and recognized. It is also important to ensure that evaluation processes are transparent and consistent, fostering fairness and trust among academic staff.

This dimension is also closely related to human-centered principles. The assessment systems used are fair and inclusive, allowing all academics an equal opportunity to be recognized and promoted. This way, the power to evaluate performance becomes an important tool for achieving meaningful, lasting change by aligning incentives with institutional goals.

6.4 Continuous Professional Development and Digital Capability Building

The fourth dimension focuses on training skills and competencies for use in the digital university—the skills of the job change as the job changes. The digital transformation brings new tools and practices, new expectations, and new ways to learn; in fact, continuous learning is key.

The framework provides a capacity-building tool – professional development. It helps academics navigate adaptive career trajectories and adjust to evolving performance requirements. The expertise and skills to be acquired should be centered around digital pedagogy, data analytics, artificial intelligence, and collaborative technologies. These programmes should be practical, up to date, and in line with institutional priorities.

This dimension is directly related to the strategic alignment. Development activities should foster the development of skills required to support institutional aims. It also has implications for performance assessment, as connecting development to career advancement can boost motivation and involvement. If learning is valued and rewarded, education is more likely to be invested in.

This dimension also relates closely to inclusion. Digital confidence, experience, and access to resources are not uniform across academics. Institutions must therefore take steps to ensure equitable opportunities for capability development, so that all staff can meaningfully engage in digital transformation.

This dimension highlights the preeminence of lifelong learning. It allows academic careers to be more flexible and resilient to a shifting world. The other aspects of the framework are ineffective if they are not continuously developed.

6.5 Human-Centered and Inclusive Talent Systems

The fifth dimension focuses on the development of academic careers grounded in human needs and values. Whilst technology is a big part of digital transformation, it is the people who put it in place and maintain it that make the difference.

Human-centered means independent, creative, and free thinking. Such values are essential in academic pursuits and must be safeguarded during the shift. Digital tools enhance these attributes: innovation, collaboration, and knowledge creation.

An important aspect of this dimension is inclusion. Digital transformation can generate access gaps and disparities in opportunities, resources, and development programs. Inclusive talent systems are those in which all academics can access new roles and be supported by institutional initiatives (Aftimos & Al Saeed, 2023).

Within the framework, this dimension serves as a moderating factor as it affects the other dimensions. Career pathways can be flexible and offer new opportunities, but if they are not supported by inclusive policies, not all pathways will be accessible to everyone. Similarly, evaluation systems need to be clear and equitable to foster trust and equity.

Well-being is also a necessity. Expanded workload and pressure can exist in hybrid roles and responsibilities. Supporting change means universities need to ensure it does not negatively impact academic staff's well-being. Effective management, job clarity, and achievable workloads are therefore essential.

This dimension reinforces the idea that sustainable change depends on people. Academics who feel valued, supported, and included are more likely to help their institution succeed and to be engaged in and supportive of change.

6.6 Integration of the Framework

These five dimensions are all interdependent and reinforcing. Strategic alignment provides direction by connecting talent systems to institutional goals. There is room for adaptation and mobility due to flexible career pathways. Performance evaluation systems reward diverse forms of contribution. Professional development builds academics' capacities, and human-centered systems foster sustainability through inclusion, equity, and well-being.

These relationships are not necessarily linear. If one dimension is changed, the others change too. For instance, when flexible career pathways are proposed, the evaluation systems need to be modified. Similarly, greater professional development, flexibility, and adaptability can result in greater engagement with inclusive practices across all dimensions.

The framework, therefore, functions as a whole system. It is dependent on the interaction and alignment of all five dimensions. Single interventions will have little impact. A comprehensive strategy involving policy, practice, and institutional culture is needed for universities.

6.7 Conclusion

This framework offers a comprehensive model for understanding and redesigning academic careers in the digital university. By identifying the key dimensions and clarifying their relationships, it provides both analytical and practical value.

By focusing on alignment, flexibility, recognition, development, and inclusion, the framework highlights the key elements that shape academic careers in a digital context. It shows that digital transformation is not only about technology, but also about people, roles, and systems. Universities that align their talent systems with digital transformation are likely to be better positioned for innovation, adaptability, and long-term sustainability.

7. CONTRIBUTION, CONCLUSION, KEY INSIGHTS, AND FUTURE RESEARCH

7.1. Contribution of the Study

The chapter adds to the existing body of literature on digital transformation in higher education by refocusing academic careers as a key aspect of institutional transformation. A lot of literature available now is about technologies, digital infrastructures, and governance. All these are considerations; they tend to leave out the human aspect of change. This chapter aims to fill this missing link, demonstrating that technology is not the only factor challenging universities; people, practices, and institutional culture also do so.

One of the major features of the chapter is the perspective that digital transformation is a process of workforce change. It illustrates how digital technologies change the way teaching, research, collaboration, and engagement with external stakeholders are conducted. These changes have a direct impact on career, professional identity, and institutional expectations. This includes talent management as a strategic force, highlighting these dynamics and broadening the conversation about digital transformation.

Theoretically, the chapter brings together strategic human resource management, digital transformation theory, and boundaryless career theory into a single analytical framework. This integration supports a broader understanding of the evolution of academic careers toward greater flexibility, hybridity, and interdisciplinarity. It demonstrates that academic life is no longer linear but dynamic and evolving in digital environments.

The chapter also contributes by offering a conceptual framework for rethinking academic careers in the digital university. It is a framework that brings together institutional strategy, governance arrangements, and talent programmes in a unified model. It offers theory-based insights into the transformation of academic careers through digitalization and how academic institutions can align human resource systems with digital strategies.

In addition, the chapter builds on existing work on higher education transformation by moving beyond engagement with technology to focus on the consequences of that engagement for the academic workforce. This chapter brings together the relatively under-researched topic of academic career transformation. This topic has been underexplored in previous research, which focuses on digital learning platforms and institutional innovation. It demonstrates that digital transformation necessitates a new approach to job design, job performance measurement, and career advancement systems.

In practice, the chapter outlines implications for university leaders and human resource managers. It offers a framework for redesigning academic career systems to enable digital transformation. Interdisciplinary/innovation-oriented academic positions have been encouraged at institutions such as Arizona State University (ASU), and the recognition of the roles of teaching, engagement, and 'digital scholarship' has grown within the promotion system at University College London (UCL). While the scope and context of these efforts vary, they show an increasing trend toward adapting academic career systems to the needs of digital universities. The framework is flexible and adaptable, and it focuses on alignment with institutional strategy and talent development practices. Importantly, it recognizes that there are many different higher education contexts and does not offer a single solution that fits all.

The chapter also offers insights for policy discussions on risks arising from inadequate digital transformation management. These include a lack of capability, unequal access to digital resources, role ambiguity, and workload pressures. Highlighting these issues provides a basis for developing more inclusive and equitable higher education policies.

7.2 Conclusion and Key Insights

There are several important lessons from this analysis. To begin with, careers in academia are increasingly flexible, multi-disciplinary, and boundary-spanning. The traditional linear career trajectory is being replaced by more flexible career paths that involve multiple aspects of teaching, research, leadership, digital innovation, interdisciplinary research, and external engagement. The changes mean universities need to rethink their tacit assumptions about academic trajectories and career outcomes.

Second, academic contribution is being redefined by digital transformation. The use of technology in teaching, research, knowledge sharing, innovation, and leadership is increasingly gaining importance as activities of digital scholarship. However, many institutional systems continue to reward traditional measures of success, creating tensions between new expectations and existing career systems.

Third, for successful transformation, institutional alignment is needed. Digital strategies need to be reinforced by governance arrangements, leadership practices, promotion systems, and talent management frameworks. When these are not connected, digital initiatives will result in weak long-term effects and a fragmented outcome.

Fourth, there are several challenges with digital transformation. Institutional effectiveness and staff well-being can suffer due to capability gaps, inequitable access to digital resources, workload intensification, and role ambiguity. Long-term investments in professional development, policies, and organizational cultures are necessary to address these issues.

In addition, universities need to build on, rather than weaken, the values of higher education by fostering innovation. Academic freedom, intellectual diversity, scholarly integrity, and critical inquiry remain vital pillars of the university. The most successful institutions will be those that are technologically advanced, have embraced these timeless principles, and have developed career systems that can meet the changing demands of academic work.

7.3 Future Research Directions

The following are a few future research opportunities that emerge in higher education with digital transformation, talent management, and academic careers.

First, the conceptual framework developed in this chapter needs to be tested in future studies in a variety of institutional and national settings. Comparative research would help better understand how the academic career is transformed across academic institutions with varying degrees of digital maturity.

Second, qualitative research is needed to examine the experiences of academic personnel in digital universities. This kind of research would provide insights into how scholars navigate these multiple roles, manage their workload, and cope with changing expectations for performance.

Third, greater emphasis is needed on the role of leadership in digital transformation. The competencies, strategies, and decision-making processes of university leaders to manage digital change and talent systems should be studied.

In addition, there is a need for additional research on the long-term impacts of the digital transformation on academic well-being, job satisfaction, and retention. It is valuable to be aware of these outcomes to enable sustainable workforce development in higher education.

Lastly, policy-oriented research is needed to explore the role of national higher education systems in the quest for equitable digital transformation.

REFERENCES

Abhari, K. (2025). Employee participation in digital transformation: From digitalization sentiment to transformation predisposition. *Information & Management*, *62*(8), 104212. Advance online publication. DOI: 10.1016/j.im.2025.104212

Aftimos, S., & Al Saeed, F. (2023). Cultural diversity: Profiling done right! In *Global Citizenship and Its Impact on Multiculturalism in the Workplace* (pp. 113–128). IGI Global Scientific Publishing. DOI: 10.4018/978-1-6684-5436-7.ch005

Aftimos, S., & Diab-Bahman, R. (2025). AI-driven talent management: Transforming workforce strategies in the digital age. In M. Lowe & Y. Luximon (Eds.), *creativity, innovation, and entrepreneurship. AHFE international conference* (AHFE Open Access, Vol. 166, pp. 29–58). AHFE International. https://doi.org/DOI: 10.54941/ahfe1006110

Aftimos, S., & Diab-Bahman, R. (2026, June). "To AI or Not to AI?"—When Synergies Collide. In *Proceedings* (Vol. 142, No. 1, p. 8). MDPI.

Aftimos, S., & Khafash, M. (2026). Embedding talent management in the digital transformation of universities in Kuwait. In *Organizational change, innovation, and consumer behavior in the digital economy* (pp. 29–58). IGI Global Scientific Publishing. DOI: 10.4018/979-8-2600-1453-0.ch002

Al-Rashidi, F., Diab-Bahman, R., & Al-Enzi, A. (2021). The impact of socio-economic factors on human capital investments. *International Journal of Entrepreneurship*, *25*, 1–14.

Alhogail, A., & Mirza, A. (2011). Implementing a virtual learning environment (VLE) in a higher education institution: A change management approach. *Journal of Theoretical and Applied Information Technology*, *31*, 42–52.

Benson, T. A., Cohen, A. L., & Buskist, W. (2005). Rapport: Its relation to student attitudes and behaviors toward teachers and classes. *Teaching of Psychology*, *32*(4), 237–239.

Blankesteijn, M. L., & Ghorbani, A. (2025). Embracing the digital horizon: Future scenarios for the Dutch higher education system. *Futures*, *174*, 103702. Advance online publication. DOI: 10.1016/j.futures.2025.103702

Boone, C. G., Pickett, S. T. A., Bammer, G., Bawa, K., Dunne, J. A., Gordon, I. J., Hart, D., Hellmann, J., Miller, A., New, M., Ometto, J. P., Taylor, K., Wendorf, G., Agrawal, A., Bertsch, P., Campbell, C., Dodd, P., Janetos, A., & Mallee, H. (2020). Preparing interdisciplinary leadership for a sustainable future. *Sustainability Science*, *15*(6), 1723–1733. DOI: 10.1007/s11625-020-00823-9 PMID: 32837574

Börner, K., Contractor, N., Falk-Krzesinski, H. J., Fiore, S. M., Hall, K. L., Keyton, J., Spring, B., Stokols, D., Trochim, W., & Uzzi, B. (2010). A multi-level systems perspective for the science of team science. *Science Translational Medicine*, *2*(49), 49cm24. Advance online publication. DOI: 10.1126/scitranslmed.3001399 PMID: 20844283

Carmo, J. E. S., Lacerda, D. P., Klingenberg, C. O., & Piran, F. A. S. (2025). Digital transformation in the management of higher education institutions. *Sustainable Futures : An Applied Journal of Technology, Environment and Society*, *9*, 100692. DOI: 10.1016/j.sftr.2025.100692

Collings, D. G., & Mellahi, K. (2009). Strategic talent management: A review and research agenda. *Human Resource Management Review*, *19*(4), 304–313. DOI: 10.1016/j.hrmr.2009.04.001

Dahlstrom, E., Brooks, D. C., & Bichsel, J. (2014). *The current ecosystem of learning management systems in higher education: Student, faculty, and IT perspectives*. EDUCAUSE Center for Analysis and Research.

Diab-Bahman, R. (2024). *Sustainable business in the Arab region: Corporate social responsibility vs culture*. Emerald Publishing Limited. DOI: 10.1108/9781835493267

Diab-Bahman, R., & Al-Enzi, A. (2021). The emotional impact of COVID-19 on undergrads: Hybrid open access. *Clinical Schizophrenia & Related Psychoses*, *15*(2). Advance online publication. 10.71/CSRP.RBAE.170521

Diab-Bahman, R., Al-Enzi, A., Sharafeddine, W., & Aftimos, S. (2022). The effect of attendance on student performance: Implications of using virtual learning on overall performance. *Journal of Applied Research in Higher Education*, *14*(3), 1175–1192. DOI: 10.1108/JARHE-04-2021-0135

Diab-Bahman, R., & Bahman, T. A. (2022). Forensic accounting and corporate governance. In *Handbook of research on the significance of forensic accounting techniques in corporate governance* (pp. 150–166). IGI Global Scientific Publishing. DOI: 10.4018/978-1-7998-8754-6.ch008

Gandy, R., Harrison, P., & Gold, J. (2018). Talent management in higher education: Is turnover relevant? *European Journal of Training and Development, 42*(9), 597–610. DOI: 10.1108/EJTD-11-2017-0099

Gerli, F., Bonesso, S., & Pizzi, C. (2015). Boundaryless career and career success: The impact of emotional and social competencies. *Frontiers in Psychology, 6*, 1304. Advance online publication. DOI: 10.3389/fpsyg.2015.01304 PMID: 26388809

Glazier, R. A. (2016). Building rapport to improve retention and success in online classes. *Journal of Political Science Education, 12*(4), 437–456. DOI: 10.1080/15512169.2016.1155994

Haque, S. M. S., Shaha, S., & Sharmin, S. (2024). Future-proofing the workforce: Training and development in the digital age. *European Journal of Human Resource Management Studies, 7*(2). Advance online publication. DOI: 10.46827/ejhrms.v7i2.1637

Harris, A., Jones, M., & Baba, S. (2013). Distributed leadership and digital collaborative learning. *British Journal of Educational Technology, 44*(6), 926–939. DOI: 10.1111/bjet.12107

Howaniec, H., Karyy, O., & Pawliczek, A. (2022). The role of universities in shaping talents—The case of the Czech Republic, Poland, and Ukraine. *Sustainability (Basel), 14*(9), 5476. DOI: 10.3390/su14095476

Jing, M. (2025). Higher education digital academic leadership: Understanding leadership roles in digital transformation. *Education Sciences, 15*(5), 606. DOI: 10.3390/educsci15050606

Kelley, S. (2022). Employee perceptions of the effective adoption of AI principles. *Journal of Business Ethics, 178*(4), 871–893. DOI: 10.1007/s10551-022-05051-y PMID: 35818389

Kharchenko, A., Nalyvaiko, O., Kreydun, N., Sheiko, A., Ptushka, A., Khatuntseva, S., Zotova, L., & Kharkiv, N. K. (2024). Digital technologies as a factor in transforming university learning. *Revista Romaneasca Pentru Educatie Multidimensionala, 16*(4), 97–126. DOI: 10.18662/rrem/16.4/909

Koseda, E., Cohen, I. K., McIntosh, B., & Cooper, J. (2024). Internationalisation and digital transformation in higher education: The impact of Education 4.0 on teaching, learning and assessment. *Active Learning in Higher Education.*

Lammers, W. J., & Gillaspy, J. A. (2013). A brief measure of student–instructor rapport predicts student outcomes. *Teaching of Psychology, 40*(4), 314–317.

Lei, J., Hall, J. A., Wang, Q., & Alenezi, M. (2023). Digital learning and digital institutions in higher education. *Education Sciences, 13*(1), 88. DOI: 10.3390/educsci13010088

Mishra, L., Gupta, T., & Shree, A. (2020). Online teaching-learning in higher education during lockdown. *International Journal of Educational Research Open, 1*, 100012. DOI: 10.1016/j.ijedro.2020.100012 PMID: 35059663

Modi, R. K., & Garg, R. (2025). The Role of Artificial Intelligence in Transforming Higher Education: Opportunities and Challenges. *Exploresearch, 02*(02), 59–65. DOI: 10.62823/ExRe/2025/02/02.53

Muilenburg, L. Y., & Berge, Z. L. (2005). Student barriers to online learning. *Distance Education, 26*(1), 29–48. DOI: 10.1080/01587910500081269

Murphy, E., & Rodríguez-Manzanares, M. A. (2012). Rapport in distance education. *International Review of Research in Open and Distance Learning, 13*(1), 167–190. DOI: 10.19173/irrodl.v13i1.1057

Onan, G. (2024). Digital Transformation and Digital Leadership in Higher Education Institutions: Insights from the Literature. *International Journal of New Approaches in Social Studies, 8*(2), 198–213. DOI: 10.38015/sbyy.1587587

Palmer, C. L., Teffeau, L. C., & Pirmann, C. M. (2009). *Scholarly information practices in the online environment : themes from literature and implications for library service development*. 57.https://www.researchgate.net/publication/230800450_Scholarly_Information_Practices_in_the_Online_Environment_Themes_from_the_Literature_and_Implications_for_Library_Service_Development

Pham, D. H. (2021). The professional development of academic staff in higher education institutions. *Journal of Teacher Education for Sustainability, 23*(1), 115–131. DOI: 10.2478/jtes-2021-0009

Piccoli, G., Ahmad, R., & Ives, B. (2001). Web-based virtual learning environments. *Management Information Systems Quarterly, 25*(4), 401–426. DOI: 10.2307/3250989

Raes, A., Detienne, L., Windey, I., & Depaepe, F. (2020). Hybrid learning environments. *Computers & Education, 143*, 103682. Advance online publication. DOI: 10.1016/j.compedu.2019.103682

Rapanta, C., Botturi, L., Goodyear, P., Guàrdia, L., & Koole, M. (2020). Online University Teaching During and After the Covid-19 Crisis: Refocusing Teacher Presence and Learning Activity. *Postdigital Science and Education, 2*(3), 923–945. DOI: 10.1007/s42438-020-00155-y PMID: 40477148

Scanlon, E. (2018). Digital Scholarship: Identity, Interdisciplinarity, and Openness. *Frontiers in Digital Humanities*, *5*, 3. Advance online publication. DOI: 10.3389/fdigh.2018.00003

Seabolt, B., & Arends, B. (2000). *Remaining real in a virtual world.*

Sejdiu, N. P., & Sejdiu, S. (2025). The quiet transformation of higher education in the AI era. *Open Research Europe*, *5*, 249. DOI: 10.12688/openreseurope.20715.1 PMID: 40963694

Sharafeddine, W., Diab-Bahman, R., & Al-Enzi, A. (2024). The impact of fasting on workplace productivity and well-being: A review of fasting in Ramadan. *International Journal of Productivity and Quality Management*, *41*(1), 32–48. DOI: 10.1504/IJPQM.2024.136191

Singun, A. J. (2025). Unveiling the barriers to digital transformation in higher education institutions: A systematic literature review. *Discover Education*, *4*(1), 37. Advance online publication. DOI: 10.1007/s44217-025-00430-9

Tang, J., Huang, P., & Yan, S. (2025). Digital transformation in higher education: Logical framework, practical dilemmas, and implementation approaches. *Frontiers in Psychology*, *16*, 1565591. Advance online publication. DOI: 10.3389/fpsyg.2025.1565591 PMID: 41280162

Teker, S., Teker, D., & Basak TAVMAN, E. (2025). STRATEGIES FOR DIGITAL TRANSFORMATION OF UNIVERSITIES. *Http://Jtie.Upol.Cz/Doi/*, *17*(1), 147–166. https://doi.org/DOI: <ALIGNMENT.qj></ALIGNMENT>10.5507/Jtie.2025.005.Html

Walker, A., & White, G. (2013). *Technology-enhanced language learning*. Oxford University Press.

Wentzel, K. R. (2009). Students' relationships with teachers. In the *Handbook of motivation at school.*

Wilson, J. H., & Ryan, R. G. (2013). Professor–student rapport scale: Six items predict student outcomes. *Teaching of Psychology*, *40*(2), 130–133. DOI: 10.1177/0098628312475033

Wilson, J. H., Ryan, R. G., & Pugh, J. L. (2010). Professor–student rapport scale. *Teaching of Psychology*, *37*(4), 246–251. DOI: 10.1080/00986283.2010.510976

Zabalawi, I., Kordahji, H., & Aftimos, S. (2024). Digital transformation in universities: Strategic framework, implementation tools, and leadership. In *Higher education in the Arab world: Digital transformation* (pp. 145–210). Springer Nature Switzerland. DOI: 10.1007/978-3-031-70779-7_8

Zhukabayeva, T., Baumuratova, D., Zholshiyeva, L., Karabay, A., & Abdrakhmanov, K. (2025). Digital Transformation in Higher Education: Toward a National Model of Digital University in Kazakhstan Through Global and Local Comparison. *Sustainability 2025, Vol. 17, Page 11132, 17*(24), 11132. https://doi.org/DOI: 10.3390/su172411132

Chapter 4

Reimagining Talent Management in Higher Education:
A Strategic Shift Toward Digital Transformation

Ankita Pathak
http://orcid.org/0000-0002-8068-8874
Institute of Business Management, GLA University, India

Ashish Jaswal
http://orcid.org/0000-0001-5077-6702
Sadhu Vaswani Institute of Management Studies for Girls, Pune, India

Majdi Anwar Quttainah
http://orcid.org/0000-0002-6280-1060
Kuwait University, Kuwait

ABSTRACT

The rapid digital transformation in higher instruction is altering the process of recruitment, development and retention in academic and administrative areas. This study investigates the strategic digitisation of talent management within the higher education sector and examines how emerging technologies, like data analytics, artificial intelligence (AI) and integrated human resources information systems (HRIS), are changing the operation. Digital talent management enables institutions to move towards proactive with data-based strategies. It is necessary in order to achieve sustainability, flexibility as well as academic excellence among colleges

DOI: 10.4018/979-8-3373-8959-2.ch004

and universities. The research emphasis on combining technical capability with human-centered management techniques which will lead to the development of both strong, sustainable ecosystems of talent.

1. INTRODUCTION

1.1 Changing Landscape of Higher Education

Institutions of higher education have been undergoing significant shifts as a result of advancements in technology; globalization of education; and shifts in the expectations of society. Today's universities have expanded their traditional boundaries of classroom and have joined together to become a community of scholars rather than isolated individuals. They exist as part of an interconnected and competitive global educational system. The rapid adoption of digital technology; hybrid and online learning delivery methods; increases the international collaborative academic research projects etc. Afifa (2026) witness the changed the manner in which universities provide, administer and assess education. Universities now have to create knowledge and also respond quickly to changes in technology, job market, and changing student needs and expectations. In this environment, institutions have to make changes to their organizational structure and management practices to become more flexible and adaptable. Digital technologies will play an important role in all aspects of an institution's operations, such as how they teach; collaborate on research; manage their administrative processes; and supervise their employees (Azuwandri, 2026). Consequently, institutions need to rethink on traditional ways of managing their academic and administrative workforce.

1.2 The Growing Importance of Talent in Academic Institutions

Higher education institutions consider human capital to be one of the most important and valuable assets they possess. The combination of faculty, researchers, and administrative personnel is the driving force behind an institution's reputation, research output, teaching effectiveness, and capacity for innovation. Universities are experiencing increased competition globally for skilled academics and staff which state that hiring and managing their talent is crucial to sustain their institutional performance (Bolander et al., 2017). Talent management in higher education refers to the effective and efficient attraction, development, retention of high quality faculty to provide an environment which promotes innovation and collaboration. It ensure their success as educators and researchers. The management of academic talent is rapidly becoming more complicated as universities need to balance multiple faculty responsibility such as teaching, research, collaboration across disciplines and services within their institutions (Cappelli & Keller, 2014). Furthermore, faculty members must be able to incorporate recent development related to technological tools and methods. They need to adapt to new digital learning environments and use the latest global research networks.

1.3 Limitations of Traditional Talent Management Systems

Many universities still use traditional administrative systems that restrict their ability to strategically plan for their workforce, even though talent management is becoming more significant. With traditional approaches, many institutions have disconnected data systems, manual record keeping, and performance appraisal procedures that do not relate to the overall goals of their institution (Bradley, 2016). These issues create difficult for organizations to have a complete picture of their employee skills and abilities. Institutions need to look to employee's career development, and gaps in skills. The recruitment of faculty and staff can be time-consuming and ineffective, and professional development initiatives are frequently implemented without systematic evaluation of their impact (Benavides et al., 2020). These challenges hinder an institution's ability to react to changes in the academic field or in technology. With the increasing complexity and competition in higher education, institutions need advanced methods for managing talent strategically and promoting long-term institutional growth.

1.4 Emergence of Digital Transformation in Higher Education

The digital transformation of organizations across all industries, including higher education, has been a major factor in reshaping how organizations operate. Universities are increasingly using digital infrastructures such as LMSs, Research Collaboration software, Data Analytics tools, and Integrated HRIS applications (Al Hashimi et al., 2021). The use of these technologies enables universities to manage their information better and provides the ability to facilitate remote work. It would lead to developmental decisions. In regards to effective talent management, universities can use digital tools to improve their recruitment process, perform continuous monitoring of performance, provide competency-based development programs, and improve the efficiency of workforce planning.

Digital tools help to improve various function like talent management, recruitment, and continuous performance monitoring. Digital tools also support competency-based development programs along with data-driven workforce planning (Bygstad et al., 2022). Digital transformation is much more than just adopting technology; it also includes cultural changes in organizations, leadership practices, and institutional governance. Successful digital transformation necessitates that an organization's overall academic mission is aligned with its technology systems.

1.5 Purpose and Objectives of the Study

This research analyzes how digital transformation impacts talent management strategies within colleges and universities. The goal is to develop a theoretical framework that illustrates how digital talent management systems have the potential to enhance workforce development and transform an institution's agility. It also improve institutional performance. In order to achieve these objectives, this study will

(1) Identify the evolution of the concept of talent management as it relates to institutes of higher education.
(2) Describe how digital technology is transforming traditional talent management practices.
(3) Assess potential strategic advantages and disadvantages related to digitally enhanced talent management systems.
(4) Provide insights relating to the implications of digitally enhanced talent management strategies to institutional leadership, governance and human resource professionals.

This study will add literature to the current body of literature in relation to digital transformation within institutes of higher education. It will shed the light on how institutions can take advantage of technology based innovations in order to develop a talent development strategy. It also focuses on the needs of the individual employee.

2. CONCEPTUAL FOUNDATIONS OF TALENT MANAGEMENT

In knowledge-based organizations like colleges and universities, human talent is one of the major strategic resources an organization has. Many industries consider that technology and physical infrastructure is more important than workforce's talents. The workforce of higher education institutions are primarily responsible for the intellectual contributions through research, and develop through teaching (Chong et al., 2026). It can serve to society by engaging in community service. In addition to the academic workforce, administrative support staff assist in the administration of the institutions and the overall operation of the academic system.

Since human talent is so vital, colleges have to find a way to identify, develop and retain people in order to fulfill their strategies and objectives. Talent Management is capable to provides a integrated system of human resource functions which coordinate and develop the strategic framework to strengthen an organization's capacity (Collings et al., 2022). Rather than focusing on traditional personnel administration functions, talent management focuses on developing the long-term workforce, planning strategically, and aligning the competencies of people with the priorities of the college or university.

2.1 Meaning and Evolution of Talent Management

The term “talent management” refers to an organized and planned method for discovering, developing, motivating and keeping employees who contribute to organization perform . Talent management first became a popular term in the late 1990s where organizations understood the link between sustainable competitive advantage and a high quality and creative workforce. Early discussions about talent management focused primarily on discovering high potential employees and building leadership pipelines that would enable long-term growth of the organization.

Today's talent management is much more integrated across the entire workforce with an understanding that an organization's success does not depend only on a select group of high performing employees, but also on the overall ability. It also focuses on level of engagement and ability to work together to contribute in overall success of an organization. It includes many different organizational practices such as workforce planning, competency development, performance management and career development (Collings & Mellahi, 2009). These practices will help to ensure that organizations are continually developing the required skills and capabilities to respond to an ever changing institutional environment.

Talent Management's evolution is influenced by the changing nature of work especially in knowledge intensive industries. The expansion of global workforce, and greater use of digital technology have altered how organizations identify and nurture talent (Cotter et al., 2026). Higher education are using more flexible and data-driven approaches to develop their workforces. This also reflects a larger shift away from traditional personnel administration towards strategically managing human capital.

2.2 Talent Management in the Higher Education Context

Originally, talent management practices were established in the business world, but now they are also relevant to the university sector. Academic institutions are located in environments where intellectual capital and academic expertise are crucial for success. The major areas on which faculty contribute are teaching, conducting research and sharing knowledge; while the administrative professionals handle and administer the complex processes related to admissions, research administration, student services and other aspects of the university.

Talent management in higher education must incorporate strategies that cater to the distinctive qualities of academia. In most corporate settings, productivity is determined primarily by profit margin measured against other similar business units (El Garem, 2026). In contrast, the evaluation of employee productivity in higher education includes an assessment of teaching performance, research output, academic administration, and involvement in community service. This productivity assessment in higher education is more complex by the due to dimensions of academic employment.

A strong focus on professional growth is another characteristic of an academic career. Faculty members focus on developing themselves for years through research training, mentoring, and collaborative skill-sets before they are ready to proceed. Universities must create environments in which continuous development and growth are encouraged(Dogan & Arslan, 2026). Professional administrators must also develop themselves in developing environments, such as digital infrastructure, analytics, and strategic planning. the alignment of talent management practices with the differentiated aspects of working with academics, would produce a professional workforce that would support academic improvements and produce innovative educational institutions.

2.3 Strategic Importance of Academic and Administrative Talent

The effectiveness of a higher education institution is dependent on both the academic and administrative staff's commitment to the mission and vision of that institution. It is the faculty member's work - teaching, research and scholarship - that largely defines the intellectual character of the institution. A faculty member's ability to develop new knowledge, assist students learn successfully and work with other discipline areas also significantly impact both the institution's reputation and the institution's contributions to research.The teaching, research, and scholarly contributions of faculty members shape universities' intellectual identities. The capacity of universities to generate knowledge, mentor students, and collaborate across disciplines is a significant factor determining their institutional reputation and their impact on research activities (Fahad et al., 2026). Universities that have high calibre academic talent have greater potential to attract competitive research funding, form international collaborations and recruit high-performing students. Therefore, the development and retention of talented faculty is a central strategic priority for many universities.

The role of an administrative professional is critical in supporting the operational and strategic side of higher education. The complexity of the operations of higher education institutions is growing, so effective administration is necessity for administering academic programs, managing financial resources, coordinating research initiatives, and implementing technology systems. Skilled administrators ensure that institutional processes are working smoothly so that faculty can focus on their teaching responsibilities (Gandy et al., 2018). Talent is especially important in today's competitive globalized world of education because many universities want to attract highly qualified scholars and professional staff members. Institutions that invest in workforce development and supportive cultures are more likely to sustain academic excellence and long-term institutional stability. The recognition of talent as a strategic resource incentivizes universities to be proactive in workforce planning, mentorship, and professional development.

2.4 Key Dimensions of Talent Management in Universities

Talent management in universities consists of several interconnected dimensions which support the development and effective utilization of human capability. The key dimension is acquiring talent, which involves recruiting individuals with expertise aligned with the academic mission and strategic priorities of the institution. The recruitment methods should focus not only on the areas of specialization that the candidates have but also on their ability to engage in innovative instruction and to perform interdisciplinary research (Gkrimpizi et al., 2024). Recruitment methods should not only evaluate candidates based on their qualifications. It also evaluate their ability to promote innovations in the classroom and engage in interdisciplinary research and institutional collaboration with colleagues.

Professional development or ongoing learning opportunities are the second aspect of best practices in management of talent. Universities should provide opportunities for faculty and staff to improve their knowledge and skills throughout their careers. They should offer funding for research projects, design workshops to improve skills, mentorship, networking opportunities to connect with colleagues working on similar scholarly activities, etc (Hannan, 2023). These opportunities will allow faculty to continue to adapt and adjust their teaching practice and research.

One of the key components to effectively manage talent is through performance management. Institutions use performance evaluation methods to identify individual contributors and help them develop to reach their full potential. They also provide individuals with the opportunity to advance in their careers (Jani et al., 2023). Performance evaluations need to create a balance between accountability and fairness by recognizing the different roles and responsibilities that are associated with academic work.

Higher Education Institutions rely on hiring and retaining Employees to sustain their overall institutional capacity. Employee Engagement will significantly support building a culture of Employee Engagement through Intellectual Curiosity, Collaboration, and Fulfillment. Universities develop commitment from employees and reduce turnover by establishing a clear career development path, a solid recognition structure, and a supportive organizational culture. The successful integration of these three factors will create an effective talent pool to support the long-term viability of the institution.

3. DIGITAL TRANSFORMATION IN HIGHER EDUCATION

Digital technologies have led to the structural change of both academic and administrative processes in higher education institutions. The introduction of digital technology to the university is much more than just implementing new technology. It involves reconfiguring how the institution produces, delivers and manages knowledge. Today's universities produce electronic infrastructure necessary for supporting distance learning communities, research collaboration, data-based management decision-making, and integration (Huang et al., 2026). These changes lead to an increase in operational efficiency at the university as well as allow the university to compete in the global academic networks.

Digital transformation has become an important component of an institution's strategy. Universities are no longer using digital technologies to become more efficient, but rather incorporating digital technologies into longer-term institutional development plans. The use of Digital Platforms allows institutions to coordinate complex academic activities, and manage large amounts of information. It also assist in responding more effectively to the rapidly changing demands of students, faculty and external stakeholders. As the global and competitive environment for higher education continues to grow, strategic partnerships with digital technology are now imperative to maintain institutional sustainability and driving innovation.

The use of technology also impacts the management of Human Resources within universities. Technology provides integrated approach to support faculty, administrative professionals and leadership teams within the institution (Hussain & Shoukat, 2026). Digital infrastructures provide the institution with greater opportunity to build its capacity, provide for professional development and to advance evidence-based management. It also provides a more coordinated approach to managing and sharing information.

3.1 Scope and drive of Digital Transformation in Higher Education Institutions

Universities' digital transformation encompasses numerous multi-functional aspects. Digital technologies have supported many online and blended forms of learning and teaching which allow for greater access to education. It provide flexibility in the number of ways to the students in achieve their education. Research activities can now occur across institutions and continents, with the help of advanced computing tools, digital libraries, and collaborative online platforms. It further facilitate academic collaboration among different institutions and researchers. Most universities have also started to utilize integrated information systems in order to provide more support for their administrative tasks. It has also improve how institutions manage their data and coordinate with one another.

The impact of digital transformation continues to redefine governance and strategic planning. University administrators ensure that digital infrastructure will support their long-term academic goals. It also ensure that any technology should be used responsibly and ethically. Therefore digital transformation is a comprehensive institutional change that combines technology capabilities, strategic vision and organizational learning.

There are several interrelated factors contributing to the increasing digitalization of higher education institutions. One of the main drivers of this phenomenon is the rapid evolution of information and communication technologies that have generated new avenues for delivering education and managing academic systems (Kaputa et al., 2022). The ability of an institution to effectively deliver services creates new ways of operating more efficiently. It also allows for a more responsive approach to shift education requirements through delivery methods such as cloud services, collaborative tools and advanced data management systems.

The shift towards digitalization in education is also impacted by changing student expectations. Today's students are looking for education systems that are flexible and allow them to access a range of courses, which accommodate their different learning styles, professional needs, and physical locations. Digital platforms also allow educational institutions to create the environments that encourage students to learn through the use of asynchronous learning, multimedia interaction, and collaborative exchange of knowledge (Khan et al., 2026). It has prompted many universities to rethink their traditional teaching methods.

Digital transformation also has an increasing impact on the competitiveness of institutions. They are evaluated on their teaching innovations, research output, and level of international activity. Digital infrastructures provide visibility to institutions by enhancing their opportunities for international collaboration and improving institutional administrative efficiency. Many governments are implementing policies and funding strategies to promote the use of digital technologies as part of an overall strategy for modernizing the education system. All of these factors together provide compelling reasons for universities to make and invest in digital transformation.

3.2 Role of Technology in Organizational and HR Transformation

Advances in technology have dramatically changed the ways in which universities organize their internal systems and employ their staff. Digital technology allows universities' managers and administrators to more effectively and efficiently use digital systems to conduct university's activities. It allow more efficient administrative processes, academic coordination of academic operations, and improved inter-departmental communication (Kasmia & M'hamed, 2023). Digital systems also allow increased transparency, eliminate redundancies, and improve collaboration of faculty and staff among university departments.

Digital technology supports the Human Resource Department of universities in managing their faculty. Kornita and Tampubolon (2026) stated that Digital technology allows for greater integration of faculty expertise, research output, and educational development into one central data repository. It allows the use of the data to make more informed and effective decisions related to recruitment, promotion, and future planning of an institution.

In addition, digital technology provides opportunities to faculty and staff for improving their knowledge and skills through digital learning environments. Digital technology also plays an important role in improving academic collaboration. Electronic means of communication enable faculty to work together on interdisciplinary research, build global knowledge, and collaborations (Khushk et al., 2026). It can also share resources across institutional lines, and communicate more easily and effectively about their work or area of expertise. As a result of these technological advancements, universities can also develop more flexible and adaptive academic organizations.

3.3 Impact of Hybrid Learning and Global Academic Competition

Hybrid learning models are shaping and defining the current and future structure and operation of higher education. A hybrid learning model provides students with the opportunity to learn using both traditional face-to-face approaches and digital formats. In a hybrid learning model, students can access their course materials either in person at their respective academic institution, or online. This new model of learning allows universities to reach larger and wider groups of students than was previously possible. facilities have begun using more creative and varied approaches to teach by incorporating digital-based learning and interactive learning into the classroom environment.

At the same time, hybrid learning has increased competition among academic institutions at an international level. Universities now operate in a global educational marketplace and students have access to courses and degree programs from education institutions around the world (Kumar et al., 2026). Digital technology enables universities to provide educational content to students regardless of their geographic location. It create more opportunities for students, and increasing competition among educational institutions.

Universities must increase their investments in technological infrastructure, professional development, and innovative program development to meet the competitive advantage. Consequently, student with degrees and certifications would be able to compete globally. Leikuma-Rimicane et al. (2022) stated that universities will provide educational opportunities to learners who are either unable or unwilling to travel to an education institution. Digitalization is now a primary factor in determining the relevance of higher education systems today

4. CONCEPT AND INTEGRATION OF TECHNOLOGY WITH HUMAN RESOURCE PRACTICES

The combination of technology and human resource (HR) processes is one of the foundational components of the digital transformation of talent management in higher education institutions. Colleges and universities are transiting their operations from conventional administrative models to more agile and data-driven models (Loidl, 2026). The digitization of human resources has changed how academic and non-academic talent is attracted, developed, engaged, and retained. This change is not simply an operational change to improve existing processes but a strategic change of aligning human capital management to the institution's mission and goals. It will help in responding to the competitive and globalized nature of today's academic environment.

One of the main reasons for this change is due to the increasing implementation of HRIS and cloud-based talent management systems that automate traditional HR processes such as recruitment, onboarding, employee payroll, and performance evaluations. Maharani et al. (2026) stated that automation of these functions allows for streamlining of HR processes and decreased administrative workload. An HRIS increases efficiency within HR departments. More importantly, HRIS provides a centralized and real-time view of all employee data. It enables organisations to make data-based purchasing decisions. In institutions of higher education, faculty perform multiple functions such as teaching, research, and service. Human Resource Information Systems (HRIS) enable Higher Education institutions to assess employees performance using a holistic approach and align each employee's contribution to the institution's strategic objectives.

HR management has become a more complex task by the introduction of artificial intelligence (AI) and machine learning (ML) into the management of talent. With AI-enabled HR systems, time can be managed much more effectively. AI enables HR can evaluate multiple data to eliminate biased evaluation of job candidates. Additionally, predictive analytics can be used for identification and analysis of workforce trends, as well as identification and forecasting of skill gaps. Predictive analytics can also assist HR with the ability to forecast employee turnover, thereby improving their overall workforce management (Mayer et al., 2026). Predictive analytics are essential for the long-term planning of a high-performing workforce and thus have a major effect on the overall quality of the academic output of the institution.

The importance of digital learning & development platform in transforming HR processes cannot be understated. LMSs and online training modules are an integral component of continuous professional development - providing instructors and staff with opportunities for flexible, personalized learning. These platforms are able to connect with performance management systems to provide a framework for individual development plans based on competency assessments and career goals. As technology continues to evolve rapidly, and educational philosophies shift towards blended and online formats, upskilling on a regular basis (Zhang, 2026). It is essential to ensure that quality of instruction and relevance of institutions are maintained.

Technology integration creates additional opportunities for organizations to enhance employee engagement and experience. Digital tools, such as employee self-service portals, mobile applications for HR-related functions, and virtual collaboration platforms, can provide employees with improved autonomy and accessibility. Additionally, these digital tools help facilitate clear and effective communication, feedback, and recognition (Young et al., 2026). As a result, they can contribute to an organizational culture that is more inclusive, responsive, and agile. Faculty autonomy is highly valued at institutions of higher education, and an organization's technology can support decentralized decision-making while maintaining general institutional coherence.

The data analytics in Human Resources (HR) practices provides organizations with an evidence-based approach to their decisions. This is an essential aspect of the strategic management of talent. Big data allows organizations to identify patterns. Organizations may analyze data around employee performance, employee engagement, employee retention, and employee diversity (Yadav et al., 2026). Analytics will allow organizations to develop specific interventions and retention strategies tailored to diverse groups, as well as inclusion initiatives. All of these types of patterns can be identified using analytics. Organizations can use analytics to identify inequitable or unfair promotion rates and workloads across employee segments. Organizations can also use analytics to reform policies that are inequitable or unfair. Analytics provides organizations with equity and transparency within the academic institution.

The incorporation of technology into HR processes comes with multiple benefits; however, it also has some challenges. The areas of data privacy, cybersecurity and ethical use of A.I. all need to be addressed diligently in order to maintain compliance with regulations and keep stakeholder trust (Wahyuningtyas, 2015). Also, digitalization will serve as an impediment towards successful usage of digital tools. Institution can become digitally literate by investment and can implement change in management activities. It will ensure that transition from traditional practices to digital seamless.

4.1 Role of Digital Platforms in Talent Ecosystems

Digital Technologies and Platforms will continue developing Data and Talent Intelligence. Advanced analytics are a key feature of digital technologies, which give an organization the ability to analyze and understand the employee's experience, performance, and engagement. Higher education can target specific employees by implementing dedicated programs for them. Vignieri and Santoni (2026) stated that digital technologies also help higher education to develop strategic hiring practices, customized faculty development programs, and evidence-based retention strategies. Furthermore, organizations can use predictive analytics to find high-performing faculty or develop new researchers. Predictive analytics also support succession planning and leadership development.

Continuous education, competence development, and lifelong learning are equally important elements. Digital technology provides access to digital learning platforms such as LMS, MOOC, micro-credentials, which allow faculty and staff to participate in lifelong education. Digital learning platforms also create personalized pathways for developing skills for both higher education and the workplace (McDonnell et al., 2017). Continuous upskilling and reskilling is a requirement to remain competitive and innovative in Talent Ecosystems.

Digital platforms also significantly improve the employee experience and increase the employee's engagement. Digital tools such as collaboration tools, virtual communication tools, and employee engagement applications create more collaborative and inclusive office environments. Digital tools also create real-time feedback, peer recognitions and transparent communication within the workplace. These three characteristics are essential for cultivating a sense of belonging, and an organizational commitment to the organization. In higher education, more emphasis is given on intellectual autonomy and collegiality Swailes (2016). Digital tools assist in balancing the need of individuals to work independently and the desire of the institution to obtain common goals.

There are challenges associated with the use of digital platforms in talent ecosystems such as interoperability between platforms, data governance issues, and a lack of user acceptance. Organizations should ensure that all systems can connect with each other efficiently as per the standards. In addition, organizations must handle the concern related to privacy, ethical use of algorithms, and digital surveillance. It ensure that all stakeholder retain trust in the organization. Additionally, organizations will need to put significant resources into training and change management to address the varying degrees of skill with technology amongst faculty and staff in their organizations.

4.2 Strategic Alignment between Institutional Goals and Talent Systems

The alignment between an institution's goals and its talent systems, would contribute in achieving the institution's mission, vision and long-term competitive position within higher education. Talent systems cannot remain as solely administrative; they must become strategic enablers of academic excellence, productivity in research, and sustainability of institutions through digital transformation.

Institutions must align their talent strategies with institutional priorities such as global rankings, research impact, teaching quality, and collaborations within industry. In recruitment process institute should look for faculty and staff that have knowledge and skill set which match the emerging disciplines and strategic research areas. The use of digital recruitment, candidate screening and selection is one of the most important features of HR technology. With the help of advanced applicant tracking systems (ATS) and AI-assisted tools, universities can quickly handle thousands of applications and identify the best applicants for academic, research. Institutional needs to use structured screening methods, competency-based filters and data-driven shortlists to accelerate hiring processes while improving their quality. It will reduce biasness and increase transparency in selection methods (Moghtadaie & Taji, 2016). The integration of talent analytics and workforce planning increase clarity of workforce competencies. It can forecast the employee attrition and determine skill gaps exist at institutions. This helps institutions develop proactive hiring and transition management and capacity planning strategies, thereby ensuring talent management strategies are future-based and not reactive.

Additionally, while designing the performance management systems, institute should incorporate metrics that meets with the goals of the institution. The goals of institute are such as quality of publication, innovations, and how engaged students are, and its overall impact on society. Varma et al. (2021) stated that digital dashboards are used to continuously monitor key performance indicators (KPIs) related to labour such as teaching effectiveness, research output and institutional service. This will make performance evaluation process more evidence- and data-based. This measure individual performance are consistently align with institutional priorities.

The use of integrated talent systems and technologies will allow institutions to keep real time track of their employee's capabilities. Data-driven analytics will help institutions identify gaps in skill levels and forecast talent needs as well as create targeted development strategies. Hence, workforce planning will be proactive as there is continues change in pedagogical models and technology (Thomas et al., 2026). Digital tools like self-service portals, mobile HR apps, and real-time feedback assist in augmenting employee experience and engagement. It give the employee more autonomy, and better access to HR services. It provide them clarity of what they do and how it contribute to institution mission increase the levels of engagement and commitment to the organization.

Professional development should be strategically aligned with institutional goals. The training, learning and development platforms available to faculty and staff should provide competency-based and personalized training programs. The designed programs should support innovation in teaching, digital pedagogy and interdisciplinary research. This will not only help the individual faculty and staff member to improve performance, but will also result in the institution's capacity to adapt, innovate and remain relevant to current educational trends (Tathavadekar & Mahankale, 2026). With the use of learning management systems (LMS), online certification services and micro-learning tools, faculty and staff can participate in continuous self-paced skill development. Staff members can use these systems to develop a learning path aligned with emerging areas such as digital pedagogy, interdisciplinary research and working with industry. It will improve individual skills and preparing institutions to be more responsive.

Leadership development and succession planning are equally vital for maintaining alignment across multiple layers of an organization. Identifying and developing the high-potential faculty and administrative staff will help ensure that the institution's strategic direction and governance can be sustained over time (Mohamed Hashim et al., 2022). In addition, digital talent analytics can provide information about leadership competencies and identify when someone is ready to lead.

The establishment of a performance-driven and accountable organizational culture is essential. Digital solutions provide fair and transparent employee evaluation systems which create fairness, produce predictable expectations. When employees understand how their jobs support the broader institution's goals, they are more likely to be engaged and committed to their jobs. Institute should consider various factors like resistance to change, lack of digital preparedness, and potential conflict between academic freedom and management systems for achieving the alignment.

Institutions must implement a balanced, human-based approach that respects academic values while utilizing the efficiency of technology-based systems. Successful talent management requires alignment with the institution's strategy. Universities operate in an ever-changing environment. It need to balance teaching excellence, research productivity, and community engagement all together . Aligning talent management systems with institutional goals encourages faculty and staff to direct their effort toward the institution's growth.

Digital solutions can facilitate the achievement of this alignment by connecting the competencies of the workforce to the objectives of the institution. University leaders can identify faculty member's areas of expertise and voice their ranking with respect to priority areas for future research. It also uncover areas of potential faculty development in new disciplines, and implement initiatives to support the long-term success of the institution. Thus, talent management will now become part of the institution's strategy rather than simply an administrative function.

5. STRATEGIC BENEFITS OF DIGITAL TALENT MANAGEMENT

Higher Education institution can maintain a competitive edge by using digital technologies in their Talent Management processes. As today's universities face rapidly changing technology, shifting student expectations, and increasing global pressure to perform academically, effective human capital management has never been more essential. Digital talent management tools help universities not only gain insight into their current employees' skill sets and capabilities but also can help them foster ongoing growth and connect their human resources to their long-term strategic goals.

Unlike traditional administrative systems, digital solutions provide real-time visibility into workforce dynamics so that institutions can anticipate problems, proactively take action, and coordinate academic and administrative functions (Muchsam et al., 2026). Institutions create an efficient and connected ecosystem by integrating of competency, performance, and development data into one platform .In addition to operational efficiency benefits, digital talent management supports a culture of transparency, accountability, and support.

Most importantly, digital talent management provides institutions with the ability to adapt to change. Digital talent management systems enable universities to make evidence-based decisions, foster collaboration and encourage ongoing learning, which builds a resilient workforce that can continue to innovate and excel academically into the future.

5.1 Evidence-Based Decision Making

Digital talent management has a significant strategic benefit because it allows evidence-based decision-making. Institution generate the data about faculty related to their expertise and professional development. These data can help in university planning when organized and analyzed properly. Digital systems offer universities structured insights about their workforce, so they can make better choices on recruiting, training, and resource allocation. It increase the accuracy and consistency of their decision-making.

In addition, data-driven systems can create both transparency and accountability. It has ability to track faculty members' performance indicators and professional contributions and keep record of these activities (Muda, 2026). The documentation, can engage the faculty members in positive discussions with leadership related to their performance indicators and contributions to the organization. This aids in aligning individual professional development with the organization's overall goals.

5.2 Talent Retention and Engagement

Retention of skilled faculty and experienced leaders is crucial for organizational sustainability and continuity. Digital talent management systems facilitate retention by providing a transparent, supportive and developmentally-oriented environment for the institution's employees (Tapsir et al., 2026). The use of digital systems allows employees to see the various career paths available to them, how they have performed against those career pathways and what opportunities exist to grow. This visibility increases employees' motivation to reach their fullest potential and improves their sense of connection to the institution. In addition, easier access to learning resources and collaborative projects increase employees' professional engagement (Tariq et al., 2026). Digital systems allow for more interactive communication through feedback and recognition systems. When employees feel that they are part of an organisation, valued, supported, and connected with the goals of the organisation, their commitment and engagement to an institution will increase dramatically in the long run.

5.3 Identification of Skill Gaps and Competency Mapping

Digital talent management helps organisations to systematically identify skill gaps and to map what competencies their workforce have. In a rapidly changing academic world, ongoing evaluation of faculty's capabilities will be important for all institutions. Digital platforms keep comprehensive records on qualifications, expertise and research interests. The information can be analysed to find gaps in emerging areas like digital teaching, interdisciplinary research, or new academic areas. Taamneh et al. (2022) stated that competency mapping will support targeted and efficient professional development. Institutions will be able to identify specific learning needs through competency mapping and be able to create focused learning interventions. It will address the identified learning needs. Therefore, this development will contribute meaningfully to building institutional capacity.

5.4 Institutional Agility and Innovation

Agility in institutions has become extremely important for fast changing academic and technological contexts. Digital talent systems will enhance institutional agility by providing real-time information about the areas of expertise within the institutional workforce. It enable institutions to deploy their talents in a timely and efficient manner.

Digital talent systems also support institutional adaptation to structural changes, such as new programs, partnerships, and research initiatives. Digital talent systems provide flexibility in workforce planning and continuous learning for the future.

6. ORGANIZATIONAL AND ETHICAL CHALLENGES

There are many clear organizational advantages of digital talent management, but have complexity in terms of organizational and ethical challenges. Institution before implementing the digital system should understood and deal appropriately with those challenges. The shift towards digital transformation requires Universities to find a balance between innovation and core academic values (Shafiee & Goodarzi, 2026). A primary concern associated with digital talent management includes how workforce sensitive data is managed. Universities collect very detailed levels of information related to academic performance, research outputs and professional evaluations. It is therefore essential that digital infrastructure continues to grow, but that workforce sensitive data is kept private, secure and used in a responsible manner. Sheri et al. (2021) stated that any challenges would lead towards decline in trust in an institution and may result in negative legal and reputation outcomes for a university. The use of digital technologies is changing current professional practices of performing their job responsibilities due to new data driven technology (Shifa et al., 2026). This transition requires leadership, strong communication and ongoing support from the institution and assurance that the transition is meaningful.

6.1 Data Privacy and Security Concerns

The problems of data privacy and security are among the greatest challenges posed by digital talent. Universities have large quantities of data about their employees' performance, credentials, and the activities they engage in. Therefore the use of robust data protection within digital HR systems is plays a vital role. Universities should implement secure digital infrastructures supported by encryption, access controls, and other comprehensive data governance frameworks. The development and implementation of clear protocols for monitoring data usage and responding to data breaches will help protect the integrity of the institution (Sattari-Ardabili & Narimani, 2026). The importance of ethical transparency is equally considerable. Faculty and staff need detailed explanations about how their data is gathered, held and utilized in the decision-making process. Transparent practices not only promote compliance, but also foster trust and validate the legitimacy of digital systems.

6.2 Digital Skill Gaps among Faculty and Staff

Digital talent systems will primarily rely on the users' abilities to use technology and their knowledge of digital tools. There are many faculty members and staff that show they are not on the same level of digital literacy, as they can utilize available technology differently (Rozi et al., 2026). Faculty members must learn and use new tools available to them for research collaboration, teaching innovation, and professional documentation, while school administration will require the ability to manipulate digital workflows and analyze data for administrative purposes. The development of true digital transformation in higher education would hinder without sufficient support, gaps in technology proficiency (Salama & Hinton, 2023). The higher education must implement and support continued skill development through structured training, mentoring, and available education resources.

6.3 Resistance to Technological Change

One of the biggest barriers to change in higher education is actually Resistance. Many academic settings are characterized by an atmosphere of independent thought and Academic Freedom. Many people view Digital Systems as intrusive and too 'managerial' in nature; thus many academic professionals are resistant to adopting new technologies for many different reasons. It include increased supervision, loss of autonomy, and uncertainty about how these new technologies will affect existing practices and institutions. If these issues are not addressed, resistance to change will seriously stunt the progression of digital initiatives and negatively affect the overall value (Pittman et al., 2026). Therefore, it is critical that institution leaders engage faculty and staff in open dialogue, communicate clearly about the need for and benefits of Digital Systems. It should involve all stakeholders in the design and implementation of these systems in order to create commitment from users and convert their resistance to acceptance of Digital Systems.

6.4 Governance and Regulatory Issues

Digital talent management poses significant governance and regulatory issues as well. Universities need to ensure that the digital systems they use should meet the legal obligation such as data privacy, employment law and ethics. They also need to create clear governing bodies to dictate and define the levels of authority, responsibility and accountability for managing the digital platforms (Pelser, 2026). Coordination between different departments is very important to eliminate fragmentation and create consistency within systems and their operations. Furthermore, regular monitoring and evaluation will provide a strong basis for governance of technology. Continuous monitoring will allow higher education institutions to identify and mitigate risk, evaluate the effectiveness of their systems. They also need to adapt new policies as technology and regulations continue to change

6.5 Balancing Technology with Academic Values

Universities are facing the challenge of keeping the technology systems aligned with the fundamental values of academic life. Universities are not simply places of administration; they are intellectual bibliographies based on scholarship, mentorship, and autonomy in their academic professions. If universities overutilize digital metrics to assess academic performance, then they risk misconstruing or minimizing the substantial contribution to academia (Putranto, 2026). Many important aspects of academia is mentorship; interdisciplinary collaboration; and community engagement which are difficult to quantify but remain an integral part of the institutional mission. Digital technologies should support in decision-making, rather than dominating it.

7. STRATEGIES FOR EFFECTIVE DIGITAL TALENT TRANSFORMATION

The process of effectively transforming talent through digital technology at the higher education level goes far beyond simply adopting new technologies. Successful transformations occur when there is organizational alignment of leadership, employee skills and abilities, governance, and cultural elements of the organization (Pathak & Mishra, 2025). Institutions should view digital transformation as a strategic initiative that enhances human capacity, increases collaboration. It also increase the ability of an institution to respond to their respective communities rather than simply being seen as a technical enhancement.

A successful transformation also depends on the establishment of digital practices into the academic and administrative operations through collaboration among leadership. Academic faculty, and staff programs focused on developing a culture that appreciates innovation, rewards, supports and encourages ongoing education; and implementation of mechanisms for shared accountability. Institutions that develop these characteristics within their culture are in the best position to sustain long-term transformation and continue to be competitive in the rapidly changing academic environment.

7.1 Leadership Commitment and Strategic Vision

A strong commitment to digital transformation by leadership and a clearly articulated strategy are the foundation for continuous digital transformation within an institution. Leadership at the institution level is critical in establishing a strategic direction that aligns with the institution's mission through digital talent initiatives (Pathak & Quttainah, 2026). The development of a clear strategic vision will allow digital talent to be integrated into the long-term planning of the institution rather than treated as isolated initiatives. The commitment of leaders must be demonstrated by how they allocate resources, invest in capabilities and communicate transparently to their institutions. leaders must establish clarity and decrease the ambiguity of institutional trust during times of transformation.

7.2 Building Digital Competencies in Academic Institutions

Digital talent systems ultimately rely on the quality of the individuals that work with them. The development of digital competency in faculty and administrative staff is therefore a key strategic priority for institutions. The competencies of faculty and administrative staff extend beyond basic technical knowledge. Peddi and Manoharan (2026) stated that faculty can utilize digital platforms for research collaboration, data-based decision making, innovative teaching and professional development. Institutions should provide structured training, peer learning, mentoring and ongoing upskilling opportunities to establish an effective transition to a digital workforce. Institutions that develop a digitally confident workforce will ensure that the adoption of technology will lead to significant improvements in performance, collaboration and innovation..

7.3 Human-Centered Management Approaches

Technology can improve efficiency at work but how effective technology is depends on its ability to complement the academic work of all users. It is possible to create a digital environment that does not restrict professional autonomy and academic work. . The collaboration create user-friendly systems that accurately reflect the realities of academic work such as collaboration, mentoring, and interdisciplinary collaboration. It is essential to balance technology capabilities and the needs of the user for managing effectiveness and acceptance.

7.4 Creating Sustainable Digital Talent Ecosystems

Sustainable and integrated talent ecosystems are the building blocks of long-term success in digital talent transformation. These talent ecosystems connect the core functions of an organization such as recruiting, developing, managing performance, collaborating, while forming one integrated digital framework. It provide connectivity between the multiple functions throughout an organization. Digital platforms will assist in sharing of knowledge, fostering collaboration across different disciplines (Oksana, 2026). It will create opportunities for continuous learning, and help to bridge organizational boundaries. The result is a more dynamic, interconnected, and strategic approach to talent management. These ecosystems also build institutional resiliency by providing the capacity to adapt, innovate, and collaborate.

8. MANAGERIAL IMPLICATIONS

University officials need to create a more proactive and strategy for effective use of digital talent system. Leaders can no longer solely manage the work from administrative perspective but they must be involved in the development of talent strategies that utilize digital capabilities in support of the institution's goals. Institution should identify human resources as an important strategic asset which leads to overall development plan (Ogogo & Qureshi, 2026). Leaders also need to create an environment that encourages continued learning and innovation, which may require additional training and support. Since digital systems are changing the way faculty and staff do their jobs, leaders need to provide direction, open communication, and ongoing support to their faculty and staff.

Finally, administrators have to find the right balance between efficiency and maintain the academic integrity as they integrate technology into the academic process. Digital tools can help to improve the method institution use to tracks performance. Digital tools cant replace the institution's core purposes, which are teaching, research, and knowledge creation. Strong, and effective leadership will ensure that advancement in technology enhance the performance rather than weaken the academic institution's value and mission.

8.1 Policy Implications for Educational Governance

Digital talent management requires additional considerations regarding educational governance and policy frameworks. Institutions which heavily relies on digital technologies require regulatory frameworks that are robust and flexible in order to promote accountability, fairness and the ethical use of data. Governance frameworks must also have clearly defined inputs and outputs in order to manage data, system integration and institutional oversight. In the frameworks, policies must stipulate how faculty data related to faculty performance, faculty development, and research activities are being collected, stored, and used (Naufalin et al., 2026). The purpose of these well-defined policies is to protect the interests of academic staff and also ensure that institutions practice responsibly.

Governance will also not limit innovation if the policy framework create appropriate balance between technological advancements, academic integrity and ethical conduct. Regulatory bodies can further promote innovation through capacity building in the field of digital technology. It will promote inter-institutional collaboration and promote knowledge sharing across the higher education sector

8.2 Implications for HR and Talent Development Professionals

As organizations undergo digital transformation, human resources (HR) functions transit from administrative role and duties to strategist for organizational development, talent management, and workforce planning. One significant implication of this digital transformation make HR professionals to develop new capabilities to manage both data analytics and digital systems. HR professionals will also be able to analyse workforce data to identify performance, productivity, and skills gaps. It will create greater opportunities for stronger decision making based on evidence.

HR professionals will also support professional development through digital systems. It can create targeted development programs, provide mentorships and collaboration opportunities, and establish knowledge-sharing cultures in their academic communities. HR professionals bridge the digital and human aspects of HR to ensure that digital tools complement rather than supplant the human aspect of talent management.

9. FUTURE RESEARCH DIRECTIONS

The increased use of digital technology to manage workforce talent in higher education will create opportunities for future research. The current research has examined how the transformation process with the use of digital technology influences the organization. Yet many aspects of managing digital talent is yet to be explored. There is an urgent need for more substantive and contextually relevant research to assess the effectiveness of aligning a university's technological capabilities with the human-centred nature of academic work. Assessing the long-term effects of digital talent management initiatives on organizational outcomes is a key area for future research. Although many universities are implementing digital systems, there are few empirical studies on how digital systems may impact institutional performance, faculty productivity, and research collaboration outcomes (Musakuro, 2022). Longitudinal study designs are important in assessing how digital talent management initiatives evolve over time, and contribute to both institutional development and growth through adaptability and academic excellence.

Another key area of research is understanding the experiences and perceptions of faculty and professional staff in higher education systems. Faculty and professional staff do not experience digital systems in the same way; rather, their engagement with digital systems will vary due to their discipline, career stage, and institutional context.

The systems of higher education vary widely in terms of governing structures, regulations and culture. Therefore, research into how digital technology is used to manage talent will give institutions an understanding of what works best and what constraints may exist within their region's specific environment (Naoum et al., 2026). The research can assist the institutions in developing flexible and scalable frameworks which enable them to implement their digital transformation in various academia domainsThe different systems of higher education vary widely in terms of governing structures, regulations and culture. Therefore, research into how digital technology is used to manage talent will give institutions an understanding of what works best and what constraints may exist within their region's specific environment. Through this research, institutions can develop flexible/scalable frameworks to enable them to implement their digital transformation efforts across various types of academia. Technology advancements such as advanced analytics, smart digital platforms, and collaborative technologies are rapidly changing the way that educational institutions are structured and success is measured in relation to their academic workforce. The future direction of research should examine the impact of these new technologies on decision-making, professional relationships, and the overall ecosystem in an educational setting. The role of these technologies in terms of functionality, ethics, culture, and institution will be identified in the research..

Technology advancements such as advanced analytics, smart digital platforms, and collaborative technologies are rapidly changing the way that educational institutions are structured and success is measured in relation to their academic workforce. The future direction of research should examine the impact of these new technologies on decision-making, professional relationships, and the overall ecosystem in an educational setting.

Higher education institutions have very different governance models, regulatory frameworks, and cultures. There is the opportunity to learn from the best practices and the constraints of digital talent management practices in higher education institutions through this research. The findings will develop scalable and flexible digital transformation frameworks for higher education institutions. Advanced analytics, intelligent digital platforms, and collaboratively designed technologies continue to shape the way we organize and measure the performance of the academic workforce. Future research should also focus on how the tools affect decision making, professional relationships, and the academic enterprise as a whole; and should also identify the benefits of these tools from functional, ethical, cultural, and institutional perspectives.

10. CONCLUSION

The digital transformation taking place in higher education has significantly changed how universities manage and develop their human resources.As academic institutions have developed into technology-based entities, they are being pushed toward adopting new strategic talent management approaches. It is integrated both vertically and horizontally across other organizations.

The study examined the development of digital talent management in higher education, including foundational concepts, operational practices, strategic advantages, and associated drawbacks. The study revealed, how digital tools can lead to greater data-driven, more structured, and more proactive approaches to manage both academic and administrative talent. Furthermore, the study emphasizes the need for alignment between talent systems that support the institution's priorities and the global competitive environment faced by today's higher education institutions. The study's findings that technology alone does not result in transformational change. The success of digital talent initiatives is reliant on effective leadership, a well-developed governance structure, and the continued investment on faculty and staff's professional development. Additionally, the implementation of digital systems must respect and supports the key values of higher education. Digital talent management should be viewed as a strategic driver for building capability and resiliency of institutions. When digital systems for talent management are designed and implemented well, it create supportive environments for generating knowledge. It develop employees on regular basis; and create innovative solutions to problems. The alignment of technology with-human knowledge uplift the academic values. Universities are not only bringing change but become leaders in circulating change. It is shaping the globe's future regarding digital system.

REFERENCES

Afifa, U. K. (2026). Integrated Islamic School Management: Leaders' Policies and Stakeholders' Responses. *Social Criticism of Islamic Studies*, *1*(1), 41–55.

Al Hashimi, A. S. A., Azmin, A. A., & Junoh, M. Z. M. (2021). Talent management in higher education: A critical review. *International Journal of Education. Psychology and Counseling*, *6*(44), 155–166.

Azuwandri, A. (2026). The Role Of Digital HR In Improving Indonesian Human Resource Competence In The Era Of Industry 4.0 Transformation. *Focus of Human Resource Management Journal*, *1*(1), 31–36.

Benavides, L. M. C., Tamayo Arias, J. A., Arango Serna, M. D., Branch Bedoya, J. W., & Burgos, D. (2020). Digital transformation in higher education institutions: A systematic literature review. *Sensors (Basel)*, *20*(11), 3291. DOI: 10.3390/s20113291 PMID: 32526998

Bolander, P., Werr, A., & Asplund, K. (2017). The practice of talent management: A framework and typology. *Personnel Review*, *46*(8), 1523–1551. DOI: 10.1108/PR-02-2016-0037

Bradley, A. P. (2016). Talent management for universities. *Australian Universities' Review. The*, *58*(1), 13–19.

Bygstad, B., Øvrelid, E., Ludvigsen, S., & Dæhlen, M. (2022). From dual digitalization to digital learning space: Exploring the digital transformation of higher education. *Computers & Education*, *182*, 104463. DOI: 10.1016/j.compedu.2022.104463

Cappelli, P., & Keller, J. R. (2014). Talent management: Conceptual approaches and practical challenges. *Annual Review of Organizational Psychology and Organizational Behavior*, *1*(1), 305–331. DOI: 10.1146/annurev-orgpsych-031413-091314

Chong, L. Y. Q., Lim, T. S., & Nipo, D. T. (2026). Human resource analytics adoption and its impact on talent management and operational performance: Evidence from Malaysian firms. *Journal of Modelling in Management*, *21*(4), 1–20. DOI: 10.1108/JM2-06-2025-0307

Collings, D. G., & Mellahi, K. (2009). Strategic talent management: A review and research agenda. *Human Resource Management Review*, *19*(4), 304–313. DOI: 10.1016/j.hrmr.2009.04.001

Collings, D. G., Vaiman, V., & Scullion, H. (2022). Talent management: A decade of developments.

Cotter, J. J., O'Brien, F., & Kelly, É. V. (2026). Integrating Knowledge Management, Project Management, and Human Resource Management for Organisational Resilience in the Construction Industry. *Buildings (Basel, Switzerland)*, *16*(3), 511. DOI: 10.3390/buildings16030511

Dogan, M., & Arslan, H. (2026). Empowering Academics in the Digital Age: Navigating the Transformation of Higher Education. *European Journal of Education*, *61*(1), e70420. DOI: 10.1111/ejed.70420

El Garem, R. A. (2026). HR digital transformation: Enhancing human resource management through technology. *Future Business Journal*, *12*(1), 5. DOI: 10.1186/s43093-025-00703-7

Fahad, S., Khan, I. U., Bibi, A., & Sarwar, A. (2026). The Impact of Multi-Dimensional Engagement on Talent Retention and Organizational Performance: The Mediating Role of Employee Engagement in the Nursing Workforce. *Journal of Political Stability Archive*, *4*(1), 208–226. DOI: 10.63468/jpsa.4.1.12

Gandy, R., Harrison, P., & Gold, J. (2018). Talent management in higher education: Is turnover relevant? *European Journal of Training and Development*, *42*(9), 597–610. DOI: 10.1108/EJTD-11-2017-0099

Gkrimpizi, T., Peristeras, V., & Magnisalis, I. (2024). Defining the meaning and scope of digital transformation in higher education institutions. *Administrative Sciences*, *14*(3), 48. DOI: 10.3390/admsci14030048

Hannan, S. A. (2023). Development of digital transformation in higher education institutions. *Journal of Computer Science & Computational Mathematics*, *13*(01), 1–8. DOI: 10.20967/jcscm.2023.01.001

Huang, Z., Sulaiman, N., Yunus, M. M., & Li, X. (2026). Analysis of Blended Learning in Higher Education Based on CiteSpace (2001-2024). *Electronic Journal of e-Learning*, *24*(1), 138–161. DOI: 10.34190/ejel.24.1.4290

Hussain, S. M., & Shoukat, L. (2026). Administrative Dysfunction in Pakistan Higher Education: A Qualitative Exploration of Institutional Sclerosis, Democratic Deficits, and Post-Colonial Persistence. *Social Science Review Archives*, *4*(1), 977–993. DOI: 10.70670/sra.v4i1.1616

Jani, A., Muduli, A., & Kishore, K. (2023). Human resource transformation in India: Examining the role digital human resource technology and human resource role. *The International Journal of Organizational Analysis*, *31*(4), 959–972. DOI: 10.1108/IJOA-08-2021-2886

Kaputa, V., Loučanová, E., & Tejerina-Gaite, F. A. (2022). Digital transformation in higher education institutions as a driver of social oriented innovations. In *Social innovation in higher education: Landscape, practices, and opportunities* (pp. 61–85). Springer International Publishing. DOI: 10.1007/978-3-030-84044-0_4

Kasmia, N. B., & M'hamed, H. (2023). Digitalization of higher education: Impacts on management practices and institutional developement. A literature review. *Conhecimento & Diversidade, 15*(39), 56–82. DOI: 10.18316/rcd.v15i39.11135

Khan, G. F., Bhatt, A. S., Siddiqui, M. H., & Mishra, M. (2026). Impact of Strategic Leadership Styles and Leadership Support on Employee Engagement in Indian Higher Education. *International Review of Management and Marketing, 16*(2), 253–262. DOI: 10.32479/irmm.21493

Khushk, A., Zhiying, L., Yi, X., & Aman, N. (2026). AI-driven HR transformation in Chinese automotive industry: Strategies and implications. *Business Process Management Journal, 32*(1), 30–50. DOI: 10.1108/BPMJ-11-2023-0915

Kornita, S. E., & Tampubolon, D. (2026). Bridging Skill Gaps in the Palm Oil Workforce: A Mixed-Methods Training Needs Assessment of Plantation Workers in Kampar Regency, Indonesia. *Journal of Cultural Analysis and Social Change*, 1400-1408.

Kumar, M., Najeeb, A., Rajora, H., & Rani, P. (2026). Privacy in the Digital Workplace: Reforming Data Protection Law for Monitoring and HRIS. In *Legal Frameworks of Human Resource Management Reform* (pp. 37-54). IGI Global Scientific Publishing.

Leikuma-Rimicane, L., Baloran, E. T., Ceballos, R. F., & Medina, M. N. D. (2022). The role of higher education in shaping global talent competitiveness and talent growth. *International Journal of Information and Education Technology (IJIET), 12*(11), 1211–1220. DOI: 10.18178/ijiet.2022.12.11.1741

Loidl, V. (2026). Designing Human-Centered Organizations: Practical Insights and Future Research Opportunities. *Journal of Organizational Behavior Review, 8*(1), 100–126.

Maharani, H., Amaliah, I., & Nurhayati, N. (2026). Resilience of Alpha Generation: Digital Resiliency, Organizational Culture, and Talent Management. *International Journal of Science. Technology & Management, 7*(1), 90–97.

Maharani, H., Amaliah, I., & Nurhayati, N. (2026). Resilience of Alpha Generation: Digital Resiliency, Organizational Culture, and Talent Management. *International Journal of Science. Technology & Management, 7*(1), 90–97.

Mayer, S., Abou Refaie, R., & Uebernickel, F. (2026). The challenges and opportunities of hybrid education with location asynchrony: Implications for education policy. *Policy Futures in Education, 24*(1), 82–104. DOI: 10.1177/14782103231224507

McDonnell, A., Collings, D. G., Mellahi, K., & Schuler, R. (2017). Talent management: A systematic review and future prospects. *European Journal of International Management, 11*(1), 86–128. DOI: 10.1504/EJIM.2017.081253

Moghtadaie, L., & Taji, M. (2016). Study of the performance of faculty members according to talent management approach in higher education. *Educational Research Review, 11*(8), 781–790.

Mohamed Hashim, M. A., Tlemsani, I., & Matthews, R. (2022). Higher education strategy in digital transformation. *Education and Information Technologies, 27*(3), 3171–3195. DOI: 10.1007/s10639-021-10739-1 PMID: 34539217

Muchsam, Y., Maulana, M. A., Cegunawan, C., & Yuda, M. S. (2026). Digital Industry: Talent Mapping and Triple Helix Partnerships for Strengthening Services Exports. *The Eastasouth Management and Business, 4*(02), 511–522. DOI: 10.58812/esmb.v4i02.852

Muda, F. P. (2026). Implementation of the balanced scorecard in higher education performance management: A comparative study between Indonesia and international cases. *Klabat Journal of Management, 7*(1), 1–22. DOI: 10.60090/kjm.v7i1.1333.1-22

Musakuro, R. N. (2022). A framework development for talent management in the higher education sector. *SA Journal of Human Resource Management, 20*, 1671. DOI: 10.4102/sajhrm.v20i0.1671

Naoum, R. F., Szakadáti, T., & Balogh, G. (2026). Artificial Intelligence (AI) in human resource management (HRM): a systematic review of its dual impact on diversity, equity, and inclusion (DEI). *Management Review Quarterly*, 1-72.

Naufalin, L. R., Indrawati, C. D. S., Indriayu, M., & Noviani, L. (2026). Bridging Religiosity and Digital Competence: The Mediating Role of Digital Ethics in Higher Education. *Munaddhomah: Jurnal Manajemen Pendidikan Islam, 7*(1), 92–108. DOI: 10.31538/munaddhomah.v7i1.2455

Ogogo, A. U., & Qureshi, A. (2026). Comparative Study On Talent Identification And Talent Retention: Nigeria As A Developing Country And The Western World. *INTERNATIONAL JOURNAL OF ADVANCES IN SIGNAL AND IMAGE SCIENCES*, 353-371.

Oksana, K. R. A. V. C. H. U. K. (2026). Human-centric digital leadership for HRM 5.0 ecosystem readiness. *ORA E INTELIGENTE I DEZVOLTARE REGIONALĂ, 10*(01), 55–85.

Pathak, A., & Mishra, S. (2025). An Empirical Exploration of MOOC Effectiveness Towards Participants' Intention-Fulfilment and Learners' Satisfaction. Vision. *The Journal of Business Perspective, 29*(1), 67–80. DOI: 10.1177/09722629211054170

Pathak, A., & Quttainah, M. A. (2026). Charting the Future: AI's Evolving Role in Human Capital Management. In Mehra, P., Olga Titovna, E., Agrawal, S., Kansra, P., & Stefanovic, M. (Eds.), *AI-Enabled Workforce Management for Hybrid Workplaces* (pp. 69–96). IGI Global Scientific Publishing., DOI: 10.4018/979-8-3373-5871-0.ch003

Peddi, S., & Manoharan, G. (2026). Ethical Guidelines for the thoughtful Implementation of AI in Higher Education. *EthAIca: Journal of Ethics. AI and Critical Analysis*, (5), 409.

Pelser, A. M. (2026). Human-Centric and Sustainable Digital Transformation: Are Higher Education Institutions Ready to Manage and Develop Talent in the Age of AI?. *Észak-magyarországi Stratégiai Füzetek, 22*(04), 20-28.

Pelser, A. M. (2026). Human-Centric and Sustainable Digital Transformation: Are Higher Education Institutions Ready to Manage and Develop Talent in the Age of AI?. *Észak-magyarországi Stratégiai Füzetek, 22*(04), 20-28.

Pittman, J., Anderson, J., Bentley, E., Clanton, C., Hammonds, L. S., McCoy, K. T., Otts, J. A., Riley, B. H., & Sturm, T. A. (2026). Gap analysis methodology for mapping baccalaureate and graduate nursing curricula to the AACN essentials: A step-wise approach. *Journal of Professional Nursing : Official Journal of the American Association of Colleges of Nursing, 63*, 26–32. DOI: 10.1016/j.profnurs.2025.12.009 PMID: 41796558

Putranto, S. A. E. (2026). Human Resource Analytics and Data-Driven Decision Making: Implications for Talent Acquisition and Retention Strategies. [JUMPER]. *Journal Management & Economics Review, 3*(8), 439–452.

Rozi, A., Junengsih, J., Alam, S., Pawar, A., Sumarjo, W., & Sunarsi, D. (2026). Impact of HR Management on AI Implementation and Data Protection in Indonesian Manufacturing. [IJCITSM]. *International Journal of Cyber and IT Service Management, 6*(1), 51–64. DOI: 10.34306/ijcitsm.v6i1.226

Salama, R., & Hinton, T. (2023). Online higher education: Current landscape and future trends. *Journal of Further and Higher Education*, *47*(7), 913–924. DOI: 10.1080/0309877X.2023.2200136

Sattari-Ardabili, F., & Narimani, M. (2026). Hybrid education as a new paradigm in higher education. *Revista Mexicana de Investigación e Intervención Educativa*, *5*(1), 51–57. DOI: 10.62697/rmiie.v5i1.272

Shafiee, M., & Goodarzi, S. (2026). The role of employer branding in talent management: Analysis of key strategies and tools. *The International Journal of Organizational Analysis*, *34*(1), 99–114. DOI: 10.1108/IJOA-10-2024-4900

Sheri, A. A., Nori, N. R., & Gupta, S. K. (2021). The role of strategic intelligence in enhancing effective talent management: A study on some academic institutions of Duhok Governorate. [AJNU]. *Academic Journal of Nawroz University*, *10*(2), 137–155. DOI: 10.25007/ajnu.v10n2a929

Shifa, S., Abbas, S. J., & Muhammad, K. K. (2026). HR Analytic as a Strategic Tool: Predicting Talent Retention and Performance. *The Critical Review of Social Sciences Studies*, *4*(1), 387–395. DOI: 10.59075/vhtstj93

Swailes, S. (2016). The cultural evolution of talent management: A memetic analysis. *Human Resource Development Review*, *15*(3), 340–358. DOI: 10.1177/1534484316664812

Taamneh, A. M., Taamneh, M., Alsaad, A., & Al-Okaily, M. (2022). Talent management and academic context: A comparative study of public and private universities. *EuroMed Journal of Business*, *17*(4), 731–751. DOI: 10.1108/EMJB-08-2020-0088

Tapsir, S. H., Yusof, R., & Hashmi, A. (2026). Transformational leadership, Green HRM and top management commitment: Pathways to sustainability in Malaysian higher education. *Journal of Applied Research in Higher Education*, *18*(2), 478–494. DOI: 10.1108/JARHE-09-2024-0493

Tariq, J., Shahab, H., & Zahoor, H. (2026). Talent Management in Organizational Landscape: A Systematic Review of Literature. *Policy Journal of Social Science Review*, *4*(2), 351–369.

Tathavadekar, V. P., & Mahankale, N. R. (2026). Digital HR for sustainable value chains: Bridging tech maturity and green talent in emerging economies. *Strategic HR Review*, *25*(1), 28–34. DOI: 10.1108/SHR-07-2025-0067

Thomas, S., Nair, D. S., Joseph, J., Srampical, S. G., & Cleetus, R. S. (2026). Examining the sustainable integration of artificial intelligence in human resource digitalization in the context of Industry 4.0. *European Public & Social Innovation Review*, *11*, 1–14. DOI: 10.31637/epsir-2026-2044

Varma, R. R., Umesh, I. M., Nagesh, Y. N., & Kumara Swamy, K. S. (2021). Digital transformation in higher education institutions-an overview. *International Journal of Applied Engineering Research: IJAER*, *16*(4), 278–282.

Vignieri, V., & Santoni, R. (2026). Open innovation in the public sector: Managing knowledge assets for public value creation through dynamic performance management. *International Journal of Public Sector Management*, **•••**, 1–28. DOI: 10.1108/IJPSM-03-2025-0103

Wahyuningtyas, R. (2015). An integrated talent management system: Challenges for competitive advantage. *International Business Management*, *9*(4), 384–390.

Yadav, M., Dewasiri, N. J., & Aquino Jr, P. G. (2026). The Legal Challenges and Opportunities of Using AI in HR Functions. *Legal Frameworks of Human Resource Management Reform*, 55-88.

Young, K., Küçük, Z. D., Delahunty, T., Dempsey, M., & Maglaperidze, N. (2026). Evaluating the impact of a digital competency-based placement model on STEM pre-service teachers' digital competence and teaching experiences. *Teaching and Teacher Education*, *175*, 105466. DOI: 10.1016/j.tate.2026.105466

Zhang, C. (2026). Digital Empowerment in Design: A Literature Review of Design Ecosystem Service Platforms. *Review of Economic Assessment*, *5*(1), 24–58. DOI: 10.58567/rea05010002

Chapter 5
Brains Meet Bots: AI and Data in Academic Talent Management Practices in Higher Education Institutions

Sapheya Aftimos
http://orcid.org/0000-0002-5810-9856
Australian University, Kuwait

Matt Aftimos
http://orcid.org/0009-0005-2809-0700
Bryant University, USA

Azar Aftimos
MSM, Kuwait

ABSTRACT

Artificial intelligence and data analytics are transforming how higher education institutions attract, develop, and retain talent. HEIs are entering a digital era that extends beyond operational change to encompass deeper cultural and strategic transformation. This chapter proposes a six-pillar framework: strategic alignment, continuous learning, adaptive culture, data capability, ethical governance, and human-centered design. The framework examines transformation across four levels: institutional, HR, academic unit, and individual. It also addresses emerging ethical and governance challenges linked to the increasing reliance on algorithmic decision-making in academia. To achieve sustainability, innovation, and global competitiveness, universities must align technological capabilities with core academic values. The chapter concludes that the future of academic work lies in the productive coexistence of human expertise and intelligent systems, where data-driven insights enhance, rather than replace, the scholarly process.

DOI: 10.4018/979-8-3373-8959-2.ch005

1. INTRODUCTION: WHY AI AND TALENT NOW?

Higher education institutions (HEIs) stand or fall on the strength of their human resources (Schaap et al., 2025). Architecture, rankings, and endowments matter, but academic capability is what sustains institutional innovation and reputation. Faculty members shape research agendas, attract funding, mentor doctoral students, build international partnerships, and define the intellectual character of their institutions. In an environment marked by global competition, demographic change, and economic pressure, HEIs cannot treat talent as a purely administrative issue; it is a strategic asset.

Meanwhile, artificial intelligence (AI) and advanced analytics are reshaping organizational decision-making. Across sectors, algorithmic systems support recruitment, forecast staff turnover, personalize development, and generate near real-time performance insights (Tursunbayeva et al., 2025). Practices that were once reactive and intuition-led are becoming more data-informed and predictive. In corporate settings, HR functions are evolving from record keeping to analytics-enabled strategic partnering. HEIs are not exempt. They already operate in data-rich environments (e.g., learning management systems and research databases), yet much of this data remains underused in workforce decision-making.

Tensions follow. HEIs have invested heavily in digital technologies for teaching, administration, research, and student services. Digital transformation (DT) strategies typically prioritize research infrastructure, learning analytics, and online delivery, while talent management (TM) is often treated separately and still relies on traditional processes, fragmented data, and collegial practices that resist formalization. In many institutions, digitalization and human capital strategy run in parallel: one stream focuses on platforms and infrastructure, while the other revolves around recruitment committees, promotion panels, and professional development. These streams are rarely integrated (Aftimos & Khafash, 2026).

HEIs therefore risk modernizing tools while leaving assumptions about talent unchanged. They may adopt AI enabled systems without understanding how they reshape academic careers, standards, and culture. Or they may avoid AI on ethical grounds and lose opportunities to improve transparency, equity, and strategic coherence. The question is whether to use AI than how to embed it in a values-based TM strategy.

Academic work adds further complexity. Academic careers combine teaching, research, supervision, community engagement, and institutional service, and performance unfolds over long time horizons. Research impact may take years to materialize, teaching quality blends quantitative and qualitative evidence, and disciplinary norms shape what counts as excellence. Governance is also distinctive: many decisions rely on collegial processes and peer review rather than hierarchical control. These features make AI-enabled TM both potentially valuable and inherently sensitive in HEIs.

One example is that predictive analytics could support more systematic recruitment by placing global talent pools or flagging unconscious bias in shortlisting. Promotion decisions could be made more transparent by using data dashboards. Personalized development recommendations may assist academics in the early stages of their careers to navigate complex career paths. However, those tools might also minimize academic performance to narrow metrics, enhance managerialism, or lead to surveillance perceptions. With autonomy and trust being the key factors in the context, morale and legitimacy can be compromised with poorly designed AI systems.

These tensions are amplified by the pace of technological change. Generative AI, automated screening, and increasingly sophisticated research analytics are already redefining expectations for productivity and skills. HEIs face pressure to remain competitive, innovative, and digitally capable. Leaders are asked to make strategic workforce decisions under uncertainty, from anticipating skills gaps to redesigning roles. Data can provide clarity, but poorly governed data practices and unethical AI use can undermine the very values that differentiate higher education from other sectors.

AI in academic TM cannot be treated as a set of tools. It raises questions of mission, academic values, governance, and stakeholder trust. HEIs need clarity on why data is collected, what decisions can be supported by algorithms, and where human judgment must remain decisive. Benefits also depend on capability building: without data literacy among HR professionals, academic leaders, and faculty, even advanced systems will underperform.

The chapter brings together AI, data driven HR practices, and the higher education context. It considers how AI and analytics can be used across the academic TM life cycle including recruitment, development, performance, and retention. It also examines why data informed decision-making matters for institutional sustainability and addresses the ethical, governance, and cultural dilemmas raised by algorithmic systems in academia.

The chapter also develops a framework tailored to HEIs. It treats AI as a strategic enabler that complements human expertise without undermining academic values. By aligning technology, talent strategy, and ethical governance, HEIs can move beyond fragmented digital initiatives toward responsible, data driven academic TM.

2. CONCEPTUAL FOUNDATIONS

This chapter uses three linked lenses: strategic talent management, DT in higher education, and AI and data driven HRM. Together they show that AI enabled academic TM is more than a technology upgrade. It is an institutional change that reshapes decision making, roles, and governance, and must be understood within the distinctive context of HEIs.

2.1 Strategic Talent Management in Higher Education

Strategic talent management (STM) has become a key focus in contemporary HR research, particularly in the work of Scullion and Collings (2011). At its core, STM involves systematically identifying, developing, deploying, and retaining people who create disproportionate value for organizational performance and sustainability. In corporate contexts, this logic is tied to competitive advantage, innovation, and resilience. In HEIs, however, it requires careful translation and contextualization.

A first difference is academic autonomy. Unlike most corporate employees, academics have substantial professional independence in setting research agendas, shaping pedagogy, and building external collaborations. This autonomy reflects academic freedom and intellectual inquiry. TM therefore cannot rely on standardized structures and tightly managed career tracks. It must balance strategic alignment with intellectual independence. Poorly designed AI systems that enforce rigid evaluation or predictive career models can conflict with these values.

A second feature is professional identity. Academic work is anchored in disciplinary communities that often extend beyond institutional boundaries, and many academics identify more with their discipline than with their employer. This shapes career choices, collaboration networks, and mobility. STM in HEIs must therefore support disciplinary excellence while also building organizational commitment. Data and AI can illuminate collaboration patterns, research impact, and skill development, but they must respect the social and epistemic foundations of academic work.

A third significant difference is long career cycles. Academic careers are processes for decades, where the extended training period, tenure system, and research directions change. The benefits of the investments in the early career can be observed only many years later. This time aspect is a challenge to short-term, performance-based models prevalent in corporate talent systems. More strategic decision-making can be aided by predictive analytics and longitudinal workforce planning, but it must consider uncertainty, non-linear career paths, and the dynamism of knowledge production.

A fourth difference is that academic performance is multidimensional. Academic work combines teaching, research, supervision, and institutional service, whereas many corporate roles prioritize a narrower set of measurable outputs. Each domain creates value through different competencies. Teaching quality includes student engagement, curriculum development, and mentoring. Research impact may be reflected in publications, grants, and societal contribution. Service includes leadership, governance, and community engagement. TM should integrate these contributions rather than privilege one at the expense of others. AI and analytics can help document diverse contributions, but poorly calibrated systems can still default to a narrow set of indicators.

Academic talent markets are also further distinguished by global mobility. HEIs are competing on the international level to attract scholars, doctoral students, and postdoctoral scholars. Global networks, international collaborations, and transnational labor markets shape academic careers. The STM in HEIs is thus in need of a global orientation. International recruitment and retention strategies can be supported with the help of data analytics, but institutions must solve the challenges of diversity, inclusion, and equal access to opportunities.

The above characteristics indicate that STM in higher education should be adaptive, relational, and contextual. Rather than blanket adoption of corporate models, HEIs require structures that appreciate academic values, governance traditions, and work that is knowledge driven. AI and data systems should then be incorporated into a more comprehensive concept of academic careers and institutional missions.

2.2 Digital Transformation in Higher Education

Higher education is being transformed by DT in ways that are profound but uneven. What began as the adoption of information technologies is now framed as a shift in how institutions create, deliver, and sustain value. This change affects teaching, research, governance, and institutional identity (Díaz-García et al., 2022; Zabalawi et al., 2024).

The platformization of education is one of the significant dimensions. The teaching and learning have been shifted to learning management systems, digital assessment tools, and online collaboration platforms. HEIs are becoming more digital ecosystems, made up of technology providers, global education platforms, and open knowledge networks. These advances make access and flexibility more open, but they are also accompanied by competition and new demands regarding digital capability. Digital pedagogical skills, instructional design, and technology-enhanced learning should therefore be the academic competencies to be considered in talent strategies.

Another major change is remote and hybrid work. The COVID-19 pandemic facilitated the process of normalizing the distributed academic work, including virtual teaching and remote research collaboration. This trend of hybrid models is now common in many institutions. Such a change has an impact on recruitment, engagement, and retention. HEIs can attract global talent without necessarily having to do a physical relocation. However, they must deal with distributed teams, digital collaboration, and the evolving work-life balance demands. Despite these transitions being able to be supported by data and analytics, they also present the challenges of monitoring, trust, and autonomy.

The emergence of learning environments characterized by abundant data also explains the extent of change. Digital systems are capturing more student engagements, learning outcomes, and engagement patterns. These data streams give information about the effectiveness of teaching, curriculum, and student achievement. Nonetheless, they also need the emergence of novel data interpretation and ethical governance capabilities. Members of the faculty are supposed to work with learning analytics, change the pedagogical approaches, and collaborate with data experts. This brings about new developmental needs and career trajectories.

Academic roles are also being redefined because of DT. There is an increase in the blurring of boundaries between teaching, research, and professional practice. Scholars are required to work with interdisciplinary work, industry collaborations, digital scholarship, and public engagement. New roles such as digital educators, specialists in research data, and leaders of academic innovation are now emerging. TM systems will have to shift away, however, towards more flexible and hybrid career models, rather than the old academic models.

These transformations shape competitiveness and capability. HEIs that connect DT with talent strategies can innovate more effectively, respond to external pressures, and remain relevant. When digitalization is treated as a purely technical initiative, fragmentation grows, skills gaps widen, and performance can decline. Alignment between DT and TM is therefore a strategic necessity.

2.3 AI and Data-Driven HRM

The evolution of HRM offers the third conceptual pillar of this chapter. In the past, the HR functions of most organizations were based on administrative functions that included payroll, compliance, and personnel records. Discipline has, over the years, moved towards strategic and evidence-based approaches. The recent phase in this development is data-driven HRM.

Workforce management is changing through AI, predictive analytics, and intelligent decision support. These tools can detect patterns in large datasets, anticipate talent needs, and inform recruitment, development, and retention. The shift moves HR from reactive responses to more proactive, strategic action. Rather than responding to turnover after it occurs, organizations can flag risks earlier and design targeted retention plans. Decisions can draw on professional experience alongside data driven evidence (Aftimos & Diab-Bahman, 2025; Marler & Boudreau, 2017).

This change is still uneven in higher education. Most institutions hold large volumes of data on faculty performance, student outcomes, and research productivity, but these sources are often siloed. Integrating them can support a more holistic approach to talent. For example, predictive models can help identify early-career academics who may need additional support. Analytics can also inform workforce planning for emerging areas such as data science or sustainability. Finally, smart systems can recommend individualized career pathways and professional development options.

Even so, AI in HR raises serious concerns. Algorithms can reproduce historical inequities when training data reflects structural bias. Some systems lack transparency and accountability, raising questions about justification and contestability. An excessive focus on quantitative measures can erode trust and collegiality in academic settings. These risks are especially salient in HEIs, where legitimacy and fairness are central to institutional culture (Tursunbayeva et al., 2022; Barocas & Selbst, 2016).

AI based HR therefore requires balancing technological potential with ethical control. Human judgment remains essential, particularly in value laden decisions such as appointment, promotion, and leadership selection. The aim is not to replace decision makers, but to strengthen deliberation with better evidence and, where appropriate, predictive insight.

STM, DT, and AI-driven HRM give a potent conceptual base in which to appreciate the future of academic workforce management. The integration of these concepts provides an opportunity to improve institutional sustainability, agility, and innovation. However, this integration requires critical thinking, sensitivity to contexts, and ethical alertness. In the following sections, this foundation will be built to examine how AI and data may be implemented throughout the academic TM life cycle, without jeopardizing the unique values and missions of higher education.

3. AI AND DATA ACROSS THE ACADEMIC TALENT MANAGEMENT LIFE CYCLE

AI and analytics are influencing TM across HEIs, yet academic careers are long, multidimensional, and shaped by disciplinary and institutional cultures (Adamakis & Rachiotis, 2025). When used well, AI can support more strategic and consistent decisions across the talent life cycle. When used poorly, it can amplify unfairness, weaken trust, and threaten professional autonomy. The following sections consider how AI may shape attraction, development, performance, and retention, and the tensions HEIs must manage.

3.1 AI in Academic Talent Attraction and Recruitment

Higher education recruitment has been based on peer networks, academic reputation, and committee-based decision-making. As much as the practices contribute to collegiality and disciplinary legitimacy, they contribute to closed networks and unconscious bias. HEIs are transforming the way they find and utilize global talent by using AI and analytics.

AI-based talent source and global search are among the most important developments. Digital platforms and large academic databases are now giving institutions the opportunity to find potential candidates by their publication records, citation networks, collaboration patterns, and research impact. These will enable HEIs to shift to a proactive global search instead of passive recruitment. This is especially useful in the new areas where talent competition is intense. Analytics of academic profiles can also assist institutions in knowing research directions, interdisciplinary collaborations, and social change, which provides more information compared to the traditional screening of CVs.

Another shift is AI assisted screening. These systems can process large volumes of data, flag relevant experience, and identify alignment with institutional priorities. Predictive hiring models can analyze historical hiring and performance data to detect patterns linked to longer term performance, retention, and research productivity. The promise is greater efficiency and consistency, particularly where recruitment is large scale.

Nevertheless, the developments present significant dangers. The issue of algorithmic bias is one of the primary areas of concern. Predictive models can replicate past inequalities by gender, race, or institutions, in case historical data have such inequalities (Barocas & Selbst, 2016; Naoum et al., 2026). Indicatively, hiring algorithms can be biased towards applicants of prestigious institutions or overarching research paradigms and thus perpetuate the hierarchies. Disciplinary differences are also to be considered. Metrics that are meaningful in the natural sciences may not be applicable in the humanities or the arts. The excessive use of quantitative-based indicators can also exclude those scholars whose work is innovative but cannot be easily measured.

It is thus important that there be transparency. HEIs should make sure that AI systems are explainable and that human judgment is at the center stage. The AI ought to assist search committees and not substitute them. AI can be used responsibly to promote diversity, extend the search around the world, and decrease the administrative load. Applied unthinkingly, it can reduce intellectual diversity and undermine trust.

3.2 AI in Academic Development and Career Pathways

The process of academic development has been traditionally based on mentoring, learning with peers, and institutional workshops. AI opens the prospect of more data-driven career paths that are more personalized.

Customized faculty development is one of the promising ways of its use. Through evaluation of teaching, research, collaboration, and the use of digital tools, AI systems will be able to create customized development plans. These may involve suggestions for pedagogical training, leadership programs, or interdisciplinary collaboration. This strategy goes in line with the trend of lifelong learning in the academic profession, whereby skills need to change in relation to technological and societal transformation.

Another aspect of change is skills and competency mapping. Digital pedagogy, data literacy, and interdisciplinary collaboration are some of the emerging competencies that AI can discover. Institutions can track the available skills in the academic workforce and find gaps in capability. This facilitates strategic planning of the workforce and dedicated investment in professional development.

Analytics around the productivity of research is also getting sophisticated. Instead of talking only about the number of publications, advanced analytics can analyze collaboration networks, interdisciplinary impact, and knowledge diffusion. These lessons can assist the newly graduated academics in negotiating complicated research conditions and establishing viable academic careers. Simultaneously, they can reinforce the institutional strategy as they are able to see emergent areas of strength.

A further development is teaching analytics and digital pedagogy. Learning management system data will give insights into the engagement of students, course design, and outcomes of learning. AI can facilitate reflective teaching practice by finding patterns and proposing improvements. Recommendation systems in learning can enable scholars to create new methods of teaching, embrace new technologies, and improve student education.

However, these innovations also raise serious questions. It is also possible that development will be overly data-driven, and academic growth will be reduced to quantifiable products. Mentorship, peer engagement, and intellectual discovery can be impoverished if AI systems focus on efficiency rather than depth. The issue of privacy also arises where sensitive information regarding performance and behavior is utilized to inform development (Tursunbayeva et al., 2022; European Data Protection Board, 2018).

The major challenge is to make sure that AI facilitates agency and not control. Individual growth ought to enable scholars to create their own careers rather than limit them to career patterns. AI has the potential to transform lifelong academic careers positively when planned appropriately and offer more opportunities, personalized support, and institutional capacity.

3.3 AI in Performance and Promotion Systems

Performance evaluation and promotion are among the most sensitive processes in academic life. They shape career trajectories, resource allocation, and institutional culture. Traditionally, decisions rely on peer review, disciplinary norms, and deliberation. AI introduces both opportunities and tensions.

The combination of multi-source data to be evaluated is one of the significant changes. HEIs are increasingly integrating research output, teaching evaluations, student outcomes, grant performance, and service contributions. AI will be able to combine these streams of data and create detailed performance data. Real-time feedback should be offered to academics via transparent and dynamic dashboards so that they can take a more proactive career management approach.

Research impact metrics are changing at a fast pace. In addition to citation counts, AI has the capability to monitor influence in society, policy engagement, interdisciplinary collaboration, and dissemination of knowledge. These wider pointers are in line with the increasing demands that academic assignments help to address social issues. Nevertheless, they also raise debates about how impact should be defined and measured.

New opportunities are also provided by teaching quality analytics. Other data that can give deeper information about the teaching effectiveness are student engagement data, learning outcomes, and peer feedback. AI can determine trends in courses and contribute to evidence-based teaching enhancement. Open reporting could improve the accountability and rewards relating to teaching excellence.

Despite these benefits, the issue of over-quantification is still strong. Opponents claim that metrics may cause distortion of academic priorities, strategic behavior, and decrease intellectual risk-taking. Distrust and unwarranted dependency on algorithmic assessment can destroy collegiality. The argument is reminiscent of wider issues regarding managerialism in HEIs and the possible loss of academic freedom (Zuboff, 2019; Tursunbayeva et al., 2022).

The challenge, hence, does not lie in the question of whether to employ metrics or not, but rather the matter of balancing between quantitative and qualitative judgment. The use of AI must increase transparency and fairness and maintain the deliberative and peer-based aspects of academic assessment. Institutions should make sure that performance systems are an embodiment of various types of academic contributions.

3.4 AI and Academic Retention and Engagement

The issue of retention and engagement is becoming a strategic concern in higher education. Academic mobility is being transformed by global competition, pressure at work, and the transformation of career expectations. AI and analytics provide emerging tools to aid the sustainability of the workforce.

Predictive retention analytics will be able to detect the initial indicators of disengagement, including a decrease in research output, collaboration, or excessive workload. These insights can be used to offer specific assistance, mentorship, or professional growth by institutions. This is proactive as it goes beyond reactive resignation.

Another application is well-being and burnout monitoring. Workload, teaching intensity, and digital engagement data can also assist the institutions in detecting patterns of stress. These findings are useful in a scenario where the levels of academic burnout are on the increase. They, however, also have ethical issues with surveillance and privacy. Trust is essential. The surveillance should be open and encouraging as opposed to reproving (European Commission High-Level Expert Group on Artificial Intelligence, 2019; UNESCO, 2021; Tursunbayeva et al., 2022).

Another opportunity is career mobility. AI can scrutinize internal and external career paths and assist academics in investigating new job markets, interdisciplinary endeavors, or leadership. This is in line with the changing demands of flexible and boundary-spanning careers.

There is also an increase in internal talent markets. Online activities have the potential to pair scholars with research initiatives, instructional developments, and management opportunities. This improves the cooperation and agility of institutions. It also promotes interdisciplinary knowledge sharing and innovation.

This phase of the talent life cycle brings out the point of sustainability best. The higher the chance of retaining talent and maintaining the performance of the institution, the higher the use of AI in HEIs aims to ensure engagement, development, and well-being. Nonetheless, success is pegged on the ethical design, cultural compatibility, and the trust of the stakeholders.

Throughout the academic TM life cycle, AI and data have a great strategic potential. They facilitate better decision-making, personalized support, and proactive planning of the workforce. However, they also put a strain on the conventional standards of independence, teamwork, and professional discretion. The future of academic TM will hinge on the way the institutions negotiate this balance by integrating technological capability with academic values and ethical governance.

4. DATA-INFORMED DECISION MAKING AND INSTITUTIONAL SUSTAINABILITY

So far, the discussion has focused on what AI and analytics can do across stages of the academic talent life cycle. Tools, however, do not transform institutions on their own. The deeper shift lies in how decisions are made. Data driven decision making is not just dashboards or predictive models, but a move from ad hoc intuition toward systematic evidence in shaping academic workforce strategy. When linked to purpose, this shift can support institutional sustainability.

4.1 From Intuition to Evidence in Academic Workforce Strategy

HEIs have long relied on professional judgment, peer review, and collegial consultation to manage academic talent. These practices are central to academic culture, but they can also be shaped by informal assumptions, incomplete information, and short-term pressures. Workforce decisions, such as hiring priorities, succession planning, and leadership appointments, may therefore be reactive rather than guided by long-term evidence.

Data-informed approaches can strengthen, rather than replace, professional judgment by combining evidence on research output, teaching demand, enrollment trends, collaboration networks, and retirement projections. For example, instead of hiring only when vacancies arise, HEIs can anticipate future disciplinary needs based on student demand, funding trends, and societal priorities.

In short, evidence can improve transparency and strategic consistency, but it cannot substitute for mission-driven choices. Academic environments are value-laden and context dependent, so human deliberation remains essential when interpreting data and setting priorities.

4.2 Workforce Planning in Uncertain Environments

The environment in which higher education operates is volatile and uncertain. Shifts influence institutional stability in public funding, demographic changes, technological disruption, and geopolitical tensions. Under these circumstances, academic workforce planning becomes a difficult undertaking. Tenure systems and long career cycles create a lack of flexibility, and the need for rapid changes in knowledge domains creates the need to have new capabilities.

Under uncertainty, AI and predictive analytics can assist in improving workforce planning. The effects of declines in enrollment, a reduction in funding, or new research priorities can be simulated with scenario modeling tools. Anticipatory systems can help identify areas of potential skill shortage or overcapacity. Longitudinal data may provide information on patterns in career advancement, retirement trends, and mobility flows.

Such abilities enhance institutional foresight. HEIs will be able to anticipate changes instead of responding to the crisis. They will be able to invest strategically in new fields, reskill the current faculty, and implement better succession planning. In this regard, resilience is strengthened by data-informed workforce planning.

However, uncertainty cannot be eliminated using algorithms. Assumptions in data and models shape the predictions. Disruptions will always occur unexpectedly. Human leadership will still play a critical role in scenario interpretation, weighing trade-offs, and workforce decisions in accordance with the values of the institution.

4.3 Alignment Between Institutional Strategy and Talent Analytics

Mismatch between the institutional strategy and the TM practices is one of the persistent issues in higher education. The most common strategic plans contain ambitious objectives related to digital innovation, interdisciplinary research, community engagement, and international partnerships. Nevertheless, the recruitment, development, and promotion systems can be stuck in traditional disciplinary silos and performance indicators.

Talent analytics can play as a bridge between practice and strategy. Connecting workforce data with strategic goals can help HEIs to make sure that the hiring, development, and evaluation processes support the institutional priorities. As an example, when the institution aims to enhance interdisciplinary research, analytics can detect collaboration trends and highlight structural obstacles. In case DT is a strategic goal, competency mapping can show digital skills gaps across faculties.

This alignment enhances coherence. TM, therefore, becomes a facilitator of strategy rather than a parallel administrative function. It also enhances accountability. Workforce indicators allow leaders to track the progress of strategic goals based on actual capabilities and not symbolic commitments.

However, alignment must not turn into strict conformity. Academic institutions thrive on diversity of thought and intellectual exploration. Data-driven alignment should give room for innovation that does not conform to set strategic themes. In this case, too, strategic focus and academic freedom are to be balanced through human judgment.

4.4 Data, Agility, Resilience, and Innovation

Agility and resilience are now central to debates on institutional sustainability. Agile institutions adjust quickly to emerging conditions. Resilient institutions absorb shocks without losing their core identity. Data informed decision making can support both.

To begin with, real-time analytics can improve agility. Leaders can access updated data on staffing levels, workload distribution, and performance patterns through dashboards, enabling earlier interventions rather than delayed responses.

Second, data enhances resilience through informed resource allocation. Evidence-based decisions can be made by the HEIs on where to invest, consolidate, or innovate when faced with financial constraints. Open information minimizes speculation and maximizes the legitimacy of hard times.

Third, analytics can be useful in innovation, as they can recognize new opportunities. Collaboration network analysis can also show some unforeseen interdisciplinary relationships. New funding priorities can be indicated by research trend analytics. Skills mapping has the capacity to discover latent abilities within the institution. These lessons favor strategic experimentation and knowledge recombination.

However, innovation also requires creativity, intellectual risk-taking, and human imagination. Data can point out patterns, but it does not create vision. Institutional sustainability demands that there be a balance between analytical rigor and exploration.

4.5 The Role of Human Judgment Alongside AI

Human judgment remains indispensable in academic workforce management because it brings contextual understanding, ethical sensitivity, and institutional wisdom that AI cannot replicate. Academic leadership requires navigating competing values, disciplinary cultures, and long-term mission commitments; tasks that cannot be delegated to algorithms.

Human judgment is a key tool in the interpretation of data, challenging assumptions, and ensuring fairness. A predictive model can determine a faculty member as being at risk of leaving because of performance indicators. This signal should be interpreted by a leader in the context of a more extended picture, which encompasses personal situation, institutional level of climate, and career desires. On the same note, performance dashboards can show disparities across departments, but resource allocation decisions need to be discussed and debated.

Trust is also essential. Scholars tend to deal with data-driven systems when they feel that these systems support them rather than dominate them. It is essential to have clear communication on how data is gathered, reviewed, and utilized. Inclusion in the system design may lead to greater legitimacy and less opposition.

Finally, AI should function as decision support, not as an autonomous decision maker. The aim is a hybrid approach in which analytics increase transparency and help surface potential bias, while accountable leaders and peer-based processes retain responsibility for judgments and trade-offs.

Data-informed decision-making should not become technocratic control. When embedded in clear governance, transparent communication, and academic values, analytics can support sustainability, resilience, and innovation. Without these safeguards, the same systems can erode trust and weaken the mission they are meant to advance.

5. ETHICAL, GOVERNANCE, AND CULTURAL CHALLENGES

Integrating AI and data into academic TM raises ethical, governance, and cultural questions. HEIs are knowledge making organizations and civic institutions, legitimized by trust, equity, and freedom of thought. For that reason, AI in HR cannot be treated as a purely technical or efficiency driven initiative. It must be grounded in institutional values, transparent governance, and cultural sensitivity. This section reviews key issues that emerge when data and algorithms intersect with academic work.

5.1 Ethical Risks

Bias and discrimination are two of the most popularly discussed ethical concerns. AI systems are trained with past data, and the academic labor markets have been historically unequal and based on gender, race, geography, and institutional prestige. If these patterns are used and embedded in training data, predictive models may reproduce and amplify them. For instance, recruitment algorithms may discriminate in favor of candidates who have attended elite HEIs or dominant research traditions and thus restrict intellectual diversity. Equally, performance analytics can be disadvantageous to scholars in up-and-coming or interdisciplinary disciplines where more traditional measures can be less suitable. Ethical application of AI thus demands ongoing auditing, bias detection, and corrective mechanisms. Efficiency is not the only desired goal, but equity and inclusion are as well.

The other major challenge is transparency and explainability. A lot of sophisticated AI systems can be viewed as complex models with their internal logic that can hardly be interpreted. However, academic settings are very much dependent on justification and shared responsibility. Hiring, promotion, or resource allocation decisions must be justifiable and verifiable. When academic staff lacks the knowledge of how algorithmic recommendations are formed, trust is breached. Institutions should consequently focus on explainable AI, and it is important to make sure that data-driven processes are open to human questioning. Clear information on data sources, assumptions, and constraints should be communicated (European Commission High-Level Expert Group on Artificial Intelligence, 2019; Organisation for Economic Co-operation and Development, 2019; UNESCO, 2021).

The issue of academic freedom is also another area of concern. The autonomy of scholars to explore knowledge without any unnecessary interference has long been held by the HEIs. The application of data to track research productivity, teaching engagement, or digital behavior can produce the impression of being monitored. These anxieties reflect more general arguments regarding digital capitalism and data mining highlighted in the works of scholars such as Shoshana Zuboff (Zuboff, 2019). Although there can be a healthy behavior between monitoring and development, it can also be seen as an act of control by the managers. Academic risk-taking and creativity can be reduced if scholars feel that they are under constant observation. The moral theories need to be clear in the distinction between proximate analytics and intrusive surveillance.

Data ownership and privacy are two closely connected concepts. Scholarly work generates volumes of digital data in the form of education management systems, research databases, and collaboration tools. One would wonder who the owner of this data is, how and where it is used, and how long it remains stored. The faculty might not be comfortable with the analysis of their teaching, research, and communication data without their permission. Institutions need to have a clear policy on the rights, consent, and access to data. This involves the safeguarding of sensitive personal data and allows only authorized analytical use. In international partnerships, data transfers and flows across jurisdictions increase the complexity.

These are not ethical issues that are likely to hinder the use of AI, but an indication that AI needs to be designed and managed responsibly. HEIs can be at the frontline to come up with ethical standards that balance innovation with human dignity.

5.2 Governance and Accountability

There is a need for ethical awareness to be translated into robust governance structures. One of the prerequisites is institutional data governance. This entails a proper structure of data collection, storage, access, sharing, and deletion. Roles and responsibilities need to be delineated by governance structures so that data use will be in a manner that is consistent with institutional mission and values. In the absence of such frameworks, adoption of AI will be fragmented, duplicative, and subject to misuse.

Another very important dimension is regulatory compliance. Consent, transparency, and accountability standards are found in data protection laws (e.g., in the European Union General Data Protection Regulation). HEIs all over the world must deal with dissimilar environments governed by regulations. In certain regions, the regime of protecting the data is robust and enforceable. In some others, the regulatory frameworks are changing or disproportionate. Institutions must adopt flexible and principled informative approaches that meet both legal and ethical expectations (European Data Protection Board, 2018).

Cross-functional management is necessary since AI in TM is in the interplay of HR, IT, legal, academic leadership, and institutional research. Governance is not possible without collaboration in these areas. Oversight committees, ethics boards, and data governance councils can offer multidisciplinary perspectives. Academic staff and faculty representatives should be involved in the processes of governance to increase the level of legitimacy and trust. Involvement of stakeholders will create a sense of ownership (Wu et al., 2024).

Another area of concern is risk management. AI presents operational, reputational, and strategic risks. Biased recruitment algorithms may result in legal and public criticism. Data breaches may harm the institutional reputation. Excess dependence on predictive models is a potential cause of strategic errors. HEIs need to thus incorporate AI governance into wider institutional risk frameworks. Frequent audits, contingency plans, and scenario planning are needed.

Global variation further makes governance more complicated. The systems of higher education vary in terms of the traditions of governance, regulatory framework, and cultural expectations. A robust central government could provide coordinated data strategies in certain settings. In other ones, decentralized structures and academic autonomy demand more participatory strategies. The institutions need to conform the governance models to the local situations without sacrificing ethics.

5.3 Professional and Cultural Resistance

Apart from the technical and regulatory issues, the most significant challenges may be cultural. Powerful professional norms, disciplinary identities, and traditions of self-government mark academic communities. Antipathy toward AI is also indicative of a more fundamental identity, power, and institutional change apprehension.

The main area of concern in algorithms is trust. Scholars might be concerned about the ability of algorithm systems to reproduce the depth of academic activity. Aspects of bias, reductionism, and loss of nuance are often brought up. Technical expertise cannot be used to impose trust. It should be constructed out of openness, involvement, and value manifestation. Building confidence may be achieved through pilot projects, open dialogue, and co-design processes.

Another crucial aspect is fear of managerialism. Over the past decades, the growing roles played by managerial practices in HEIs have raised concern among many academics. Artificial intelligence analytics can be seen as a continuation of managerial authority, performance, and more active monitoring, and a decrease in collegial rule. When AI is connected to control instead of help, it is probable that resistance will grow. Institutions should thus present AI as one that will facilitate academic work and not a surveillance and control tool.

These issues are closely associated with professional identity and autonomy. The values that influence academic careers include intellectual autonomy, peer recognition, and contribution to the field of study. Systems that seem to standardize or in any way quantify these values can be perceived to be a threat. To implement this properly, it is necessary to be sensitive to differences in disciplines and to understand that there are various kinds of academic contributions.

Digital capability gaps also represent a practical and cultural challenge. Many scholars and human resource experts have not developed data literacy and the use of AI tools. New systems can cause anxiety, exclusion, or dependence on technical experts in the absence of proper training and support. It is therefore necessary to have capability building. It is not only technical skills; it is also the sense of ethics and critical awareness of data literacy.

The solution to cultural resistance will involve leadership, dialogue, and common purpose. HEIs' change is not usually linear. It entails negotiation, testing, and adaptation. This implies that academic communities that participate in the formation of AI systems have a higher chance of success.

5.4 Power, Voice, and Participatory Decision Making

The increasing application of artificial intelligence in academic TM is not a technical or ethical concern only. Here is the deeper reality. It also transforms power in HEIs. Recruitment, promotion, development, and retention decisions are increasingly based on data systems and predictive models as well as algorithmic recommendations. This move also brings very important concerns regarding who sets the rules, who owns the data, and who is the ultimate beneficiary of these systems.

The use of AI in most organizations may lead to a concentration of power in the top management, the human resource departments, or even external technology providers. In case algorithms mediate decision-making, academic departments and collegial decision-making processes that have long ruled academic work may lose power. This may cause a conflict between managerial efficiency and academic self-governance. Leaders can consider AI as a source of uniformity, transparency, and strategic focus. Nevertheless, scholars might find it a control or standardization mechanism, which does not allow them to recognize disciplinary variation and scholarly judgment. These are not mere resistance to change. They are indications of greater anxieties about independence, professionalism, and the future of academic governance.

It is due to this fact that voice and representation are the key aspects of responsible AI adoption. The data-driven decisions usually involve academics, professional staff, and students, but hardly involve them in the design and evaluation of the systems that influence such decisions. Such non-involvement may undermine legitimacy and trust. Participatory styles of governance lead to a solution. Engaging stakeholders during the initial stages will bring up issues, enhance transparency, and make AI solutions reflective of academic values and institutional missions. Faculty committees, advisory boards, and pilot consultations are some of the mechanisms that can be used in establishing common ownership instead of forced change.

Co-creation and inclusion are also compelling to the traditions of collaboration in higher education. HEIs are discursive communities founded on a production of knowledge through debate, criticism, and peer-to-peer. Applying these principles to the process of DT enhances ethical integrity and functionality. When involved in system design, various stakeholders can provide contextual knowledge that may decrease bias, increase fairness, and usability. Digital capability and confidence may also be developed in this process, which will, in the long term, be more meaningful in terms of human AI collaboration.

Meanwhile, it should be noted that larger institutional and national settings influence the concepts of power and participation. There is variation in higher education systems in terms of traditions of governance, regulatory environment, and managerial authority. AI may support centralized control and performance-driven cultures in certain systems. It can facilitate transparency, fairness, and more participatory decision-making in others. Global sensitivity is thus necessary. Institutions should not bring in technological models that would go against the local values or systems of governance.

It is therefore important to note that ethical, governance, and cultural issues are not peripheral issues but the key determinants of success. HEIs that begin to apply AI to TM without addressing these dimensions will endanger the trust, legitimacy, and institutional cohesiveness. On the other hand, the ones that give preference to ethical design, clear governance, and cultural fit can utilize AI to enhance academic values. This sets the stage for the next section, which develops a framework for ethical and strategic AI-driven TM in higher education.

6. ETHICAL AND STRATEGIC AI-DRIVEN TALENT MANAGEMENT FRAMEWORK FOR HEIS

The preceding discussion shows that AI and data analytics can strengthen academic talent management (TM) only when they are embedded in institutional strategy, governance, and culture. Rather than adopting disconnected tools, HEIs need an integrated, values-based approach. This section proposes the Academic AI TM Model (AATM Model): a six-pillar, four-level framework that integrates

AI across recruitment, development, performance, and retention while prioritizing augmentation over automation and protecting academic values.

6.1 The Six Pillars

6.1.1 Pillar 1: Strategic Alignment

The question of purpose is the fundamental aspect of any AI-based system of talent deployment. HEIs are not like corporations in the sense that their missions are not confined to efficiency or financial performance. Their goal is to advance knowledge, educate future generations, and contribute to society. AI initiatives that are not directly associated with these objectives will be at risk of being fragmented or having unintended effects.

Strategic alignment entails that institutional priorities through which talent analytics can be utilized include transformation into digital, interdisciplinary research, global interaction, and impact on society. For instance, recruitment algorithms must be based on the philosophy of diversity, inclusion, and intellectual pluralism at the institution. The development systems should reinforce emerging fields of knowledge and innovation. Performance analytics is supposed to support the balance between teaching, research, and service, and not prioritize the limited outcomes.

Coherence between planning processes is also stressed in this pillar. Shared data and long-term vision should guide workforce planning, institutional strategy, and resource allocation. In this regard, AI becomes a strategic enabler, rather than a technical add-on.

In practice, predictive analytics can help universities anticipate emerging research areas and plan staffing proactively (e.g., by analyzing publication, funding, and collaboration trends). Used this way, talent acquisition shifts from vacancy-led hiring to strategic capacity building.

6.1.2 Pillar 2: Human-Centered Design

One of the principles of this framework is that AI needs to support human judgment, rather than take the place of it. Academic work entails creative, interpretive, and moral reasoning. These processes can be supported using algorithmic systems and can never be replicated. Human-centered design consequently prioritizes academics, HR personnel, and institutional leaders in the adoption of AI.

This includes participatory design, whereby users are involved in the design and testing of AI systems. Faculty participation increases legitimacy, and systems carry diversity in terms of discipline. Flexibility is also given importance in human-centered approaches. Instead of providing standardized routes, AI must be able to provide information that can be interpreted and adopted by individuals based on their career aspirations.

Augmentation also means preserving deliberative processes. Leadership teams, recruitment committees, and even promotion panels should use AI-generated insights into their systems but not make final decisions. This ensures collegial and peer-based academic governance.

For example, AI can surface patterns (e.g., collaboration or innovation signals) that inform peer review and self-reflection, while final evaluations remain deliberative and human led.

6.1.3 Pillar 3: Ethical Governance

Trust is built on the foundation of ethical governance. It includes transparency, accountability, fairness, and respect for privacy. The HEIs are best placed to become the forefront of ethical AI since they are both knowledge creators and consumers.

Transparency involves explainable mechanisms and openness in the use of data. Stakeholders will need to know how analytics inform decisions. Fairness entails bias and inclusive design through continuous auditing. Accountability will make sure that there are clear lines of responsibility for the decisions made with the help of AI.

Academic freedom is also covered in this pillar. Professional autonomy and intellectual diversity should be supported by the systems instead of being limited. There are many risks of data-driven control and the significance of governance that safeguards human agency.

Many universities are establishing AI ethics boards, audit routines, and oversight committees for high-stakes TM uses (e.g., hiring and promotion) to monitor bias, transparency, and compliance over time.

6.1.4 Pillar 4: Data Capability

Technology alone is not transformative. Institutions must build the human and organizational capability to interpret and use data effectively, including digital literacy, analytical skills, and critical AI awareness among HR professionals, academic leaders, and faculty.

Development of capability ought to be involved with both technical and ethical competencies. Leaders must know the strategic implications of analytics. HR specialists need to turn data into working knowledge of the workforce. Scholars need the ability to work with teaching and research analytics. Data scientists and subject experts need to work together in an interdisciplinary manner.

It is also important to invest in data infrastructure. Integrated data systems allow holistic views, whereas disjointed systems negatively impact effectiveness. The development of governance and capability should go hand in hand.

In practice, integrated data systems that link HR data with teaching and research indicators can reveal workload imbalances and capability gaps, supporting more transparent development and resource decisions without removing human judgment.

6.1.5 Pillar 5: Adaptive Culture

The most challenging part of transformation is usually cultural alignment. HEIs have strong traditions, decentralized governance, and diverse disciplinary norms. Adoption of AI thus necessitates an adaptive culture that is founded on trust, dialogue, and shared purpose.

Participation is central. Scholars must take part in the creation of AI efforts instead of being mere consumers. The use of open communication regarding the goals, risks, and benefits leads to increased legitimacy. Confidence to trust is achieved when systems are seen to be enablers as opposed to coercive.

Experimentation is also adopted in adaptive cultures. The success of all initiatives will not be the same. It is necessary to learn through failure and make changes in the strategies. This attitude changes the compliance with innovation.

6.1.6 Pillar 6: Continuous Learning

The final pillar recognizes that AI and DT are ongoing, not one off projects. Institutions need cycles of feedback, review, and adjustment so systems improve over time rather than remaining fixed after implementation.

New strategies in recruitment, development, and retention can be piloted. Data gathered in these projects can be used to make changes in scaling and improvement. Periodic examination will make sure that systems are in accordance with institutional objectives and ethics.

Constant learning also involves keeping a check on external developments. Technological changes, shifts in regulations, and curriculum developments mean that changes are necessary. HEIs must be agile and reflective.

6.2 A Multi-Level Framework for Implementation

To bring these pillars into practice, the framework works at four levels, which are interdependent. Each level supports the others. This means that the success of adoption cannot be brought about by technology, but through an alignment in terms of strategy, structures, and normal academic work.

6.2.1 Institutional Level

At the institutional level, leadership determines the strategic purpose, moral values, and distinctiveness of governance that influence the application of AI in TM. This involves investment in data capabilities and digital infrastructure, as well as long-term workforce planning. The policies are set at this level to define the role of AI in sustaining, innovating, and competing globally. In terms of institutional mission and academic values, there must be alignment to ensure that technological adoption will enhance and not destroy the identity of the university. There is also trust that is created through clear communication and supervision throughout the academic community.

6.2.2 HR Function Level

The HR role is the core part of the strategy to incorporate analytics throughout the life cycle of talent. This is by incorporating AI in recruitment, development, performance, and retention, and making sure that there are fairness, transparency, and accountability. HR professionals are translators between institutional strategy and practice. They are also at the forefront in capability development, promoting digital literacy, and fostering collaboration between technology, academic, and administrative stakeholders. Through this, HR turns into an evidence-based decision-making unit and not an administrative unit.

6.2.3 Academic Units Level

Faculties and departments are important to put AI systems into perspective. They analyze data according to standards of discipline, instructional methods, and research priorities. Such a locality leads to more relevance and legitimacy. It also provides flexibility, whereby it acknowledges that various disciplines have different values on various types of knowledge, influence, and performance. The involvement at this level enhances ownership and curbs resistance.

6.2.4 Individual Academic Level

At the individual level, AI promotes career growth, mobility, and well-being. Academics use insights to make decisions during teaching, research, collaboration, and leadership journeys. Here, it is empowerment and agency. The use of AI instead of substituting professional judgment improves reflection, learning, and informed career preferences.

Figure 1. AATM model

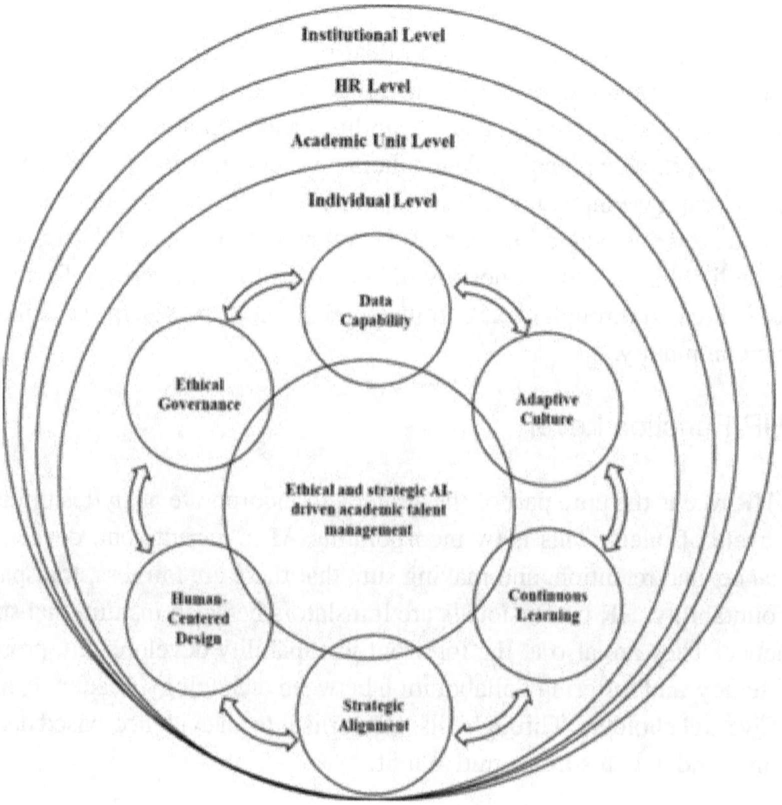

Figure 1 shows the AATM Model as a multi level framework for ethical and strategic AI enabled academic TM. Responsible, AI driven TM sits at the center and is supported by six interdependent pillars (strategic alignment, human centered design, ethical governance, data capability, adaptive culture, and continuous learning). The outer layer sets out four implementation levels: individual, academic unit, HR function, and institution. The model emphasizes coordination: leadership defines purpose and governance, HR embeds analytics across the TM life cycle, academic units interpret insights within disciplines, and individuals use insights to support career growth and well being.

This framework is fundamentally different from other models that deal with TM and DT in three essential ways. To begin with, this framework has been purposely designed to integrate academic values with technology, rather than viewing digitalization solely as an operational or technical improvement. Most of the dominant strategies for TM and DT in the world of strategic HRM are rooted in the corporate sector and are focused on efficiency, automation, and performance optimization. In contrast, universities operate under an entirely different logic due to collegial governance, discipline autonomy, and the value of producing knowledge as a public good. Therefore, this framework integrates the academic values of higher education into the development and implementation of AI-based technologies, thereby making it clear that decisions regarding technology adoption in higher education cannot be made independently of academic identity, intellectual freedom, and the overall mission of the institution.

Another difference is that this framework acknowledges that the impact of AI on academic work is experienced on four interrelated levels: institutional strategy, organizational systems, professional roles, and individual academic practice. Most other models examine only the impact of AI on a single level, organizational performance or individual productivity; as a result, those models tend to underestimate the complete impact of AI on academic work. This framework's multi-level approach illustrates how strategic priorities inform technology investments, how those investments change how we manage human resources and govern, and how, ultimately, those investments are reflected in how we perform the work of teaching, research, and service. By employing this multi-level view of transformation, this framework provides a more in-depth understanding of transformation as a systemic process rather than as a series of isolated interventions.

The framework's core components of human-centered design and ethical governance directly guide digital TM, rather than being treated as secondary components of it; prior frameworks tended to deal reactively with ethical issues, often after systems had been implemented. This framework is different because principles of fairness, transparency, accountability, and inclusivity will be built into the design, deployment, and evaluation of AI systems from the outset. This issue is particularly important in the academic context because algorithmic decision-making processes affect the recruitment process, advancement within an organization, distribution of workload among employees, and recognition of the academic contributions of employees. By making ethical governance and human-centered design primary components, the framework acknowledges that AI use within academia is not just a technical concern, but also a normative concern, with significant implications for both the professional identity of academics, equity among professors, and trust in academia by both those employed within it, as well as the general public.

7. CONCLUSION

This chapter argues that introducing AI and data analytics into academic talent management (TM) is not simply a technological upgrade; it is a strategic and cultural shift in how HEIs attract, develop, evaluate, and retain academic talent. AI can enable more proactive, integrated, and evidence-informed decisions (e.g., workforce planning, global talent mapping, personalized development, and more transparent performance systems). Yet these gains depend on aligning analytics with academic values, governance traditions, and trust-based professional cultures.

The chapter also shows that AI's promise cannot be separated from its risks. Algorithmic bias, limited explainability, privacy concerns, and surveillance perceptions can undermine equity, collegiality, and academic freedom. Over-reliance on narrow metrics may distort academic priorities and amplify managerialism. These tensions make AI-enabled TM in universities an ethical and governance challenge as much as a technical one.

To address this, the chapter proposes the AATM Model, which integrates six pillars (strategic alignment, human-centered design, ethical governance, data capability, adaptive culture, and continuous learning) across four interdependent levels (institution, HR function, academic units, and individual academics). The model positions AI as an enabler of responsible, sustainable TM: institutional leadership sets direction and safeguards values, HR translates strategy into practice, academic units contextualize analytics within disciplines, and individuals use insights to support growth and well-being.

A core implication is augmentation rather than automation: AI should strengthen, not replace, scholarly judgment. HEIs that balance data-informed decision-making with academic wisdom can become more agile, resilient, and inclusive, recognizing diverse contributions and evolving career paths while preserving deliberation, mentorship, and critical inquiry.

Conversely, unreflective adoption can trigger resistance, mistrust, fragmentation, and reputational harm when AI is experienced as control rather than support. Weak data governance can reduce decision quality, increase legal and ethical exposure, and create strategic drift when analytics initiatives are disconnected from institutional mission and values.

Looking ahead, academic work will continue to evolve through digital scholarship, open science, global research networks, and hybrid teaching models. AI will increasingly support discovery and collaboration, but core higher education values, academic freedom, collegiality, public engagement, and social responsibility, remain non-negotiable. The task is not to preserve unchanged traditions, but to reinterpret these values in digitally mediated workplaces.

Future academic TM depends on partnership, not substitution: academics can use analytics while remaining critical and ethical decision makers, and leaders can use predictive insights while retaining deliberation and dialogue. HEIs that treat AI as a strategic, ethical, and human-centered change aligning technology with academic values, investing in capability and culture, and practicing participatory governance will be better positioned to adapt and to shape the future of higher education.

REFERENCES

Adamakis, M., & Rachiotis, T. (2025). Artificial Intelligence in Higher Education: A State-of-the-Art Overview of Pedagogical Integrity, Artificial Intelligence Literacy, and Policy Integration. *Encyclopedia, 5*(4), 180. DOI: 10.3390/encyclopedia5040180

Aftimos, S., & Diab-Bahman, R. (2025). AI-Driven Talent Management: Transforming Workforce Strategies in the Digital Age. *Creativity. Innovation and Entrepreneurship, 166*(166). Advance online publication. DOI: 10.54941/ahfe1006110

Aftimos, S., & Khafash, M. (2026). Embedding talent management in the digital transformation of universities in Kuwait. In *Organizational change, innovation, and consumer behavior in the digital economy* (pp. 29–58). IGI Global., DOI: 10.4018/979-8-2600-1453-0.ch002

Barocas, S., & Selbst, A. D. (2016). Big data's disparate impact. *California Law Review, 104*(3), 671–732.

Díaz-García, V., Montero-Navarro, A., Rodríguez-Sánchez, J. L., & Gallego-Losada, R. (2022). Digitalization and digital transformation in higher education: A bibliometric analysis. *Frontiers in Psychology, 13*, 1081595. DOI: 10.3389/fpsyg.2022.1081595 PMID: 36533011

European Commission High-Level Expert Group on Artificial Intelligence. (2019). *Ethics guidelines for trustworthy AI*. European Commission.

European Data Protection Board. (2018). *Guidelines on automated individual decision-making and profiling for the purposes of Regulation 2016/679*. EDPB.

Marler, J. H., & Boudreau, J. W. (2017). An evidence-based review of HR analytics. *International Journal of Human Resource Management, 28*(1), 3–26. DOI: 10.1080/09585192.2016.1244699

Naoum, R. F., Szakadáti, T., & Balogh, G. (2026). *Artificial intelligence (AI) in human resource management (HRM): A systematic review of its dual impact on diversity, equity, and inclusion (DEI)*. Management Review Quarterly., DOI: 10.1007/s11301-025-00580-y

Organisation for Economic Co-operation and Development. (2019). *OECD AI principles*. OECD.

Schaap, L., Nijland, F., Cents-Boonstra, M., & Vanlommel, K. (2025). A framework supporting the innovative capacity of higher education institutions: An integrative literature review. *Sustainability (Basel), 17*(14), 6517. DOI: 10.3390/su17146517

Scullion, H., & Collings, D. G. (2011). *Global talent management*. Routledge. DOI: 10.4324/9780203865682

Tursunbayeva, A., Fernandez, V., Gallardo-Gallardo, E., & Moschera, L. (2025). Artificial intelligence and digital data in recruitment: Exploring business and engineering candidates' perceptions of organizational attractiveness. *European Management Journal*. Advance online publication. DOI: 10.1016/j.emj.2025.03.002

Tursunbayeva, A., Pagliari, C., Di Lauro, S., & Antonelli, G. (2022). The ethics of people analytics: Risks, opportunities and recommendations. *Personnel Review*, *51*(3), 900–921. DOI: 10.1108/PR-12-2019-0680

UNESCO. (2021). *Recommendation on the ethics of artificial intelligence*. UNESCO.

Wu, C., Zhang, H., & Carroll, J. M. (2024). AI governance in higher education: Case studies of guidance at Big Ten universities. *Future Internet*, *16*(10), 354. DOI: 10.3390/fi16100354

Zabalawi, I., Kordahji, H., & Aftimos, S. (2024). Digital transformation in universities: Strategic framework, implementation tools, and leadership. In Badran, A., Baydoun, E., Hillman, S., & Mesmar, J. (Eds.), *Higher education in the Arab world*. Springer., DOI: 10.1007/978-3-031-70779-7_8

Zuboff, S. (2019). *The age of surveillance capitalism: The fight for a human future at the new frontier of power*. Profile Books.

Chapter 6
Artificial Intelligence in Higher Education:
Integrating Governance, Education, and Professional Training Systems

Mohamed Amine Frikha
http://orcid.org/0000-0002-6737-1370
Applied College, King Faisal University, Saudi Arabia

ABSTRACT

This chapter examines the transformative role of artificial intelligence (AI) in reshaping higher education through the integration of academic learning and vocational training. It explores how AI supports industry-aligned curricula, adaptive learning environments, and skills-based education that enhance graduate employability and workforce readiness. The chapter also highlights the emergence of intelligent governance systems in higher education institutions, where data-driven decision-making and human–AI collaboration improve institutional performance and talent management. Drawing on governance, socio-technical, and human capital theories, the chapter proposes a comprehensive framework for understanding AI-enabled educational transformation. In addition, it addresses critical challenges related to ethics, algorithmic bias, data privacy, and the need for responsible and sustainable AI governance in higher education

DOI: 10.4018/979-8-3373-8959-2.ch006

1. INTRODUCTION

In an era defined by digital disruption, intensifying global competition, shifting demographic profiles, and heightened demands for accountability, AI is no longer treated merely as a technological upgrade. The rapid evolution of artificial intelligence (AI) is fundamentally reconfiguring the operational, managerial, and strategic foundations of higher education institutions (HEIs). Artificial intelligence (AI) is arguably the driving technological force of the first half of this century, and will transform virtually every industry, if not human endeavors at large (Holmes et al. 2019)

This shift marks a structural departure from conventional bureaucratic models toward dynamic, digitally integrated environments. Historically, higher education relied on fragmented administrative routines, static workforce planning, and hierarchical leadership structures. Today, AI-enabled predictive analytics, intelligent automation, and generative applications are reshaping these practices across the institutional lifecycle. From faculty recruitment and retention to workload optimization, performance assessment, succession planning, and curriculum mapping, AI is increasingly embedded within strategic planning and talent management frameworks (Wu et al., 2024). Consequently, universities are evolving into adaptive organizations that continuously align internal operations with external labor market signals, ensuring that institutional strategy remains responsive, evidence-based, and forward-looking (Hossain and Rafat, 2026).

Central to this transformation is AI's capacity to bridge academic education and professional training. By enabling industry-aligned curricula, skills-based pedagogies, and practice-oriented learning environments, AI enhances graduate employability and accelerates work-integrated learning pathways. Intelligent tutoring systems, adaptive assessment platforms, and simulation-based training modules allow learners to develop applied competencies in real time, while conversational AI and virtual assistants streamline administrative support and learner engagement (Chan & Colloton, 2024).

Human capital theory highlights the shifting value of workforce competencies, as routine administrative and instructional tasks become automated while distinctly human capabilities emotional intelligence, creative problem-solving, ethical reasoning, and digital fluency grow strategically indispensable (Nair et al., 2025). Socio-technical systems theory further explains the interdependence between AI infrastructures and social structures, emphasizing that successful integration depends on organizational readiness, digital leadership, and stakeholder inclusion. Furthermore, sustainability and Environmental, Social, and Governance (ESG) perspectives underscore that AI adoption must align with principles of equity, institutional resilience, and responsible innovation to ensure long-term societal and organizational value creation (Markova et al., 2026).

Yet, the institutionalization of AI also introduces significant governance and ethical challenges. Algorithmic bias, opaque decision-making processes, data privacy vulnerabilities, cybersecurity risks, and unequal digital access can erode institutional trust and reinforce structural inequities if oversight remains fragmented (Slimi and Carballido, 2023; Lam, 2026). The growing reliance on AI-driven evaluation, learning analytics, and management systems also raises critical questions regarding academic autonomy, faculty agency, and pedagogical integrity. In response, HEIs are progressively establishing AI ethics committees, compliance-by-design protocols, and algorithmic accountability frameworks to safeguard educational quality, ensure transparency, and align technological adoption with social legitimacy (Bhaskar et al., 2026; Wu et al., 2024).

Against this backdrop, this chapter argues that AI-driven change in higher education represents far more than operational modernization; it constitutes a structural reconfiguration of governance systems, educational models, and professional training architectures. Drawing on governance, socio-technical, and human capital theories, the chapter develops a comprehensive conceptual framework that examines how AI reshapes institutional leadership, teaching and learning ecosystems, talent development, and strategic decision-making. It advances a multi-capital governance perspective encompassing technical, human, governance, and sustainability capital to evaluate the long-term organizational and economic implications of AI adoption. Ultimately, the chapter contributes to the emerging discourse on responsible and sustainable AI institutionalization by emphasizing the need for governance systems that balance innovation with transparency, equity, academic integrity, and the integrated mission of higher education in both academic and professional training domains (Szostak, 2025).

2. BACKGROUND AND LITERATURE REVIEW

This section synthesizes current scholarship on artificial intelligence (AI) in higher education, organized around four interrelated themes: (1) the historical trajectory of digital transformation in higher education institutions; (2) AI applications across governance, academic education, and professional training systems; (3) theoretical foundations that explain how AI integration yields workforce-ready outcomes; and (4) critical challenges and ethical considerations. Collectively, these strands establish that professional training is not a peripheral function of AI adoption, but rather the direct result of strategically integrating institutional governance, pedagogical innovation, and labor market responsiveness.

2.1 Digital Transformation Trajectories in Higher Education

Today, investment in education must be strengthened by improving job opportunities in high-quality alternative jobs similar to those in the public and private sectors. The digital evolution of higher education has unfolded through multiple interconnected and overlapping phases shaped by technological innovation, globalization, changing labor market expectations, and institutional modernization pressures. Over the past three decades, higher education institutions have progressively transitioned from conventional administrative and teaching models toward digitally integrated ecosystems capable of supporting intelligent governance, adaptive education, and industry-oriented professional training systems. This transformation reflects not only technological advancement but also a structural redefinition of the university's role within the knowledge economy and workforce development landscape.

The earliest phase of digital transformation, commonly associated with the 1990s and early 2000s, focused primarily on administrative digitization. During this period, universities adopted student information systems (SIS), financial management platforms, human resource management systems, and basic learning management systems (LMS) such as Blackboard and Moodle (Hossain and Rafat, 2026). The principal objective of these technologies was operational efficiency through the automation of manual administrative processes, record management, and communication functions. Although these systems improved institutional coordination and reduced administrative burdens, their impact on professional training and workforce readiness remained relatively limited. Educational delivery continued to rely predominantly on traditional classroom-based pedagogies, while industry integration and competency-based training models were still underdeveloped.

The second phase of digital transformation emerged during the 2010s and was characterized by enhanced connectivity, scalability, and global accessibility. Universities increasingly adopted digital technologies not only to manage institutional processes but also to expand access to education beyond physical campuses. The rise of cloud ecosystems such as Google Workspace and Microsoft Teams enabled collaborative and flexible learning environments, while MOOCs democratized access to educational content on a global scale.

Despite these advancements, the second phase remained fragmented in many institutions because educational technologies often operated in isolated digital silos with limited interoperability. While students gained broader access to online knowledge and technical skills development opportunities, stronger integration between higher education and professional training systems was still relatively weak. Industry partnerships, digital credentialing mechanisms, and employability-oriented curricula remained underdeveloped, limiting the capacity of universities to fully align educational outcomes with evolving workforce needs.

The current phase of digital transformation, emerging strongly in the post-pandemic era, is defined by intelligent integration and AI-driven institutional ecosystems. Advances in machine learning, predictive analytics, natural language processing, generative AI, and intelligent automation have enabled universities to move beyond simple digitization toward fully integrated and data-driven institutional architectures (Wu et al., 2024). In this phase, AI technologies are increasingly embedded across governance systems, educational delivery, talent management processes, and professional training infrastructures.

This new transformation paradigm reflects a shift from digitization, which involves converting analog information into digital formats, to digitalization, where workflows and institutional operations are redesigned around digital technologies, and finally toward full digital transformation, where institutional missions, governance structures, and value creation models are fundamentally reconfigured through intelligent systems (Hossain and Rafat, 2026). AI now enables universities to function as adaptive and continuously evolving learning ecosystems capable of responding dynamically to labor market changes, technological disruption, and emerging competency requirements.

One of the most significant characteristics of this phase is the growing integration between academic education and professional training systems. AI-powered adaptive learning platforms, intelligent tutoring systems, simulation-based environments, digital twins, and competency-mapping tools are enabling universities to provide personalized, practice-oriented, and industry-aligned learning experiences.. As a result, professional training is no longer treated as a peripheral activity but rather as a central strategic function integrated into institutional governance and educational design.

Furthermore, AI-driven micro-credentialing systems, digital badges, and competency-based certification models are reshaping how universities validate learning outcomes and professional skills. These mechanisms support lifelong learning pathways and allow institutions to respond more flexibly to rapidly changing industry expectations. In leading AI-enabled higher education ecosystems, universities are increasingly collaborating with industry partners to co-design curricula, internship programs, and applied training initiatives that enhance graduate employability and workforce readiness.

The COVID-19 pandemic further accelerated this transformation by exposing the limitations of traditional educational infrastructures and highlighting the strategic importance of digital resilience. Universities worldwide rapidly adopted remote learning systems, AI-supported learning analytics, virtual laboratories, and intelligent student support services to maintain educational continuity. This period demonstrated that digital transformation is no longer optional but has become essential for institutional sustainability, competitiveness, and long-term resilience.

At the governance level, intelligent integration also enables universities to improve strategic planning, resource allocation, quality assurance, and performance monitoring. AI-supported governance systems facilitate real-time decision-making through continuous data analysis, enabling institutions to anticipate risks, optimize operations, and strengthen accountability mechanisms. Consequently, higher education governance is progressively evolving from static and bureaucratic management structures toward agile, predictive, and evidence-based governance ecosystems.

Overall, the trajectory of digital transformation in higher education illustrates the gradual emergence of AI-enabled universities that integrate governance, education, and professional training within unified digital ecosystems. This evolution reflects a broader institutional shift in which universities increasingly position themselves not only as providers of academic knowledge but also as strategic actors in workforce development, innovation ecosystems, and lifelong professional learning.

Table 1.

Phase and Time Period	Key Technologies and Applications	Adoption Metrics	Impact on Professional Training and Workforce Readiness	Representative Data Sources
Phase 1: Administrative Digitization (1990s–2000s)	• Student Information Systems (SIS) • Financial/HR management platforms • Basic LMS (e.g., Blackboard, Moodle) • Email & intranet portals	• LMS adoption: about 35% of HEIs globally by 2005 (EDUCAUSE, 2006) • SIS implementation: about 60% of research universities (Hossain and Rafat, 2026) • Digital record-keeping: about 45% administrative tasks automated	• Limited direct impact on professional training • Indirect benefits: improved enrollment tracking, basic skills documentation • Training remained largely classroom-based, industry-aligned curricula rare	(Hossain and Rafat 2026); UNESCO (2008)
Phase 2: Connectivity & Scalability (2010s)	• MOOCs and OER platforms • Cloud collaboration (Google Workspace, Microsoft Teams) • Mobile learning apps • Learning analytics dashboards	• MOOC enrollment: >110 million learners globally by 2019 (Class Central, 2020) - Learning analytics use: about 42% of institutions for retention interventions	• Expanded access to skills content, but limited credential recognition • Early industry partnerships for digital badges (~15% of programs) • Graduate employability metrics rarely integrated into platform design	World Bank (2021)
Phase 3: Intelligent Integration (AI-Driven) (2020s–Present)	• AI-powered adaptive learning & tutoring • Predictive analytics for retention & career pathways • Simulation/ digital twin training environments • AI-mediated labor market intelligence & micro-credentialing	• AI tool adoption: about 54% of HEIs globally (2024), projected 79% by 2027 (Wu et al., 2024) • Institutions using AI for curriculum alignment: about 38% (2024) • Micro-credential programs with AI verification: about 22% growth YoY (2023–2025)	• Direct linkage between academic performance and skills mapping • Competency-based credentials recognized by 65+ industry partners in leading ecosystems	Wu et al. (2024); Hossain and Rafat (2026); OECD (2025)

Table 1 illustrates the progressive evolution of digital transformation in higher education from basic administrative digitization toward fully integrated AI-driven

institutional ecosystems. The comparison between the three phases demonstrates that technological advancement in universities has evolved from operational efficiency objectives to broader strategic goals centered on intelligent governance, adaptive education, and professional workforce preparation. While early digitalization efforts primarily improved administrative coordination and information management, later phases increasingly emphasized accessibility, scalability, and learner connectivity through cloud technologies and online learning environments.

The current phase of intelligent integration represents a fundamental shift in institutional strategy, where AI technologies are no longer isolated support tools but core infrastructures shaping governance, teaching, learning, and professional training systems simultaneously. In this context, universities are increasingly adopting AI-enabled mechanisms to align academic curricula with labor market expectations, personalize learning pathways, strengthen competency-based education, and enhance graduate employability outcomes. This evolution reflects the growing recognition that higher education institutions must operate not only as knowledge providers but also as dynamic talent development ecosystems capable of supporting continuous professional training and lifelong learning.

Furthermore, the table highlights how AI-driven ecosystems contribute to stronger collaboration between universities and industry actors through micro-credentialing systems, simulation-based learning, digital internships, and workforce analytics. Such developments reinforce the strategic role of AI in bridging the gap between academic education and practical professional competencies (Pang et al. 2025). Consequently, digital transformation in higher education increasingly represents a comprehensive institutional reconfiguration in which governance systems, educational models, and professional training architectures become interconnected components of a unified intelligent ecosystem.

2.2 AI Applications and the Emergence of Integrated Professional Training

The growing convergence between artificial intelligence, institutional governance, and workforce development has significantly expanded the strategic role of higher education institutions (HEIs) within contemporary knowledge economies. While earlier digital transformation initiatives in universities primarily focused on administrative efficiency and online learning accessibility, recent AI-driven developments increasingly emphasize the integration of academic education with professional training and employability outcomes. In this context, AI is not only transforming teaching and governance processes but also reshaping how universities design competency-based curricula, anticipate labor market demands, and support lifelong learning pathways. Consequently, understanding AI adoption in higher education requires a multidimensional perspective that connects governance systems, pedagogical innovation, human capital development, and professional training within a unified institutional framework. The following review therefore examines the evolution of digital transformation in HEIs and explores how AI-enabled ecosystems are progressively redefining the relationship between higher education, workforce readiness, and sustainable institutional development.

2.2.1 AI in Institutional Governance: Enabling Training-Aligned Decision-Making

Artificial intelligence is fundamentally reshaping governance structures within higher education institutions (HEIs), transforming them from traditionally hierarchical and experience-driven administrative systems into adaptive, data-informed, and strategically responsive governance ecosystems. Historically, institutional governance in universities relied heavily on manual reporting procedures, retrospective performance assessments, fragmented communication channels, and leadership decisions grounded primarily in institutional precedent and human judgment. While such approaches supported administrative continuity, they often lacked the agility and predictive capacity required to respond effectively to rapidly changing labor market conditions, technological disruption, demographic shifts, and increasing accountability pressures. The emergence of AI-driven governance systems has significantly altered this paradigm by enabling universities to integrate real-time analytics, predictive intelligence, and automated decision-support mechanisms into institutional leadership and strategic planning processes (Wu et al., 2024).

One of the most significant contributions of AI to institutional governance lies in its capacity to support evidence-based strategic decision-making. Predictive analytics systems can process large volumes of institutional and external data to forecast enrollment trends, identify student attrition risks, optimize resource allocation, and anticipate future workforce skill demands. These systems enable university leaders to move beyond reactive administrative management toward proactive and anticipatory governance models capable of responding dynamically to environmental uncertainty. For example, AI-driven forecasting models allow institutions to anticipate emerging disciplinary needs and redesign academic programs in alignment with evolving industry requirements. As a result, governance decisions increasingly reflect real-time labor market intelligence rather than static historical assumptions.

AI also strengthens governance efficiency through intelligent automation and advanced data management capabilities. Natural language processing technologies increasingly automate policy analysis, accreditation documentation, compliance reporting, and institutional communication processes, reducing administrative burdens while improving operational consistency and transparency. Similarly, algorithmic dashboards and integrated business intelligence platforms provide institutional leaders with continuous visibility into key performance indicators related to student success, faculty productivity, employability outcomes, financial sustainability, and institutional rankings. These technologies facilitate more agile governance structures where strategic adjustments can be implemented rapidly based on continuously updated institutional data.

Importantly, the integration of AI into governance systems extends beyond administrative modernization and increasingly serves as the strategic foundation for aligning higher education with professional training and workforce development objectives. Through machine learning algorithms and labor market analytics, universities can identify emerging skill shortages, anticipate future occupational transformations, and evaluate the relevance of existing curricula against industry needs. Consequently, governance systems become active coordination mechanisms that continuously align academic programs, competency frameworks, and professional training initiatives with external economic and technological realities.

This governance transformation also influences talent management and institutional workforce planning within HEIs themselves. AI-supported systems increasingly inform faculty recruitment strategies, succession planning, workload optimization, and professional development initiatives. Universities can identify areas where specialized expertise is needed to support emerging AI-enabled disciplines and industry-oriented training programs. In this context, governance becomes directly connected to institutional capacity-building and the long-term sustainability of workforce-oriented educational ecosystems.

Furthermore, AI-enabled governance strengthens collaboration between universities and external stakeholders, particularly industry partners, professional organizations, and vocational training providers. Through data-sharing platforms, predictive workforce analytics, and partnership intelligence systems, universities are increasingly able to co-design curricula, internship pathways, simulation-based training programs, and micro-credentialing initiatives that respond directly to labor market expectations. These collaborative governance mechanisms support the emergence of integrated learning ecosystems where academic education and professional training are no longer separated but strategically interconnected components of institutional missions.

Another important dimension of AI-driven governance concerns quality assurance and institutional accountability. Governments, accreditation agencies, and international ranking systems increasingly require universities to demonstrate measurable outcomes related to employability, graduate competencies, sustainability performance, and institutional effectiveness. AI systems facilitate continuous monitoring and evaluation by generating real-time evidence regarding program quality, student engagement, learning outcomes, and career placement indicators. Such capabilities enhance institutional transparency while supporting data-driven policy adjustments and continuous organizational improvement.

However, the growing reliance on AI within governance systems also introduces important ethical and managerial challenges. Algorithmic decision-making may unintentionally reinforce institutional biases, particularly when predictive models rely on historically uneven data related to admissions, student performance, or employment outcomes. Similarly, excessive dependence on automated governance systems may reduce human oversight, weaken participatory decision-making processes, and create concerns regarding accountability, transparency, and institutional autonomy. Consequently, many HEIs are beginning to establish AI governance frameworks that incorporate ethical review mechanisms, algorithmic auditing procedures, stakeholder participation models, and compliance protocols designed to ensure responsible and equitable AI adoption (Bhaskar et al., 2026).

Overall, AI-driven institutional governance represents a foundational pillar in the transformation of higher education toward integrated education-and-training ecosystems. Rather than functioning solely as administrative support technologies, AI systems increasingly shape strategic leadership, institutional adaptability, workforce alignment, and professional training integration. Governance therefore evolves into a dynamic coordination mechanism through which HEIs continuously align academic programming, talent development, industry collaboration, and employability objectives within intelligent and sustainable institutional ecosystems.

Figure 1. AI-driven institutional governance for training-aligned decision-making in higher education

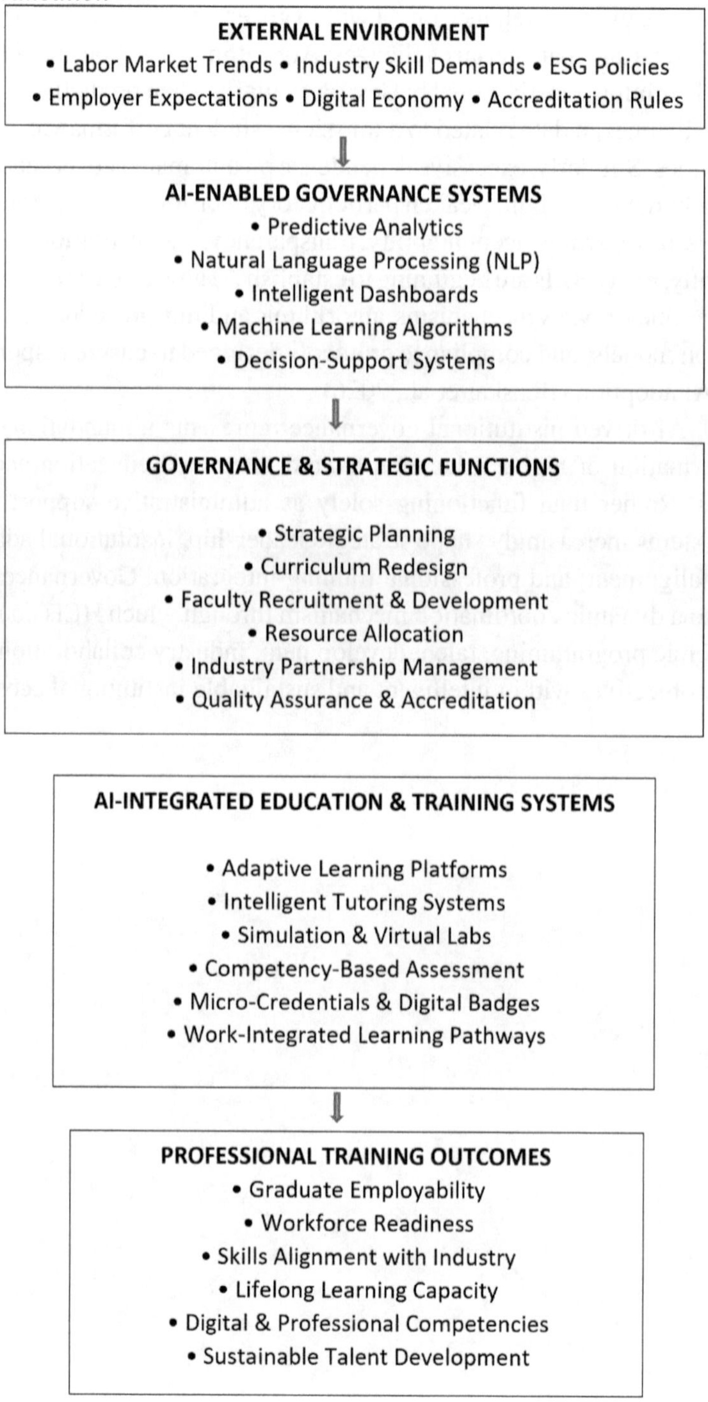

Figure 1 illustrates how AI-enabled governance systems function as the strategic coordination mechanism linking institutional leadership, academic education, and professional training within higher education ecosystems. The framework demonstrates that AI technologies such as predictive analytics, intelligent dashboards, and machine learning tools support evidence-based governance and enable universities to align curricula, resource allocation, and workforce development strategies with evolving labor market demands. Through this integration, higher education institutions increasingly evolve into adaptive and data-driven ecosystems that simultaneously enhance educational quality, graduate employability, and long-term institutional sustainability.

2.2.2 AI in Academic Education: Building Competency Foundations for Professional Practice

Artificial intelligence is significantly transforming academic education by enabling more personalized, adaptive, and competency-oriented learning environments across higher education institutions (HEIs). Traditionally, university teaching models relied heavily on standardized instructional approaches, fixed curricula, and generalized assessment systems that often struggled to accommodate diverse learner needs, learning styles, and career aspirations. Although such models facilitated mass education, they frequently limited individualized support, practical skill development, and responsiveness to rapidly evolving labor market expectations. The integration of AI into teaching and learning environments is reshaping this paradigm by enabling institutions to deliver more flexible, data-driven, and learner-centered educational experiences capable of preparing students for increasingly complex professional environments.

One of the most influential applications of AI in academic education is the emergence of adaptive learning systems. These platforms utilize machine learning algorithms and learning analytics to continuously monitor student performance, engagement patterns, and competency progression in real time. Based on these insights, AI systems dynamically adjust instructional content, difficulty levels, pacing, and learning pathways according to individual learner profiles and educational needs. Students who demonstrate mastery of specific concepts can progress more rapidly, while those experiencing difficulties receive additional explanations, remedial activities, and personalized support. This adaptive capability enhances learner engagement, improves knowledge retention, and promotes more equitable educational outcomes by reducing the limitations associated with one-size-fits-all instructional models (Chan & Colloton, 2024).

Intelligent tutoring systems further strengthen AI-supported education by providing individualized academic assistance traditionally associated with human mentoring. Through natural language processing and conversational AI technologies, these systems can deliver immediate feedback, explain complex concepts, answer student questions, and guide learners through problem-solving processes. Unlike conventional static e-learning platforms, AI tutors respond interactively to learner behavior and cognitive performance, thereby supporting continuous and self-directed learning. In disciplines requiring procedural understanding and analytical reasoning such as engineering, medicine, computer science, and business analytics intelligent tutoring systems increasingly serve as scalable mechanisms for reinforcing applied competencies and professional problem-solving skills.

Generative AI technologies are also expanding the pedagogical capabilities of higher education. AI-assisted curriculum design tools help educators develop competency-based learning materials, interdisciplinary teaching modules, case studies, and simulation exercises aligned with industry expectations and emerging professional standards. In addition, generative AI can support automated assessment design, personalized feedback generation, and research mentorship by assisting students with literature exploration, conceptual organization, academic writing support, and data interpretation. These technologies enable educators to devote greater attention to higher-order pedagogical functions such as critical discussion, mentorship, creativity development, and experiential learning facilitation.

Beyond improving instructional efficiency, the strategic importance of AI in academic education lies in its role in building foundational competencies required for professional practice and workforce readiness. AI-supported learning environments increasingly emphasize competency-based education models in which academic progression is linked to demonstrable skills acquisition rather than solely time-based course completion. Through continuous competency tracking systems, universities can monitor learner development across technical, analytical, interpersonal, and digital competencies that are directly relevant to professional environments.

AI-mediated formative assessment systems play a critical role in this transformation. Unlike traditional summative assessments that primarily measure end-point academic achievement, AI-driven assessment systems provide continuous diagnostic feedback throughout the learning process. By analyzing student interactions, response patterns, and performance trajectories, AI systems identify knowledge gaps, misconceptions, and competency deficiencies in real time. This enables both learners and educators to implement targeted interventions that strengthen professional readiness and applied skill development. Consequently, assessment becomes an ongoing developmental mechanism rather than merely an evaluative process.

Interdisciplinary project simulations and immersive learning environments further illustrate how AI bridges academic education and professional training. AI-powered virtual laboratories, scenario-based simulations, augmented reality environments, and digital twins allow students to engage with realistic professional challenges within controlled and scalable educational settings. For example, medical students can practice diagnostic procedures through AI-supported virtual patients, engineering students can simulate industrial systems management, and business students can participate in AI-driven market strategy simulations. These experiential learning environments strengthen decision-making, collaboration, communication, and problem-solving capabilities that are essential for contemporary professional practice.

Moreover, AI facilitates stronger alignment between academic curricula and labor market expectations through real-time workforce intelligence. By analyzing employer demands, industry reports, job market trends, and emerging occupational competencies, AI systems assist universities in continuously updating course content, learning outcomes, and professional certification pathways. This dynamic curriculum alignment helps reduce the gap between academic knowledge and workplace requirements while ensuring that graduates possess competencies relevant to rapidly evolving industries (Nair et al., 2025).

AI also contributes to improving educational accessibility and inclusion. Intelligent accessibility tools including speech recognition systems, automated transcription services, multilingual translation technologies, and personalized support applications help accommodate students with diverse linguistic, cognitive, and physical needs. These technologies expand participation opportunities and support more inclusive educational ecosystems capable of serving increasingly diverse learner populations. In addition, AI-enabled remote learning systems enhance flexibility for working professionals, lifelong learners, and geographically dispersed students seeking continuous professional development.

However, the integration of AI into academic education also raises important pedagogical and ethical concerns. Excessive dependence on automated systems may risk reducing human interaction, weakening critical thinking development, and encouraging passive learning behaviors if not carefully designed. Generative AI tools additionally create challenges related to academic integrity, originality, authorship, and assessment validity. Concerns also persist regarding algorithmic bias, unequal access to advanced learning technologies, and the potential commercialization of educational data. As a result, HEIs are increasingly adopting responsible AI governance frameworks that emphasize transparency, ethical oversight, faculty training, and balanced human AI collaboration within educational environments.

"These concerns are consistent with broader scholarship on AI ethics, which argues that transparency, accountability, fairness, and human oversight are essential principles for responsible AI deployment (Bostrom & Yudkowsky, 2014)."

Overall, AI-driven academic education represents a foundational mechanism through which higher education institutions build the competencies, adaptability, and professional readiness required in contemporary labor markets. Rather than functioning solely as instructional support technologies, AI systems increasingly shape the cognitive, analytical, technical, and interpersonal capacities that underpin professional practice. Academic education therefore evolves into an intelligent and continuously adaptive competency-development ecosystem where theoretical learning, applied skills acquisition, and workforce preparation become deeply interconnected dimensions of higher education transformation.

2.2.3 Professional Training as the Direct Outcome of AI Integration

One of the most transformative consequences of AI integration within higher education institutions (HEIs) is the emergence of intelligent, adaptive, and industry-responsive professional training ecosystems. Traditionally, professional training in universities was frequently treated as a secondary or peripheral function, often separated from core academic structures and implemented through internships, vocational modules, or isolated career-development initiatives. Such approaches typically relied on static curricula, periodic industry consultation, and generalized employability models that struggled to keep pace with rapidly evolving labor market conditions. The integration of AI across governance systems, educational delivery, and institutional decision-making has fundamentally altered this paradigm by positioning professional training as a central strategic outcome of digitally integrated higher education ecosystems.

AI enables universities to bridge the long-standing gap between academic instruction and workforce preparation through the continuous synchronization of educational systems with labor market intelligence, competency development frameworks, and professional performance requirements. In this context, professional training is no longer viewed merely as supplementary experiential learning but rather as an integrated and continuously evolving institutional process embedded within the entire educational lifecycle.

A central mechanism supporting this transformation is the use of real-time labor market intelligence systems. AI algorithms increasingly analyze large-scale datasets derived from online job postings, employer recruitment platforms, professional certification databases, industry reports, economic forecasts, and workforce analytics systems to identify emerging occupational trends and evolving competency demands (Hossain & Rafat, 2026). Through machine learning and predictive analytics, universities can detect future skill shortages, anticipate sectoral transformation, and identify competencies associated with high-growth industries such as artificial intelligence, cybersecurity, renewable energy, healthcare technologies, logistics automation, and digital finance.

This capability allows HEIs to dynamically redesign curricula, update training modules, embed industry-recognized certifications, and develop stackable micro-credential programs aligned with real-time labor market expectations. Unlike traditional curriculum revision processes that often require years to implement institutional changes, AI-supported workforce intelligence systems enable universities to respond more rapidly and strategically to technological disruption and changing employment conditions. Consequently, professional training becomes increasingly proactive, anticipatory, and adaptable rather than reactive and static.

Another major contribution of AI integration is the expansion of simulation-based and immersive professional training environments. These technologies are particularly valuable in disciplines where practical experience, procedural precision, and risk management are essential. For example, medical students can engage in AI-supported virtual diagnostic simulations, engineering students can interact with digital replicas of industrial systems, aviation trainees can practice flight procedures through intelligent simulators, and business students can participate in AI-driven strategic decision-making exercises.

Such immersive environments significantly strengthen experiential learning by enabling repeated practice, adaptive feedback, and competency refinement without the operational risks or resource constraints associated with real-world professional settings. Moreover, AI systems can personalize simulation complexity according to learner progression, thereby supporting differentiated skill development pathways. This transformation enhances not only technical proficiency but also higher-order competencies such as decision-making, teamwork, communication, adaptability, and crisis management that are increasingly demanded in modern professional environments.

AI also revolutionizes professional training through competency-based assessment and intelligent credentialing systems. Traditional assessment models in higher education have often prioritized theoretical knowledge acquisition over demonstrable professional competencies. In contrast, AI-supported assessment systems continuously evaluate learner performance across multiple dimensions, including technical execution, analytical reasoning, collaboration, creativity, communication, and problem-solving capabilities (Wu et al., 2024). Through learning analytics and machine learning algorithms, these systems generate comprehensive competency profiles that provide a more nuanced understanding of professional readiness.

This capability has accelerated the growth of digital badges, micro-credentials, competency portfolios, and AI-verified certifications that signal applied skills and workforce preparedness to employers. Unlike conventional degree structures that may not fully capture granular competencies, AI-enabled credentialing systems provide transparent and verifiable evidence of practical skill acquisition. Consequently, employers increasingly value competency-based credentials that demonstrate measurable readiness for professional tasks and industry-specific challenges.

Personalized learning-to-employment pathways further illustrate how AI integration transforms professional training into a continuous developmental process extending beyond graduation. AI-driven recommender systems analyze learner profiles, academic performance, career interests, behavioral patterns, and labor market opportunities to match students with internships, apprenticeships, mentorship programs, professional certifications, and continuing education opportunities (Chan & Colloton, 2024). These systems facilitate individualized professional development trajectories that evolve according to both learner aspirations and market dynamics.

As a result, HEIs increasingly function as lifelong professional development ecosystems rather than institutions limited to degree delivery. Graduates continue interacting with university-based AI systems through upskilling programs, reskilling initiatives, executive education modules, and continuous learning platforms designed to support long-term employability and career adaptability. This reflects a broader transformation in which universities shift from knowledge providers toward strategic partners in workforce development and lifelong learning.

Importantly, AI-driven professional training also strengthens collaboration between universities and industry stakeholders. Through integrated digital platforms and workforce analytics systems, employers increasingly participate in curriculum co-design, competency framework development, simulation design, and assessment validation processes. Such partnerships ensure stronger alignment between academic preparation and real-world professional requirements while improving graduate employability outcomes. In advanced AI-enabled ecosystems, industry actors can directly contribute to identifying emerging competencies, evaluating training relevance, and supporting applied learning opportunities through digital collaboration infrastructures.

However, the expansion of AI-enabled professional training also introduces important challenges and risks. Excessive dependence on labor market analytics may encourage over-specialization and narrow vocational alignment at the expense of broader intellectual development, creativity, and critical inquiry. Similarly, unequal access to advanced AI infrastructures may reinforce disparities between well-resourced and underfunded institutions, potentially creating new forms of educational inequality. Ethical concerns also arise regarding learner data privacy, algorithmic bias in career recommendation systems, and the commercialization of competency tracking platforms.

Consequently, responsible governance frameworks are increasingly necessary to ensure that AI-enabled professional training remains equitable, transparent, and educationally balanced. Many HEIs are therefore implementing AI ethics policies, participatory governance models, quality assurance mechanisms, and data protection frameworks designed to safeguard learner rights while supporting innovation and institutional adaptability.

Overall, AI integration transforms professional training from a static, course-based supplement into a continuous, intelligent, and data-driven ecosystem directly embedded within higher education governance and academic structures. Rather than preparing students solely for existing occupations, AI-enabled HEIs increasingly cultivate adaptive, interdisciplinary, and future-oriented competencies capable of supporting long-term employability within rapidly evolving knowledge economies. Professional readiness thus emerges as one of the most visible and measurable outcomes of institutional digital maturity and intelligent educational transformation.

2.3 Theoretical Foundations: Linking AI Integration to Professional Training Outcomes

Understanding why AI yields enhanced professional training requires grounding in complementary theoretical lenses:

- Governance Theory elucidates how institutional policies, accountability structures, and data-driven leadership align academic programming with labor market realities.
- "Socio-technical systems theory, originally developed by Eric Trist and Fred Emery, emphasizes that organizational performance depends on the joint optimization of technological and social systems (Trist & Emery, 1960). In higher education, AI integration therefore requires alignment between digital infrastructures, institutional culture, leadership practices, and stakeholder participation."
- Human Capital Theory, originating in the work of Theodore Schultz and Gary Becker, views education and training as investments that enhance individual productivity and economic value (Becker, 1964). Within AI-enabled higher education, this perspective helps explain why institutions increasingly emphasize competencies such as critical thinking, digital fluency, and adaptive problem-solving."

Together, these perspectives support a *multi-capital governance framework* that evaluates AI integration through four interrelated dimensions: technical capital (AI infrastructure, data analytics), human capital (learner competencies, faculty expertise), governance capital (policy alignment, industry partnerships), and sustainability capital (equitable access, lifelong learning pathways) (Markova et al., 2026). Within this model, professional training is not an isolated output, but the strategic convergence point where all four capitals interact to produce measurable workforce readiness.

2.4 Challenges and Critical Considerations in AI-Enabled Professional Training

Despite its transformative potential, AI-driven professional training introduces significant ethical, operational, and equity-related challenges:

- Algorithmic Bias in Skills Matching: Recommendation systems may reinforce occupational segregation or overlook non-traditional career pathways if training on historically biased employment data (Slimi and Carballido, 2023; Lam, 2026).
- Credential Fragmentation and Validation: The proliferation of AI-issued micro-credentials risks confusing employers unless standardized quality assurance and interoperable verification frameworks are established (Wu et al., 2024).
- Industry Dependency and Academic Autonomy: Over-alignment with immediate labor market demands may compromise broader educational goals, critical inquiry, and long-term adaptability (Chan & Colloton, 2024).
- Equity in Access to Advanced Training: High-fidelity simulations, AI tutors, and industry-partnered practicums require significant infrastructure, potentially widening skill gaps between well-resourced and underfunded institutions (Nair et al., 2025).
- Data Privacy in Competency Tracking: Continuous performance monitoring across academic and professional settings raises concerns about learner consent, data ownership, and long-term digital footprints (Bhaskar et al., 2026).

In response, leading HEIs are developing layered oversight mechanisms: AI ethics review boards, algorithmic impact assessments for training algorithms, transparent credentialing standards, and participatory design processes that include students, faculty, and industry stakeholders (Bhaskar et al., 2026; Wu et al., 2024). These efforts underscore that responsible professional training integration requires proactive governance not reactive compliance.

2.5 Synthesis: Professional Training as the Strategic Outcome of AI Integration

The literature reviewed above demonstrates that AI in higher education is no longer confined to administrative automation or pedagogical experimentation. When strategically integrated across governance structures, academic systems, and industry partnerships, AI produces professional training as a direct, measurable institutional outcome. Rather than treating workforce preparation as a post-graduation concern,

AI-enabled HEIs embed skills development, competency assessment, and career pathway alignment into the core academic lifecycle.

This chapter builds on that insight by advancing a multi-capital governance framework that positions professional training not as a peripheral function, but as the strategic culmination of AI-driven institutional integration. The framework examines how technical, human, governance, and sustainability capitals interact to produce equitable, industry-aligned, and ethically grounded training ecosystems. The following sections detail this framework, outline implementation pathways, and propose policy recommendations for HEIs seeking to transform AI adoption into sustained graduate employability and lifelong professional development.

3. CONCEPTUAL FRAMEWORK: MULTI-CAPITAL AI GOVERNANCE MODEL IN HIGHER EDUCATION

Building on the preceding analysis, this section develops a multi-capital governance framework to explain how artificial intelligence (AI) integration transforms higher education institutions (HEIs) into interconnected ecosystems where governance, academic education, and professional training converge. Grounded in socio-technical systems theory, human capital economics, and institutional governance perspectives, the framework positions professional training not as an isolated institutional function, but as the emergent outcome of dynamic interactions among four mutually reinforcing forms of capital: technical capital, human capital, governance capital, and sustainability capital. Rather than treating AI adoption as a discrete technology initiative, this model frames it as a leadership-driven innovation process that requires systemic alignment, ethical oversight, and continuous capacity building. The framework is designed to be operationalized by institutional leaders, policymakers, and educational researchers seeking to translate AI potential into measurable, equitable, and sustainable professional training outcomes.

3.1 Technical Capital: AI Infrastructure and Intelligent Systems

Technical capital encompasses the computational, data, and algorithmic infrastructure that enables AI integration across institutional processes. This includes machine learning architectures, learning analytics platforms, natural language processing (NLP) engines, generative AI applications, predictive modeling systems, and interoperable data pipelines embedded within administrative, academic, and training environments. Crucially, technical capital extends beyond hardware and software procurement to include data governance standards, system interoperability, algorithmic transparency, and the capacity for continuous model refinement (Hossain & Rafat, 2026; Wu et al., 2024).

In the context of professional training, technical capital enables:

- Real-time labor market analytics and skills forecasting: AI scrapes and analyzes job postings, industry certification trends, and economic indicators to identify emerging competencies, enabling dynamic curriculum updates and targeted training modules.
- Adaptive learning and competency-based progression: Intelligent tutoring systems and algorithmic pacing adjust content delivery, assessment difficulty, and feedback frequency based on individual learner performance, ensuring mastery before advancement.
- Simulation-based and immersive training environments: Digital twins, virtual labs, and AI-driven scenario generators allow learners to practice complex professional tasks from clinical decision-making to engineering troubleshooting in risk-free, scalable settings.
- Automated credentialing and digital verification: Blockchain-integrated AI systems issue, track, and validate micro-credentials, providing employers with verifiable, tamper-resistant evidence of applied skills and continuous professional development (Chan & Colloton, 2024).

The maturity of technical capital determines an institution's capacity to transition from fragmented digital tools to fully integrated intelligent ecosystems. However, technical capital alone is insufficient; without strategic governance, human capacity, and ethical safeguards, advanced infrastructure risks becoming underutilized, misaligned with pedagogical goals, or prone to algorithmic drift (Slimi and Carballido, 2023).

3.2 Human Capital: Learner and Faculty Capability Development

Human capital represents the evolving competencies, cognitive capacities, and professional dispositions of students, faculty, and administrative staff within AI-enabled environments. As AI automates routine cognitive, analytical, and administrative tasks, human capital becomes increasingly concentrated in advanced, distinctly human capabilities that machines cannot easily replicate or ethically substitute (Nair et al., 2025).

Key dimensions of human capital in AI-integrated HEIs include:

- Critical thinking and complex problem-solving: The ability to interpret AI-generated insights, question algorithmic assumptions, contextualize data within disciplinary frameworks, and make judgment-based decisions.
- Digital literacy and AI fluency: Competence in interacting with, evaluating, and co-designing AI tools rather than passively consuming them; understanding prompt engineering, model limitations, and data provenance.
- Ethical reasoning and responsible AI use: Navigating bias, transparency, data privacy, intellectual property, and the societal implications of automated decision-making in academic and professional contexts.
- Interdisciplinary and adaptive learning skills: Capacity to synthesize knowledge across domains, continuously upskill, and pivot in response to shifting labor market demands and technological disruptions.

Within professional training systems, human capital is continuously shaped through AI-supported feedback loops, competency tracking, and personalized learning pathways that align individual development with industry needs. Faculty transition from content deliverers to learning architects, designing AI-augmented pedagogies that emphasize mentorship, ethical deliberation, and applied practice. Learners engage in continuous skill formation, where academic knowledge is rapidly translated into professional readiness through iterative, data-informed training cycles. Importantly, human capital development requires intentional investment in faculty professional learning, student AI literacy programs, and cross-functional collaboration between academic units and career services (Hossain and Rafat, 2026)

3.3 Governance Capital: Institutional Leadership and Decision Intelligence

Governance capital refers to the institutional capacity to strategically manage AI integration through data-driven leadership, policy frameworks, stakeholder co-design, and accountability mechanisms.

AI enhances governance capital by enabling:

- Predictive institutional planning and scenario modeling: Forecasting enrollment trends, resource allocation needs, program viability, and financial sustainability under varying economic and demographic conditions.
- Evidence-based curriculum and workforce alignment: Using labor market intelligence and graduate outcome data to guide program development, faculty hiring priorities, and industry partnership strategies.

- Automated compliance and quality assurance: Streamlining accreditation reporting, audit trails, learning outcome assessments, and regulatory documentation through NLP and automated workflow systems.
- Transparent performance monitoring and reporting structures: Real-time dashboards that track graduate employability, skill acquisition, training effectiveness, and equity metrics across departments and learner demographics.

In professional training ecosystems, governance capital ensures that learning outcomes are continuously aligned with evolving industry standards, ensuring institutional responsiveness and strategic coherence. Crucially, effective governance capital requires distributed leadership models that empower both positional leaders (provosts, deans, vice presidents) and non-positional innovators (faculty developers, instructional designers, student advocates, industry liaisons) to co-create AI policies, ethical guidelines, and training pathways (Wu et al., 2024; Bhaskar et al., 2026). Governance capital also mediates external political and funding pressures, translating policy mandates into internally coherent innovation strategies that protect academic autonomy while advancing workforce readiness.

3.4 Sustainability Capital: Equity, Ethics, and Long-Term Institutional Resilience

Sustainability capital captures the ethical, social, and long-term developmental dimensions of AI integration. It ensures that technological advancement does not compromise equity, inclusion, academic integrity, or institutional legitimacy. In an era of rapid automation, skills polarization, and digital fragmentation, sustainability capital acts as the moral and strategic anchor that guides responsible, future-ready innovation (Markova et al., 2026)

Core elements include:

- Ethical AI governance and algorithmic accountability: Establishing institutional review boards, algorithmic impact assessments, transparency protocols, and human-in-the-loop escalation pathways to prevent bias and ensure explainability.
- Data privacy protection and responsible analytics use: Safeguarding student and employee data through informed consent frameworks, data minimization, anonymization, secure storage, and clear data ownership policies.
- Equal access to AI-enabled learning infrastructures: Ensuring that simulation tools, AI tutors, broadband connectivity, and credentialing platforms are accessible across socioeconomic, geographic, disability, and first-generation learner divides.

- Alignment with ESG (Environmental, Social, Governance) principles: Embedding sustainability metrics into institutional strategy, including carbon footprint reduction from digital infrastructure, community workforce impact, lifelong learning pathways, and long-term economic resilience.

In the context of professional training, sustainability capital safeguards against over-automation, skills polarization, and unequal access to advanced training systems. It ensures that AI-mediated skill development promotes inclusive workforce participation, ethical professional practice, and lifelong learning pathways that adapt to economic and social shifts. Without sustainability capital, AI integration risks exacerbating digital divides, producing narrow vocational outcomes, or eroding public trust in higher education's societal mission (Lam, 2026; Slimi and Carballido, 2023).

3.5 Interaction Mechanisms and System Dynamics

The four forms of capital do not operate in isolation; rather, they interact dynamically through reinforcing feedback loops, co-evolutionary processes, and emergent system behaviors. Conceptualized through a socio-ecological and systems-thinking lens, the multi-capital framework operates as a continuous cycle of enablement, direction, application, and regulation:

- Technical capital enables data-driven governance: AI infrastructure generates the analytics, predictive insights, and real-time feedback that inform strategic decision-making, policy formulation, and resource allocation.
- Governance capital directs human capital development: Leadership frameworks, institutional priorities, and ethical guidelines shape faculty development, curriculum design, learner competency targets, and professional training pathways.
- Human capital generates applied competencies for professional training: Educators, learners, and industry partners translate institutional strategy and technological tools into actionable skills, pedagogical innovations, and workforce-ready capabilities.
- Sustainability capital regulates and legitimizes the entire system: Ethical oversight, equity safeguards, data privacy standards, and long-term resilience metrics ensure that innovation remains socially responsible, academically sound, and institutionally viable.

Figure 2. Multi-capital AI governance model: System interactions and convergence on professional training outcomes

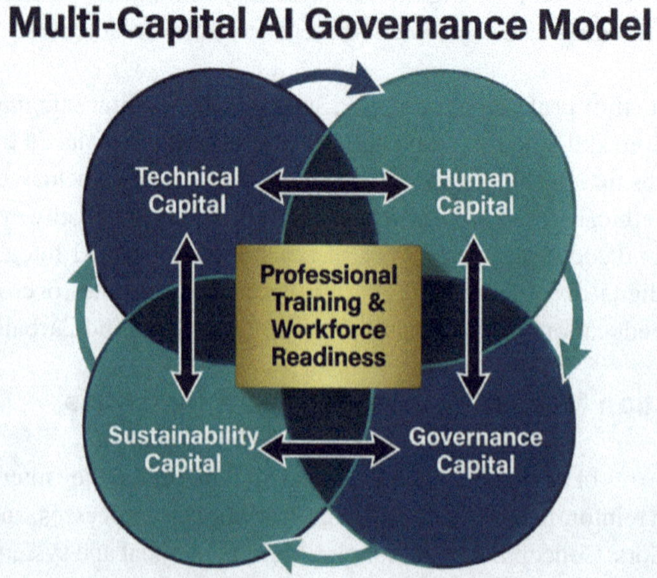

These interactions produce a self-reinforcing ecosystem in which professional training emerges as a continuous, adaptive, and AI-mediated institutional output rather than a discrete educational stage. Disruptions in one capital (e.g., inadequate digital literacy, biased algorithms, opaque governance, or unequal access) can cascade across the system, degrading training quality and institutional trust. Conversely, strategic investments in any capital can generate multiplicative benefits across the others, accelerating innovation diffusion and workforce alignment (Hossain and Rafat, 2026; Wu et al., 2024).

3.6 Positioning Professional Training within the Framework

Within this model, professional training is conceptualized as the strategic convergence point of all four capitals. It is the institutional space where:

- Technical systems translate labor market data, learner analytics, and competency frameworks into actionable, personalized learning pathways.
- Governance structures align academic programming, resource allocation, faculty incentives, and industry partnerships with real-time workforce intelligence and policy mandates.

- Human capital is continuously developed through competency-based learning, faculty mentorship, iterative skill application, and reflective professional practice.
- Sustainability principles ensure ethical oversight, equitable access, inclusive credentialing, and long-term career resilience for diverse learner populations.

This positioning reframes professional training as the final integrative outcome of AI-driven higher education transformation, rather than an auxiliary function or post-graduation add-on. It demonstrates that workforce readiness is not achieved through isolated vocational modules or reactive career services, but through a systemic, leadership-driven architecture that embeds skills development, ethical reasoning, and industry alignment into the core academic lifecycle. By operationalizing the multi-capital governance model, HEIs can transform AI adoption from a tactical IT initiative into a strategic, equity-centered innovation engine that produces measurable, sustainable, and socially responsible professional training outcomes.

The following section applies this framework to a real-world institutional case, demonstrating how leadership practices, policy interpretation, and stakeholder agency operationalize these capitals to achieve integrated educational and training transformation.

4. CONCLUSION: TOWARD INTEGRATED, ETHICAL, AND FUTURE-READY HIGHER EDUCATION

This chapter has argued that artificial intelligence (AI) in higher education represents far more than a technological upgrade or operational efficiency tool. Rather, AI functions as a structural catalyst that enables the profound integration of institutional governance, academic education, and professional training systems into coherent, adaptive, and purpose-driven ecosystems. Through the development and application of a multi-capital governance framework encompassing technical capital, human capital, governance capital, and sustainability capital this analysis demonstrates that professional training and workforce readiness are not peripheral outcomes of AI adoption but the emergent, strategic convergence point of dynamically interacting institutional capacities.

The central contribution of this work lies in reframing AI integration as a leadership-driven innovation process that requires systemic alignment, ethical oversight, and continuous capacity building across four interdependent domains. Technical capital provides the intelligent infrastructure adaptive learning platforms, predictive analytics, simulation environments, and automated credentialing systems that enables data-informed decision-making and personalized learning pathways.

Human capital ensures that faculty, students, and staff develop the critical digital literacy, ethical reasoning, and adaptive competencies necessary to leverage AI tools meaningfully rather than passively consume them. Governance capital establishes the policy frameworks, accountability mechanisms, and stakeholder co-design processes that translate technological potential into institutional practice while safeguarding academic integrity and strategic coherence. Sustainability capital anchors the entire system in principles of equity, inclusion, data privacy, and long-term resilience, ensuring that innovation advances social legitimacy alongside operational effectiveness.

When these four capitals interact synergistically, professional training emerges not as a discrete vocational add-on but as a continuous, intelligent, and ethically grounded institutional output. AI-enabled higher education institutions increasingly function as learning-to-employment ecosystems where theoretical knowledge, applied skill development, and career pathway alignment are seamlessly integrated throughout the academic lifecycle. This transformation reflects a fundamental redefinition of the university's mission: from knowledge transmission toward talent development; from degree conferral toward competency validation; from institutional silos toward collaborative, industry-responsive networks.

Theoretical, Practical, and Policy Implications

Theoretically, this chapter advances three intersecting scholarly conversations. First, it extends innovation leadership theory by distinguishing creativity (idea generation) from innovation (systemic implementation) and clarifying how educational leaders translate AI-enabled experiments into scalable institutional practices. Second, it operationalizes socio-technical systems theory for higher education contexts, demonstrating that AI integration succeeds through deliberate alignment of algorithms, workflows, cultural norms, and regulatory structures not through technological superiority alone. Third, it enriches human capital and equity scholarship by centering sustainability capital, challenging narrow employability metrics and arguing that equitable AI integration requires continuous attention to who benefits, who is excluded, and how institutional legitimacy is maintained amid rapid technological change.

Practically, the multi-capital framework offers actionable guidance for institutional leaders navigating AI integration. Leaders are encouraged to: (1) diagnose institutional readiness across all four capitals before deploying new technologies; (2) sequence interventions strategically, recognizing that capitals develop interdependently; (3) cultivate cross-capital synergies by designing initiatives that simultaneously strengthen multiple domains; (4) monitor feedback dynamics to balance innovation acceleration with equity safeguards; and (5) center equity by design, embedding accessibility, inclusion, and algorithmic fairness into procurement and implementation processes from the outset.

At the policy level, the framework underscores several imperatives. Accreditation bodies and government funders should develop flexible AI governance guidelines that encourage innovation while safeguarding quality and transparency. Public institutions serving diverse, under-resourced populations require sustained investment in both technical infrastructure and human capacity development. Policy processes should mandate inclusive participation from faculty, students, industry partners, and community representatives in AI planning and oversight. Finally, evaluation frameworks should track not only short-term employment outcomes but also learner wellbeing, ethical reasoning, civic engagement, and career resilience over time.

Limitations and Future Directions

While the multi-capital framework offers a robust conceptual foundation, several limitations warrant acknowledgment. First, the model is derived primarily from scholarship and practice in well-resourced, English-speaking higher education contexts; its applicability to Global South institutions, community colleges, or non-Western epistemological traditions requires further empirical testing. Second, the rapid evolution of AI technologies particularly generative AI and autonomous agents means that technical capital specifications will require continuous updating. Third, the framework assumes a baseline of institutional stability; its utility in crisis contexts (e.g., financial exigency, political interference, pandemics) remains untested.

Future research should pursue three priorities: (1) comparative institutional studies examining how different governance traditions, resource environments, and cultural values shape AI integration trajectories; (2) longitudinal impact assessments tracking how AI-mediated professional training affects graduate career mobility, earnings trajectories, and civic participation disaggregated by demographic characteristics to assess equity impacts; and (3) participatory design research centering marginalized voices in co-designing AI tools and governance protocols, ensuring that innovation reflects diverse needs and epistemologies.

Final Reflection: Leadership for an AI-Enabled Future

The integration of artificial intelligence into higher education represents not a technological endpoint but an ongoing leadership challenge (Daner Sun et al. 2026). As institutions navigate the tensions between innovation and integrity, efficiency and equity, automation and human agency, the multi-capital governance framework offers a compass rather than a blueprint. It reminds leaders that sustainable transformation requires more than purchasing powerful tools or issuing bold strategic plans;

it demands cultivating the technical infrastructure, human capabilities, governance structures, and ethical commitments that enable AI to serve the enduring mission of higher education: advancing knowledge, developing talent, and contributing to the public good.

Professional training, reconceptualized through this lens, becomes not a vocational add-on but a holistic outcome of integrated institutional ecosystems where learners develop not only job-ready skills but also critical digital literacy, ethical reasoning, and adaptive capacity for lifelong learning. In an era of accelerating change, this is the ultimate promise of AI-enabled higher education: not to replace human judgment with algorithmic certainty, but to augment human potential through thoughtful, equitable, and purpose-driven innovation.

Questions for Reflection

How does your institution currently define and measure "innovation" in AI adoption? In what ways could the multi-capital framework help diagnose gaps between technological investment and meaningful professional training outcomes?

When balancing efficiency gains with equity commitments, what governance mechanisms could ensure that AI integration advances inclusion rather than exacerbating existing disparities?

Which stakeholder groups are currently underrepresented in your institution's AI planning processes, and what structural changes would enable their meaningful participation in co-designing professional training pathways?

How might educational leaders cultivate the courage to pause or redirect AI initiatives when evidence suggests unintended harms without succumbing to risk aversion that stifles beneficial innovation?

FUNDING

This work was supported by the Deanship of Scientific Research, Vice Presidency for Graduate Studies and Scientific Research, King Faisal University, Saudi Arabia [Grant No. KFU264030].

REFERENCES

Becker, G. S. (1964). *Human Capital: A Theoretical and Empirical Analysis, with Special Reference to Education*. University of Chicago Press.

Bhaskar, P., Khan, M., & Bhaskar, P. (2026). Establishing an AI Ethics Governance Committee in Higher Education: A Theoretical Framework. In Kalafat Çat, A., Yetgin, M., & Sarker, J. (Eds.), *Navigating Modern Digital Communication Ethics and Law* (pp. 105–124). IGI Global Scientific Publishing., DOI: 10.4018/979-8-3373-1702-1.ch004

Bostrom, N., & Yudkowsky, E. (2014). The Ethics of Artificial Intelligence. In Frankish, K., & Ramsey, W. M. (Eds.), *The Cambridge Handbook of Artificial Intelligence* (pp. 316–334). Cambridge University Press., DOI: 10.1017/CBO9781139046855.020

Chan, C. K. Y., & Colloton, T. (2024). *Generative AI in Higher Education: The ChatGPT Effect* (1st ed.). Routledge., DOI: 10.4324/9781003459026

Emery, F. E., & Trist, E. L. (1960). Socio-Technical Systems. In Churchman, C. W., & Verhulst, M. (Eds.), *Management Sciences: Models and Techniques* (Vol. 2, pp. 83–97).

Holmes, W., Bialik, M., & Fadel, C. (2019). *Artificial Intelligence in Education: Promises and Implications for Teaching and Learning*. Center for Curriculum Redesign.

Hossain, M. Z., & Rafat, S. O. G. (2026). Artificial Intelligence-Driven Talent Management in Higher Education: Ethical, Strategic, and Socio-Technical Perspectives. *Journal of Artificial Intelligence and Technological Development*, *48*(1), 33–44. DOI: 10.59324/jaitd.2026.2(2).03

Lam, T. (2026). The importance of ethics, governance and leadership in meeting the artificial intelligence challenge in higher education: A critical review. *Cogent Education*, *13*(1), 2636441. Advance online publication. DOI: 10.1080/2331186X.2026.2636441

Markova S. V. Alieva A. B. Dadova M. Kh.. (2026). The impact of integration of artificial intelligence and ESG principles on the development of the innovation economy in education. ekonomika i upravlenie problemy resheniya. 2/5(167):84-94 DOI: 10.36871/ek.up.p.r.2026.02.05.011

Nair, S., Banka, K., & Pandya, A. (2025). *Humanizing AI in Higher Education: Rethinking HR, Ethics, and Skill Development for University Employees in the SDG Era*. INTI Journal., DOI: 10.61453/INTIj.202560

Pang, H., Dong, S., Tan, P., Wang, H., & Li, J. (2025), From data to decisions: AI-Augmented geoscience and engineering in natural gas industry, Natural Gas Industry B, Volume 12, Issue 2, PP 101-109, ISSN 2352-8540, DOI: 10.1016/j.ngib.2025.04.001

Slimi, Z., & Carballido, V. B. (2023). Navigating the Ethical Challenges of Artificial Intelligence in Higher Education: An Analysis of Seven Global AI Ethics Policies, TEM Journal. Volume 12, Issue 2, PP 590-602, ISSN 2217-8309, DOI: DOI: 10.18421/TEM122-02

Sun, D., Ba, S., Cha, Y., Yu, J., Chiang, F.-K., & Hai, M. D. Cher-Ping Lim (2026), Empowering university teachers in higher education: A generative AI-responsive competency framework, Computers and Education: Artificial Intelligence, Volume 10, 2026,100542, ISSN 2666-920X, DOI: 10.1016/j.caeai.2026.100542

Szostak, M. (Ed.). (2025). *Organizations, Humanism and AI: An Aesthetics Approach* (1st ed.). Routledge., DOI: 10.4324/9781003662723

Wu, C., Zang, H., & Carroll, J. M. (2024). AI Governance in Higher Education: Case Studies of Guidance at Big Ten Universities. Arxiv, Computer Science. https://doi.org//arXiv.2409.02017DOI: 10.48550

Chapter 7
Postgraduate Studies as a Training Space for Digital Leadership

Edgar Oliver Cardoso Espinosa
http://orcid.org/0000-0001-7588-9439
Instituto Politécnico Nacional, Mexico

ABSTRACT

The objective of this chapter is to determine the implications of digital leadership in postgraduate training in order to integrate them as a key component in this level educational. Digitalization and technological advances have encouraged companies to transform their structures, processes, business models, and organizational strategies. To achieve digital transformation in organizations, leadership is the key factor in establishing the vision, driving change, and fostering an organizational culture that embraces innovation and digital disruption in operational processes. Digital leadership is characterized by the ability to guide organizations through digital transformation, integrating technological tools into operations and processes to achieve strategic objectives. Digital leadership is responsible for designing and implementing strategies aimed at the digital transformation of the organization through the incorporation and sustainable use of technological tools that enable organizational success.

INTRODUCTION

Since the mid-20th century, education has been considered one of the main factors determining a country's economic growth. Investment in education fosters sustained economic growth and strengthens the quality of the workforce (Schultz,

DOI: 10.4018/979-8-3373-8959-2.ch007

1961; Lucas, 1988; Barro, 1996; Becker et al., 1993). In the 21st century, technology is considered the main driver of economic growth, although it is linked to education and training of the human capital and research as means to acquire and generate new knowledge, innovative products, and thus add value to national economies (Escamilla-Mejía et al., 2025)[1].

It has been proven theoretically and empirically that the training and development of human capital is the way to add value to the capabilities of the individual that allow him to successfully carry out specialized activities that require the use of technology (Escamilla-Mejía et al., 2025).

Digitalization and technological advances have encouraged companies to transform their structures, processes, business models, and organizational strategies. The information age has created an environment that demands flexibility, adaptability, and speed in industrial sectors to avoid stagnation and falling behind the competition (Zulu et al., 2023).

This landscape, resulting from technological innovations, has led organizational leaders to seek strategies to remain relevant and competitive in the market. Thus, it is the responsibility of digital leadership to interrelate the human, material, and financial resources that allow the organization to thrive in this competitive environment that digital transformation entails (Khan et al., 2022).

According to Westerman et al. (2014), the continuous evolution of digital technologies has transformed the nature, dynamics, processes, and operations of contemporary organizations. The digital revolution has fostered the emergence of a new leadership style and organizational culture, which must adapt to the new conditions and demands of the digital age (Bharadwaj et al., 2013).

Thus, digital transformation has become a fundamental driver for the success of organizations and enables the growth of industries and countries. This transformation involves the integration of emerging technologies such as Artificial Intelligence (AI), big data, cloud computing, and automation to improve efficiency, agility, and customer satisfaction.

Vial (2019) and Kayanja et al. (2025) define digital transformation as a process with the objective of improving an entity by generating significant changes in its operations through technological tools, digital communication and connectivity in combination with strategic use by the members of the organization.

However, digital transformation is not just about a technological upgrade but also involves an organizational change that requires visionary leadership to address the difficulties and complexities to ensure that the transformation aligns with the organization's objectives and market demands.

Digital transformation involves a strategic renewal that leaders must adopt to ensure the sustainable success of the organization through innovation, changing its processes and acquiring new capabilities to create competitive advantages (Mamoun & Mousa, 2018).

Digital transformation leads to greater operational efficiency, improved customer experiences, and fostered innovation (Ahsan, 2025). Organizations and their members who adopt and implement digital transformation are better positioned to respond to market disruptions and maintain their competitive advantage (Probojakti et al., 2025).

To achieve digital transformation in organizations, leadership is the key factor in establishing the vision, driving change, and fostering an organizational culture that embraces innovation and digital disruption in operational processes. In this sense, a leader guides the digital transformation, which involves changes in the mindset of the organization's members, interdepartmental collaboration, and continuous learning.

Therefore, the leader's strategic communication becomes the primary mechanism for achieving a vision aligned with digital initiatives and organizational objectives. Communication then enables each member of the organization to understand the purpose and impact of digital transformation, thus empowering them to work collaboratively using new technologies (Tebenko et al., 2024).

Research on digital leadership has recognized its importance in improving organizational performance and profitability. However, theoretical frameworks are needed to identify the skills of digital leaders (Hanelt et al., 2021).

Based on the above, the objective of this chapter is to determine the implications of digital leadership in postgraduate education to integrate it as a key component at this educational level. The questions guiding this chapter are:

- What is digital leadership?
- What are the competencies that comprise digital leadership?
- What is the influence of digital leadership on organizations?
- What is the relevance of postgraduate studies as a training ground for digital leadership?

BACKGROUND

During the 20th century, leadership in organizations was hierarchical, with each top-down decision based on experience and intuition. Technological development facilitated access to information across various areas of the organization and fostered openness to new ways of communicating and working collaboratively and inclusively (Dittes et al., 2019).

Therefore, a new leadership paradigm, known as digital leadership, has emerged. Currently, a leader needs to recognize the challenges of a digital ecosystem to organize teams that foster innovation and growth through the diversified use of technological tools (Cortellazzo et al., 2019).

Digital leadership determines direction, influences others, initiates sustainable change through access to information, and builds relationships to anticipate key changes for future organizational success. To achieve this, the digital leader's objective must be to foster employee engagement and job satisfaction for the organization's sustainable future (Pongton & Suntravuth, 2019; Tanucan et al., 2022).

Digital leadership is the ability of organizational leaders to identify technologies relevant to the organization to encourage all members to implement them in their activities (Rudito & Sinaga, 2017).

Digital leadership is the ability to lead organizations through technological transformations while maintaining alignment with organizational objectives. A digital leader's fundamental role is to guide their organization through digital change and ensure their teams possess the necessary skills to thrive in a technological world (Madanchian & Tahedoost, 2025).

Digital leadership is characterized by the ability to guide organizations through digital transformation to integrate technological tools into operations and processes to achieve strategic objectives (Cheng et al., 2025). A digital leader fosters a digital culture, encourages innovation, and drives organizational change (Wang et al., 2022). According to Kane (2019), digital leaders combine technical competence, strategic vision, and change management skills.

A digital leader who implements digital strategies improves decision-making processes, enhances employee productivity, and fosters a culture of continuous improvement (Ahsan, 2025). Digital leadership enables organizations to maintain a competitive position by motivating greater responsiveness to the market (Probojakti et al., 2025).

The digital transformation of leadership focuses not only on the knowledge and use of technological tools but also on organizational adjustments, changes in processes and the psychology of the members to achieve the innovations necessary for the organization (Eckhardt et al., 2018). It has been recognized that digital transformation in the organization not only fosters productivity but also promotes collaboration, innovation and positioning by reducing the costs of operations (Attaran et al., 2019).

Job satisfaction stems from the technological infrastructure used by employees, adapted to their work processes, which allows for greater job performance. This situation is explained by the impact of digital leadership in promoting a suitable work environment that guarantees learning, cooperation, and a digital work culture (Gruman & Saks, 2018).

Therefore, a digital leader must possess a high degree of digital literacy to lead effectively in a technological environment, enabling them to guide their teams through digital transformations and foster a culture of continuous learning and adaptation

(Avolio et al., 2014). Digital leadership positively influences the commitment of members by facilitating better communication, collaboration, trust and job satisfaction (Agustina et al., 2020; Rüth & Netzer, 2020). A good digital leader possesses attributes such as digital literacy, openness to new ideas, and the ability to enable members to use technology efficiently (Bai et al., 2020).

The importance of digital leadership lies in boosting organizational performance and employee engagement in the technological environment (Albrecht et al., 2018). A digital leader is someone who successfully uses technological tools to inspire and influence their team members and teams, creating an environment that values creativity and adaptability. The relevance of digital leadership lies in its contribution to advancing the sustainable development of countries by aligning with the UN Sustainable Development Goals (SDGs), which emphasize the need for interconnected action among government, civil society, and the private sector. Thus, organizations are fundamental to the design and implementation of sustainable practices (Soergel et al., 2021).

According to the United Nations (2024), global progress towards the SDGs is shown in Figure 1.

Figure 1. Proportion of countries (United Nations, 2024)

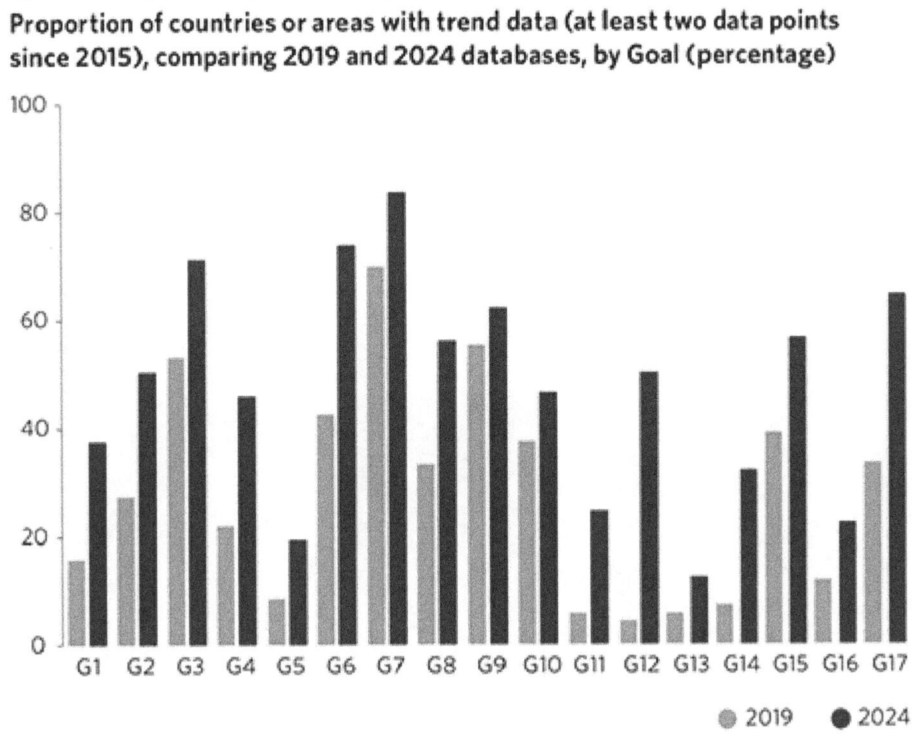

Figure 1 identifies the level of achievement of the SDGs, as well as the comparison from 2019 to 2024. Figure 1 shows that each of the SDGs has been in increasing evolution during this period. The variability in national data coverage is reflected differently across the different Goals, with significant shortcomings in priority development areas such as gender equality (Goal 5), climate action (Goal 13) and peace, justice and institution building (Goal 16).

Based on Figure 1, the potential for organizations to significantly contribute to achieving the SDGs through digital leadership is identified, as this can be the driving force behind integrating sustainability into the organization's vision (Saxena et al., 2021). Digital technologies encourage organizations to reduce both inefficiencies and environmental impacts. Furthermore, technological tools create new avenues for engaging with diverse stakeholders, enabling organizations to collaborate with government, communities, and other local, regional, national, and even international organizations.

Similarly, digital leadership is a key factor in developing an organizational culture aligned with the SDGs (Martínez-Peláez et al., 2023). Through the strategic integration of technologies, an organization incorporates sustainability into its business operations, ensuring its long-term viability. Furthermore, a digital leader fosters a collaborative and inclusive organizational culture focused on three key areas: social, environmental, and economic. As shown in Figure 2.

Figure 2. Organizational culture oriented towards the SDGs

Based on Figure 2, it is important to foster structural changes in organizational culture within organizations to achieve the SDGs. These changes are based on four pillars: 1) Promoting digital transformation through continuous innovation; 2) Integrating collaboration and inclusion among members and organizational areas; 3) Positioning the economic, social, and environmental sustainability approach in organizational processes; and 4) Evaluating results from a combined social, envi-romental, and economic perspective.

Thus, digital leadership is a strategic factor in contributing to the achievement of the SDGs because it integrates sustainability into the core values and operations of organizations (Jayashree et al., 2022). Digital leaders are the actors who effectively use technological tools to implement environmentally sustainable practices aimed at promoting social responsibility and driving organizational growth, thereby aligning organizational activities with the global sustainable development agenda (Khuntia et al., 2018).

According to Bughin et al. (2019), organizations with digital leadership are twice as likely to report superior profitability and achieve their strategic objectives. Jones and Wynn (2021) emphasize that digital leadership incorporates technical expertise and forward-thinking leadership to understand the link between digital transformation and sustainable development. Digital leaders who align digital strategies with the SDGs will contribute not only to their organization's resilience and competitiveness but also to ensuring a sustainable future.

Therefore, Cann (2016), digital transformation will contribute to global economic growth through advanced technologies such as artificial intelligence (AI), cloud computing, big data, and the Internet of Things. This type of digitalization encourages organizations to be more agile and responsive to market demands, facilitating innovation in their offerings of goods and services.

Digital leadership has become a strategic factor for the digital transformation of organizations. A digital leader combines traditional leadership skills with the implementation of emerging technologies to generate disruptive changes in organizations (Espina-Romero & Guerrero-Alcedo, 2022). Zeike et al. (2019) define digital leadership as the skills acquired to drive digital change and leverage technological options that strengthen the organization. Mihardjo et al. (2019a) consider that digital leadership encompasses a way of thinking and acting based on knowledge of the application of digital technologies within leadership, with the goal of generating value for the organization.

Digital leadership is the strategic factor for organizations to survive in the new digital age by adapting and transforming strategies to achieve business objectives and successfully drive the digital transformation of the business. Digital leaders utilize and enhance the company's digital assets, giving them different skills and perspectives than traditional leaders. However, many organizations fail to grasp the value of digital leaders, leading to poor performance and irreparable failures. The main function of digital leadership is to guide an organization in a highly technological and constantly evolving context to achieve competitiveness and the achievement of the Sustainable Development Goals (SDGs) (Fennelly et al., 2022; Sarfraz et al., 2022; Saraih et al., 2022; Tanucan et al., 2022).

Digital leadership is the use of an organization's digital resources to achieve its objectives at both the organizational and individual levels. This requires a digital leader to possess a set of competencies that enable the organization to advance through the transition and meet the challenges posed by the digital environment. The competencies that constitute digital leadership are providing vision and mission; creating growth opportunities; motivating team members to think innovatively;

fostering vertical and horizontal teamwork; promoting communication between teams and organizations; developing and driving organizational strategies; and fostering cooperation.

Similarly, in this new digital environment, adaptation to an organizational culture with a digital focus is required, one capable of processing and analyzing information to transform it into knowledge as a source of productivity. Therefore, it is necessary to train members of the organization in digital skills (Alvarez, 2023). Integrating technology into an organization's processes is a complex challenge, requiring infrastructure, development, and training of human capital for the effective use of digital tools. The importance of technology lies in designing platforms that facilitate relationships between organizations and their customers, adding value and satisfaction (Sosa et al., 2018).

Given this digital landscape, organizations must have professionals trained in digital leadership to make decisions that allow them to position themselves in the market segment in which they compete, as well as boost the growth of their members and guarantee the quality of their digital assets (Alshehab et al., 2022; Espina-Romero, 2023).

Furthermore, the digital space has established new demands and conditions for companies, requiring them to adapt and implement change processes. To achieve this, digital leadership is a crucial variable because it is responsible for defining the digital business strategy. Organizations also recognize the need to create and cultivate a new type of leadership so that the organization can adapt structurally and operationally to remain competitive in the sector. However, there is no established program for digital leadership training at the postgraduate level.

In this sense, the postgraduate level focuses on the training of high-level human capital through a training process aimed at developing a set of relevant capabilities that allow the graduate to design and implement strategies that impact the organizations in which they work. Therefore, postgraduate studies, as a training space, must update their academic programs to focus on developing digital leadership skills and competencies. For comparison, Table 1 shows the competencies of traditional leadership in relation to digital leadership.

Table 1. Comparative table

Competence	Traditional leadership	Digital Leadership
Vision	Consistency, but incremental change	Technological innovation
Adaptability	Adaptation to gradual change	Rapid response to technological change
Continuous learning	Previously acquired skills and knowledge	Improving skills and incorporating a learning culture
Collaboration and inclusion	Vertical decision-making	Inclusive decision-making through technology
Flexibility	Rigidity	High flexibility to cater to different generations
Digital literacy	Non-existent or limited	Highly proficient in technological tools
Self-knowledge	Non-existent	Capacity for self-criticism
Digital communication	Non-existent	Use of collaborative platforms, instant messaging, and videoconferencing
Emotional intelligence	Non-existent	Ability to understand, regulate and manage emotions

Source: Prepared from Sainger (2025).

Based on Table 1, a digital leader possesses a forward-looking vision for the organization's sustainability by predicting industry trends. They also continuously incorporate technological tools to achieve organizational goals. Furthermore, the digital leader designs and implements strategies focused on adapting to technological changes to promote innovation in organizational processes. In this way, they foster continuous personal learning and promote it among team members, generating synergy and collaborative work through the ongoing development of each member's skills.

Therefore, digital leadership is not solely associated with the use of technology but rather involves a set of competencies aimed at promoting a shift in organizational focus toward sustainability through innovative process management (Avolio et al., 2014). The digital transformation promoted by the digital leader involves the transformation of the business model, operational transformation, and transformation of the customer interaction strategy (Westerman et al., 2014).

Developing a digital vision is essential for organizations seeking to be competitive in a rapidly changing technological environment. A digital vision serves as a strategic plan that aligns technological advancements with objectives to ensure that every digital initiative contributes to long-term growth and innovation. A digital vision enables organizations to transition from traditional methods to more agile, technology-driven models, thereby fostering efficiency, scalability, and sustainability (Westerman et al., 2014).

An effective digital vision is adaptable and scalable, allowing the organization to adapt as new technologies emerge. Digital transformation is not a one-time event, but an ongoing process that requires monitoring to adjust organizational strategies.

This means that the digital leader must foster an understanding of the importance of digital transformation among members of the organization. Therefore, continuous communication about the digital vision is required, focusing on its alignment with the mission and objectives. This, in turn, generates commitment to digital initiatives within the organization.

Emotional intelligence, for its part, is relevant because it allows digital leaders to build strong relationships, communicate effectively, and inspire teams. Emotional intelligence encompasses self-awareness, self-regulation, empathy, and motivation. Furthermore, it fosters a positive and high-performing work environment where team members feel heard, valued, and motivated to embrace digital transformation (Higgs & Dulewicz, 2016).

DISCUSSION

Digital leadership presents challenges for organizations to consolidate their transformation:

- Resistance to change: Employees feel threatened by new technologies that will replace them. The leader addresses this through communication, training programs, and change management strategies focused on presenting the advantages.
- Implementation of initiatives: They require interdisciplinary collaborations, investment, and alignment with regulatory and ethical criteria.
- Cybersecurity risks, data privacy and technological changes: Designing strategies that foster long-term success and sustainability.

Figure 3. Role of digital leadership

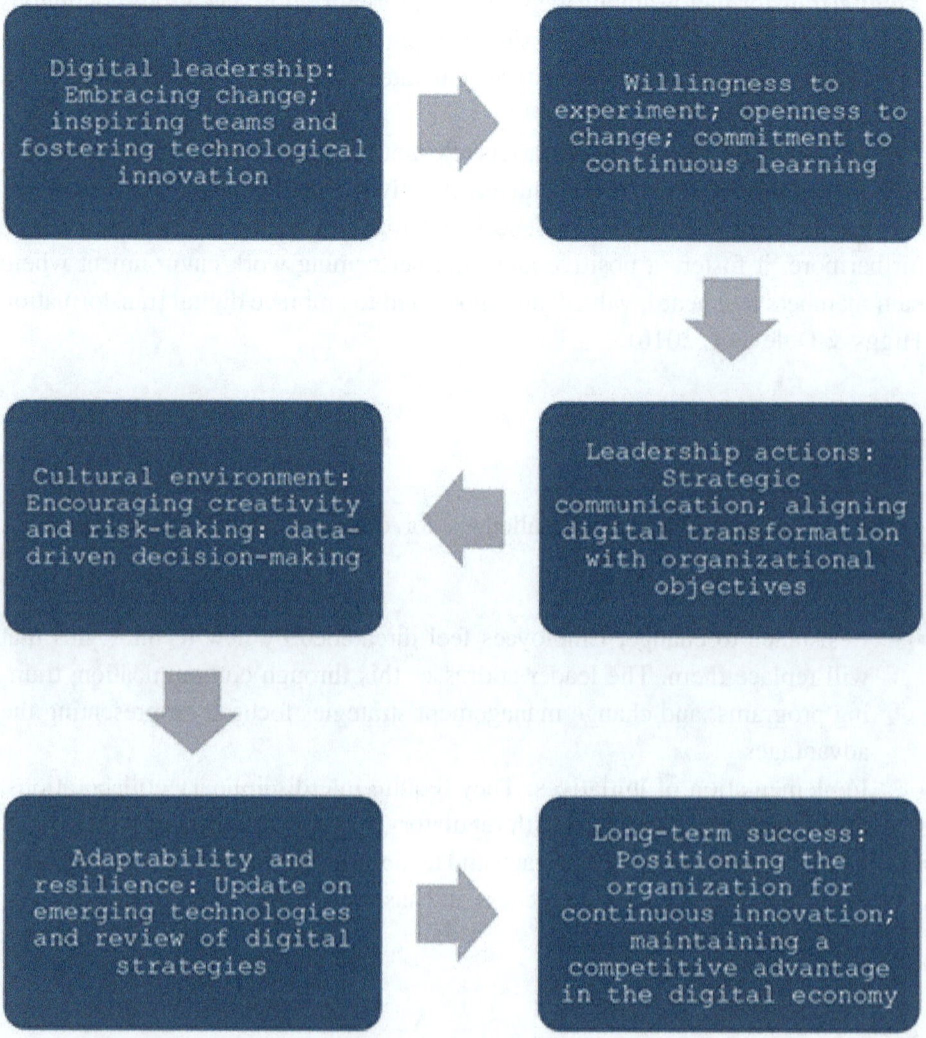

Based on Figure 3, digital leadership involves the exercise of diverse, interrelated functions aimed at the digital transformation of the organization. Digital leadership consists of six main functions:

- The first is the vision of organizational change focused on motivating change and integrating teams that foster technological innovations in the organization's areas and processes.

- The second is openness to change oriented toward modifications in the behaviors of members and operational processes, making continuous learning the fundamental axis for achieving this.
- The third is the alignment of organizational objectives with the vision of digital transformation and the establishment of horizontal and vertical communication channels.
- The fourth is the promotion of an organizational environment conducive to openness to change and creativity that enables digital transformation.
- The fifth is adaptability and resilience to change at both the individual and organizational levels. It is necessary to recognize that technological changes imply continuous modifications in the behaviors of members but also allow them to position themselves as human talent within the organization.
- The sixth is the long-term strategic vision aimed at generating competitive advantages in the digital economy through the incorporation of technological innovations in each of the organization's operational processes.

As organizations continue to adopt digital transformation, there is a need to train members in technological skills to ensure their use of tools to improve their performance and contribute to growth.

However, it is necessary to foster other types of skills in the members such as critical thinking, problem-solving and adaptability to successfully take advantage of new technologies in their work environments.

Figure 4. Digital leadership to develop the talent

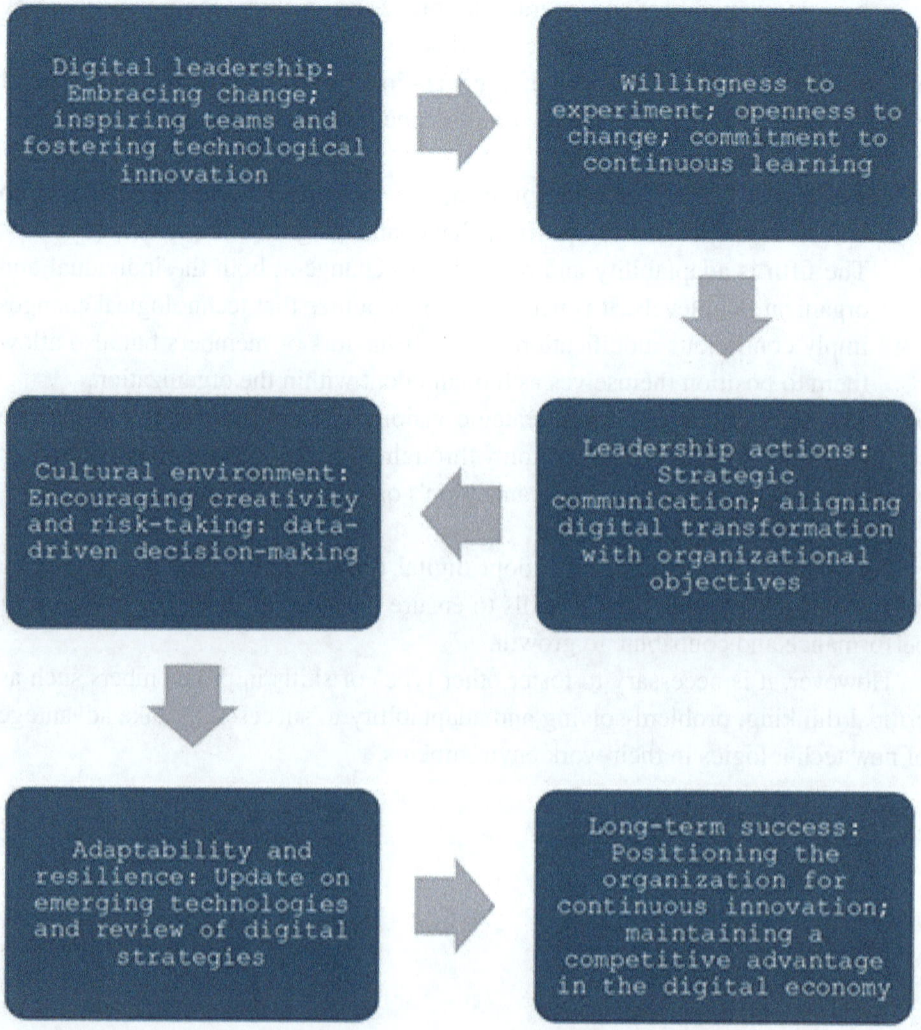

Based on Figure 4, digital leadership is a strategic factor for digital transformation in organizations. A digital leader is a change agent who promotes substantial modifications in the organization they lead to maintain its permanence and sustainability.

Thus, digital leadership requires professional training to promote digital transformation within the organization. According to Ranga & Etzkowitz (2013); Etzkowitz & Leydesdorff (2000), the knowledge economy requires human talent trained at the postgraduate level to generate and transfer knowledge within organizations, thereby fostering the economic and social development of countries. Živković & Panić (2020); Živković & Panić (2024) establish the relevance of developing high-quality human capital capable of driving fundamental changes based on emerging technologies, with the aim of incorporating them into organizations.

This training must be provided at the postgraduate level. Postgraduate studies are geared towards generating high-quality human capital, providing individuals with a range of competencies that enable them to position themselves in the job market (Groen, 2021).

Postgraduate training involves three main pillars: skills, human talent development, and continuous learning. These pillars allow for intervention in organizational culture and strategic alignment. Organizational culture must be modified through a mentoring process led by the digital leader to promote collaboration and technological innovation in operational areas, as well as to foster the inclusion of diverse technological tools and recognize the existence of team members with varying levels of technological proficiency. Strategic alignment must be transformed to incorporate technologies that enable the achievement of organizational objectives and thus consolidate the organization's sustainability. To achieve this, the digital leader must promote human talent management focused on training in the use of technological tools.

Based on the above, it is necessary to promote teleworking, hybrid teams and digital collaboration tools within the organization, as these have become integral components of the work environment, transforming the functioning of organizations and the interaction between their members. Furthermore, they increase job satisfaction and employee retention, as well as improving work-life balance.

The hybrid team model allows organizations to combine the advantages of remote work with the collaborative advantages of face-to-face interactions, thus fostering collaboration and group cohesion. Digital collaboration tools play a fundamental role in facilitating the smooth functioning of teams. Their importance lies in enabling communication and information exchange regardless of physical location, thereby fostering productivity, a sense of belonging, and the ability to track activities.

This implies that the fundamental skills of a digital leader are technological literacy and adaptability due to:

- Digital literacy is not limited to understanding how technological tools and platforms work, but also to having the perspective to know which of them are likely to be used to achieve the organization's objectives;
- Digital leadership needs to become familiar with concepts such as AI, cloud computing, data analytics, and automation, recognizing if they are not experts.
- Due to constant technological change, a digital leader identifies its implications for the organization and therefore makes modifications to strategies, as well as guiding its members in the transitions when introducing a new technological tool.

Based on the above, it is relevant to foster a culture of continuous learning within the organization, encourage the exploration of new digital tools, and create an environment where change is viewed as an opportunity for growth. Therefore, digital literacy enables a leader to make informed decisions, while adaptability ensures the gradual adoption of technological opportunities, thus positioning the organization for sustainable success (Matsunaga, 2024).

Therefore, the digital transformation in the organization based on the exercise of the digital leader involves the following phases shown in Figure 5.

Figure 5. Phases of digital transformation

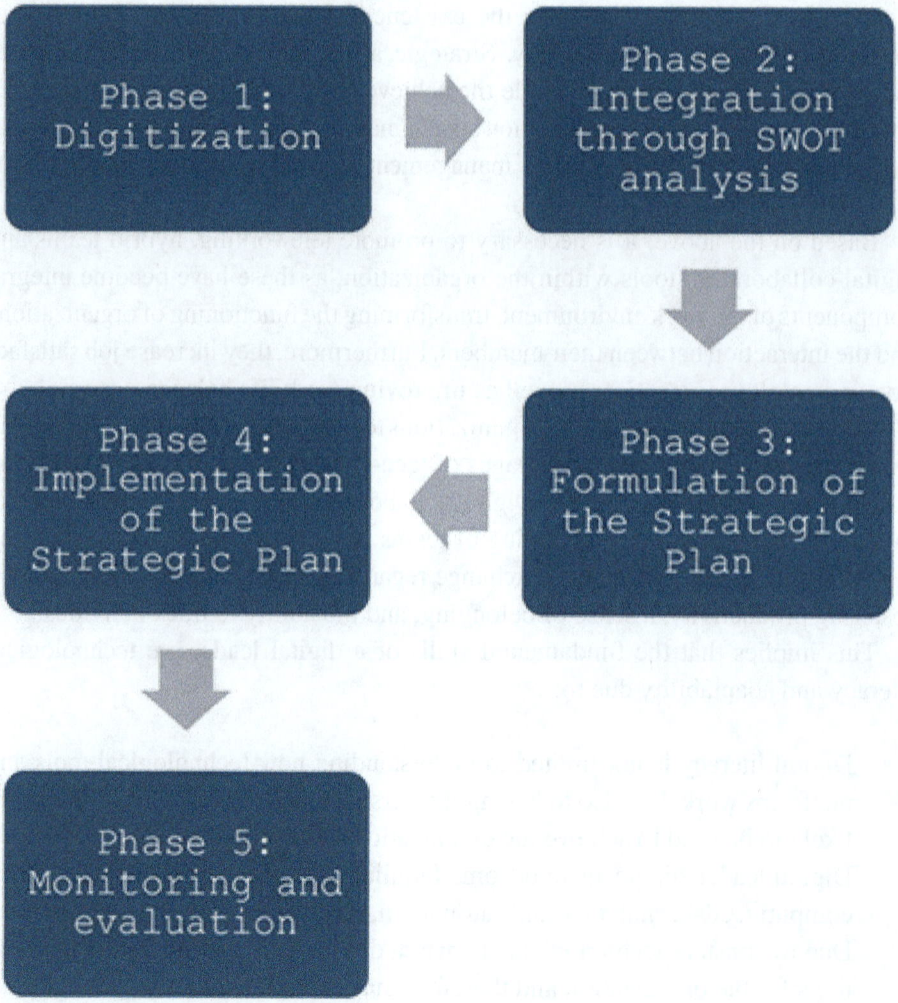

Based on Figure 5, there are five stages of digital transformation according to Wengler et al. (2021); Bresciani et al. (2021); Razia & Awwad (2022); Razia et al. (2022): The first is the organization's recognition of the need to use technological tools in its processes. At the organizational level, this implies identifying a need to incorporate technology, recognizing its future importance for productivity, efficiency, and sustainability.

The second part addresses internal and external analysis (SWOT). The former focuses on determining the resources and skills needed to begin the digital transformation, while the latter identifies the opportunities associated with digitalization by analyzing the economic, cultural, and technological context. Both enable the design and implementation of digital transformation strategies for the organization.

The third step is the formulation of the strategic digital transformation plan, which defines the actions, resource allocation, goals, objectives, timelines, and indicators to leverage the benefits of technologies and their impact on productivity, cost reduction, and process innovation, while also aligning with the organization's vision and strategic objectives.

The fourth is the implementation of the strategic plan, which requires the participation of the members, promoting a culture of collaboration and highlighting the importance of digital transformation. The fifth is monitoring and evaluation to determine the progress in the use of technologies to take corrective actions or strengthen the actions that have allowed the integration of digital tools into the organization's processes.

It is important to recognize that all organizations are influenced by technology, making the digital leader the agent of change for survival (Jasim et al., 2024). Digital leadership focuses on fostering innovation, organizational change, and developing a culture of continuous learning for the gradual adoption and integration of technological tools.

As Gledson et al. (2024) indicate, organizations find themselves in disruptive environments due to technological development, so vision, trust, responsibility and resilience are skills inherent to digital leadership that allow promoting technological innovation in each organization.

Therefore, postgraduate training in digital leadership is required. As Manetti et al. (2022a) mention, educational programs must constantly review their training practices and academic content to stay current and implement the necessary adjustments to fulfill their mission of developing high-quality human capital. In this context, postgraduate studies must move beyond the traditional pedagogical model toward new approaches focused on providing quality education to students, recognizing the importance of digital leadership training (Ramírez-Montoya et al., 2022).

This has led postgraduate programs to recognize the importance of digitally transforming their training practices to integrate the changes resulting from scientific and technological advancements. Furthermore, organizations, immersed in a constantly evolving environment due to technological development, require the ongoing training and development of their human capital to foster a learning culture focused on the introduction and use of digital tools.

As confirmed by Valencia (2005), investment in human capital in the country generates significant social benefits for the economy, exceeding individual benefits. These social benefits are related to the development of human capital and the development of new technologies that foster organizational innovation. In this sense, human capital comprises a diverse set of competencies that must be developed through postgraduate training, enabling graduates to contribute to the advancement of both public and private organizations.

For its part, higher education has a relevant role to play in fulfilling goal 8.2: Achieving higher levels of economic productivity through diversification, technological upgrading and innovation, as well as adding value and intensive use of labor; and goal 8.3: Promoting growth through entrepreneurship, creativity and innovation, formalization and growth of micro, small and medium-sized enterprises (United Nations, 2018).

It is also recognized that, given the rapid pace of technological advancements, the role of digital leadership has become the driving force reshaping organizational performance. The education sector, responsible for providing training services, represents an opportunity to leverage these technologies (Namatovu & Kyambade, 2025; Kyambade et al., 2024). In this sense, governments must invest in education that is profitable for both individuals and organizations (Aghion et al., 2009).

FUTURE STUDIES

Future research to be carried out includes:

- Design of instruments to assess the acquisition of digital leadership skills
- Implementation of active methodologies as strategies to promote digital leadership learning in postgraduate studies
- Studies on the influence of Artificial Intelligence as an emerging technology in organizations and its impact on digital leadership
- Qualitative research focused on obtaining testimonies from key digital leaders to expand knowledge about leadership and digital transformation in organizations.

CONCLUSION

It is important to recognize the existence of a multigenerational workforce within organizations, which presents an opportunity for digital leadership. This situation means that each age group possesses different levels of digital literacy. In this sense, older employees require more time and mentorship to adapt to the use of new technologies, while younger employees, being digital natives, do not need it.

Thus, the digital leader becomes the talent to address this diversity and promote inclusion. Furthermore, they foster a more dynamic and innovative work environment by promoting intergenerational cooperation and learning, leveraging the unique capabilities of each generation in terms of knowledge, experience, and wisdom.

Digital leadership implies the need to adopt flexible styles that address the diversity of the organization's members. A younger employee prefers a more autonomous approach, while an older one values more direct communication and guidance. Governments must prioritize investments in higher education while addressing access gaps, so policies must align with SDGs 4 and 8. Therefore, more research on investment in education is needed.

The challenges of digital leadership are:

- Resistance to change: Members of the organization resist change due to fear of the unknown or a lack of skills in managing and using digital tools.
- Digital divide: Unequal access in organizations and members due to a lack of connectivity and access to devices and even limited infrastructure.

To overcome the challenges of digital leadership, the following is proposed:

- Building a culture of continuous learning where the leader fosters ongoing professional development in acquiring new skills related to the management and use of emerging technologies. This also involves mentorship and online learning resources to facilitate their assimilation by team members.
- Investment in digital infrastructure: Governments need to collaborate with organizations to invest in providing digital infrastructure so that they can incorporate it into their processes and thus contribute to the SDGs.
- Public-private partnerships: Collaboration between the public and private sectors will contribute resources and technical knowledge to the development of digital infrastructure and thus promote digital literacy.
- Inclusion and diversity: By implementing digital transformation and sustainability, an organization, through digital leadership, fosters diversity in terms of gender, ethnicity, and socioeconomic background, creating a collaborative environment and strong, sustainable relationships.

REFERENCES

Aghion, P., Boustan, L., Hoxby, C., & Vandenbussche, J. (2009). The Causal Impact of Education on Economic Growth: Evidence from U.S. *Brookings Papers on Economic Activity*, *1*(1), 1–73.

Agustina, R., Kamdi, W., Hadi, S., Muladi, S., & Nurhadi, D. (2020). Influence of the principal's digital leadership on the reflective practices of vocational teachers mediated by trust, self-efficacy, and work engagement. *International Journal of Learning. Teaching and Educational Research*, *19*(11), 24–40. DOI: 10.26803/ijlter.19.11.2

Ahsan, M. J. (2025). Cultivating a culture of learning: The role of leadership in fostering lifelong development. *The Learning Organization*, *32*(2), 282–306. DOI: 10.1108/TLO-03-2024-0099

Albrecht, S., Bakker, A., Gruman, J., Macey, W., & Saks, A. (2018). Employee engagement in the digital age. *Human Resource Management Review*, *28*(3), 227–238.

Alshehab, A., Alfozan, T., Gaderrab, H., Alahmad, M., & Alkandari, A. (2022). Identifying significant elements of the digital transformation of organization in Kuwait. *Indonesian Journal of Electrical Engineering and Computer Science,* 26(1), 318–325. https://doi.org/. i1.pp318-325DOI: 10.11591/ijeecs.v26

Alvarez, L. (2023). Liderazgo digital: El nuevo estilo para gerenciar. *Revista Científica Internacional*, *6*(1), 61–72. DOI: 10.46734/revcientifica.v6i1.64

Attaran, M., Attaran, S., & Kirkland, D. (2019). The need for digital workplace: Increasing workforce productivity in the information age. [IJEIS]. *International Journal of Enterprise Information Systems*, *15*(1), 1–23. DOI: 10.4018/IJEIS.2019010101

Avolio, B., Sosik, J., Kahai, S., & Baker, B. (2014). E-leadership: Re-examining transformations in leadership source and transmisión. *The Leadership Quarterly*, *25*(1), 105–131. DOI: 10.1016/j.leaqua.2013.11.003

Bai, C., Dallasega, P., Orzes, G., & Sarkis, J. (2020). Industry 4.0 technologies assessment: A sustainability perspective. *International Journal of Production Economics*, *229*, 107776. DOI: 10.1016/j.ijpe.2020.107776

Barro, R. (1996). *Determinants of Economic Growth: A Cross-Country Empirical Study* (5698). https://doi.org/DOI: 10.3386/w5698

Becker, G. S., Murphy, K. M., & Tamura, R. (1993). Human Capital, Fertility, and Economic Growth. In *Human Capital: A Theoretical and Empirical Analysis, with Special Reference to Education* (3rd ed., pp. 323–350). The University of Chicago Press. DOI: 10.7208/chicago/9780226041223.001.0001

Bharadwaj, A., Sawy, E., Pavlou, A., & Venkatraman, N. (2013). Digital business strategy: Toward a next generation of insights. *Management Information Systems Quarterly*, *37*(2), 471–482. DOI: 10.25300/MISQ/2013/37:2.3

Bresciani, S., Ferraris, A., Romano, M., & Santoro, G. (2021). *Building a digital transformation strategy, digital transformation management for agile organizations: A compass to sail the digital world*. Emerald Publishing Limited., DOI: 10.1108/978-1- 80043-171-32021100

Bughin, J., Deakin, J., & O'Beirne, B. (2019). Digital transformation: Improving the odds of success. *The McKinsey Quarterly*, *22*, 1–5.

Cann, O. (2016). *$100 trillion by 2025: The digital dividend for society and business*. World Economic Forum. https://www.weforum.org/press/2016/01/100-trillionby -2025-the-digital-dividend-for-society-and-business/

Cheng, Z., Jin, X., & Kwak, W. J. (2025). Using the new positive aspect of digital leadership to improve organizational sustainability: Testing moderated mediation model. *Acta Psychologica*, *255*, 104963. DOI: 10.1016/j.actpsy.2025.104963

Cortellazzo, L., Bruni, E., & Zampieri, R. (2019). The role of leadership in a digitalized world: A review. *Frontiers in Psychology*, *10*, 1938. DOI: 10.3389/fpsyg.2019.01938

Dittes, S., Richter, S., Richter, A., & Smolnik, S. (2019). Toward the workplace of the future: How organizations can facilitate digital work. *Business Horizons*, *62*(5), 649–661. DOI: 10.1016/j.bushor.2019.05.004

Eckhardt, J., Ciuchta, M., & Carpenter, M. (2018). Open innovation, information, and entrepreneurship within platform ecosystems. *Strategic Entrepreneurship Journal*, *12*(3), 369–391. DOI: 10.1002/sej.1298

Escamilla-Mejía, M. G., Alfaro-Ponce, B., Aali-Bujari, A., & Hernández-Veleros, Z. S. (2025). Differentiated Impact of Higher Education by Gender, Age, and Income Level on Economic Growth: Evidence for OECD Countries. *Multidisciplinary Journal of Educational Research*, *15*(1), 72–90. DOI: 10.17583/remie.15206

Espina-Romero, L. (2023). Collaboration and interdisciplinarity in scientific research: Fostering synergy to address current challenges. *IPSA Scientia. Revista Científica Multidisciplinaria*, *8*(2), 8–9. DOI: 10.25214/27114406.1627

Espina-Romero, L., & Guerrero-Alcedo, J. (2022). Fields Touched by Digitalization: Analysis of Scientific Activity in Scopus. *Sustainability (Basel), 14*(21), 14425. DOI: 10.3390/su142114425

Etzkowitz, H., & Leydesdorff, L. (2000). The dynamics of innovation: From national systems and 'mode 2' to a triple helix of university-industry-government relations. *Research Policy, 29*(2), 109–123. DOI: 10.1016/S0048-7333(99)00055-4

Fennelly, O., Grogan, L., Reed, A., & Hardiker, N. (2022). Use of standardized terminologies in clinical practice: A scoping review. *International Journal of Medical Informatics, 149*, 104431. DOI: 10.1016/j.ijmedinf.2021.104431

Gledson, B., Zulu, S. L., Saad, A. M., & Ponton, H. (2024). Digital leadership framework to support firm-level digital transformations for Construction 4.0. *Construction Innovation, 24*(1), 341–364. DOI: 10.1108/CI-12-2022-0328

Gruman, J. A., & Saks, A. M. (2018). Performance management and employee engagement. *Human Resource Management Review, 28*(2), 155–168. DOI: 10.1016/j.hrmr.2017.11.007

Hanelt, A., Bohnsack, R., Marz, D., & Antunes Marante, C. (2021). A systematic review of the literature on digital transformation: Insights and implications for strategy and organizational change. *Journal of Management Studies, 58*(5), 1159–1197. DOI: 10.1111/joms.12639

Higgs, M., & Dulewicz, V. (2016). *Leading with emotional intelligence*. Palgrave Macmillan. DOI: 10.1007/978-3-319-32637-5

Jasim, T. A., Khairy, H. A., Fayyad, S., & Al-Romeedy, B. S. (2024). Digital leadership and creative performance in tourism and hotel enterprises: Leveraging strategic agility and organizational learning culture. *Geo Journal of Tourism and Geosites, 54*(2 supplement), 872–884. DOI: 10.30892/gtg.542spl11-1262

Jayashree, P., El Barachi, M., & Hamza, F. (2022). Practice of sustainability leadership: A multi-stakeholder inclusive framework. *Sustainability (Basel), 14*(10), 6346. DOI: 10.3390/su14106346

Jones, P., & Wynn, M. (2021). The leading digital technology companies and their approach to sustainable development. *Sustainability (Basel), 13*(12), 6612. DOI: 10.3390/su13126612

Kane, G. (2019). The technology fallacy: People are the real key to digital transformation. *Research Technology Management, 62*(6), 44–49. DOI: 10.1080/08956308.2019.1661079

Kayanja, W., Kyambade, M., & Kiggundu, T. (2025). Exploring digital transformation in higher education setting: Theshift to fully automated and paperless systems. *Cogent Education, 12*(1), 2489800. DOI: 10.1080/2331186X.2025.2489800

Khan, M., Zubair, S., & Malik, A. (2022). Digital leadership and its influence on organizational success: A case study in the private sector. *Journal of Organization and Management, 36*(4), 46–59.

Khuntia, J., Saldanha, T., Mithas, S., & Sambamurthy, V. (2018). Information technology and sustainability: Evidence from an emerging economy. *Production and Operations Management, 27*(4), 756–773. DOI: 10.1111/poms.12822

Kyambade, M., Namuddu, R., Mugambwa, J., & Namatovu, A. (2024). I can't express myself at work: Encouraging socially responsible leadership and psychological safety in higher education setting. *Cogent Education, 11*(1), 2373560. DOI: 10.1080/2331186X.2024.2373560

Lucas, R. E.Jr. (1988). On the mechanics of economic development. *Journal of Monetary Economics, 22*(1), 3–42. DOI: 10.1016/0304-3932(88)90168-7

Madanchian, M., & Taherdoost, H. (2025). The Digital Leader's Toolkit: Essential Skills and Competencies, Tech-Driven Leadership. In M., Madanchian & H. Taherdoost (Eds.), *Strategies to Maximize Business Potential with Emerging Technologies*, (pp. 21-43). https://doi.org/DOI: 10.1108/978-1-83708-046-520251002

Mamoun, A., & Mousa, M. (2018). Business model innovation as strategic process: A case study of China's most innovative firms. *Global Business and Management Research, 10*(2), 1–18.

Manetti, A., Lara-Navarra, P., & Sánchez-Navarro, J. (2022a). Design process for the generation of future education scenarios. *Comunicar, 73*(73), 33–44. DOI: 10.3916/C73-2022-03

Martínez-Peláez, R., Ochoa-Brust, A., Rivera, S., Félix, V. G., Ostos, R., Brito, H., Félix, R. A., & Mena, L. J. (2023). Role of digital transformation for achieving sustainability: Mediated role of stakeholders, key capabilities, and technology. *Sustainability (Basel), 15*(14), 11221. DOI: 10.3390/su151411221

Matsunaga, M. (2024). The role of digital literacy in leadership. In *Employee uncertainty over digital transformation: Mechanisms and solutions* (pp. 139–188). Springer Nature Singapore. DOI: 10.1007/978-981-99-8409-1_4

Mihardjo, L., Sasmoko, S., Alamsjah, F., & Elidjen, E. (2019). Digital leadership impacts on developing dynamic capability and strategic alliance based on market orientation. *Polish Journal of Management Studies*, *19*(2), 285–297. DOI: 10.17512/pjms.2019.19.2.24

Namatovu, A., & Kyambade, M. (2025). Leveraging AI in academia: University students' adoption of ChatGPT for writing coursework (take home) assignments through the lens of UTAUT2. *Cogent Education*, *12*(1), 2485522. DOI: 10.1080/2331186X.2025.2485522

Pongton, P., & Suntravuth, S. (2019). Communication satisfaction, employee, engagement, job satisfaction, and job performance in higher education institution. *ABAC Journal*, *39*(3), 90–110.

Probojakti, W., Utami, H. N., Prasetya, A., & Riza, M. F. (2025). Driving sustainable competitive advantage in banking: The role of transformational leadership and digital transformation in organizational agility and corporate resiliency. *Business Strategy and the Environment*, *34*(1), 670–689. DOI: 10.1002/bse.4005

Ramírez-Montoya, M. S., McGreal, R. y Obiageli Agbu, J.-F. (2022). Horizontes digitales complejos en el futuro de la educación 4.0: luces desde las recomendaciones de UNESCO. *RIED-Revista Iberoamericana de Educación a Distancia, 25*(2), 09-21. https://doi.org/DOI: 10.5944/ried.25.2.33843

Ranga, M., & Etzkowitz, H. (2013). Triple Helix Systems: An Analytical Framework for Innovation Policy and Practice in the Knowledge Society. *Industry and Higher Education, 27*(4), 237-262. [REMOVED HYPERLINK FIELD]https://doi.org/DOI: 10.1016/j.caeo.2023.100151

Razia, B., & Awwad, B. (2022). *A comprehensive review of blockchain technology and its related aspects in higher education* (pp. 553–571). Technologies, artificial intelligence and the future of learning post-COVID-19: The crucial role of international accreditation.

Razia, B., Awwad, B., & Taqui, N. (2022). The relationship between artificial intelligence (AI) and its aspects in higher education. *Development and Learning in Organizations*, *37*(3), 21–23. DOI: 10.1108/DLO-04-2022-0074

Rudito, P., & Sinaga, M. F. (2017). *Digital mastery, Membangun kepemimpinan digital untuk memenangkan era disrupsi*. Gramedia Pustaka Utama.

Rüth, R., & Netzer, T. (2020). The key elements of cultural intelligence as a driver for digital leadership success. *Leadership, Educaton, Personality. An Interdisciplinary Journal*, *2*(1), 3–8.

Sainger, G. (2025). Fostering a Sustainable Future: The Role of Digital Leadership in Cultivating an SDG-Oriented Organisational Culture. In Jasola, M., & Singh, N. (Eds.), *Digital Transformation Of Business World: A Managerial Perspective* (pp. 97–112). Emerald Insight., DOI: 10.1108/978-1-83662-046-420251007

Saraih, E., Wong, S., Asimiran, S., & Khambari, M. (2022). Contemporary communication conduit among exemplar school principals in Malaysian schools. *Research and Practice in Technology Enhanced Learning*, *17*(1), 4. Advance online publication. DOI: 10.1186/s41039-022-00179-x

Sarfraz, M., Ivascu, L., Abdullah, M., Ozturk, I., & Tariq, J. (2022). Exploring a Pathway to Sustainable Performance in Manufacturing Firms: The Interplay between Innovation Capabilities, Green Process and Product Innovations and Digital Leadership. *Sustainability (Basel)*, *14*(10), 5945. DOI: 10.3390/su14105945

Saxena, A., Ramaswamy, M., Beale, J., Marciniuk, D., & Smith, P. (2021). Striving for the United Nations (UN) sustainable development goals (SDGs): What will it take? *Discover Sustainability*, *2*(1), 1–14. DOI: 10.1007/s43621-021-00029-8

Schultz, T. W. (1961). Investment in Human Capital. *The American Economic Review*, *51*(1), 1–17. https://www.jstor.org/stable/1818907

Soergel, B., Kriegler, E., Weindl, I., Rauner, S., Dirnaichner, A., Ruhe, C., Hofmann, M., Bauer, N., Bertram, C., Bodirsky, B. L., Leimbach, M., Leininger, J., Levesque, A., Luderer, G., Pehl, M., Wingens, C., Baumstark, L., Beier, F., Dietrich, J. P., & Popp, A. (2021). A sustainable development pathway for climate action within the UN 2039 Agenda. *Nature Climate Change*, *11*(8), 656–664. DOI: 10.1038/s41558-021-01098-3

Sosa, E., Salinas Ibañez, J., & de Benito, C. (2018). Factores que afectan la incorporación de Tecnologías Emergentes en el aula: Una mirada desde expertos (docentes) Iberoamericanos. *Revista Espacios*, *39*(2), 1–15.

Tanucan, J., Negrido, C., & Malaga, G. (2022). Digital Leadership of School Heads and Job Satisfaction of Teachers in the Philippines during the Pandemic. *International Journal of Learning. Teaching and Educational Research*, *21*(10), 1–18. DOI: 10.26803/ijlter.21.10.1

Tebenko, V., Kutsai, N., Shashyna, M., Omelianenko, O., & Bakushevych, I. (2024). Digital transformation in business: The impact of technology on efficiency, innovation and competitiveness. *Economic Affairs*, *69*(Special Issue), 307–315. DOI: 10.46852/0424-2513.1.2024.32

United Nations. (2018). *Sustainable Development Goals*. United Nations.

United Nations. (2024). *The sustainable development goals report 2024*. United Nations. Retrieved September 4, 2024, from https://www.un.org/sustainabledevelopment/ progress-report

Valencia, M. (2005). El capital humano, otro activo de su empresa. *Entramado*, 1 (2), 20 – 33. https://www.redalyc.org/pdf/2654/265420471004.pdf

Vial, G. (2019). Understanding digital transformation: A review and a research agenda. *The Journal of Strategic Information Systems*, *28*(2), 118–144. DOI: 10.1016/j.jsis.2019.01.003

Wang, T., Lin, X., & Sheng, F. (2022). Digital leadership and exploratory innovation: From the dual perspectives of strategic orientation and organizational culture. *Frontiers in Psychology*, *13*, 902693. DOI: 10.3389/fpsyg.2022.902693

Wengler, S., Hildmann, G., & Vossebein, U. (2021). Digital transformation in sales as an evolving process. *Journal of Business and Industrial Marketing*, *36*(4), 599–614. DOI: 10.1108/JBIM-03-2020-0124

Westerman, G., Bonnet, D., & McAfee, A. (2014). *Leading digital: Turning technology into business transformation*. Harvard Business Press.

Zeike, S., Bradbury, K., Lindert, L., & Pfaff, H. (2019). Digital leadership skills and associations with psychological well-being. *International Journal of Environmental Research and Public Health*, *16*(14), 2628. Advance online publication. DOI: 10.3390/ijerph16142628

Živković, Ž., & Panić, M. (2020). Development of science and education in theWestern Balkan countries: Competitiveness with the EU. *Scientometrics*, *124*(3), 2319–2339. DOI: 10.1007/s11192-020-03554-x

Živković, Z., & Panić, M. (2024). PhD studies in transition conditions – the basis for educational system and economic development: A case study Serbia. *Serbian Journal of Management*, *19*(2), 339–355. DOI: 10.5937/sjm19-53172

Zulu, S. L., Saad, A. M., Ajayi, S. O., Dulaimi, M., & Unuigbe, M. (2023). Digital leadership enactment in the construction industry: Barriers undermining effective transformation. *Engineering, Construction, and Architectural Management*, *31*(10), 3493–3514. DOI: 10.1108/ECAM-05-2022-0491

ADDITIONAL READING

Aroca, M. (2025). Habilidades Contemporáneas Adaptadas a la Gestión Del Talento Humano En La Era Digital. *PSICOLOGÍA UNEMI, 9*(16), 69-78. https://ojs.unemi.edu.ec/index.php/faso-unemi/article/view/2197

Arroyo Monreal, M., & Hermoso Traba, R. (2019). *Current needs in talent management: 4.0 solutions*. Zaragoza University. https://core.ac.uk/download/pdf/290000833.pdf

Basco, A. I., De Azevedo, B., Harraca, M., & Kersner, S. (2020). *Latin America in motion: Competencies and skills in the Fourth Industrial Revolution*. Inter-American Development Bank., DOI: 10.18235/0002132

Chiu, T. K. F., Xia, Q., Zhou, X., Chai, C. S., & Cheng, M. (2023). Systematic literature review on opportunities, challenges, and future research recommendations of artificial intelligence in education. *Computers and Education: Artificial Intelligence, 4*(100118), 100118. Advance online publication. DOI: 10.1016/j.caeai.2022.100118

Dung, D. A., Toan, N. T., Minh, N. D., & Anh, N. Q. (2026). Reimagining quality: Artificial intelligence, governance and the politics of data in higher education. *Higher Education for the Future, 13*(1), 50–73. DOI: 10.1177/23476311251386123

Filippi, E., Bannò, M., & Trento, S. (2023). Automation technologies and their impact on employment: A review, synthesis and future research agenda. *Technological Forecasting and Social Change, 191*, 122448. DOI: 10.1016/j.techfore.2023.122448

Mora-Sánchez, D., & Guerrero-Marín, L. (2020). Industria 4.0: El reto en la ruta hacia las organizaciones digitales. *Estudios De La Gestión: Revista Internacional De Administración, 8*, 186–209. DOI: 10.32719/25506641.2020.8.7

OECD. (2024). The potential impact of artificial intelligence on equity and inclusion in education, In *OECD artificial intelligence papers*. Organisation for Economic Co-Operation and Development (OECD). https://doi.org/DOI: 10.1787/dee339a8-en

Rodríguez-Alegre, L. R., Trujillo-Valdiviezo, G., Egusquiza-Rodríguez, M. J., & López-Padilla, R.-P. (2021). Revolución industrial 4.0: La brecha digital en Latinoamérica. *Revista Arbitrada Interdisciplinaria Koinonía, 6*(11), 147–162. DOI: 10.35381/r.k.v6i11.1219

Zhu, J., Zhang, Y., Qiu, T., & Pan, Y. (2025). Graduate Education in China. In Feng, Z., Wang, Q., & Liu, N. (Eds.), *Education in China and the World*. Springer., DOI: 10.1007/978-981-97-7415-9_6

ENDNOTES

[1] This chapter is a research product funded by the Instituto Politécnico Nacional-México [SIP number 20260574]

Chapter 8
Prioritising Digital Talent Initiatives in Universities: Evidence From Turkey

Tuğçe Şimşek
http://orcid.org/0000-0003-3256-4348
Gümüşhane University, Turkey

Aybala Şimşek
Burdur Mehmet Akif Ersoy University, Turkey

Ahmet Bahadır Şimşek
Gümüşhane University, Turkey

ABSTRACT

Universities are under growing pressure to advance digital transformation, yet priorities in digital talent management often remain unclear. This chapter develops a document-based multi-criteria decision framework to identify and compare such priorities across universities of different institutional scale in Türkiye. Drawing on public strategic plans, quality reports, distance education documentation, and staff development texts from Anadolu, Sakarya, and Tarsus Universities, the study constructs a decision matrix covering three initiatives and six evaluation criteria. Criterion weights are calculated through entropy, and initiative rankings are generated with TOPSIS. The findings show that digital infrastructure support has the strongest discriminating power. Strengthening distance education and LMS infrastructure emerges as the top priority, followed by a needs-based in-service training system and a digital competence development programme. The chapter offers a transparent and transferable framework for setting scale-sensitive digital transformation priorities in higher education.

DOI: 10.4018/979-8-3373-8959-2.ch008

INTRODUCTION

Digital transformation in higher education is often described as a technical upgrade that has accelerated in recent years. Its institutional significance, however, runs much deeper. Benavides et al. (2020) show that digital transformation in higher education entails a multi-layered reorganisation that extends beyond teaching processes to management, service delivery, and stakeholder relations. Mohamed Hashim et al. (2022) likewise argue that it is closely tied to strategic orientation, organisational agility, and long-term competitive capacity. Bisri et al. (2023), in turn, emphasise that digital initiatives rarely generate their intended effects in the absence of leadership, strategic clarity, organisational culture, and implementation consistency. What is changing, then, is not simply the technological toolkit of the university. What is changing is the way the institution organises learning, circulates knowledge, develops its staff, and governs change.

The problem, therefore, is not technology adoption in itself. In higher education, digital transformation is frequently discussed through platforms, data systems, online learning environments, and technical infrastructure. Yet these structures do not operate in isolation once they enter institutional life. Gkrimpizi et al. (2023) show that barriers to digital transformation in higher education cannot be reduced to technological constraints alone; strategic, organisational, cultural, and human factors are equally decisive. Similarly, Marks et al. (2020) demonstrate that the absence of a holistic vision, insufficient digital competence, and fragmented data structures can weaken organisational progress. The real institutional question is thus broader than which technologies should be adopted. It concerns how these technologies become meaningful within the university and what forms of human capacity are required to sustain them.

For that reason, the human dimension of digital transformation cannot be treated as peripheral. Bond et al. (2018) show that digital media use in higher education has expanded considerably, but that this use often remains confined to narrow and relatively basic functions. Nurhas et al. (2021) further demonstrate that the rapid digitalisation of the pandemic period placed substantial pressure on pedagogical preparation, workflow design, coordination, and institutional support systems. Taken together, these studies point to a recurring pattern. Universities may be able to mobilise technologies quickly, yet institutional learning and workforce preparedness do not always advance at the same pace. When that gap widens, digital transformation becomes less a coherent strategic trajectory than a patchwork of partial adjustments.

At this point, the human resources dimension becomes a strategic threshold rather than a secondary concern. Razali et al. (2024) show that research on talent management in higher education has expanded significantly in recent years and has been closely linked to institutional sustainability, performance, and competitive advantage. Ramaditya et al. (2022) likewise suggest that talent management practices are positively associated with university performance, particularly when they reinforce organisational learning and transformation capacity. At the same time, Allui and Sahni (2016) note that research on strategic human resource management in higher education remains fragmented, especially in relation to the connection between institutional strategy and investments in people. This makes the relationship between digitalisation and talent management impossible to treat as a side issue. The success of digital transformation depends not only on installing systems, but on developing the knowledge, skills, organisational support, and role configurations that allow those systems to become part of institutional routine.

This challenge is intensified by the nature of academic work itself. Naidoo-Chetty and du Plessis (2021) show that academics operate under growing job demands, time pressure, and multi-role expectations. Robson and Mavin (2014) similarly argue that the effectiveness of training and development depends on the alignment of programme design, staff perceptions, and organisational context. Decramer et al. (2013) further demonstrate that performance management systems can have far-reaching consequences for staff satisfaction. Read together, these studies suggest that digital initiatives directed at the academic workforce cannot be reduced to training provision or the introduction of new tools. Each new digital arrangement also reshapes workload, role definitions, evaluation procedures, and institutional expectations. Under such conditions, the key managerial question is not whether digital talent initiatives matter, but which initiatives should be prioritised first and on what organisational basis.

That question places the study squarely within a decision-making problem. Universities are often expected to respond to several needs at once: digital competence development, distance education and learning management system infrastructures, redesigned in-service training systems, assessment mechanisms, and governance arrangements. Yet most institutions cannot invest in all of these areas with equal intensity or at the same pace. Mustafa and Goh (1996) show that multi-criteria decision-making approaches can support complex higher education management problems such as resource allocation and prioritisation. Hashemi Petrudi et al. (2022) likewise demonstrate that such frameworks provide analytical clarity in multidimensional institutional settings. In this context, prioritising digital talent initiatives is not simply a matter of listing preferences. It requires the joint assessment of strategic alignment, human resource impact, digital infrastructure support, implementation maturity, traceability, and governance support.

Türkiye provides an analytically valuable setting for examining this problem. The reason is not that the country represents a universal model, but that it combines system-wide digital transformation pressures with marked institutional variation. Kuzu (2020) shows that university strategic plans in Türkiye increasingly foreground digital transformation, often with a strong emphasis on learning technologies and distance education. Keskin et al. (2022), examining the official websites of Turkish state universities during the early pandemic period, demonstrate that institutions did not provide pedagogical and technical support to teaching staff with the same intensity during the emergency transition to distance education. Aytar and Arslan (2024) further show that although the rhetoric of the digital age is visible in Turkish university strategic plans, institutional priorities and preparedness levels are unevenly distributed. Türkiye is therefore a useful context precisely because digitalisation is a shared pressure, whereas institutional responses differ in terms of scale, resources, strategy, and infrastructure.

This context also sharpens the research gap. The digital transformation literature has generated substantial insight into technical and organisational change. The talent management and human resources literature has illuminated staff development, performance, workload, and institutional capacity. The multi-criteria decision-making literature, for its part, has shown how complex institutional preferences can be structured systematically. Yet studies that bring these three strands together in a document-based and comparative framework remain limited. We know that universities are affected by digital transformation. We also know that the human resources dimension is critical. What is addressed much less systematically is which digital talent initiatives universities appear to prioritise, and how such priorities can be analysed in a structured way.

This study addresses that gap by prioritising digital talent initiatives through a document-based multi-criteria decision-making framework across universities in Türkiye representing different institutional scales. In doing so, it moves the digital transformation debate beyond a general narrative of modernisation and into the terrain of institutional priority setting. It also repositions the discussion of talent management from a largely normative field of best practice to a decision problem shaped by resource allocation, institutional visibility, and organisational commitment. The contribution of the study lies here. Rather than focusing only on the technical dimensions of digitalisation or on isolated human resources subthemes, the chapter analytically identifies which initiatives assume greater priority within a comparative document-based design.

The scope of the study should be stated clearly from the outset. The chapter does not seek to measure the actual implementation success of universities or to capture the full experience of digital transformation. Instead, it examines the traces of institutional priorities that become visible in official documents. Put differently, the study asks which initiatives universities have institutionalised more strongly within the field of digital talent management. Framing the problem in this way brings the human dimension of digital transformation onto a more measurable analytical ground.

The next section develops that ground conceptually and clarifies the relationship between digital transformation and digital talent management.

1. CONCEPTUAL BACKGROUND

This section clarifies the conceptual architecture of the chapter. Its central question is straightforward: how should the relationship between digital transformation in higher education and the prioritisation of digital talent initiatives be understood? Answering that question requires more than defining the key concepts in isolation. It requires showing the chain through which organisational restructuring creates new demands on human capacity and, in turn, turns those demands into a problem of prioritisation. The discussion therefore proceeds in three steps: first, it conceptualises digital transformation as organisational restructuring; second, it explains why this restructuring places human capacity at the centre; and third, it shows why the resulting pressures produce a need to rank digital talent initiatives rather than treat them as equally urgent.

In this study, digital transformation is not understood as the mere addition of technical innovations to an existing organisation. Benavides et al. (2020) show that digital transformation in higher education simultaneously affects teaching, administration, stakeholder engagement, and the flow of information. Mohamed Hashim et al. (2022) likewise emphasise its close relationship with strategic orientation and organisational agility. Bisri et al. (2023), meanwhile, show that the success of transformation depends on the alignment of leadership, strategic clarity, organisational culture, and implementation consistency. Read together, these studies suggest that digital transformation should be understood as a reconfiguration of the university's operating logic. What changes is not only the technological environment, but also the processes, roles, coordination mechanisms, decision channels, and learning capacities through which the institution functions.

This understanding also clarifies why digital transformation cannot be explained without reference to human capacity. Gkrimpizi et al. (2023) show that barriers to digital transformation in higher education extend across strategic, organisational, cultural, and human dimensions. Bond et al. (2018) similarly note that, despite the visible spread of digital tools, their use in teaching and learning often remains limited to relatively basic functions. Nurhas et al. (2021) further demonstrate that rapid digital transitions place significant pressure on pedagogical preparation, workflow design, and institutional coordination. The underlying conclusion is consistent across these studies. Technology does not produce transformation automatically. Transformation deepens only when technical infrastructures are matched by the human capacity required to interpret, implement, adapt, and sustain them.

At that point, talent management can no longer be treated as a merely supportive human resources activity. Allui and Sahni (2016) emphasise that strategic human resource management in higher education must be linked more directly to organisational strategy. Ramaditya et al. (2022) connect talent management to organisational performance, knowledge management, and transformation capacity. Razali et al. (2024), moreover, show that research on talent management in higher education has intensified rapidly and is increasingly framed in strategic terms. In this light, talent management refers to the identification, development, support, and retention of human capacity in line with institutional objectives. Under digital conditions, however, that definition broadens further. Rincón-Rodríguez et al. (2025) show that talent management in higher education must now be considered alongside technological skills, data literacy, digital agility, and adaptability to change. Digital talent management, in this study, is therefore defined as the strategic design and governance of the competencies, learning mechanisms, role adjustments, and support structures that universities require under conditions of digital transformation.

This definition needs to be specified within the university context. Universities are not conventional service organisations. They combine teaching, research, societal engagement, and administrative coordination within the same institutional space, while also operating through academic autonomy, disciplinary diversity, and multiple stakeholder expectations. Naidoo-Chetty and du Plessis (2021) show that academics work under intensifying workloads, time pressure, and role multiplicity. Robson and Mavin (2014) emphasise that training and development are effective only when programme design, staff perceptions, and institutional context are aligned. Decramer et al. (2013) likewise show that performance management systems have significant consequences for staff satisfaction. Taken together, these studies indicate that interventions targeting academic staff rarely produce a single effect. A new digital platform, for instance, changes not only technical routines but also workflows, role expectations, training needs, and the logic of evaluation. Digital talent management in higher education is therefore not a narrow skills issue; it is a management problem tied to the rebuilding of institutional capacity.

Once this point is established, the conceptual chain becomes clearer. As digital transformation intensifies, universities become more dependent on technological systems and digitally mediated forms of coordination. That dependence, in turn, exposes gaps between existing human capacity and the level of performance expected from staff and institutions. As these gaps become visible, multiple initiatives emerge at once: digital competence development, stronger infrastructure, redesigned in-service training, governance arrangements, and monitoring mechanisms. The result is not simply a longer list of needs. It is a problem of choice. Universities cannot invest in all initiatives with the same intensity, on the same timeline, or with the same institutional payoff. For that reason, the human dimension of digital transformation becomes, conceptually, a problem of prioritisation rather than a generic call for improvement.

This relationship comes into sharper focus when strategic planning and organisational visibility are brought into the picture. Biondi and Russo (2022) show that strategic planning and performance management are mutually constitutive in universities. Kuzu (2020) likewise demonstrates that while strategic plans often foreground digital transformation, this emphasis is not distributed with the same depth or content across institutions. Aytar and Arslan (2024) further show that the rhetoric of the digital age is visible in the strategic plans of Turkish universities, yet institutional priorities and preparedness levels vary markedly. These findings suggest that digital talent management needs do not arise only from internal organisational pressures. They are also shaped by what the institution chooses to formalise, render visible, and attach to strategic meaning. From this perspective, document-based analysis is not merely a convenient source of data. It is conceptually appropriate for tracing how institutional priorities are articulated and stabilised.

Within this framework, digital talent initiatives are organised in this study around three focal areas. The first is digital competence development programmes, which encompass arrangements designed to strengthen the ability of academic and administrative staff to use digital tools effectively, work in digital environments, engage with data, and align their practice with pedagogical needs. The second is the strengthening of distance education and learning management system infrastructure, understood not simply as the presence of technology but as its sustainable, scalable, and process-aligned operation within the institution. The third is a needs-analysis-based in-service training system, where training is designed not as an ad hoc activity but as a structured response linked to institutional requirements, development goals, and evaluation mechanisms. What unites these three areas is that each connects the human dimension of digital transformation to institutional capacity. They therefore provide the conceptual basis from which the study's alternatives are derived.

The chapter, then, rests on four propositions. First, digital transformation in higher education should be understood as institutional restructuring rather than mere technical change. Second, this restructuring places human capacity at the centre of organisational adaptation. Third, the university context, because of its functional complexity and layered expectations, renders talent management more differentiated and context-sensitive. Fourth, this entire configuration turns digital talent management into a prioritisation problem that requires the structured ranking of initiatives. The next section shows how the literature has addressed these issues in a fragmented manner and where the present study locates its contribution.

2. LITERATURE REVIEW

The literature on digital transformation in higher education has expanded substantially, but this expansion has not always produced conceptual integration. Closely related problems are often examined on separate analytical planes. Some studies focus on digital infrastructure and online learning capacity; others turn to organisational strategy and human resources; still others address complex institutional choices through multi-criteria decision-making methods. This fragmentation is partly a sign of the field's richness. At the same time, it leaves an important gap. Technical transformation, human capacity, and prioritisation are not separate realities inside universities, yet the literature often treats them as if they were. For that reason, this review is organised around three strands: digital transformation in higher education, talent management and human resource transformation, and multi-criteria decision-making. The aim is not simply to catalogue prior studies, but to show where these strands converge and where they still leave the central problem unresolved.

The first strand consists of studies on digital transformation in higher education. Its earlier and more dominant orientation has focused on the visible instruments of digitalisation and their operational consequences. Bond et al. (2018), examining the use of digital media by students and academic staff in Germany, show that while digital tools are widespread in universities, they are often used in fairly limited ways. Keskin et al. (2022), analysing the official web content of Turkish state universities during the early pandemic period, likewise show that institutions could implement technical arrangements rapidly during the transition to emergency distance education, but could not organise pedagogical and institutional support with the same intensity. These studies make an important contribution because they render the visible face of digitalisation—tools, platforms, and access—empirically traceable. Their limitation, however, is that the deeper logic behind institutional choices often remains implicit. Why one initiative acquires greater priority than another is rarely addressed directly.

A second cluster within this strand approaches digital transformation at a more institutional level. Benavides et al. (2020), in their systematic review, show that digital transformation simultaneously affects teaching, management, stakeholder relations, and information flow. Mohamed Hashim et al. (2022) connect digital transformation to strategy, managerial agility, and organisational sustainability. Marks et al. (2020), through a digital maturity framework, demonstrate that weak data integrity, insufficient digital competence, and the absence of a shared vision constrain transformation capacity. Bisri et al. (2023) further identify leadership, strategic clarity, cultural alignment, and implementation consistency as central success factors. This body of work makes an important contribution by moving digitalisation from the level of tools to that of organisational restructuring. Even so, it pays less systematic attention to a key downstream question: which human-resource-related initiatives should institutions prioritise in response to these pressures? The literature defines the pressure well, but does not always treat its implications for institutional priority-setting as an analytical problem in its own right.

A third cluster within the digital transformation literature concentrates on strategic plans and documentary visibility. Kuzu (2020), analysing university strategic plans, shows that the discourse of digital transformation is visible in institutional documents, though often concentrated around distance education and learning technologies. Aytar and Arslan (2024) likewise show that the rhetoric of the digital age is present in Turkish university strategic plans, while the priorities and readiness levels articulated under that heading vary across institutions. This finding matters because it suggests that universities do not merely experience digital transformation; they also frame it through documentary language and strategic signalling. Yet these studies, for all their strength in documenting institutional visibility, stop short of translating documentary traces into a structured set of action priorities. The digital transformation literature therefore offers broad explanatory power, from technical infrastructure to organisational strategy, but remains limited in placing the prioritisation of digital talent initiatives at its centre.

The second strand of literature centres on talent management and human resource transformation. A dominant tendency here is to link talent management in higher education to organisational performance and strategic capacity. Razali et al. (2024), in their bibliometric analysis, show that the field has expanded rapidly in recent years and has clustered around performance, competitiveness, and sustainability. Ramaditya et al. (2022) examine the relationship between talent management practices in higher education and performance through the lens of knowledge management and transformation capacity. Allui and Sahni (2016) argue that strategic human resource management in universities is often implemented in ways that remain disconnected from institutional strategy, and that a more integrated framework is therefore needed. Collectively, these studies shift human resources from the margins of higher education administration to the centre of organisational strategy. What remains less developed, however, is the question of which initiative should take priority under which conditions.

A second cluster within this strand focuses on staff development, competence requirements, and changing role expectations. Robson and Mavin (2014) show that training and development in universities are effective only when staff perceptions, institutional context, and implementation design are aligned. Rincón-Rodríguez et al. (2025) further argue that, in the 4.0 era of human talent management, universities must account for digital agility, data literacy, and adaptability to change. These studies make the capability demands of the digital age much more visible. Yet the same limitation persists. The literature is strong in identifying which competencies matter, but weaker in specifying how institutions should prioritise the initiatives designed to build them. The informational base is rich; the logic of prioritisation remains underdeveloped.

A third cluster addresses academic labour, workload, performance, and retention. Naidoo-Chetty and du Plessis (2021) show that academic staff increasingly work under heavy workload, role multiplicity, and time pressure. Decramer et al. (2013) demonstrate that performance management culture and system design have decisive consequences for staff satisfaction. Ashraf (2019) likewise shows that working conditions and staff retention have indirect but significant effects on educational quality. This body of research makes clear that human resource decisions in universities are not merely administrative preferences; they directly shape institutional life and the quality of education. Yet within this strand too, the question of which initiatives should be prioritised under conditions of digital transformation remains secondary. The human dimension is foregrounded, but the problem of selecting between competing initiatives is not.

The third strand consists of studies on multi-criteria decision-making and prioritisation. Its core contribution lies in structuring multi-dimensional problems within systematic decision spaces rather than leaving them at the level of isolated judgement. Mustafa and Goh (1996) show that multi-criteria models have long been applicable to higher education management problems such as planning and resource allocation. Hashemi Petrudi et al. (2022) demonstrate the usefulness of a multi-criteria framework for complex educational problems by structuring performance measurement in higher education through the Fuzzy Delphi and Best-Worst Method. Zhang and Liu (2023), in evaluating the quality of online teaching through Entropy and TOPSIS, show that a multi-dimensional criterion structure can make decision outcomes more interpretable. Karakaş et al. (2016), by examining university staff work behaviour performance through Entropy-based TOPSIS, likewise show that human-resource-related variables can be handled within an MCDM framework. Methodologically, this literature is highly robust. It makes relative differences between alternatives visible and translates complex preferences into a structured numerical form.

Even here, however, an important limitation remains. A large share of current MCDM applications relies on expert judgement, survey data, or performance outputs from a single organisation. What is usually measured is outcome performance, whereas traces of organisational priority and documentary orientation occupy a less central place. As a result, the methodological instrument is strong, but the problem definition is not always linked to organisational visibility or document structure. This is a particularly important gap for the prioritisation of digital capability initiatives, because universities often make decisions not only through enacted practice but also through document-based strategic orientation. Institutional priorities are frequently visible in strategic plans, quality reports, distance learning documents, and staff development texts. Yet the MCDM literature remains limited in converting that visibility directly into decision inputs.

Taken together, these three strands produce a clear analytical picture. The digital transformation literature explains technical and organisational change. The talent management literature makes visible the human-capacity and organisational-development dimensions of that change. The MCDM literature provides the tools needed to structure prioritisation. What remains limited is research that brings these strands together within a document-based and comparative framework for analysing digital talent initiatives in higher education. That is the precise point at which the present study intervenes. Universities face digital transformation pressures, confront human resource challenges, and must make choices under constrained conditions. Yet the literature still does not adequately bring these pressures, capacities, and prioritisation logics onto the same analytical plane. Table 1 summarises this configuration.

Table 1. Analytical summary of the three strands of literature

Literature strand	Dominant focus	Gaps in the literature
Digital transformation in higher education	Infrastructure, digital maturity, institutional strategy, barriers to transformation	Priority order of human resource initiatives
Talent management and HRM	Competence, performance, workload, development, retention	Systematic prioritisation across initiatives
Multi-criteria decision-making	Criterion-based weighting and ranking	Document-based and comparative organisational priority analysis

The pattern captured in Table 1 defines the knowledge gap addressed in this study. Research on digital transformation in higher education clarifies the pressures that drive institutional change. Talent management studies deepen the human-capacity dimension of that picture. Multi-criteria decision-making studies, meanwhile, provide the analytical basis for prioritisation. Even so, research that comparatively evaluates universities' digital talent initiatives through publicly available institutional documents and ranks them systematically remains limited. The present study therefore brings technical transformation, human capacity, and decision analytics into the same comparative framework.

3. METHODOLOGY

This study employs a document-based, comparative multi-criteria decision-making design to prioritise digital talent initiatives across three universities in Türkiye representing different institutional scales. The design is analytical rather than statistically representative. Its purpose is to compare patterned institutional variation across deliberately selected cases, rather than to estimate how all universities in Türkiye would rank the same initiatives. In line with Bowen's (2009) understanding of document analysis, the study treats institutional documents not as background material but as empirical traces of organisational priorities and implementation logic. Accordingly, the institutional effects of digital transformation are examined through strategic plans, quality documents, materials relating to distance learning infrastructure, and texts focused on staff development. An initiative that recurs across institutional documents, has an operational counterpart, and is supported by monitoring mechanisms is taken to signal institutional priority. For that reason, the study relies on publicly available institutional traces rather than subjective statements. In this way, the decision problem is relocated to an analytical framework that examines, through documentation, which initiatives universities appear to support more systematically and institutionalise more strongly within the field of digital talent management.

The study uses purposeful case selection. Anadolu University, Sakarya University, and Tarsus University were chosen not as a representative sample of Turkish higher education, but as analytically contrasting cases that make institutional scale visible within a common national context. The selection was guided by three considerations: variation in institutional scale, the availability of comparable and publicly accessible document sets, and the presence of documentary material across strategic planning, quality assurance, distance learning infrastructure, and staff development. This design makes it possible to examine how universities of different scale render digital talent priorities visible in their official documents, while maintaining a shared analytical basis for comparison. The aim, therefore, is not statistical generalisation, but analytically grounded comparison across cases with different institutional capacities and document ecologies.

The dataset comprises five document groups. The first group consists of strategic plans. These documents reveal the underlying decision-making logic regarding institutional goals, capacity development, digitalisation strategies, and human resources. The second group comprises internal institutional evaluation reports and quality assurance documents. These texts make it possible to assess the extent to which plans have been translated into structures that are traceable and assessable. The third group comprises official pages and documents relating to the distance learning centre, the learning management system, and the digital learning infrastructure. The fourth group consists of in-service training plans, staff development announcements, human resources policies, and relevant guidelines. The fifth group comprises supplementary institutional documents such as digital transformation coordination, technical frameworks, activity reports, and training evaluation tools. The document universe was bounded prior to coding in order to preserve comparability across cases. Four criteria guided document selection: the document had to be published by an official institutional source, be publicly accessible, contain content directly related to digital transformation and talent management, and provide insight into current institutional practices.

The analysis unit comprises digital talent initiative alternatives derived from the consolidation of recurring themes within the documents. This approach creates an intermediate layer that transforms the document corpus into a decision matrix. The texts were first scanned using open coding logic, after which themes with a high degree of organisational recurrence were brought together. However, conceptual proximity alone was not deemed sufficient for inclusion in the final set of alternatives. For an alternative to be included in the decision matrix, it was required to leave a direct or partially direct trace in the relevant university documents; in other words, it had to have a concrete counterpart in strategic, operational or evaluation documents. As a result of this process, three alternatives were identified. These are the digital competence development programme, the strengthening of distance learning and the LMS infrastructure, and the in-service training system based on needs analysis. Although the education and HR analytics and evaluation system, along with the digital transformation governance and coordination model, appeared analytically meaningful in the document review, they were not included in the final decision matrix because they did not provide direct documentary support with the same clarity and at a comparable level across all universities. Consequently, the existence of alternatives is linked not to abstract conceptual proximity, but to the degree of textual visibility and institutional concreteness.

The evaluation criteria were formulated by combining dimensions highlighted in the literature on digital transformation and talent management with recurring structural patterns identified in the document review. Thus, the decision problem has been balanced on both theoretical and empirical grounds. Six criteria have been identified. Strategic alignment refers to the extent to which the initiative is explicitly incorporated into the organisation's strategic plan and quality documents. The impact on human resources and talent indicates the initiative's potential influence on the competence development, role transformation and organisational capacity of academic or administrative staff. Digital infrastructure support measures the initiative's relationship with technical systems, LMS, distance learning infrastructure, data flow and IT capacity. Implementation maturity reflects the degree to which the initiative has been institutionalised in the form of plans, programmes, guidelines or activities, rather than remaining merely at the level of rhetoric. Traceability and assessability indicate whether the initiative can be measured within reports, surveys, performance indicators or quality cycles. Governance support, meanwhile, is based on the existence of relevant coordination units, organisational structures, policy documents or corporate accountability mechanisms. Table 2 presents the criteria set alongside the alternatives.

Table 2. Alternatives and criteria used in the decision matrix

Alternatives	Criteria
Digital competence development programme	Strategic alignment
Strengthening distance learning and LMS infrastructure	Human resources and talent impact
In-service training system based on needs analysis	Digital infrastructure support
	Implementation maturity
	Traceability and evaluability
	Governance support

The document coding process was carried out in two stages. In the first stage, the documents were read, and phrases related to digitisation, human resources, competence development, distance learning, evaluation, coordination and infrastructure were extracted. In the second stage, these phrases were grouped under a set of criteria and a score between 1 and 5 was generated for each alternative. The logic behind the coding goes deeper than a simple frequency count. The mere mention of a concept in the text was not deemed sufficient. The fact that the relevant initiative was listed as a target in the strategic document, had authorisation for implementation in the operational document, and was linked to a monitoring mechanism in the quality document resulted in a higher score. Consequently, the scoring system measures both visibility and organisational intensity. The scoring scale used in Table 3 is provided.

Table 3. Document-based scoring scale

Score	Definition
1	Very weak document trace
2	Limited and indirect documentary evidence
3	Moderate visibility
4	Robust and transparent document support
5	Very strong, multi-document and institutional support

Once the coding was completed, a separate decision matrix was created for each university. Subsequently, an integrated matrix was obtained for the purpose of comparative evaluation. At this stage, each row of the matrix represents an alternative, and each column represents a criterion. The general decision matrix is defined as $X = \left[x_{ij}\right]$. Here, $i = 1,2,\ldots,m$ denotes the alternatives, and $j = 1,2,\ldots,n$ denotes the criteria. In the study,$m = 3$ and$n = 6$ were adopted. Each cell of the matrix represents the document-based score of the relevant alternative with respect to the relevant criterion. Thus, the qualitative document data has been converted into a numerical decision space through a controlled coding process.

Criterion weights were calculated using the Entropy method. Entropy is an objective weighting approach that measures the information content and discriminatory capacity of each criterion. The logic is simple. If a criterion produces values that are very close to one another across all alternatives, that criterion carries limited information for the decision problem. Conversely, a criterion that distinctly distinguishes the alternatives contains more information and receives a higher weight. Therefore, Entropy uses the amount of information arising from the data's own internal structure rather than subjective priorities assigned by the decision-maker from the outside.

The first step of the Entropy algorithm is the column-wise normalisation of the decision matrix. As all criteria are defined in terms of utility, the following transformation has been used.

$$p_{ij} = \frac{x_{ij}}{\sum_{i=1}^{m} x_{ij}}$$

Here, `$p_{ij}$` denotes the normalised ratio of the alternative `$i$` under the criterion `$j$`. In the second step, the entropy value is calculated for each criterion.

$$e_j = -k\sum_{i=1}^{m} p_{ij} \ln\left(p_{ij}\right)$$

In this equation, ` ` is the entropy value of the ` ` criterion. The constant ` ` maps the entropy value to the range between 0 and 1. In the third step, the degree of differentiation for each criterion is determined.

Here, as increases, the criterion's discriminatory power increases. In the final step, the criterion weights are calculated.

Thus, an objective weight vector satisfying the condition is obtained. This vector quantitatively indicates which columns of the decision matrix carry higher information.

The ranking of alternatives was performed using the TOPSIS method. The fundamental assumption of TOPSIS is that the most suitable alternative is the one closest to the positive ideal solution and furthest from the negative ideal solution. This method was chosen because, in multi-criteria decision-making problems, it considers not only the total score but also the relative position with respect to the ideal solution. In the first step, the decision matrix is normalised using the vector norm.

In the second step, the weights obtained via entropy are multiplied by the normalised matrix to produce a weighted normalised matrix.

In the third step, the positive ideal solution and the negative ideal solution are determined. As all criteria are utility-oriented, the positive ideal solution consists of the column maximums, whilst the negative ideal solution consists of the column minimums.

In the fourth step, the Euclidean distance of each alternative from the positive and negative ideal solutions is calculated.

In the final step, the relative proximity coefficient is determined.

As this value approaches 1, the alternative's proximity to the ideal solution increases. Accordingly, the alternatives are ranked from highest to lowest, yielding a priority sequence. This ranking indicates which digital capability initiative is stronger in terms of document-based organisational visibility, maturity and distinctiveness.

The reliability of the method is supported by three mechanisms. The first mechanism is document triangulation. The same initiative has been tracked across strategic plan, quality report and operational document levels as far as possible. The second mechanism is explicit coding rules. Criterion definitions and the scoring scale were fixed prior to coding, thereby limiting retrospective interpretation bias. The third mechanism is sensitivity analysis. By introducing limited deviations in entropy weights, the extent to which the TOPSIS ranking changed was tested. This assessed whether the results were overly dependent on a single set of weights.

The study is based solely on publicly available institutional documents, and this creates a clear methodological boundary. A direct equivalence between document visibility and actual practice cannot be assumed. Some universities may have stronger practices than their public documents reveal, whereas others may produce a more visible documentary profile. Accordingly, the findings support analytic rather than statistical generalisation. They show how digital talent priorities become institutionally visible across the selected cases; they do not claim to describe the entire higher education system in Türkiye. For this reason, the resulting ranking should be interpreted as a prioritisation output shaped by institutional intent, institutional visibility, and institutional maturity. The study therefore presents its findings not as absolute truth, but within the logic of document-based decision support. In that sense, it moves the discussion of digital talent management away from abstract discourse and repositions it within a measurable, traceable, and comparable decision framework.

4. FINDINGS

The analysis was conducted across three alternatives and six criteria. The flow of findings is structured to follow the logic of the calculation chain. First, the discriminatory power of the criteria was determined, followed by a demonstration of how this weighting structure affects the relative positioning of the alternatives.

The first analytical layer consists of criterion weights. The entropy approach measures not the normative importance of the criteria, but the extent to which they distinguish between alternatives. Therefore, the weights obtained here indicate which column carries higher information content within the decision space. As the column values of a criterion converge, its discriminatory capacity weakens, whilst the weight of columns that create more distinct differences between alternatives increases. The results have produced a distinct asymmetry in this regard. The highest discriminatory power among the criteria emerged in the digital infrastructure support dimension. Governance support ranked second, whilst the remaining four criteria showed a closely clustered distribution. This structure is of critical importance for understanding why the subsequent ranking step concentrated in favour of a specific alternative.

Table 4. Entropy-based criterion weights

Criterion	Entropy value	Differentiation coefficient	Weight
K1 Strategic alignment	0.9947	0.0053	0.0923
K2 HR and talent impact	0.9952	0.0048	0.0836
K3 Digital infrastructure support	0.9713	0.0287	0.5031
K4 Application maturity	0.9947	0.0053	0.0923
K5 Traceability and assessability	0.9947	0.0053	0.0923
K6 Governance support	0.9922	0.0078	0.1365

Table 4 shows that the digital infrastructure support criterion stands out clearly from the other criteria with a weight value of 0.5031. This finding indicates that the K3 column produces the highest differentiation among the alternatives. The conclusion to be drawn from this is not that digital infrastructure support is the most important criterion in conceptual terms. A narrower and more accurate interpretation is as follows. When considering the three alternatives under examination, the highest discriminatory power in the decision matrix was generated in this dimension. Similarly, the fact that governance support ranks second with a weight of 0.1365 indicates that this criterion also has a relatively high capacity to distinguish between the alternatives. The criteria of strategic alignment, implementation maturity and traceability are clustered at the same weight level. The human resources and talent impact criterion, however, has the lowest value at 0.0836. This does not indicate the insignificance of the criterion, but rather that it produces more limited variation among the current alternatives. Consequently, the decision structure requires the weights to be interpreted not on a normative basis, but according to a distributional logic.

Once the criterion weights were determined, the position of the alternatives in the TOPSIS space was calculated. At this stage, the weighted normalised matrix was used as a basis, and positive and negative ideal solutions were defined for each criterion. The positive ideal solution represents the reference point containing the highest weighted normalised value for each criterion. The negative ideal solution, on the other hand, indicates the opposite reference point composed of the lowest values. Once the position of each alternative is determined between these two boundaries, the ranking shifts from a total score logic to a geometric proximity logic. Thus, the performance of the alternatives is evaluated not merely on the basis of how strong they are, but on how closely they approach the ideal profile.

Table 5. Positive and negative ideal solutions

Criterion	Positive ideal solution	Negative ideal solution
C1	0.0611	0.0489
K2	0.0514	0.0412
K3	0.3836	0.2302
K4	0.0611	0.0489
K5	0.0611	0.0489
K6	0.0853	0.0640

As shown in Table 5, the widest range again appears in the K3 column. The value observed as 0.3836 in the positive ideal solution drops to 0.2302 in the negative ideal solution. The difference between them is greater than the differences observed in the other criterion columns. This is consistent with the Entropy findings and demonstrates that the digital infrastructure support dimension also constitutes a decisive axis in the TOPSIS analysis. A relatively distinct divergence is also present in the K6 column. In contrast, the difference between the ideal and counter-ideal values in the K1, K2, K4 and K5 dimensions is more limited. Consequently, the final ranking of the alternatives becomes more sensitive to the distribution pattern, particularly in K3 and, to a lesser extent, in K6.

This structure becomes clearer when the distances of the alternatives from the ideal solution are calculated. The Euclidean distance to the positive ideal and the distance to the negative ideal were determined separately for each alternative. Subsequently, the relative proximity coefficient was calculated, and the alternatives were ranked according to this coefficient. A value approaching 1 indicates that the alternative is approaching the ideal profile. Low values, on the other hand, indicate that the alternative remains relatively closer to the negative ideal.

Table 6. TOPSIS distances and proximity coefficients

Alternative	Distance from the positive ideal solution	Distance from the negative ideal solution	Proximity coefficient
A1 Strengthening distance learning and the LMS infrastructure	0.0160	0.1559	0.9070
A2 Digital skills development programme	0.1564	0.0103	0.0617
A3 Needs-based in-service training system	0.1544	0.0266	0.1471

Table 6 shows that the first alternative stands out clearly in the decision space. A1's distance from the positive ideal solution is 0.0160. The fact that the same alternative's distance from the negative ideal is 0.1559 indicates that this option is quite close to the ideal profile but is clearly distant from the opposite profile. In contrast, an inverse pattern is observed for A2 and A3. The distance from the positive ideal for both alternatives is relatively high. Their distances from the negative ideal, however, are lower compared to A1. This distribution indicates that A1 not only ranks first but has also secured a dominant position distinct from the other alternatives.

The distinction between the alternatives in second and third place is more limited. A3's proximity coefficient was calculated as 0.1471, whilst A2's value was 0.0617. Although this difference does not appear significant, it produces a consistent superiority in the ranking. The primary reason for A3 overtaking A2 is that it possesses a more balanced profile in the traceability and governance support columns. Whilst A2 appears strong in terms of human resources and talent impact, it does not demonstrate the same intensity regarding infrastructure and governance patterns. Consequently, A2's position within the decision space has resulted in a more limited proximity coefficient.

Table 7. Final ranking

Rank	Alternative	Proximity coefficient
1	A1 Strengthening distance learning and the LMS infrastructure	0.9070
2	A3 In-service training system based on needs analysis	0.1471
3	A2 Digital skills development programme	0.0617

Table 7 summarises the final ranking. Strengthening distance learning and the LMS infrastructure ranks first. The needs-based in-service training system ranks second, whilst the digital competence development programme ranks third. This ranking is the result of the combined effect of the visibility density of the alternatives within the document set and the discriminatory structure of the criteria. A1's superiority is particularly linked to its high score in the digital infrastructure support dimension. A3, meanwhile, has overtaken A2 thanks to its more balanced criteria profile.

Reading the alternatives together clarifies the internal logic of the numerical ranking. A1 appears as an option with a technical backbone defined more clearly in the document set and one that is more directly linked to the organisational infrastructure. When combined with the weighting structure of the K3 column, this has produced a strong result in favour of A1. A3 does not possess an infrastructure advantage as strong as that of A1. Nevertheless, it has overtaken A2 due to offering a more balanced distribution in terms of traceability and governance. A2's lagging position can be attributed to the fact that, although the theme of digital competence development is visible in the documents, the institutional and technical groundwork supporting this theme does not appear as robust as in the other two alternatives . Within this framework, the ranking suggests a differentiation based on the level of institutional embedding.

University-based document patterns also support this general trend. The greater visibility of open and distance learning infrastructure at Anadolu University explains the strong result in favour of A1. At Sakarya University, the more balanced pattern provided by the documents of the distance learning centre and the in-service training structure contributes to the joint strengthening of A1 and A3. At Tarsus University, in-service training plans and direct documents relating to the distance learning system increase the visibility of A3 and, to some extent, A1. This observation demonstrates that the document density of a single university does not determine the ranking on its own; rather, the result stems from the combined effect of the three institutional patterns.

When considering the findings as a whole, two conclusions stand out. Firstly, the highest discriminatory power in the decision matrix was found in the digital infrastructure support dimension. Secondly, under this weighting structure, the alternative of strengthening distance learning and LMS infrastructure was identified as the option closest to the ideal solution. The needs-analysis-based in-service training system ranked second, whilst the digital competence development programme remained in third place. These results indicate that, within a document-based multi-criteria decision-making framework, initiatives with high organisational visibility, a more clearly defined technical foundation, and stronger traceability capabilities are positioned at the top of the rankings.

5. DISCUSSION

The findings show that the institutional ranking of digital talent initiatives in higher education cannot be explained through a simple logic of benefit. What the decision framework captures is not merely the attractiveness of an initiative in the abstract, but the degree to which it becomes institutionally visible, technically supported, and embedded within an implementable organisational structure. In that sense, the ranking reflects the interaction between documentary visibility, implementation maturity, and organisational operability. The entropy results make this especially clear. Digital infrastructure support emerged as the most discriminating criterion, which means that it differentiated the alternatives more sharply than the other dimensions within the decision matrix. The significance of this result lies not in any universal claim that infrastructure is always the most important factor, but in what it reveals about the institutional logic visible in the selected cases.

The strongest explanation for this pattern lies in the meaning of digital infrastructure support within the organisational context of universities. Entropy weights do not indicate theoretical importance; they indicate the extent to which a criterion differentiates the available alternatives. The fact that digital infrastructure support received the highest weight therefore suggests that it is the point at which the examined initiatives diverge most clearly. This is consistent with the structure of digital transformation in higher education. Infrastructure is not simply a technical layer added to existing work. It is the operational condition that allows digital teaching, administrative coordination, data circulation, and user support to function with continuity. For that reason, infrastructure often becomes the most visible point at which strategy is translated into organisational reality.

The prioritisation of distance education and learning management system infrastructure becomes more intelligible in this light. This initiative is the one most consistently reflected across strategic, operational, and support-oriented documents, and it is also the one most directly tied to day-to-day institutional functioning. What makes it especially important is that it connects the technical system to pedagogical practice and organisational coordination at the same time. The operability of online teaching, user support, access continuity, platform reliability, and data integrity all converge here. Bisri et al. (2023) argue that successful digital transformation depends on coherence among leadership, strategy, culture, and implementation. In many university settings, infrastructure is the most visible organisational expression of that coherence. It is therefore not just a technical investment. It is where the logic of transformation becomes materially actionable.

This finding also broadens how digital talent management in universities should be conceptualised. The results suggest that institutional priority does not first emerge through abstract lists of competencies. It emerges through an operational logic that makes digital work possible, sustainable, and governable. Under digital transformation pressures, universities initially confront the need to become technically and managerially operable. They then have to build organisational learning and human capacity around that operability. The ranking produced by this study reflects precisely that sequence. Digital talent management, in this sense, is not reducible to staff development alone; it is a layered relationship between system continuity, organisational learning, and competence formation.

The distribution of the second- and third-ranked alternatives requires a more nuanced interpretation. The needs-analysis-based in-service training system surpasses the digital competence development programme, and this may appear surprising at first glance. In much of the digital transformation discourse, competence development is presented as the most visible and immediate solution. The decision framework used here, however, does not reward conceptual appeal alone. It captures how evenly and institutionally each alternative is distributed across the criteria. The in-service training system performs more consistently on traceability and governance support, and that balance improves its position in the TOPSIS space. Robson and Mavin (2014) show that training and development are effective only when staff needs, organisational context, and evaluation logic are aligned. Decramer et al. (2013) similarly show that system design shapes satisfaction and organisational acceptance. In that respect, an in-service training system is more than a delivery mechanism. It identifies needs, organises intervention, monitors implementation, and produces feedback. Under conditions of digital transformation, that integrated cycle generates greater organisational value than fragmented training activity.

The third-place ranking of the digital competence development programme does not imply that this initiative is unimportant. Rather, it suggests that, within the documentary and organisational logic captured by this study, the initiative is not institutionalised as intensely as the other two. Rincón-Rodríguez et al. (2025) emphasise that human talent management in higher education must now be approached through digital agility, data literacy, and adaptability to change. Ramaditya et al. (2022) likewise link talent management practices to transformation capacity and organisational performance. The literature therefore leaves little doubt about the relevance of digital competence development. The point revealed by the ranking is different. Institutional importance and institutional embeddedness are not the same thing. Universities may recognise an initiative as valuable without formalising it with the same documentary density, governance support, or implementation maturity. The third-place position of the competence development programme appears to reflect precisely that distinction.

The Turkish context deepens the significance of these findings. Kuzu (2020) shows that the rhetoric of digital transformation is visible in the strategic plans of Turkish universities, often with particular emphasis on distance education and learning technologies. Aytar and Arslan (2024) similarly show that, although the language of the digital age appears widely in strategic documents, institutional priorities and future-oriented visions are unevenly distributed. The ranking produced in this study points in the same direction. Turkish universities face a shared pressure to digitalise, but their institutional responses vary in terms of scale, documentary density, governance capacity, and strategic transparency. The results should therefore not be read as a fixed prescription for all universities in Türkiye. A more defensible interpretation is that, across universities of different scale, the pressure of digital transformation becomes institutionally visible most clearly through the technical backbone and the organisational training cycle.

The theoretical contribution of the study becomes clear at this point. First, it brings the digital transformation literature and the talent management literature together within a shared problem of prioritisation. These fields often intersect, but they rarely advance on the same analytical plane. By defining digital talent initiatives as a structured set of institutional alternatives, the study places them within a single comparative framework. Second, the chapter converts document-based organisational visibility into decision analytics. Bowen (2009) notes that document analysis is a powerful means of uncovering organisational values, orientations, and operational logic. Here, documents are not used merely as descriptive background; they are transformed into a decision matrix. Third, the study extends the application of multi-criteria decision-making to a document-based and comparative human resources problem in higher education. Mustafa and Goh (1996) and Hashemi Petrudi et al. (2022) show the relevance of MCDM approaches in higher education settings. The present study broadens that line of work by showing how documentary traces of institutional priority can be translated into a structured ranking framework.

The managerial implications are equally important. Under digital transformation pressures, universities cannot invest in every initiative at once or with the same intensity. Resource constraints, implementation burden, and organisational capacity make sequencing unavoidable. The findings suggest that technical infrastructure and human-capacity investments should not be designed as separate tracks. The fact that distance education and learning management system infrastructure ranks first does not mean that in-service training or competence development can be postponed indefinitely. It means that a functional technical backbone forms the condition under which the other initiatives can generate consistent organisational returns. In parallel, an in-service training system organised around needs analysis and monitoring creates the learning cycle through which infrastructure use becomes more than a superficial adjustment. Competence development programmes, finally, have their greatest value when they are linked to both infrastructure and workflow. The implication for managers is therefore not to choose one initiative and ignore the others, but to treat them as a reinforcing sequence of technical backbone, organisational learning, and competence formation.

The limitations of the discussion should also be acknowledged. First, the analysis is based exclusively on publicly available institutional documents. This provides a strong basis for comparing official priorities, organisational orientations, and visible areas of practice, but it does not allow a direct equivalence between documentary visibility and actual implementation. Some universities may have stronger practices than their public documentation suggests, whereas others may document certain areas more intensely than they enact them in practice. Second, the study is based on three universities. That design offers analytical richness and comparative variation, but it also requires caution in extending the findings beyond the selected cases. Third, the entropy weights are not normative. They indicate only which criterion is more discriminating among the available alternatives in this specific decision matrix. Finally, the document-based scoring structure inevitably involves a level of abstraction. Future studies could increase explanatory depth by combining document analysis with interviews, surveys, or institutional performance data.

Overall, the study shows that the prioritisation of digital talent initiatives in higher education is shaped by the interaction of institutional visibility, technical capacity, managerial structure, and traceability. The first-place ranking of distance education and learning management system infrastructure suggests that universities often encounter digital transformation first through the logic of a functioning system. The second-place ranking of the needs-analysis-based in-service training system indicates that organisational learning and feedback form a critical intermediate layer that supports this system logic. The third-place position of the digital competence development programme, meanwhile, highlights the difference between normative value and institutional embeddedness. The broader implication is clear: the digital transformation debate in higher education needs to be reframed as a measurable relationship between technical infrastructure and human capacity, rather than a choice between them.

6. PRACTICAL IMPLICATIONS

The practical significance of this study lies in showing that digital transformation in universities does not become sustainable organisational transformation through disconnected technology projects. The findings point instead to three interdependent axes of institutional priority: a functional technical backbone, an organisational learning cycle driven by needs analysis, and role-sensitive competence development. These are not isolated investment areas. They form a sequence in which each layer strengthens the one that follows. When the technical backbone is fragile, training generates fragmented outcomes. When the organisational learning cycle is absent, infrastructure use remains shallow. When competence development is detached from everyday workflows, acquired skills do not become part of institutional memory. The practical question for university leaders is therefore not which initiative is valuable in general terms, but which initiative, in what sequence, is likely to generate the strongest organisational return.

The first practical implication is that the technical backbone should be treated as the starting point of the investment sequence. This does not refer only to software procurement or hardware upgrades. It includes the reliability of the learning management system, continuity of access, user support, data integrity, authentication, integration capacity, and responsiveness to technical failure. Universities often measure digitalisation by counting visible platforms. The more consequential question, however, is whether those platforms function reliably within organisational processes. When systems operate poorly, teaching and service delivery become discontinuous. As disruptions accumulate, user confidence declines, and the return on educational investment weakens. For senior management, the first decision is therefore to determine which technical components are indispensable to the core functioning of the institution. Budget and staffing decisions should then be aligned not with the visibility of projects, but with the removal of bottlenecks that strengthen continuity.

The second practical implication is the shift from calendar-driven training events to a process-oriented learning cycle. Universities may organise many training activities, yet a large share of these remain episodic and fail to generate institutional learning. The findings indicate that a needs-analysis-based in-service training system has greater practical value. Such a system should operate through a four-step cycle: identifying needs, designing content, implementing programmes, and monitoring impact. Without this cycle, training may produce individual participation but not institutional capacity. Human resources units should therefore move beyond the role of event organisers. Working with quality assurance structures, they need to identify training needs through documents, usage data, and recurring performance bottlenecks. At the same time, distance learning centres and IT units should support the technical interface of this process. Once this structure is in place, training ceases to be a reactive intervention and becomes a mechanism of organisational learning.

The third implication is that digital competence development should be designed as role-based capacity investment rather than as a vague developmental aspiration. In many institutions, the language of digital competence remains broad enough to sound attractive but too diffuse to guide managerial action. This creates two problems. First, it becomes unclear which skills are actually critical. Second, the connection between training and workflow weakens. A more workable approach is to define competence areas through functional clusters. For academic staff, priorities may include online course management, digital assessment, content design, and feedback processes. For administrative staff, data processing, digital document flow, online service delivery, and reporting may be more central. For middle managers, digital workflow coordination, data-informed monitoring, and cross-platform integration may be especially important. Once such a modular structure is established, competence development ceases to be an abstract promise and becomes a measurable area of institutional investment.

For this implementation chain to work, responsibilities must be allocated clearly. Decision architecture does not function simply because priorities are identified correctly; it functions when organisational roles are aligned with those priorities. Table 8 summarises this alignment at the level of roles, functions, and outputs.

Table 8. Organisational application map

Organisational actor	Primary Function	Expected Output
Senior management	To determine the order of priority and resource allocation	Alignment of strategic direction with the budget
Personnel and human resources departments	Conducting needs analysis and development planning	Goal-oriented training structure
Quality assurance units	Generating indicators and establishing a feedback loop	Traceable implementation system
Distance learning centre and IT	Ensuring technical continuity and user support	Operational infrastructure
Academic and administrative units	Generating user adoption and in-system feedback	Transformation embedded in workflows

The structure outlined in Table 8 shows that transformation cannot be sustained through single-point management. Senior management may provide direction, but implementation cannot simply be pushed downward. Staff units can identify training needs, but without quality support they cannot establish monitoring mechanisms. Technical units can keep the system operational, but without user experience they cannot identify the institution's real bottlenecks. Academic units are central to the process, yet without governance support they cannot internalise it as an institutional priority. The practical implication is therefore unambiguous. Digital talent management is not a project that can be delegated to a single unit. Even well-designed initiatives will yield fragmented results unless an internal coordination mechanism is established.

Timing matters as much as content. One of the recurrent mistakes universities make is to launch multiple initiatives at the same time and with the same intensity. This creates the appearance of action without producing institutional depth. A more workable model is based on phased progression. In the short term, technical and operational bottlenecks should be removed in order to secure access, integration, user support, and the reliability of core data. In the medium term, the institution should establish an in-service training system grounded in needs analysis. At this stage, the priority is not merely to offer training content, but to build the system itself: which need will be matched to which programme, how impact will be monitored, and where feedback will circulate. In the long term, digital competence development should be tied to career, performance, and organisational development policies. Such sequencing does not dissipate organisational energy; it ensures that each step creates the infrastructure and learning conditions for the next.

In terms of resource allocation, the decision logic developed in this study offers a filter that can be adapted to other institutions. Universities should assess digital transformation investments not only by their visibility, but also by their strategic fit, human-resource implications, technical support requirements, implementation maturity, traceability, and governance capacity. This shifts decision-making from preference-driven choice to institutionally grounded evaluation. Such a filter becomes especially valuable under conditions of fiscal pressure. All initiatives require resources, but they do not create institutional value at the same rate. Prioritisation, from a managerial point of view, is therefore not merely a technical exercise. It is a discipline of institutional judgement.

This chapter has examined the human dimension of digital transformation in higher education through the lens of priority-setting. Its starting point was clear: universities are operating under intensifying digital pressures, yet the organisational question they face is not simply how to digitalise, but which digital talent initiatives should be prioritised first. To address that problem, the study brought together digital transformation, talent management, and multi-criteria decision-making within a document-based comparative framework. In doing so, it shifted the discussion away from a generalised language of digital change and towards the institutional ordering of human-capacity investments.

The findings show that digital infrastructure support occupies the most discriminating position within the decision structure. This does not mean that infrastructure is universally the most important factor in every setting. It means that, across the selected cases and alternatives, infrastructure most sharply differentiated institutional priority. In consequence, the strengthening of distance education and learning management system infrastructure ranked first, followed by a needs-analysis-based in-service training system and then a digital competence development programme. Read together, these results suggest that universities often encounter digital transformation first through the operational demands of a functioning system, then through the organisational learning mechanisms required to sustain that system, and only then through more formalised competence-development agendas.

The chapter makes three main contributions. First, it brings the digital transformation and talent management literatures onto the same analytical plane by defining digital talent initiatives as a prioritisation problem rather than a diffuse strategic aspiration. Second, it shows how publicly available institutional documents can be transformed into a decision matrix, thereby converting organisational visibility into a structured analytical input. Third, it extends multi-criteria decision-making in higher education by applying it to a document-based and comparative human-resources problem. In this respect, the chapter does not merely borrow an existing method; it repositions that method within the analysis of institutional priority.

The managerial implications are equally direct. Universities should not treat digital transformation as a collection of disconnected projects or isolated training efforts. A more workable approach is sequential and integrated: first, establish a functional technical backbone; second, build an organisational learning cycle through a needs-based in-service training system; third, link competence development to roles, workflows, and longer-term organisational development. This sequence does not reduce digital talent management to infrastructure. It shows, instead, that technical continuity, organisational learning, and competence formation reinforce one another when managed as an integrated architecture rather than as separate agendas.

The chapter should also be read with its limits in view. The analysis is based on publicly available institutional documents and therefore captures institutional visibility rather than the full depth of practice. The selected universities provide analytical variation, but they do not support statistical generalisation to the entire higher education system in Türkiye. Even so, the study offers a clear framework for understanding how digital talent priorities become institutionally visible and how they can be ranked in a structured way. Its broader message is straightforward. In higher education, the human side of digital transformation should not be treated as an afterthought to technical change. It is itself a problem of institutional design, sequencing, and decision-making.

The theoretical value of the research is summarised in three points. To begin with, the digital transformation and talent management literatures have been collated under a common prioritisation issue. Second, publicly available organisational documents have not only been used as descriptive information, but as a data base that can be converted to decision analytics. Thirdly, a multi-criteria decision-making approach has been used to compare and assess digital talent initiatives in higher education. In this regard the research makes the correlation between technical change, capacity of human and governance more traceable. More to the point, it unites the debate of the digital transformation and human resources into the same institutional decision-making paradigm. This is where the original value of the study is found.

The implication of the findings is evident at the managerial level. Universities should not manage their digital transformation investments as a series of disconnected projects. A more operational approach is to set up a sequence architecture, initially to achieve the technical backbone then the organisational learning cycle and lastly to bind role-sensitive competency development programme to this architecture. This architecture is able to make resource allocation more uniform, evenly spread the burden of implementation, and improve the sustainability of organisational learning. This study, therefore, does not only generate a ranking but it also suggests a viable prioritisation mechanism to be adopted by university administrators.

The limitations of the findings are however evident. The study is anchored on publicly available institutional records and does not presuppose an ideal correspondence between the visibility of the documents and the practice. The three universities are compared only, and hence the results cannot be taken as a model of the whole higher education system. The priority structure described here could be tested in more detail in future studies that involve document analysis and interviews, surveys and performance data. However, the basic conclusion that this study has arrived at is evident. The relevance of digital transformation to higher education lies not as much in the fact that there is a relationship between technology and human capacity, but in the priority logic within which this relationship is created.

REFERENCES

Allui, A., & Sahni, J. (2016). Strategic human resource management in higher education institutions. Empirical evidence from Saudi Arabia. *Procedia: Social and Behavioral Sciences*, *235*, 361–371. DOI: 10.1016/j.sbspro.2016.11.044

Ashraf, M. A. (2019). Influences of working conditions and faculty retention on quality education in private universities in Bangladesh. An analysis using SEM. *International Journal of Educational Management*, *33*(1), 149–165. DOI: 10.1108/IJEM-03-2018-0121

Aytar, O., & Arslan, R. (2024). Future-shaping themes. Digital age foresight in Turkish university strategic plans. *Strategic Management*, *29*(4), 70–81. DOI: 10.5937/StraMan2300062A

Benavides, L. M. C., Tamayo Arias, J. A., Arango Serna, M. D., Branch Bedoya, J. W., & Burgos, D. (2020). Digital transformation in higher education institutions. A systematic literature review. *Sensors (Basel)*, *20*(11), 3291. DOI: 10.3390/s20113291 PMID: 32526998

Biondi, L., & Russo, S. (2022). Integrating strategic planning and performance management in universities. A multiple case-study analysis. *The Journal of Management and Governance*, *26*(2), 417–448. DOI: 10.1007/s10997-022-09628-7

Bisri, A., Putri, A., & Rosmansyah, Y. (2023). A systematic literature review on digital transformation in higher education. Revealing key success factors. *International Journal of Emerging Technologies in Learning*, *18*(14), 164–187. DOI: 10.3991/ijet.v18i14.40201

Bond, M., Marín, V. I., Dolch, C., Bedenlier, S., & Zawacki-Richter, O. (2018). Digital transformation in German higher education. Student and teacher perceptions and usage of digital media. *International Journal of Educational Technology in Higher Education*, *15*(1), 48. DOI: 10.1186/s41239-018-0130-1

Bowen, G. A. (2009). Document analysis as a qualitative research method. *Qualitative Research Journal*, *9*(2), 27–40. DOI: 10.3316/QRJ0902027

Decramer, A., Smolders, C., & Vanderstraeten, A. (2013). Employee performance management culture and system features in higher education. Relationship with employee performance management satisfaction. *International Journal of Human Resource Management*, *24*(2), 352–371. DOI: 10.1080/09585192.2012.680602

Gkrimpizi, T., Peristeras, V., & Magnisalis, I. (2023). Classification of barriers to digital transformation in higher education institutions. Systematic literature review. *Education Sciences*, *13*(7), 746. DOI: 10.3390/educsci13070746

Hashemi Petrudi, S. H., Ghomi, H., & Mazaheriasad, M. (2022). An integrated fuzzy Delphi and Best Worst Method for performance measurement in higher education. *Decision Analytics Journal*, *4*, 100121. DOI: 10.1016/j.dajour.2022.100121

Karakaş, A., Kıngır, S., & Öztel, A. (2016). Evaluation of university employees' work behaviours performance via entropy-based TOPSIS methods. *Electronic Journal of Social Sciences*, *15*(58), 1046–1058. DOI: 10.17755/esosder.67295

Keskin, S., Çinar, M., & Demir, Ö. (2022). A quantitative content analysis of Turkish state universities' official websites in terms of their preparedness and actions during emergency distance education in the early phase of the COVID-19 pandemic period. *Education and Information Technologies*, *27*(1), 493–523. DOI: 10.1007/s10639-021-10744-4 PMID: 34667430

Kuzu, Ö. H. (2020). Digital transformation in higher education. A case study on strategic plans. *Higher Education in Russia*, *29*(3), 9–23. DOI: 10.31992/0869-3617-2019-29-3-9-23

Marks, A., Al-Ali, M., Atassi, R., Abualkishik, A. Z., & Rezgui, Y. (2020). Digital transformation in higher education. A framework for maturity assessment. *International Journal of Advanced Computer Science and Applications*, *11*(12), 504–513. DOI: 10.14569/IJACSA.2020.0111261

Mohamed Hashim, M. A., Tlemsani, I., & Matthews, R. (2022). Higher education strategy in digital transformation. *Education and Information Technologies*, *27*(3), 3171–3195. DOI: 10.1007/s10639-021-10739-1 PMID: 34539217

Mustafa, A., & Goh, M. (1996). Multi-criterion models for higher education administration. *Omega*, *24*(2), 167–178. DOI: 10.1016/0305-0483(95)00053-4

Naidoo-Chetty, M., & du Plessis, M. (2021). Job demands and job resources of academics in higher education. *Frontiers in Psychology*, *12*, 631171. DOI: 10.3389/fpsyg.2021.631171 PMID: 34248738

Nurhas, I., Aditya, B. R., Jacob, D. W., & Pawlowski, J. M. (2021). Understanding the challenges of rapid digital transformation. The case of the COVID-19 pandemic in higher education. *Behaviour & Information Technology*, *42*(16), 2773–2789. DOI: 10.1080/0144929X.2021.1962977

Ramaditya, M., Maarif, M. S., Affandi, J., & Sukmawati, A. (2022). Reinventing talent management. How to maximise performance in higher education. *Frontiers in Education*, *7*, 929697. DOI: 10.3389/feduc.2022.929697

Razali, R., Arifin, M. A., Shafie, L. A., Azizan, F. L., & Ishak, M. A. M. (2024). Mapping the landscape of talent management research in higher education. A bibliometric analysis. *Cogent Business & Management*, *11*(1), 229–300. DOI: 10.1080/23311975.2023.2298300

Rincón-Rodríguez, I. C., Chaparro-Medina, J. E., Ortiz-Ortiz, E. G., Plata-Acosta, Y. I., Zarta-Botero, M., Crespo, J. E., & García-Lirios, C. (2025). Human talent management in higher education institutions. Facing challenges and taking advantage of opportunities in the 4.0 era. *Multidisciplinary Journal of Educational Research*, *15*(3), 170–181. DOI: 10.17583/remie.16140

Robson, F., & Mavin, S. (2014). Evaluating training and development in UK universities. Staff perceptions. *European Journal of Training and Development*, *38*(6), 553–569. DOI: 10.1108/EJTD-04-2013-0039

Zhang, Y., & Liu, C. (2023). Online teaching quality evaluation. Entropy TOPSIS and grouped regression model. *International Journal of Emerging Technologies in Learning*, *18*(16), 36–49. DOI: 10.3991/ijet.v18i16.41353

KEY TERMS AND DEFİNİTİONS

Coding Scheme: The predefined set of rules used to translate evidence in institutional documents into comparable criterion scores, ensuring that the same type of signal is interpreted consistently across universities.

Decision Criterion: A specific dimension used to evaluate digital talent initiatives (e.g., institutionalisation, monitoring, or operational traceability) within the multi-criteria framework.

Decision Matrix: The structured table that brings the analysis together by listing initiatives as alternatives and recording their criterion scores derived from document-based evidence.

Digital Talent Initiative: A deliberate, bounded institutional effort intended to build or strengthen digital capability through workforce development, digitally enabled work practices, or enabling infrastructures.

Digital Talent Management: The strategic set of practices through which universities develop, sustain, and deploy the digital competencies required to support digital transformation in teaching, research, and administration.

Document Analysis: A research approach that treats institutional documents as empirical traces of priorities and practices, rather than relying on self-reported perceptions.

Entropy Weighting Method: An objective weighting technique that assigns greater weight to criteria exhibiting higher informational variation in the decision matrix, indicating stronger discriminatory power.

Institutional Documents: Publicly available university records—such as strategic plans, quality assurance reports, distance education documentation, and staff development texts—used to infer the strength and visibility of initiatives.

Institutional Scale: The size-related structural capacity of a university (e.g., large, medium, small) that shapes resources, digital maturity, and the feasibility of institutionalising initiatives.

TOPSIS (Technique for Order Preference by Similarity to Ideal Solution): A ranking method that identifies the most preferred alternative as the one closest to an ideal profile and furthest from a non-ideal profile within a weighted and normalised criterion space.

Chapter 9
Faculty Upskilling for Digital Transformation:
A Model for Higher Education Institutions

Tendai Charles
http://orcid.org/0000-0002-0253-5960
The British University in Dubai, UAE

Najwan Fares
http://orcid.org/0000-0002-9796-5233
The British University in Dubai, UAE

ABSTRACT

Digital transformation in higher education institutions (HEIs) is often viewed as a technology-driven initiative, focusing on platforms, infrastructure, and process redesign. However, the success and sustainability of digital transformation fundamentally rely on talent, especially faculty capacity to implement digitally mediated teaching, assessment, student support, and research. Despite increasing investments in educational technologies, many HEIs face challenges such as fragmented professional development, inconsistent adoption of digital pedagogy, and a disconnection between upskilling efforts and talent management systems, including hiring practices, performance reviews, promotions, and workload distribution. This chapter offers a strategic response through a Digital Competency and Career-Stage Development Model (DCCSD Model), positioning faculty upskilling as a key element of talent management in digital transformation.

DOI: 10.4018/979-8-3373-8959-2.ch009

INTRODUCTION

Digital transformation has become a central organising discourse in higher education strategy. Institutions increasingly invest in learning management systems, cloud services, integrated enterprise platforms, student-experience applications, artificial intelligence (AI) tools and data infrastructures. However, the persistent challenge is not the availability of technologies alone. The more consequential challenge is whether higher education institutions (HEIs) can translate digital resources into coherent academic practice: teaching and assessment that improve learning, student support that is responsive and equitable, scholarship that uses digital methods responsibly, and governance that preserves trust and academic autonomy.

Systematic review evidence indicates that digital transformation in HEIs is complex and multidimensional, requiring attention to institutional processes, culture, leadership, pedagogical practice and organisational roles rather than a narrow focus on technology deployment (Castro Benavides et al., 2020; Farias-Gaytan et al., 2023). Critical sociotechnical perspectives similarly caution that digitalisation should not be treated as a neutral technical upgrade; digital systems redistribute work, shape institutional priorities and carry consequences for professional identity, equity and accountability (Castañeda & Selwyn, 2018). For this reason, digital transformation is better understood as institutional capability-building distributed across leaders, academic developers, professional services, IT units and faculty.

Faculty upskilling is central to this capability-building agenda, but existing approaches often display four weaknesses. First, professional learning is frequently organised as workshops or short courses detached from disciplinary teaching, assessment and the rhythms of academic work (Charles, 2025). Second, digital competence is uneven across departments, career stages and opportunity structures; faculty digital divides are multidimensional, involving access, motivation, confidence, skills and patterns of use (Soomro et al., 2020). Third, upskilling is often misaligned with talent-management systems, including recruitment, probation, workload, performance review, promotion and retention. Fourth, newer domains of academic work, especially AI literacy and learning analytics literacy, create ethical risks that cannot be managed through tool training alone.

This chapter responds to these problems by proposing the Digital Competency and Career-Stage Development (DCCSD) Model. The model positions faculty upskilling as a talent-management mechanism of digital transformation. It specifies domains of digital competence for contemporary academic work, differentiates role expectations across career stages and aligns development pathways with institutional talent practices. The DCCSD Model is advanced as a conceptual and strategic framework rather than as an empirically validated instrument. Its value lies in synthesising established competence, professional learning, AI/analytics governance and talent-management scholarship into an actionable architecture for institutional design.

The chapter's distinctive contribution is threefold. First, it moves beyond generic digital skills by anchoring competence in academic work: learning design, assessment, student engagement, analytics, AI practice, scholarship, governance and wellbeing. Second, it makes career stage analytically central, recognising that early-career faculty, mid-career programme leaders and senior academic leaders hold different responsibilities and require different forms of support. Third, it embeds faculty capability within the talent-management lifecycle, thereby connecting professional learning to workload recognition, performance development, promotion, retention and succession planning. This alignment is the model's primary innovation: digital competence is not treated as an individual deficit to be remediated but as an organisational capability to be planned, resourced, recognised and governed.

The chapter proceeds in five parts. The literature review critically synthesises scholarship on digital transformation, faculty digital competence, professional learning, AI literacy, learning analytics and talent management, with explicit comparison to established frameworks. The methodology then explains the integrative conceptual synthesis used to derive the model. The model section presents the DCCSD architecture, competency domains, career-stage pathways, talent-management alignment and governance overlay. The implementation section provides practical examples, a stakeholder checklist and evaluation indicators. The discussion clarifies limitations, ethics and a validation agenda for future empirical work.

LITERATURE REVIEW

Digital transformation as sociotechnical capability-building

Institutional strategy documents often frame digital transformation as technology modernisation: migration to cloud services, platform integration, process redesign and expanded analytics. The research literature, however, points to a broader and more demanding interpretation. Digital transformation in higher education involves technological, cultural, pedagogical, managerial and organisational change (Castro Benavides et al., 2020; Farias-Gaytan et al., 2023). Evidence from higher education contexts shows that technology use is shaped by individual perceptions, institutional norms, available support and local conditions rather than by infrastructure alone (Bond et al., 2018). Therefore, digital transformation should be evaluated not by the number of systems adopted, but by whether institutional actors develop the capability to use digital systems in ways that advance learning quality, equity, scholarship and organisational sustainability.

This sociotechnical interpretation has direct implications for faculty upskilling. Faculty capability is not merely a matter of training individuals to operate platforms. It involves enabling academics to make pedagogical, ethical and disciplinary judgements in digitally mediated environments while working within sustainable institutional arrangements. The gap in many HEIs is that digital transformation strategies are often not matched by equally coherent faculty capability strategies, especially those connected to workload, career progression and recognition.

Faculty digital competence and professional learning

Faculty digital competence has been conceptualised as more than operational proficiency. Systematic reviews emphasise that higher education teachers require pedagogical, ethical, reflective, communicative and evaluative capabilities as well as technical skills (Basilotta-Gómez-Pablos et al., 2022; Fernández-Batanero et al., 2021). Assessment of digital competence is also complex: reliable evaluation requires construct clarity, multiple evidence sources and alignment between assessment purpose and method (Sillat et al., 2021). These findings challenge institutional practices that infer competence from workshop attendance or platform-use metrics.

Professional learning scholarship further suggests that sustained change is unlikely when development is limited to isolated training events. Faculty innovation is shaped by beliefs, disciplinary cultures, institutional motives and contextual support structures (Freitas & Paredes, 2018). Effective upskilling therefore requires practice-embedded learning, peer review, mentoring, communities of practice, learning design support and workload recognition. This also requires attention to differentiated starting points: a uniform professional development pathway may unintentionally reproduce inequities if it assumes equal access, time, confidence and prior experience (Soomro et al., 2020).

Established frameworks and the remaining gap

Several established frameworks provide important foundations for faculty upskilling. DigCompEdu offers a widely recognised educator digital competence framework with six areas and 22 competences (Redecker, 2017). TPACK explains the intersection of technological, pedagogical and content knowledge required for meaningful technology integration (Mishra & Koehler, 2006). UTAUT identifies acceptance factors such as performance expectancy, effort expectancy, social influence and facilitating conditions (Venkatesh et al., 2003). Bates (2022) provides practical guidance for designing teaching and learning in digital contexts. Siemens

(2013) clarifies learning analytics as an emerging field with organisational, methodological and ethical challenges. UNESCO's AI guidance and AI competency framework foreground human agency, ethics, AI foundations, AI pedagogy and professional learning (Miao & Holmes, 2023; Miao & Cukurova, 2024). Jisc's digital capability work adds role profiles and a common language for organisational capability-building (Jisc, 2022).

These frameworks are necessary but not sufficient for the problem addressed in this chapter. Most are either competence frameworks, pedagogical integration frameworks, adoption models or policy guidance documents. They do not, on their own, specify how HEIs should align faculty digital competence with academic career stages, workload allocation, performance development, promotion, retention and succession planning. DCCSD is therefore not presented as a replacement for these frameworks. It is presented as an integrative model that translates their insights into a career-stage and talent-management architecture for HEIs.

In summary, the literature establishes that faculty digital competence is multidimensional, context-dependent and ethically consequential (*see* Table 1). The key unresolved problem is not the absence of digital competence frameworks, but the weak alignment between competence development, academic career stages and institutional talent-management systems. This is the gap addressed by the DCCSD Model (*see* Table 2)

Table 1. Structured literature matrix and gap articulation

Literature stream	Representative sources	Contribution	Unresolved limitation	DCCSD response
Digital transformation in HEIs	Castro Benavides et al. (2020); Farias-Gaytan et al. (2023); Bond et al. (2018)	Digital transformation is multidimensional and enacted through institutional culture, pedagogy, leadership and everyday practice.	The literature often identifies transformation challenges without specifying how faculty capability is embedded into talent systems.	Digital capability is treated as an organisational infrastructure that must be planned, resourced and evaluated.
Educator digital competence	Redecker (2017); Basilotta-Gómez-Pablos et al. (2022); Fernández-Batanero et al. (2021); Sillat et al. (2021)	Competence includes pedagogical, ethical, reflective, communicative and assessment dimensions, not only technical proficiency.	Existing frameworks do not consistently differentiate expectations by academic career stage or connect competence evidence to workload and recognition.	Seven role-embedded competency domains and a developmental portfolio approach are specified.
Technology integration and adoption	Mishra and Koehler (2006); Venkatesh et al. (2003); Freitas and Paredes (2018)	Meaningful technology use depends on pedagogy-content-technology integration, perceived usefulness, effort, social influence and enabling conditions.	Adoption models explain use but do not provide a full professional development and talent-management pathway.	The model embeds support, mentoring, role expectations and institutional conditions alongside competence expectations.
AI literacy and learning analytics	Siemens (2013); Grimm et al. (2023); Tenberga and Daniela (2024); Miao and Holmes (2023); Miao and Cukurova (2024)	AI and analytics require critical evaluation, privacy protection, bias mitigation, transparency and human-centred governance.	AI and analytics literacies are often treated as emerging add-ons rather than as core faculty capability domains.	AI literacy, analytics literacy and governance/ wellbeing are explicit DCCSD domains.
Talent management and sustainability	Abiwu and Martins (2022); Sun and Yoon (2025); Charles and Papadaki (2025)	Training, career development, digital self-efficacy, leadership and ethical technology integration are associated with institutional sustainability and performance.	Faculty development is frequently detached from recruitment, performance review, promotion, workload, retention and leadership pipelines.	DCCSD aligns upskilling with acquisition, development, workload, performance, recognition, retention and succession.

Table 2. Positioning DCCSD relative to established frameworks

Framework	Primary focus	Strength retained	Distinctive DCCSD extension
DigCompEdu	Educator digital competence across six areas and 22 competences.	Provides a strong competence language for educators.	DCCSD adapts competence expectations to higher education academic work, career stages, portfolio evidence and talent-management systems.
TPACK	Intersections among technological, pedagogical and content knowledge.	Prevents tool-led approaches by foregrounding pedagogy and disciplinary knowledge.	DCCSD retains the pedagogy-discipline logic but adds assessment, analytics, AI, governance, wellbeing and institutional career alignment.
UTAUT	Explains user acceptance through expectancy, effort, social influence and facilitating conditions.	Clarifies why faculty may or may not adopt technologies.	DCCSD translates adoption conditions into organisational supports, workload recognition and developmental pathways rather than focusing only on intention to use.
Teaching in a Digital Age	Practical guidance for designing teaching and learning with technology.	Supports pedagogically informed decisions about modes, media and learner needs.	DCCSD situates such design choices within a broader model of faculty capability, career progression and institutional recognition.
Learning analytics scholarship	Clarifies analytics methods, organisational capacity and ethical challenges.	Provides a foundation for data-informed teaching and decision support.	DCCSD embeds analytics literacy within faculty development while adding transparency, contestability and limits on analytics-based evaluation.
UNESCO AI guidance and AI competency framework	Human-centred AI, ethics, AI foundations, AI pedagogy and professional learning.	Provides authoritative policy and competence guidance for responsible AI in education.	DCCSD embeds AI literacy into HEI talent systems, assessment redesign, governance responsibilities and career-stage expectations.
Jisc digital capabilities	Individual digital capabilities, role profiles and organisational development resources.	Demonstrates the value of role-sensitive capability language.	DCCSD extends role sensitivity into academic career-stage development, promotion/workload alignment and digital transformation outcomes.

METHODOLOGY

Conceptual-strategic design

This chapter employs a conceptual-strategic research design. The purpose is theory-informed model building rather than hypothesis testing. Conceptual research is appropriate where a phenomenon is multidimensional and rapidly evolving, and where institutions require a framework that clarifies constructs, relationships and implementation implications (Brady et al., 2020). The DCCSD Model is therefore advanced as a focused representation of prioritised constructs and their relationships, intended to guide institutional design and future empirical testing. It should not be read as a validated measurement instrument.

The model development followed the logic of conceptual framework analysis, in which literature is treated as the source from which concepts are identified, deconstructed and related into a coherent network (Jabareen, 2009). This approach was strengthened by Brady et al.'s (2020) guidance on conceptual model development and by Naeem et al.'s (2023) coding-to-abstraction logic for moving from extracted evidence to themes and model relationships.

Source identification and inclusion logic

The evidence base was assembled through an integrative literature synthesis rather than a full systematic review. The synthesis prioritised sources with high conceptual and practical relevance for model construction. Searches and citation chaining focused on five clusters: (1) digital transformation in higher education; (2) faculty/academic development and digital pedagogy; (3) digital competence and digital capability frameworks; (4) AI literacy, generative AI and learning analytics governance; and (5) talent management, workload, recognition and sustainability in HEIs. Recent peer-reviewed studies and systematic reviews were prioritised for contemporary developments, while foundational theories and policy frameworks were retained where they remain authoritative.

Inclusion decisions were guided by four criteria: direct relevance to higher education or educator capability; contribution to at least one DCCSD domain or governance principle; methodological or theoretical credibility; and usefulness for explaining institutional implementation. Sources were excluded when they focused only on technical tool operation without relevance to academic work, when they lacked identifiable scholarly or policy authority, or when their claims could not be connected to model construction. PRISMA-P guidance informed the transparent reporting of objectives and analytic decisions (Shamseer et al., 2015), but the chapter does not claim the comprehensiveness of a PRISMA systematic review.

Analytic procedure and evidence-to-model mapping

The analysis proceeded through an adapted eight-phase sequence. First, the knowledge domain was delimited across digital transformation, faculty digital competence, professional learning, AI/analytics governance and talent management. Second, sources were categorised by analytic function: foundational framework, systematic review, empirical evidence, policy guidance or institutional practice example. Third, recurrent constructs were extracted, including digital pedagogy, assessment, engagement, data-informed practice, AI literacy, scholarship, governance, workload and recognition. Fourth, each construct was deconstructed into definitional attributes, academic work practices and institutional enabling conditions. Fifth, overlapping constructs were integrated into higher-order domains. Sixth, relationships were specified across competency domains, career-stage expectations, talent-management functions and governance principles. Seventh, internal coherence checking was undertaken to ensure the model remained interpretable to HEI leaders, HR professionals, academic developers and faculty. Eighth, the model was refined for parsimony and actionability through tables, portfolio artefacts, implementation indicators and a validation agenda (*see* Table 3).

Table 3. Evidence-to-model mapping for DCCSD construction

Evidence stream	Synthesis inference	Model design response	Where operationalised
Fragmented faculty development and short-course dependency	Professional learning needs to be practice-embedded, sustained and supported by peers, mentors and academic development infrastructure.	DCCSD organises upskilling as developmental pathways linked to authentic academic work rather than isolated tool workshops.	Seven domains; implementation playbook; stakeholder checklist
Uneven competence and multidimensional faculty digital divides	Faculty differ by opportunity, confidence, motivation, role, discipline and access to support.	The model separates career stage from proficiency and recommends formative mapping, multiple entry points and equity monitoring.	Proficiency levels; career-stage pathways; equity indicators
Tool-centric competence assessment	Digital competence assessment should be construct-aligned, formative and based on multiple sources of evidence.	DCCSD uses portfolio artefacts and peer/reflective evidence rather than attendance records or platform metrics alone.	Portfolio evidence table; evaluation safeguards
AI, analytics and datafication risks	AI and analytics introduce risks of bias, opacity, privacy infringement, surveillance and academic integrity disruption.	The model makes AI literacy, analytics literacy and governance/wellbeing constitutive domains, not optional add-ons.	Domains 4, 5 and 7; governance overlay; ethics statement

continued on following page

Table 3. Continued

Evidence stream	Synthesis inference	Model design response	Where operationalised
Weak alignment with HR and talent systems	Upskilling is fragile when competence growth is not recognised in workload, promotion, leadership and retention systems.	DCCSD aligns competency development with acquisition, probation, workload, performance, recognition, retention and succession.	Talent-management lifecycle table
Limited empirical validation of the proposed model	A conceptual model requires external review, contextual adaptation, pilot testing and measurable outcomes before strong effectiveness claims can be made.	The chapter explicitly bounds claims and proposes a staged validation plan.	Limitations; future empirical validation agenda

The methodological contribution of this section is traceability. The tables show how the model's components were not selected arbitrarily; they were derived from recurring problems and constructs across the reviewed literature and then translated into design features that HEIs can adapt and evaluate.

THE DIGITAL COMPETENCY AND CAREER-STAGE DEVELOPMENT MODEL

The DCCSD Model positions faculty upskilling as a strategic mechanism for digital transformation in HEIs. Rather than treating professional development as an adjunct activity, the model conceptualises faculty capability as an organisational infrastructure that enables digital transformation outcomes in teaching, assessment, student support, scholarship and governance. The model is explicitly developmental, career-stage sensitive, talent-system aligned and responsible by design.

The model rests on six principles: capability over tool adoption; competence embedded in academic work; developmental progression rather than one-off training; career-stage sensitivity; alignment with talent-management systems; and responsible, human-centred governance. These principles respond to evidence that digital transformation is enacted through practice, support and organisational conditions rather than through platform access alone (Castro Benavides et al., 2020; Castañeda & Selwyn, 2018).

Model architecture

Figure 1 presents the model as a layered system. The inner layer specifies competency domains for academic work. A developmental layer differentiates expectations across career stages. An organisational layer aligns those expectations with talent-management functions. An outer governance layer safeguards equity, transparency, academic autonomy, privacy, contestability and workload sustainability. A continuous improvement loop connects implementation evidence to iterative refinement.

Figure 1. The Digital Competency and Career-Stage Development (DCCSD) Model for faculty upskilling as a talent-management mechanism of digital transformation

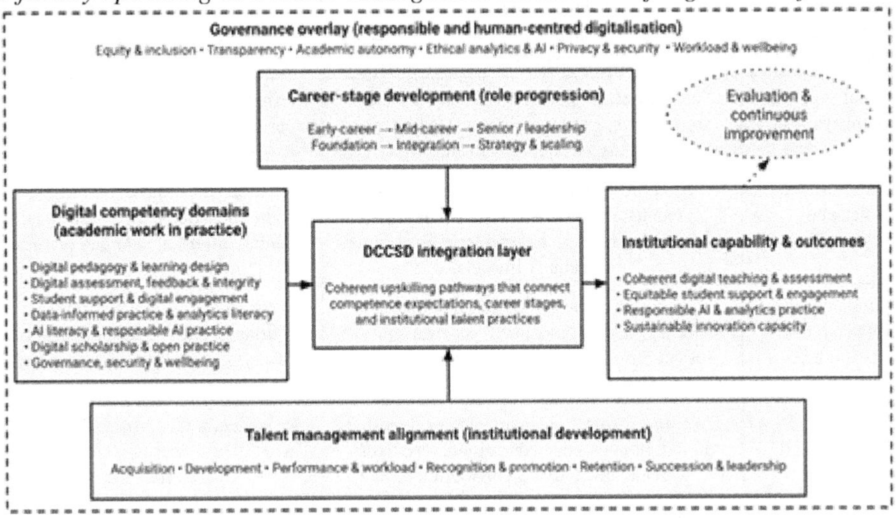

The model's theory of change can be summarised as follows: if HEIs specify domains of faculty digital competence, differentiate expectations by career stage, align development pathways with talent practices and embed governance safeguards, then faculty are more likely to enact digitally mediated teaching, assessment, student support, scholarship and leadership in sustained ways. These practices can strengthen programme-level capability and institutional digital transformation, provided that implementation is resourced and evaluated.

DCCSD competency domains

The model specifies seven competency domains. Each domain is framed as integrated knowledge, skill, judgement and disposition enacted in academic practice. The domains are intended for formative development and constructive recognition; they should not be used as punitive compliance checklists (*see* Table 4).

Table 4. DCCSD domains and indicative evidence artefacts for a developmental portfolio

DCCSD domain	Indicative evidence artefacts	Governance and risk notes
Digital pedagogy and learning design	Course blueprint; accessibility statement; peer review/observation summary; learning activities; reflective narrative linked to learning evidence.	Avoid tool-led compliance; treat accessibility and inclusion as baseline quality requirements.
Digital assessment, feedback and integrity	Assessment briefs and rubrics; staged submission designs; feedback examples; integrity-by-design documentation; moderation evidence.	Prioritise fairness and inclusion; clarify acceptable AI use; avoid disproportionate surveillance.
Student support and engagement	Communication plan; engagement artefacts; targeted support protocols; student feedback; reflections on boundary management.	Prevent communication overload; use appropriate channels; protect student and staff wellbeing.
Data-informed practice and analytics	Analytics-informed intervention plans; evaluation summaries; transparency statements; reflections on metric limitations and equity impacts.	Use analytics as decision support rather than automated judgement; ensure proportionality and privacy.
AI literacy and responsible AI	AI-use guidelines; verified AI-supported materials; student guidance; risk-management reflections; professional learning evidence.	Mitigate hallucination and bias; protect privacy and intellectual property; require transparency and verification.
Digital scholarship and open practice	Data management plans; repository deposits; digital outputs; open educational resources; evidence of digital collaboration.	Respect ethics approvals, licensing and IP; ensure secure handling of sensitive data.
Governance, security and wellbeing	Policy-compliance evidence; governance consultation contributions; workload-aware redesign documentation; wellbeing practices.	Promote participatory governance, contestability, trust and academic autonomy.

Domain 1. Digital pedagogy and learning design

The capability to design, facilitate and evaluate blended, online and technology-enhanced learning in ways that are aligned with learning outcomes, discipline expectations, accessibility and inclusion. Core practices include course blueprinting, active learning design, interaction planning, accessibility review and reflective redesign using appropriate evidence. Development evidence may include learning design maps, accessible materials, peer-review summaries and reflective narratives linked to student learning evidence.

Domain 2. Digital assessment, feedback and academic integrity

The capability to design, implement and quality-assure assessment and feedback in digital environments, including AI-aware assessment design. Core practices include authentic assessment, transparent criteria, staged submissions, feedback that supports self-regulation, moderation and explicit guidance on acceptable AI/tool use. Development evidence may include revised assessment briefs, rubrics, exemplars, feedback plans, moderation notes and integrity-by-design documentation.

Domain 3. Student support, engagement and digital communication

The capability to support students' academic progress and belonging through ethical, inclusive and sustainable digital communication. Core practices include communication routines, digital office hours, structured question-and-answer spaces, inclusive facilitation, support triage and boundary management. Development evidence may include communication plans, engagement interventions, referral protocols and reflections on student feedback.

Domain 4. Data-informed practice and learning analytics literacy

The capability to interpret and use learning-related data cautiously to inform teaching, assessment and support while recognising limitations, bias risks and privacy obligations. Core practices include metric interpretation, triangulation with qualitative evidence, intervention design, evaluation and student-facing transparency. Development evidence may include analytics-informed intervention plans, evaluation summaries, transparency statements and reflections on equity impacts.

Domain 5. AI literacy and responsible AI practice

The capability to critically evaluate and responsibly apply AI tools in teaching, assessment, scholarship and administration. Core practices include verifying AI outputs, recognising hallucination and bias, protecting privacy and intellectual property, defining discipline-specific AI norms and supporting students' responsible use. Development evidence may include AI-use statements, verified AI-supported materials, student guidance resources and reflective documentation of risk management.

Domain 6. Digital scholarship and open academic practice

The capability to conduct, communicate and steward scholarship using digital methods and infrastructures. Core practices include research data management, secure storage, open access where appropriate, digital methods, collaborative scholarship and responsible public engagement. Development evidence may include data management plans, repository deposits, open educational resources, code or datasets where ethically permissible, and evidence of digital collaboration.

Domain 7. Digital governance, security and professional wellbeing

The capability to participate in responsible governance of digital practice while sustaining professional wellbeing. Core practices include privacy and cybersecurity awareness, compliance with data-use policies, participation in AI/analytics governance, workload-aware redesign, boundary setting and ethical deliberation. Development evidence may include governance training, policy consultation contributions, workload-aware redesign documentation and wellbeing-informed communication norms.

Developmental proficiency and career-stage pathways

DCCSD distinguishes proficiency from career stage (*see* Table 5). Proficiency refers to the quality and sophistication of practice in a given domain; career stage refers to role expectations and institutional responsibilities. This distinction matters because early-career faculty may be highly proficient in some domains, while senior academics may require development in emerging domains such as AI literacy or analytics literacy. Treating career stage and proficiency separately improves developmental legitimacy and avoids deficit assumptions.

Four proficiency levels are proposed for formative use. At the Emerging level, faculty demonstrate functional use of institutional platforms with guided support. At the Practitioner level, they align digital teaching, assessment and student engagement with routine attention to inclusion and integrity. At the Integrator level, they orchestrate multiple domains within coherent disciplinary designs and may mentor peers. At the Strategist/Leader level, they shape programme or institutional practice through governance, mentoring, resourcing, ethical oversight and scaling. These levels should be used to support development conversations and recognition, not to rank faculty reductively.

Table 5. DCCSD competency focus by career stage

Domain	Early-career: foundation and adoption	Mid-career: integration and programme leadership	Senior/leadership: strategy, governance and scaling
Digital pedagogy and learning design	Design coherent blended/ online learning; apply accessibility basics; facilitate inclusive digital interaction.	Lead module/programme redesign; mentor colleagues; evaluate learning design impact.	Set institutional digital learning principles; resource learning design capacity; ensure quality assurance at scale.
Digital assessment, feedback and integrity	Implement digital assessment tools; provide timely feedback; redesign tasks for integrity and appropriate AI/tool use.	Coordinate programme assessment redesign; embed authentic assessment patterns; support moderation and integrity enactment.	Approve assessment and integrity frameworks; balance risk controls with academic autonomy; resource redesign time.
Student support and engagement	Maintain predictable digital communication; support belonging; use feedback loops to identify student needs.	Design programme-level engagement strategies; integrate advising/support systems; build peer support structures.	Set student experience strategy; ensure equitable support infrastructure; align academic and professional services.
Data-informed practice and analytics	Interpret basic dashboards cautiously; use evidence to adjust teaching; recognise limitations and bias risks.	Use analytics for programme improvement; lead intervention design; build ethical practice norms.	Establish analytics governance and transparency; oversee equity monitoring; ensure accountable use.
AI literacy and responsible AI	Use AI tools critically and transparently; teach students responsible use; apply verification and disclosure norms.	Develop discipline norms; lead AI-integrated pedagogy and assessment redesign; support staff development.	Set institutional AI principles and policy; ensure ethical oversight; align AI adoption with talent and governance systems.
Digital scholarship and open practice	Use digital tools for research productivity; adopt research data management basics; engage with open access where appropriate.	Lead adoption of discipline-relevant digital methods; mentor others; contribute to open scholarship leadership.	Set research digital strategy; resource infrastructure; align open science, data governance and ethics policies.
Governance, security and wellbeing	Follow privacy/security policies; establish sustainable digital work routines; manage boundaries.	Identify workload risks; contribute to policy refinement; lead wellbeing-aware change practices locally.	Embed wellbeing and trust in digital strategy; allocate workload fairly; ensure participatory governance and accountability.

Embedding DCCSD into the talent-management lifecycle

DCCSD's main practical innovation is its integration with institutional talent management. Upskilling remains fragile when it is not supported by HR systems, workload models, role descriptions and recognition structures. Conversely, digital transformation becomes more credible when competence expectations are matched with time, support, evidence and fair recognition. Table 6 illustrates how DCCSD can be operationalised across the talent-management lifecycle.

Table 6. Aligning DCCSD with the institutional talent-management lifecycle

Talent function	Institutional mechanisms	How DCCSD is operationalised
Acquisition	Job profiles; selection criteria; teaching portfolio expectations; induction planning.	Embed career-stage-appropriate expectations for digital teaching, assessment, AI literacy and analytics literacy; identify development needs at appointment and resource induction.
Development	Structured pathways; mentoring; communities of practice; micro-credentials; learning design and edtech support.	Provide DCCSD-aligned pathways at foundational, integration and governance levels; enable discipline-based peer learning and portfolio evidence.
Performance and workload	Workload models; annual planning; probation criteria; performance development review.	Recognise digital redesign labour, analytics-informed intervention work, AI-aware assessment redesign and digital student support; prevent hidden labour.
Recognition and promotion	Promotion criteria; teaching awards; professional accreditation; digital fellows schemes.	Reward evidence of learning design impact, inclusive assessment, responsible AI/analytics practice, digital scholarship and mentoring.
Retention and engagement	Career pathways; leadership development; wellbeing supports; innovation funding; climate initiatives.	Create transparent progression routes; support mid-career curriculum leadership; address workload and wellbeing risks.
Succession and leadership	Leadership programmes; role redesign; governance structures; strategic workforce planning.	Develop senior-stage competence in digital governance, AI/analytics ethics, transparency, equity monitoring and responsible scaling.

GOVERNANCE OVERLAY AND ETHICAL SAFEGUARDS

The governance overlay is not a peripheral addition; it is constitutive of the model. Digital transformation can create inequitable access to development, opaque use of performance data, surveillance-like analytics practices, workload escalation, academic integrity uncertainty and erosion of academic autonomy. DCCSD therefore requires HEIs to pair competence expectations with practical safeguards.

- Informed participation: faculty should understand the purposes, expected benefits and risks of competence mapping, portfolio evidence and analytics-supported interventions.

- Transparent data-use policies: institutions should state what staff and student data are collected, who can access them, how long they are retained and what decisions they may or may not inform.
- Limits on analytics-based evaluation: platform activity and dashboard data should not be used as stand-alone proxies for teaching quality or staff performance.
- Bias and equity auditing: AI and analytics tools should be reviewed for differential impacts across staff groups, disciplines, contract types and student populations.
- Contestability: faculty and students should have mechanisms to query, challenge or seek review of data-driven recommendations or AI-supported decisions.
- Academic autonomy: faculty should participate meaningfully in decisions about pedagogical models, assessment policies, AI norms and analytics implementation.
- Workload and wellbeing protection: digital redesign, AI-aware assessment work and analytics-informed student support should be recognised in workload models and monitored for hidden labour.

These safeguards are consistent with responsible learning analytics scholarship, which treats analytics as a justice-oriented and context-sensitive practice rather than as neutral measurement (Grimm et al., 2023), and with human-centred AI guidance that emphasises agency, inclusion, privacy, transparency and responsible professional learning (Miao & Holmes, 2023; Miao & Cukurova, 2024).

Regarding ethics and transparency, it should be noted that this chapter is conceptual and does not report primary human participant data. The institutional examples and scenarios are used as illustrative design patterns rather than as empirical validation of the DCCSD Model. No claims of model effectiveness are made without acknowledging the need for future external validation and implementation research. During revision, AI-assisted editorial support was used for language refinement and document preparation; the author(s) remain responsible for scholarly judgement, source verification, interpretation and final approval.

IMPLEMENTATION GUIDANCE

Implementation playbook

DCCSD can be implemented as a sequenced capability-building cycle. The sequence is intended to help HEIs move from fragmented professional development towards an integrated upskilling ecosystem.

1. Establish a shared competency language by adapting the seven DCCSD domains to local disciplines, roles and institutional strategy.
2. Conduct formative baseline mapping using self-assessment, portfolio prompts, peer dialogue and discipline-specific examples. The baseline should inform development planning and resource allocation, not punitive evaluation.
3. Design differentiated pathways aligned to career stages and proficiency levels, including induction, mentoring, design studios, communities of practice, micro-credentials and governance-focused leadership development.
4. Align talent-management systems by recognising digital redesign, AI-aware assessment work, analytics-informed support and digital scholarship in workload, performance development, promotion and recognition.
5. Implement governance safeguards for AI, analytics and staff data use, including transparency, proportionality, contestability, privacy protection and equity auditing.
6. Evaluate and iterate using capability, practice, student experience, workload, equity and institutional capability indicators. Evaluation should support learning and improvement rather than surveillance.

Public practice exemplars and transferable lessons

Because the DCCSD Model has not yet been empirically validated, institutional examples should be treated as practical analogues rather than proof of effectiveness. Three public examples illustrate how elements of the model can be operationalised.

First, the University of Edinburgh's digital skills approach, documented by Jisc, illustrates how a digital capability agenda can be connected to a wider institutional digital transformation strategy. The case describes digital skills development as part of cross-institution transformation and notes links to staff development, career and talent-management workstreams (Jisc, 2020). The transferable lesson for DCCSD is that faculty capability should be embedded in institutional strategy and career-development conversations, not left as optional self-improvement.

Second, UCL's ABC Learning Design provides a concrete example of practice-embedded and team-based learning design development. ABC uses short, structured workshops in which academic teams collaboratively storyboard learning activities and assessment in relation to outcomes; UCL reports that the approach has been used widely across the institution and integrated into programme development and review (UCL, n.d.; Young et al., 2026). The transferable lesson for DCCSD is that Domains 1 and 2 can be operationalised through collaborative design studios linked to programme approval, quality enhancement and assessment redesign.

Third, Jisc's building digital capability resources provide a sector-level example of role-sensitive digital capability language. The Jisc framework identifies six elements of digital capability and provides role profiles for teachers, students, researchers, learning technologists, educational developers, digital leaders and professional services staff (Jisc, 2022). The transferable lesson for DCCSD is that role profiles can support differentiated development. DCCSD extends this logic by adding academic career-stage progression, talent-management alignment and explicit AI/analytics governance.

Discipline- and resource-sensitive adaptation

Implementation should not assume that a single pathway fits all contexts. Discipline matters because digital scholarship, assessment integrity, AI use and evidence artefacts differ across laboratory sciences, clinical education, professional programmes, humanities, arts, social sciences and language education. Resource context also matters. High-resource institutions may implement sophisticated analytics support, learning design teams and internal micro-credentials; lower-resource institutions may begin with peer mentoring, open educational resources, low-cost assessment redesign clinics and governance templates. The common requirement is not identical infrastructure but explicit alignment among expectations, support, workload, recognition and safeguards (*see* Table 7).

Table 7. Stakeholder implementation checklist for DCCSD

Stakeholder group	Primary use of DCCSD	Practical outputs
Senior leaders	Translate digital strategy into capability investment, governance and workload policy.	Institutional DCCSD roadmap; resourcing plan; governance charter; progress dashboard.
HR and talent-management teams	Embed DCCSD language into job profiles, induction, probation, performance development, promotion and retention.	Revised role profiles; workload-recognition guidance; promotion/ recognition rubrics.
Academic developers and learning designers	Design career-stage pathways, mentoring, design studios, peer review and portfolio prompts.	Upskilling curriculum; communities of practice; portfolio templates; facilitator guides.

continued on following page

Table 7. Continued

Stakeholder group	Primary use of DCCSD	Practical outputs
Faculty and programme teams	Use DCCSD to plan development, document evidence and negotiate support for digital academic work.	Individual development plans; portfolio artefacts; programme assessment and engagement plans.
IT, data and governance units	Ensure secure systems, transparent analytics, AI governance, privacy, contestability and bias auditing.	Data-use statements; AI/analytics governance processes; risk registers; audit reports.
Students and student support services	Contribute to transparency, feedback, accessibility and responsible AI/analytics use.	Student-facing AI/analytics statements; feedback loops; support-referral protocols.

In summary, implementation requires more than a training catalogue. It requires a shared capability language, differentiated pathways, workload and recognition alignment, public governance safeguards, practical stakeholder tools and an evaluation plan that measures capability and equity without intensifying surveillance (*see* Table 8).

Table 8. Example evaluation indicators for DCCSD implementation

Evaluation focus	Indicative indicators	Potential data sources	Governance considerations
Capability development	Participation in pathways; portfolio artefact completion; peer-review outcomes; self-efficacy changes; micro-credential completion.	Professional development systems; portfolios; peer observation reports; surveys.	Use evidence formatively; avoid punitive scoring; clarify purposes.
Teaching and assessment practice	Inclusive learning design adoption; assessment redesign completion; feedback quality and timeliness; academic integrity guidance quality.	Course design reviews; LMS artefacts; moderation records; student feedback.	Respect disciplinary variation; avoid equating platform activity with quality.
Student outcomes and experience	Engagement patterns; satisfaction; progression; attainment; academic integrity incidents interpreted cautiously.	Student surveys; institutional analytics; assessment outcomes; integrity case records.	Use analytics proportionately; inform students about data use.
Equity impacts	Participation and outcomes disaggregated by discipline, contract type, career stage and staff group; accessibility improvements.	HR/PD data; accessibility audits; equity dashboards; qualitative feedback.	Use equity analysis to direct support and resources, not to stigmatise groups.

continued on following page

Table 8. Continued

Evaluation focus	Indicative indicators	Potential data sources	Governance considerations
Workload and wellbeing	Workload allocation fairness; boundary-management issues; wellbeing indicators; turnover intentions.	Workload models; pulse surveys; HR metrics; focus groups.	Protect confidentiality; use findings to redesign roles and supports.
Institutional capability	Programme-level coherence of digital curriculum; scalability of innovations; governance compliance for AI/analytics.	Quality assurance reviews; programme reports; governance audits; policy logs.	Ensure faculty representation and mechanisms of contestability.

DISCUSSION

The DCCSD Model contributes to scholarship and practice by integrating literatures that are often treated separately. Digital transformation literature explains institutional change; digital competence literature explains capability domains; technology integration and adoption theories explain pedagogical fit and enabling conditions; AI and analytics scholarship explains emerging ethical requirements; and talent-management scholarship explains how capability can be institutionalised. DCCSD synthesises these streams into a framework that connects faculty digital competence to academic career-stage development and talent-management systems.

The theoretical contribution is the model's alignment logic. DCCSD proposes that digital transformation becomes more sustainable when competence expectations, development opportunities, evidence artefacts, workload recognition, governance safeguards and career incentives are mutually reinforcing. This differentiates the model from competence-only frameworks, which may describe what educators need to know but do not fully specify how institutions should embed those capabilities into career and talent structures.

The practical contribution is the provision of implementation artefacts: a literature matrix, framework comparison, evidence-to-model mapping, competency domains, portfolio evidence, career-stage pathways, talent-management alignment, stakeholder checklist and evaluation indicators. These artefacts can support institutional leaders, HR professionals, academic developers and faculty in translating digital transformation strategy into concrete capability-building activities.

Nevertheless, implementation will surface tensions. Workload inflation is a central risk because digital redesign, AI-aware assessment and analytics-informed support require time. Surveillance risk is also significant when staff or student data are used without transparency or context. Equity risks arise when development opportunities are unevenly distributed across disciplines, contract types, campuses or career stages. Resistance should therefore not be interpreted simply as reluctance to innovate; it may signal legitimate concerns about workload, autonomy, trust, professional identity or inadequate support.

The model is also context-sensitive. HEIs in low- and middle-income settings, smaller institutions and resource-constrained departments may not be able to implement all elements simultaneously. DCCSD should therefore be adapted through phased implementation: begin with shared language, priority domains, low-cost peer support and governance basics, then scale towards portfolio evidence, workload recognition, analytics support and leadership pipelines as resources permit.

Limitations and Future Validation Agenda

The chapter's primary limitation is that DCCSD is conceptual. Although it is grounded in literature, public practice examples and internal coherence checking, it has not yet been externally validated through expert consensus, pilot implementation or longitudinal evaluation. The institutional examples are illustrative analogues and should not be interpreted as evidence that DCCSD itself improves faculty capability or institutional outcomes.

A staged validation agenda is therefore recommended. Phase 1 should involve expert review with academic developers, HR leaders, faculty representatives, digital learning leaders, data governance specialists and students to evaluate the model's clarity, relevance, completeness and feasibility. Phase 2 should involve cognitive interviews and focus groups across disciplines and career stages to test whether the domains, portfolio artefacts and career-stage expectations are interpreted consistently. Phase 3 should pilot DCCSD in selected faculties or programmes using mixed-methods evaluation, including pre/post capability self-assessment, portfolio review, workload data, staff wellbeing indicators, student experience data and equity analysis. Phase 4 should refine the model and, if a measurement instrument is developed, test reliability, validity and measurement invariance across disciplines and career stages. Phase 5 should examine longitudinal effects on programme quality, assessment design, responsible AI/analytics use, staff retention and institutional capability.

Future research should also examine disciplinary variation, faculty resistance, contract status, gendered and racialised workload patterns, resource constraints in low- and middle-income institutions, and the ethical governance of staff data. These areas are essential if digital transformation is to be evaluated not merely as technological progress but as a human-centred and equitable institutional change process.

CONCLUSION

Digital transformation in higher education is often presented as a technology-led agenda, yet sustainable transformation depends on people, practices and institutional capability. Faculty capacity to enact digitally mediated teaching, assessment, student support, scholarship and governance is central to this agenda. The challenge is that faculty upskilling is frequently fragmented, uneven and disconnected from talent-management systems.

This chapter proposed the Digital Competency and Career-Stage Development (DCCSD) Model as a conceptual and strategic framework for addressing that challenge. The model defines seven domains of faculty digital competence, differentiates expectations across career stages, aligns capability development with the talent-management lifecycle and embeds governance safeguards for equity, privacy, academic autonomy, workload sustainability and responsible AI/analytics use.

The model's core claim is that faculty upskilling should be treated as a strategic talent-management mechanism, not as a peripheral training activity. By aligning competence, career development, workload, recognition and governance, HEIs can move towards upskilling ecosystems that are academically meaningful, ethically credible and institutionally sustainable. The next step is empirical validation through expert review, pilot implementation and longitudinal evaluation.

REFERENCES

Abiwu, L., & Martins, I. (2022). Talent development as a source of sustainable competitive advantage for higher education institutions during the COVID-19 pandemic. *SA Journal of Human Resource Management, 20*, a1777. DOI: 10.4102/sajhrm.v20i0.1777

Basilotta-Gómez-Pablos, V., Matarranz, M., Casado-Aranda, L.-A., & Otto, A. (2022). Teachers' digital competencies in higher education: A systematic literature review. *International Journal of Educational Technology in Higher Education, 19*(1), 8. DOI: 10.1186/s41239-021-00312-8

Bates, A. W. (2022). *Teaching in a digital age: Guidelines for designing teaching and learning* (3rd ed.). Tony Bates Associates Ltd., https://pressbooks.bccampus.ca/teachinginadigitalagev3m/

Bond, M., Marín, V. I., Dolch, C., Bedenlier, S., & Zawacki-Richter, O. (2018). Digital transformation in German higher education: Student and teacher perceptions and usage of digital media. *International Journal of Educational Technology in Higher Education, 15*(1), 48. DOI: 10.1186/s41239-018-0130-1

Brady, S. S., Brubaker, L., Fok, C. S., Gahagan, S., Lewis, C. E., Lewis, J., Lowder, J. L., Nodora, J., Stapleton, A., Palmer, M. H., Mueller, E., Fitzgerald, C. M., Hardacker, C. T., Hebert-Beirne, J., Lavender, M., Shoham, D. A., Burgio, K., Markland, A., McGwin, G., & Constantine, M.Prevention of Lower Urinary Tract Symptoms (PLUS) Research Consortium. (2020). Development of conceptual models to guide public health research, practice, and policy: Synthesizing traditional and contemporary paradigms. *Health Promotion Practice, 21*(4), 510–524. DOI: 10.1177/1524839919890869 PMID: 31910039

Castañeda, L., & Selwyn, N. (2018). More than tools? Making sense of the ongoing digitizations of higher education. *International Journal of Educational Technology in Higher Education, 15*(1), 22. DOI: 10.1186/s41239-018-0109-y

Castro Benavides, L. M., Tamayo Arias, J. A., Arango Serna, M. D., Branch Bedoya, J. W., & Burgos, D. (2020). Digital transformation in higher education institutions: A systematic literature review. *Sensors (Basel), 20*(11), 3291. DOI: 10.3390/s20113291 PMID: 32526998

Charles, T. (2025). AI in professional development for English language teachers. In Ali, M., Fazal, S., & Ayyaz, S. (Eds.), *AI applications for English language learning* (pp. 73–92). IGI Global., DOI: 10.4018/979-8-3693-9077-1.ch004

Charles, T., & Papadaki, M. (2025). Ethical leadership in technology integration and digital education. In Soles, B., & Meyerott, T. (Eds.), *Diverse leadership perspectives in education: From K-12 to higher education* (pp. 437–454). IGI Global Scientific Publishing., DOI: 10.4018/979-8-3693-6115-3.ch016

Farias-Gaytan, S., Aguaded, I., & Ramírez-Montoya, M.-S. (2023). Digital transformation and digital literacy in the context of complexity within higher education institutions: A systematic literature review. *Humanities & Social Sciences Communications*, *10*(1), 386. DOI: 10.1057/s41599-023-01875-9

Fernández-Batanero, J. M., Román-Graván, P., Montenegro-Rueda, M., López-Meneses, E., & Fernández-Cerero, J. (2021). Digital teaching competence in higher education: A systematic review. *Education Sciences*, *11*(11), 689. DOI: 10.3390/educsci11110689

Freitas, A., & Paredes, J. (2018). Understanding the faculty perspectives influencing their innovative practices in MOOCs/SPOCs: A case study. *International Journal of Educational Technology in Higher Education*, *15*(1), 5. DOI: 10.1186/s41239-017-0086-6

Grimm, A., Steegh, A., Çolakoğlu, J., Kubsch, M., & Neumann, K. (2023). Positioning responsible learning analytics in the context of STEM identity development with a focus on under-served students. *Frontiers in Education*, *7*, 1082748. DOI: 10.3389/feduc.2022.1082748

Jabareen, Y. (2009). Building a conceptual framework: Philosophy, definitions, and procedure. *International Journal of Qualitative Methods*, *8*(4), 49–62. DOI: 10.1177/160940690900800406

Jisc. (2020). *University of Edinburgh: Building digital capability*. https://digitalcapability.jisc.ac.uk/case-studies/university-edinburgh/

Jisc. (2022). *Building digital capabilities framework: The six elements defined*. https://digitalcapability.jisc.ac.uk/what-is-digital-capability/individual-digital-capabilities/

Miao, F., & Cukurova, M. (2024). *AI competency framework for teachers*. UNESCO., DOI: 10.54675/ZJTE2084

Miao, F., & Holmes, W. (2023). *Guidance for generative AI in education and research*. UNESCO. https://www.unesco.org/en/articles/guidance-generative-ai-education-and-research

Mishra, P., & Koehler, M. J. (2006). Technological pedagogical content knowledge: A framework for teacher knowledge. *Teachers College Record*, *108*(6), 1017–1054. DOI: 10.1111/j.1467-9620.2006.00684.x

Naeem, M., Ozuem, W., Howell, K., & Ranfagni, S. (2023). A step-by-step process of thematic analysis to develop a conceptual model in qualitative research. *International Journal of Qualitative Methods*, *22*, 1–18. DOI: 10.1177/16094069231205789

Redecker, C. (2017). *European framework for the digital competence of educators: DigCompEdu* (Punie, Y., Ed.). Publications Office of the European Union., DOI: 10.2760/159770

Shamseer, L., Moher, D., Clarke, M., Ghersi, D., Liberati, A., Petticrew, M., Shekelle, P., & Stewart, L. A.PRISMA-P Group. (2015). Preferred reporting items for systematic review and meta-analysis protocols (PRISMA-P) 2015: Elaboration and explanation. *BMJ (Clinical Research Ed.)*, *349*(jan02 1), g7647. DOI: 10.1136/bmj.g7647 PMID: 25555855

Siemens, G. (2013). Learning analytics: The emergence of a discipline. *The American Behavioral Scientist*, *57*(10), 1380–1400. DOI: 10.1177/0002764213498851

Sillat, L. H., Tammets, K., & Laanpere, M. (2021). Digital competence assessment methods in higher education: A systematic literature review. *Education Sciences*, *11*(8), 402. DOI: 10.3390/educsci11080402

Soomro, K. A., Kale, U., Curtis, R., Akcaoglu, M., & Bernstein, M. (2020). Digital divide among higher education faculty. *International Journal of Educational Technology in Higher Education*, *17*(1), 21. DOI: 10.1186/s41239-020-00191-5 PMID: 41001069

Sun, T., & Yoon, M. (2025). The impact of digital transformation on faculty performance in higher education: The mediating role of digital self-efficacy and the moderating role of task-technology fit. *Frontiers in Psychology*, *16*, 1693375. DOI: 10.3389/fpsyg.2025.1693375 PMID: 41190117

Tenberga, I., & Daniela, L. (2024). Artificial intelligence literacy competencies for teachers through self-assessment tools. *Sustainability (Basel)*, *16*(23), 10386. DOI: 10.3390/su162310386

UCL. (n.d.). *ABC Learning Design @ UCL*. Retrieved June 30, 2026, from https://blogs.ucl.ac.uk/abc-ld/

Venkatesh, V., Morris, M. G., Davis, G. B., & Davis, F. D. (2003). User acceptance of information technology: Toward a unified view. *Management Information Systems Quarterly*, *27*(3), 425–478. DOI: 10.2307/30036540

Young, C., Perović, N., Havemann, L., & Shackleford-Cesare, K. (Eds.). (2026). *ABC Learning Design: Active, blended, connected and beyond*. UCL Press. https://uclpress.co.uk/book/abc-learning-design/

Chapter 10
Change Management and Organizational Culture in Digital HEIs

R. Velmurugan
http://orcid.org/0000-0002-7925-9757
Karpagam Academy of Higher Education, Coimbatore, India

K. Kumuthadevi
KPR College of Arts, Science, and Research, Coimbatore, India

D. Bhuvanendran
Nallamuthu Gounder Mahalingam College, Pollachi, India

Joji Abey
http://orcid.org/0000-0003-4176-3023
Kingdom University, Bahrain

ABSTRACT

Institutions of higher learning are being digitalized with sophisticated technologies being introduced in teaching, administration, and research. The effectiveness of adoption of technology and subsequent management of change and development of supportive organisational culture are also factors that determine success. The communication and training reduce resistance and increase the stakeholder involvement as well as development of digital competencies, which is supported by change management. In its turn, the organisational culture determines the perception and adoption of innovation by the faculty, staff, and students. An organizational culture of cooperation, innovation, and constant learning allows an effective transition toward and a constant practice of the new practices. Leadership facilitates the

DOI: 10.4018/979-8-3373-8959-2.ch010

process of transforming the institution by aligning the vision, establishing trust, and propelling the process, thus, allowing institutions to develop flexible, inclusive, and future-oriented learning environments.

INTRODUCTION

Universities and colleges are in a paradoxical situation as they are on the edge of digital transformation. Universities may be anticipated to be the most avid early adopters of the knowledge underlying technological progress as they are its producers and disseminators. However, the empirical experience is always of the same kind, that HEIs are one of the most resistant to transformational change organisations of that kind, not due to the lack of smartness or goodwill among their members but due to the fact that the scholarly business is based on the values of deliberation, collegiality, disciplinary richness, and institutional autonomy that are inherently in conflict with the speed, disruption, and standardisation that digital The key issue with this tension is navigating it, which is the main problem of this chapter.

Digital transformation of higher education is a multi-faceted, powerful impetus. The 2020 COVID-19 pandemic and the extended aftermath was a stress test that, at once, revealed the hidden ability of most universities to swiftly go digital - the transition to online classes occurred overnight and impacted over 1.5 billion learners around the world - and showed how poorly that transition would proceed otherwise, unless it was backed by a deliberate strategy, sufficient infrastructure, and cultural preparedness (Marinoni, van't Land The transition proved to be smoother in institutions that had already invested in powerful learning management systems, training in digital pedagogy and data analytics infrastructure prior to the pandemic than in institutions that depended on face-to-face interaction and paper-based processes.

In addition to the pandemic, the HEIs are still being pushed towards digital transformation by structural forces. Massification of higher education has resulted in student cohorts of unprecedented size and diversity - in terms of age, socioeconomic background, geographic location, prior educational experience, and learning preference - whose demands are increasingly beyond the means of traditional campus-based, cohort-based, credit-hour-defined degree programmes to meet (Selwyn, 2022). The emergence of lifelong learning needs, due to the disruption of the labour market caused by artificial intelligence and automation, is creating a demand of flexible, stackable and micro-credentialled learning pathways that demand institutional structures of a radically different nature than the semester based bachelors degree. Competitive pressure on traditional institutions due to global competition by platform based educational providers (Coursera, edX, Udacity and their successors) is growing, not subsiding.

To react to these forces, change is of systemic and cultural character, rather than of technical upgrading, that HEIs need to engage in. Re-implementing an old system of student information or implementing a new virtual learning environment are changes required but not sufficient; they only benefit an organisation in the long term when implemented within a transformed workflow, staff with real digital competency, decision-making based on data analysis, and an organisational culture that embraces experimentation, lifelong learning, and student-centred innovation. The disconnect between digital investment and digital transformation between procuring technology and actually transforming an institution and its approach to creating and delivering educational value is more of a change management and cultural issue (Hodges et al., 2022).

This chapter is made up of eleven substantive sections. It starts with the theoretical and practical purpose of change management in digital transformation of HEIs and looks at how effective change implementation, change communication and stakeholder engagement can be achieved and goes on to discuss training and professional development. It then moves on to the organisational culture aspects of the digital transformation such as the nurturing of innovation, leadership and the match to student expectations. As a technical and a cultural practice, data-based decision-making in HEIs is explored. The chapter ends with a synthesis of challenges and opportunities and recommendations based on the evidence analysed in the chapter.

THE ROLE OF CHANGE MANAGEMENT IN DIGITAL TRANSFORMATION

In applied organisational sense, change management is the organised methods, procedures, equipment and practices by which an organisation moves between its present state and its desired future state as well as reducing the degree of turmoil, maintenance of performance, and achieving loyalty of the members within an organisation. Change management in the particular context of digital transformation in HEIs fulfils a number of key roles: it transforms abstract strategic visions of digital futures into tangible implementation pathways; it predicts and responds to the human, cultural and political origins of resistance generated by technical change; it orders and organises change initiatives across complex, multi-stakeholder organisations in a manner that prevents initiative fatigue and contradiction; and it develops the institutional capacity,

Since the seminal unfreeze-change-refreeze model of organisational change management in the 1940s by Lewin, the theoretical underpinnings of organisational change management have been greatly developed. The modern frameworks that can be used in the context of the digital transformation of HEIs are based on various traditions. The eight-step model offered by Kotter - the establishment of urgency, the formation of a guiding coalition, the creation of a vision, the communication of the vision, empowering action, short-term wins, the consolidation of gains, anchoring the change in culture - has been popular in higher education settings due to its practical structure, but has been criticized as overly linear, disregarding the non-linear, iterative nature of institutional change within Awareness, Desire, Knowledge, Ability, Reinforcement (ADKAR model), created by Prosci, is a complementary framework at the individual level that is more and more widely used in the context of digital transformation in HEI, to fill the gap between organisational change plans and individual behavioural adoption a gap which Gartner research indicates is the cause of most digital transformation failures (Hiatt, 2022).

An emerging higher education-centric body of change scholarship stresses the need to appreciate the unique attributes of academic organisations that render generic models of corporate change management to apply imperfectly. Kezar and Holcombe (2021) hold that universities are typified by loosely coupled structures in that the constituent units (faculties, departments, research centres, professional services divisions) have great freedom not to be directed by centrally based direction), and which complicate system-wide change greatly. The traditions of shared governance, where academic workforce can become officially involved in making curriculum, policy, and strategic decisions, imply that top-down imposed digital change is usually met with opposition or outward compliance instead of internalized adoption. Effective change management within HEIs should thus involve the academic governance structures as valid places of discussion and co-design, as opposed to the barriers to surmount (Zawacki-Richter et al., 2022).

The COVID-19 pandemic created a natural experiment of change management of higher education on a global level. A systematic review of emergency remote teaching experiences in 28 countries by Rapanta et al. (2021) found that institutions that had a pre-existing capacity of digital change management, such as digital governance structures, IT support structures, and professional development infrastructure, were much more successful in the outcomes of educational continuity and staff wellbeing than those with improvisational responses. More importantly, the research revealed that the quality of previous involvement of the academic staff into the digital pedagogy as a cultural and professional developmental outcome but not a technical was the most important predictor of the teaching quality during the transition, which highlights the value of the human aspect of digital change management.

The change management of the digital transformation in HEIs should consider the unique timeline challenges of an academic organisation, as well. Processes of institutional change which could take twelve to eighteen months in a corporate setting are habitually prolonged among five to ten years in universities where the limited academic calendar, committee control cycles and staff-consultation demands slow the change process. This temporal truth has significant design implications of change management: initiatives should be designed to provide visible interim value on a regular basis - to avoid initiative fatigue and keep stakeholders engaged - and to continue to move towards long-term transformational objectives (Vial, 2021). The idea of ambidextrous-like digital leadership, which balances on the same side by leveraging the existing institutional advantages and is searching the new digital opportunities, has become popular as a paradigm of dealing with this time paradox (O'Reilly and Tushman, 2021).

STRATEGIES FOR EFFECTIVE CHANGE MANAGEMENT

Digitally transforming HEIs change management strategies should be both systemic and differentiated, systemic in terms of offering a coherent institutional framework that aligns initiatives throughout the institution, and differentiated in terms of acknowledging the change readiness, capacity and cultural specifics of various institutional units, staff groups, and stakeholder communities. There is a significant amount of evidence that the most effective HEI digital transformations can be defined through five strategic pillars, namely: the visionary leadership with distributed ownership, staged implementation with closed feedback loops, authentic co-design with academic staff, committed capability to change management, and explicit consideration of equity and inclusion aspects of digital access (Bates, 2022).

The superior results in the HEI literature have always been the use of a phaged implementation strategies that roll out digital transformation in pilot projects, incremental improvement, and full scale deployment, instead of using the so-called big bang institution-wide change implementation strategies. Picciano (2022) compared implementation strategies in forty-three American universities, and discovered that those implementing phased and pilot-led strategies had 34% higher sustained faculty adoption rates in two years than those implementing simultaneous institution-wide implementations, due to the impact of the learning-by-doing culture, visible early success, and adaptive calibration that phased strategies allow. The presence of strategic piloting in departments whose leaders are highly change-centered and who support the change gives evidence of proof-of-concept that creates institutional faith and creates champions of staff who become peer-to-peer champions when the change is rolled out to larger groups.

Co-design practices: where academic and professional personnel have a meaningful role in the design of digital processes and systems that influence them is a growingly accepted way to realise true adoption as opposed to compliance. Scanlon et al. (2021) have recorded a participatory design process of a new learning analytics platform on three Australian universities where discipline-specific working groups took part in the design of dashboards, choice of data variables, and development of intervention protocols. The researchers discovered that employees of co-design institutions expressed much more trust in the outputs of the platform, reduced privacy issues, and more integration of the insight of analytics into teaching activities than control institutions in which the platform was introduced without participatory design despite the same technical opportunities.

Institutional change management capacity (such as change management experts on the project digital transformation teams, systematic change impact appraisals before implementation, formalized mechanisms to surface and deal with staff issues) is a differentiator of more successful HEI transformations. Noesgaard and Nielsen (2021) compared Scandinavian university projects of digital transformation and discovered that institutions that had specific change management functions were much less likely to experience project failure and had a 4 times quicker time-to-adoption than institutions that used IT project managers to carry out change management functions in addition to technical duties. The authors found that managing change in complex academic organisations involves special skills in organisational psychology, engagement with stakeholders and cultural dynamics that cannot be found in, and are complementary to, technical project management competency.

Equity and inclusion in change management strategy are increasingly being seen as an ethical requirement, as well as a practical requirement towards sustainability of transformation. Planned digital transformation efforts that favor already-privileged groups of students and staff already endowed with superior devices, connectivity, and digital literacy, and impose further obstacles on under-represented groups are likely to yield counterproductive results that subvert the very equity missions of any HEI and elicit justified political backlash. Equity-conscious change management incorporates digital inclusion audit, support of less digitally confident employees and students, accessible design considerations, and community consultation into change planning at the beginning of the change process, instead of as an afterthought (Selwyn, 2022).

COMMUNICATION AND STAKEHOLDER ENGAGEMENT

Communication is not a facilitating practice of change management in digitally transforming HEIs - it is one of its key tools. The quality, consistency, transparency and bidirectionality of change communication influence the way stakeholders interpret the intent and meaning of change, whether they view leadership as credible, whether they propagate misinformation and rumour at a very fast rate (which is a sure way of filling the communication space), and finally whether they become commitmentally or resistant to change. Higher education settings, where faculty members are conditioned to view any assertion with skepticism and where institutional credibility is an asset that has been built over time and is easily lost, are especially demanding of the norms of credible change communication (Bolman and Deal, 2022).

The literature on effective change communication within the context of digital transformation of HEIs has a number of consistent characteristics. Clearness of purpose: It is essential to be clear about what is changing, why, and with a clear linkage to institutional mission and benefit to students. In a qualitative study of the perceptions of twelve American research universities regarding digital transformation, Zhu and Anagnostopoulos (2021) discovered that faculty who perceived the change in strategic justification as it led to investment in new digital capabilities displayed much lower role ambiguity, greater change commitment, and readiness to invest in acquiring new digital capabilities than did faculty who experienced change as forced by outside influences with no apparent educational rationale. Honesty about costs, risks and uncertainties - such as truthful recognition of what leaders themselves do not yet know - is found to be an especially valuable trust-building communication practice in academic cultures where intellectual honesty is a professional value.

The environment of a university is a multi-constituency place with multiple stakeholders in need of communication. Communication requirements of first-year undergraduate students, postgraduates researching, early-career academic staff, senior professors, staff in professional services, members of the governing body, and external community partners are fundamentally divergent - in terms of content, channel preference, frequency, and framing - that cannot be addressed using one-size-fits-all strategies. A survey of UK higher education institutions by Jisc (2023) of digital transformation strategies reported higher stakeholder awareness, understanding, and positive feeling towards digital transformation in institutions that used segmented, multi-channel communication methods than in those using uniform all-staff communications and those with lower socioeconomic backgrounds and students who used institutional channels less.

Bidirectional communication - organized systems of stakeholders to give feedback, express concerns, and evidence of how their input has contributed to decisions - is always reported as the least invested aspect of HEI change communication. The use of town halls, online feedback systems, focus groups, departmental roadshows and concern-reporting systems, anonymity has the dual purpose of providing real intelligence on implementation issues as well as showing respect to the views of the stakeholders that is a key to winning the trust needed to continue the engagement. In a case study of a Portuguese polytechnic university digital transformation communication programme, Queiros et al. (2022) reported that the implementation of a formalized system of academic staff feedback in an institutional digital platform connected with an institutional response protocol decreased resistance to a rollout of a new learning management system by 42 percent in six months of implementation (measured by metrics of an academic senate discussion).

The interest of students in communication on digital transformation tends to be under-valued compared to the interest of staff in the same process, but at the same time, students are the main beneficiaries of successful transformation and one of the most influential groups of stakeholders in this process. Student experience outcomes of digital systems are proven to be better in institutions where student union representatives have been actively involved in the governance of digital transformation as part of steering committees, co-design processes, and as co-authors of digital strategy documents. A review of twelve examples of student involvement in educational technology design in UK and Australian higher education institutions by Dollinger et al. (2023) indicated that student-involved design processes yielded platforms with markedly higher usability scores, a higher degree of mobile optimisation, and a higher level of support of the varied student accessibility requirements as compared to expert-designed counterparts.

TRAINING AND DEVELOPMENT INITIATIVES

The interface of digital strategy and digital practice in the Higher Education Institutions is professional development and training. Even digital systems that are conceptually developed and change communications that are the most persuasive do not lead to transformational results when staff do not possess the competencies, confidence, and pedagogical models that would make them apply technology in a manner that can really improve the quality of education. The task is daunting: the population of staff in HEIs is highly heterogeneous in terms of previous experience with digital devices, their approach to learning, availability of time and motivation to change towards digital devices (Hodges et al., 2022).

The two frameworks that are used to describe the dimensions of digital competency by the European Commission (DigComp and DigCompEdu) have become popular with European HEIs as models of how to organize their staff digital development programmes, as well as to map the progress of their staff. According to DigCompEdu, educators have six competence areas, which include professional engagement, digital resources, teaching and learning, assessment, empower learning and connecting digital competence in learners (Redecker, 2021). Research that uses the framework in the context of higher education is consistently finding that there is a bimodal distribution in staff digital competency - with a concentration at both ends of the continuum, the novice and the proficient, and a relatively sparse population between these extremes - indicating that successful development programmes need to target simultaneously the foundational digital literacy and advanced pedagogical innovation, rather than a consistent point of staff starting level.

Peer-learning models where digitally competent academic professionals are mentors, champions or advisors to colleagues in the process of deploying their digital practice are regularly more effective than formal training practices in the literature on the digital transformation of HEIs. Bond et al. (2021) meta-analysed sixty-seven studies of digital professional development in higher education, and discover that peer mentoring, communities of practice, and co-teaching set-ups yielded significantly higher and more sustained gains in digital teaching practice than workshop-based instruction, and attributed the difference to the contextual relevance, disciplinary applicability, and sustained accountability that peer-learning structures engender. Formalizing the appointment of so-called digital fellows or technology stewards programmes (whereby a small group of staff are appointed to intensive development in digital pedagogy and gain institutional recognition in exchange with peer development responsibilities) have become a cost-efficient way of scaling the development of digital competencies without directly increasing central professional development budgets.

Micro-credentialling and badging The certification of particular, granular digital competencies in the form of digital credentials that can be accumulated, displayed and constructed into portfolio records by the staff has become a common trend in HEI staff development settings. The model will deal with a long-standing motivation obstacle in the way of formal training participation: the belief that the investment of time in long training programmes is not well matched by their immediate practical payoff. Micro-credentials in particular digital teaching skills, such as designing easy online tests, working with learning analytics dashboards, writing multimedia learning materials that are interactive can allow the staff to develop the competency in small steps specifically to address immediate professional requirements, with visible credentialling to add to academic and professional promotion portfolios (Brown and Nic Giolla Mhichil, 2022).

The development of digital competencies of administrative and professional services personnel in HEIs should also respond to the needs of developing digital competencies of the staff in administrative services and professional services, the impact of which on the digital transformation is often as consequential as that of academic staff but, because of institutional investment decision views, is less visible systematically. The digital competency development needed by registry staff operating digitally transformed enrolment processes, by finance teams operating with AI-assisted procurement tools, student welfare advisors operating with digital early-intervention systems and library staff supporting digital scholarship, all have a very different requirement of digitally competence development tailored to their particular business environments and is very different to the pedagogical focus of academic development programmes. Sá and Serpa (2021) reported the presence of major performance shortfalls in HEI digital transformation projects that could be explained by insufficient investment in professional services digital development, such as the failure to adopt the system, data quality issues, and gaps in the redesign of workflows that created disturbances in the provision of services to students.

ORGANIZATIONAL CULTURE AND DIGITAL TRANSFORMATION

The most influential and the most underrated determinant of digital transformation success in HEIs is organisational culture the set of shared values, assumptions, beliefs, norms of behaviour, and symbolic practices defining an institution and meaning the behaviour of the members thereof. Technology may be acquired; strategy may be created; training may be provided; however culture cannot be imposed. It should be nurtured by means of prolonged focus on the informal dynamics - the tales individuals narrate, the heroes they glorify, the patterns of behaviour leadership paradigms and rewards, the language that shapes digital change - that comprises the experiential reality of the character of an institution (Schein and Schein, 2021).

Cultural dimensions by Hofstede and the three-level model of culture by Schein that identifies between visible artefacts, espoused values, and underlying basic assumptions, have both been used to the context of digital transformation in HEIs to shed light on the underlying deep-rooted cultural patterns that influence adoption of a technology. A study by Liang et al. (2021) used a cultural diagnostic framework to digital transformation readiness among twenty-two Asian universities and concluded that the institutions with cultures defined by high uncertainty avoidance (through the staff unwillingness to work with unpredictable or unfamiliar processes) had much slower digital adoption rates and resistance to AI-based teaching tools in comparison with institutions with cultures characterised by lower uncertainty avoidance. Importantly, the researchers concluded that these cultural patterns predicted better the results of transformation compared to institutional wealth, the quality of infrastructure or the support of senior leadership - which highlights the central role of culture in influencing digital transformation processes.

As a desired outcome of HEI transformation, the notion of digital culture has been more and more expressed in the literature, albeit under different definitions. There are common dimensions, such as: a growth mindset orientation to lifelong learning and competency building; psychological safety that is adequate to support experimentation, risk-taking and honest reporting of failure without career consequences; data literacy as a widely distributed ability to think in evidence-based ways; cross-disciplinary and collaborative working ways that do not rely on departmental or faculty silos; and a student-centred value orientation that prefigures The gap between the present cultural profile of a given institution and this desired digital culture state is a more valid indicator of the complexity of transformation and timeline than the technical complexity of intended digital systems.

The process of cultural change in HEIs is necessarily slow, non-linear and contested. The academic culture, as the result of centuries-long institutional practice and strengthened by socialisation of discipline, professional identity and traditions of governance, is not easily susceptible of strategic intervention. According to Fullan and Quinn (2021), successful cultural change in education organisations is not done by making direct attempts to change culture, which normally generate defensive responses, but by transforming the practices, relationships, and conditions that make up culture: as staff experience repeated success with new ways of working as effective and professionally rewarding, their assumptions and values begin to shift accordingly. This observation has significant implications on the strategy of digital transformation of HEI: culture change is a result of, not a precursor to, demonstrably successful digital practice, which implies that creating conditions of early success experiences is a more effective lever of cultural change than trying to change values through exhortation or training.

FOSTERING A CULTURE OF INNOVATION AND COLLABORATION

Among the most commonly mentioned cultural hopes of the HEIs that strive to undergo digital transformation are innovation and collaboration, but both tend to stay at the stage of espoused value instead of acted-upon practice when they are not backed up by certain structural circumstances and leadership practices. Educational innovation demands a workplace where academic staffs are prepared to try out new teaching and learning methods, take the risk of being initially flawed, openly share lessons of failure, and swiftly iterate to a better practice, which is not compatible with the risk-averse, individually competitive, and publication-driven cultures of many research-intensive universities (Fullan and Quinn, 2021).

Psychological safety Amy Edmondson describes the psychological safety as the shared belief that interpersonal risk-taking is safe and it is increasingly being identified as a background cultural precondition to digital innovation in HEIs. In a workplace where employees are afraid to state technological difficulties, pedagogical doubt, or discuss unsuccessful digital experimentation, not only is innovation repressed, but also their careers or performance appraisal. In contrast, where senior leaders themselves can talk publicly about their own experiences of digital learning, their own failures and misunderstandings, and where failure in digital experiments can be assessed as organisational learning and not personal failure, employees are much more likely to engage in digital experimentation, sharing knowledge with their peers, and adopting innovative practices (Edmondson and Bransby, 2023).

Structural change strategies to encourage collaborative digital innovation in HEIs involve: interdisciplinary working groups, which include academic staff members across different disciplines and educational technologists, data scientists, and student partners; focus on small grants to fund staff-led experiments on digital exploration with minimal administrative overhead; protected time to explore digital innovation built into workload models; annual digital innovation showcases that showcase and share successful experiments throughout the institution. An assessment of fifteen structures of HEI innovation programmes by Veletsianos and Kimmons (2021) established that programmes that combined financial support, protected time, peer learning community, and institutional recognition had the largest effects in terms of innovative practice diffusion - programmes composed of individual components yielded much smaller and shorter-lasting effects.

Cross-institutional collaboration: cross-institutional collaboration, via consortia, shared digital infrastructures, open educational resource projects, joint research and development projects, expands the innovation potential of individual HEIs beyond their own organisational scope. The development of national and regional digital transformation consortia, such as Jisc in the United Kingdom, SURF in the Netherlands and EDUCAUSE in the United States offer HEIs access to shared digital infrastructure, benchmarking data, professional development resources, and collaborative learning networks which would otherwise be inaccessible to individual institutions acting alone. In a study by Mwamba et al. (2023) on the effects of consortium membership on the speed of innovation in African HEI, the authors reported the average effect of being a member of the African Research Universities Alliance digital innovation network on the adoption of new educational technologies by 2.3 years compared to similar non-member institutions, attributing the effect to learning from peers, access to shared resources, and lobbying to facilitate enabling policy

LEADERSHIP'S ROLE IN SHAPING CULTURE

The most effective lever that can be used to influence organisational culture in the face of digital transformation in HEIs is leadership, which can be applied on a variety of channels at once: the priorities that a leader articulates and resources, the behaviours that a leader models personally, the narratives that a leader creates about the digital future of the institution, the staff that a leader recruits and promotes, the structural arrangements that a leader creates or maintains, and the symbol This cultural understanding of leadership as inherently a meaning-making and not a decision-making exercise is key to understanding why charismatic announcements of digital strategy with no follow-through behavioural patterns are a regular failure to induce the promised cultural change.

Top management commitment The observable, regularly sustained, and plausibly sustained support by Vice-Chancellors, Presidents, Provosts, and their respective staffs of digital transformation is both required and not enough to change the culture. Necessary, since the hierarchical organisations have their staff follow the lead of the priorities which the senior leaders are seen to take seriously; insufficient, since the cultural reach of the senior leaders in the loosely coupled academic organisations is constrained and often viewed with a grain of salt by the academic staff who value professional autonomy and peer governance. A distributed model of leadership is the most effective to have in place in HEI cultural transformation: top leaders set the strategic direction and resource priorities but the cultural change work is implemented through an extended network of change champions in middle-level roles - department heads, programme directors, digitally engaged senior academics, and professional services managers - who translate institutional vision into departmental practice and model digital behaviours within their immediate circles of influence (Jones et al., 2021

The digital leadership competency of the particular cognitive, technical and interpersonal skills needed to effectively lead digital change within educational organisations has become a unique topic of research and professional growth. Hallinger and Chatpinyakoop (2021) meta-analysed 48 studies of educational technology leadership and found four main clusters of core competencies: digital vision (the ability to communicate persuasively about the future with technology); digital literacy (adequate technical knowledge to assess, choose, and discuss about digital technologies); change leadership (the ability to overcome resistance, form alliances, and maintain momentum in a complex and long-term The research determined that leaders who exhibited all four competency clusters had a much higher number of successful digital transformation results compared to leaders who were competent in one or two dimensions.

The role of Chief Digital Officer (CDO) and Chief Information Officer (CIO) has a particularly important role in the digital transformation of HEIs, with a balance between the technical infrastructure leadership roles and the leadership of the cultural change that demands an unusually odd set of competencies. A survey of ninety-four CDOs and CIOs in UK higher education by Howell (2022) revealed that most effective incumbents were defined by: profound knowledge of the academic culture and governance; delivering technical concepts into educationally meaningful language to academic audiences; having strong collaborative relationships with both academic leaders and professional services directors; and having a consultative approach to the selection and implementation of digital systems. The paper also found that there is a considerable lack of applicants with these abilities in the labor market, who merge them in a particular way - a limitation on the digital leadership capacity of HEIs that cannot be resolved by digital strategy.

The digital transformation governance structures, such as the design of Digital Transformation Steering Committee, IT governance board, data ethics committee, and academic technology advisory committees, are indicative and perpetuate cultural values regarding decision-making power, stakeholder representation, and responsibility. When digital governance is centralized in few senior leadership teams or IT offices, institutions are likely to create digital strategies that are perceived as imposed by the leadership, which result in the compliance-without-commitment dynamics that weaken the sustainability of transformations. Those institutions that have more distributed governance architectures, meaning where the roles of academic staff, students, representatives of professional services, and external partners are substantive with respect to digital decisions, deliver slower initial decisions, but much more enduring implementation impacts since the scope of stakeholder investment in decisions reflects into a broader advocacy of their successful implementation (Zawacki-Richter et al., 2022).

ALIGNING CULTURE WITH STUDENT EXPECTATIONS

Digital HEI student experience is the final measure of cultural and technological change not in the sense of being a consumer satisfaction indicator but in the sense of how the institutions have adjusted their values, processes, and capabilities to the educational requirements and expectations of a generation whose relationship to digital technology is fundamentally different to those of the academic staff who designed their learning environment. Misalignment in this dimension has the following damaging consequences: students get educational experiences of lower quality and relevance; institutions create poor value-for-money perceptions that hurt the sustainability of their reputation and financial well-being; and the cultural credibility of the HEI being a digital organisation is diminished by the dissonance between its digital aspirations and the everyday experience of its students (Dollinger et al., 2023).

Modern learners, especially but not only members of Generation Z (born 19972012) and Generation Alpha (born 20132019), carry with them the expectations of digital interactions that are characterised by seamless, personalised, mobile-first and instant consumer digital experiences in areas such as entertainment, as well as financial services. The experience of institutional digital spaces when students are forced to use numerous logins, are not mobile-friendly, do not present information in personalised formats, and respond to time-sensitive queries asynchronously is also juxtaposed with their broader digital lives, leading to disengagement, a lack of satisfaction, and a feeling of institutional apathy (Selwyn, 2022). The cultural issue of HEIs does not lie in competing on equal footing with the consumer technology firms, but in attaining the educational counterpart, which is having a digital space that is intentionally designed to meet the learning and community needs of its students.

Student digital wellbeing - the aspect of student digital experience that considers the psychological, social, and physical health impacts of digitally intensive educational settings - has become an ever more culturally and policy relevant area of focus as the mental health stressors of digitally intensive student bodies in higher education institutions have escalated throughout the 20212026 timeframe. Orben et al. (2022) observed subtle relationships between the patterns of digital technology use and student mental health results and concluded that the quality of digital interaction and degree of student agency in the digital environment are more significant predictors of wellbeing than overall screen time - which has direct implications on HEI digital culture, with designs focused on active engagement, social connection, and learner agency considered more pedagogically and psychologically superior than passive content consumption formats.

The concept of personalised learning: the application of adaptive systems that rely on AI to personalise educational content, pacing, assessment, and support to student learning profiles is both a major challenge to both student expectations and a cultural one to the HEIs. Students are increasingly demanding that educational environments acknowledge and cater to their personal needs, strengths and interests in the manner in which recommendation algorithms and personalised interfaces have trained them to look in consumer digital services. To fulfil this promise at institutional level, it demands not merely a considerable amount of technological resources in adaptive learning platforms and learning analytics infrastructure, but a paradigm shift in the way academic personnel perceive their pedagogical mission, which is no longer to deliver standardised content but to create adaptive learning spaces and to interpret data on individual student achievement (Sá & Serpa, 2021).

DATA-DRIVEN DECISION-MAKING IN HIGHER EDUCATION INSTITUTIONS

The process of data-driven decision-making, or the systematic application of empirical data based on institutional data to support strategic, operational, and pedagogical choices, can be seen as a major opportunity and a serious cultural challenge to the digital transformation era of HEIs. The potential is great: HEIs can use their digital infrastructure to record highly valuable data regarding student learning, engagement, progression, and outcomes in the form of interaction logs in their learning management system, library access logs, assessment submission patterns, attendance logs, financial aid disbursement, mental health service utilisation, and graduate employment outcomes that, when appropriately combined and analysed, can be used to inform more effective, equitable, and personalised educational experiences on a

The issue of the culture is also significant. Historically, academic culture has given a privileged position to expert professional judgement, through disciplinary expertise, pedagogical experience and qualitative familiarity with particular student groups in educational decision making, compared to statistical analysis of population level data. This is not just conservative inertia: it represents real epistemological investments concerning the character of educational knowledge and the constraints of quantitative data in order to reflect the richness of learning. Bringing data-driven practices into academic cultures without sufficiently involving such epistemological issues produces defensive backlash as opposed to evidence-based practice (Kitchin, 2022). High-quality cultures of data-driven decision-making in HEIs are not created by trying to establish the superiority of data over professional judgement but by encouraging complementary integration: data reveals patterns and anomaly that should be addressed by a professional; professional expertise is used to interpret data in pedagogical situations and create responsive interventions.

The most advanced area of data-driven practice in digital transformation of HEI has become learning analytics, a measurement, collection, analysis and reporting of data on learning and learning contexts to understand and optimise both learning and the conditions under which learning occurs. A systematic review by Scheffel et al. (2022) of the implementation outcomes of learning analytics in 112 institution-specific case studies found that institutions with well-developed data governance systems, clear communication to students about the use of their data, and successful training of their staff on interpreting analytics, reported much higher student outcome improvements and lower rates of ethical concerns than those that implemented analytics without these facilitating conditions. The results of the study highlight the cultural and governance aspects of the effectiveness of learning analytics: without the human and institutional infrastructure that allows the use of the technology in a responsible and effectual manner, the technology is required but not sufficient.

Student privacy and consent can be considered an urgent ethical aspect of the data-driven decision-making in HEIs that needs to be addressed specifically by culture and policy. The European Union (and other similar data protection regimes around the world) pose substantial legal requirements on HEIs to collect, store, process, and share student data, but meeting legal requirements does not answer the ethical issue of what does constitute the proper scope of institutional use of data to which students themselves has a right to give their consideration. Prinsloo and Slade (2021) have discovered that views of students on institutional data use are very situation-specific: students tend to accept the use of data that is transparently disclosed, obviously helpful to their educational development, and that they are in meaningful control over, whereas they are highly concerned about the use of data that they perceive as surveillant, commercially oriented, or obscure in its intentions. Creating data cultures that respect these student viewpoints is an ethical as well as a practical institutional issue - institutions which covert student trust in data practice by being viewed as invasive are the very institutions of engagement and openness which effective learning analytics relies upon.

The role of institutional research is changing dramatically as institutional decision-making is increasingly increasingly relying on more advanced data services provided by institutional research units in HEIs, which are increasingly becoming more advanced units in terms of their ability to collect, analyze and report data. Real-time analytics, predictive modelling and machine learning-based early intervention systems that demand new technical capacities and new working relations between data professionals and academic decision-makers are supplementing the traditional institutional research model, which is focused on compliance reporting, enrolment statistics, and post hoc performance analysis. Calderon and Webber (2021) state that the change of institutional research to a strategic intelligence capability - internalised in institutional governance, trusted by the academic leadership, and with the ability to synthesise complex evidence to various audiences of stakeholders - is itself a great cultural change initiative that needs active investment and long-term support of the senior leadership.

CHALLENGES AND OPPORTUNITIES

The digital transformation landscape of HEIs can be described as a basic duality: the same forces that pose the greatest challenges (high rate of technological change, financial strain, demographic upheaval, and competition) as well as open the most crucial opportunities to institutions with the means and desire to change their cultures, competencies, and pedagogical patterns in substantive, but not cosmetic, manners. It is crucial to rigorously map this duality in order to be realistic in planning transformation as well as to be candidly involved with the complexity of the journey that HEIs are going through.

Digital equity is one of the most enduring and structurally-influenced challenges. Although digital infrastructure and provision of devices has been heavily invested in since the COVID-19 pandemic, large digital disparities exist between the student populations at HEIs along socioeconomic status, geographic location, disability, first-generation student status, and age dimensions. The rural and low-income urban connectivity variants of broadband connectivity further result in disparities in learning environment that do not warrant a complete technological response by an institutional technology strategy without parallel action on the part of the municipal, national, and international level. Assistive technology and accessible design is still an inconsistently accessible aspect of digital platforms in HEI that places exclusionary limitations on students with disabilities, which go against legal requirements as well as the educational equity commitments (Al-Fraihat et al., 2022). To tackle digital equity, it is essential to make it an essential indicator of transformation success, not a side effect and to acknowledge that equitable transformation can be slower and more costly than approaches that are not based on inequality.

The problem of cybersecurity is an increasing threat to digitally transforming HEIs that has both a strong cultural and technical aspect. The universities make a very tempting target of cyberattacks, they have valuable intellectual property, sensitive personal information, and important research infrastructure, as well as the open, collaborative network designs required by the academic culture, but limited by best practices in security. The incidence and magnitude of ransomware, data breach, distributed denial-of-service incidents against HEIs have gone up exponentially during the 20212025 period, and have resulted in massive operational, financial, and reputational impact to institutions that have fallen victim to them (Taddeo et al., 2021). Establishing cybersecurity-conscious cultures, where academic and administrative employees regularly exercise information security hygiene, notify management on suspicious activity, and are familiar with the institutional implications of security violations are as crucial as spending money on technical security infrastructure, and must be sustained and contextually relevant communication and training instead of compliance-box annual awareness training.

Financial sustainability digital transformation is a structural issue that is intertwined with governance and cultural issues. Digital transformation demands large initial investment in infrastructure, systems, training and change management - things which vie against other needs in higher education systems which are strained economically in post-pandemic times. It is methodologically hard to show digital transformation literally pays off: the payoff is often diffuse, spread within the dimensions of operational efficiency, the quality of student experience, research capacity, and staff satisfaction, and realised over timescales (usually multi-year) that are often well beyond the usual institutional planning horizons. The institutions that solely conceptualize the digital transformation in the terms of costs reduction, which is an alluringly simplistic framing, given the financial pressures, might dangerously start to establish the technology-enabled shrinkage of the educational quality and staff conditions that might cause real resistance and eventually subvert the transformation process as well as the institutional mission (Bates, 2022).

One of the greatest opportunities brought by the digital transformation, is the possibility of significantly enhancing educational equity and access both at the institutional and systems level. Digital infrastructure has made possible open and distance learning models that can bring high-quality higher education to the learners who cannot be provided with higher education through the traditional campus-based approach due to geographical, disability, caring, and financial barriers. Personalised learning based on AI can customise the learning experiences of different learners to a much better degree than delivery of standardised curricula. Learning analytics can spot at-risk students much earlier in their school careers than traditional pastoral monitoring, and intervene in real-time, targeting specific, high-risk students before they drop out of school and help them to persist, thus enabling disadvantaged students to attain completion. These opportunities cannot be realised without intentional orientation of the priorities of digital transformation to equity outcomes - a cultural choice and not a technical necessity (Dollinger et al., 2023).

The possibility to establish new types of collaboration between HEIs and their extended communities, employers, and other civic organisations as well as alumni networks with the help of digital platforms and data-sharing schemes is another major transformation dividend that is yet to be actively investigated. The ability to transfer learning achievements to employers with more flexible and trust-enhancing communication through digital credentials and blockchain-authenticated systems of transcripts opens up increased opportunities. AI-mediated engagement platforms with alumni allow institutions to build ongoing learning relationships with alumni across their career as opposed to occasional interactions at reunion events. Open data projects - the publication of institutional research and output of learning resources under open licences - can make the public value of HEI digital investment much broader than the enrolled student base, and establish the civic trust relations that underpin public funding and political support of higher education (Brown and Nic Giolla Mhichil, 2022).

CONCLUSION

This chapter has traversed the multi dimensional landscape of change management and organisational culture in the digitally transforming institutions in the higher education sector. The expedition - through the conceptual framework of change management in the theoretical world of academic organisations, the practical aspects of strategy, communication, training, and leadership, to the cultural, ethical, equity issues that infuse each aspect of digital transformation - brings about a terrain of irreducible complexity which cannot be reduced to technological implementation plans or managerial checklists. Digital transformation in HEIs is first of all a human accomplishment or nothing.

The evidence discussed in this chapter all leads to a number of general conclusions. To begin with, the digital gap between digital investment and digital transformation in HEIs is more of a cultural and human, rather than technical gap. Organisations that channel their main energy of transformation to technological acquisitions and at the same time do less investment in change management, staff training and culture building always fail to meet their transformational goals. Second, academic culture, with its own unique dedications to professional independence, collegiality, and disciplinary rigour, is not merely an impediment to digital change but an asset: critical, deliberative, evidence-appreciative nature of academic communities is precisely the scepticalism that will not allow uncritical uptake of technologies that do not really serve educational functions. This is the most important capacity that instead of trying to suppress it, harnessing it is a feature of the most successful HEI digital transformation strategies.

Third, equity should be ingrained as an intrinsic design criterion of digital transformation - not a reflex action that is undertaken once systems have been designed and implemented. The digital transformation leading to an increase in the average performance and exacerbates the disparity between the advantaged and disadvantaged groups of students is in opposition to the very nature of the educational and social purpose of the HEI. Fourth, the most effective type of data-driven decision-making is the one that does not replace professional educational judgement but supports it over the long term, allowing data scientists and academic experts to have long-term collaboration relationships and share their expertise that the other has not. Fifth, student partnership is not just a best practice in digital transformation of HEIs, but an epistemological requirement, since students are knowledgeable on the topic of their learning needs and experiences, which cannot be created by any other means by institutional designers.

The drivers of the forward path of HEI digital transformation will be forces whose full consequences are as yet unimaginable - such as the fast-growing development of generative AI, which fundamentally challenges assumptions about how knowledge is transmitted, academic integrity, and even the essence of learning that is at the heart of existing models in education. It is unclear what exactly will happen to institutions that have been investing in the development of the cultural capacity to continuously adapt the growth mindsets, psychological safety, data literacy, collaborative working style, and student-centred values that characterise digitally mature educational cultures, but it is clear that these institutions will be better placed to manage these emergent challenges and opportunities than those whose digital transformation has not attained the level of system deployment but has not been accompanied by cultural

The resulting call to action is both modest and bold: modest, in admitting that change in culture is slow, non-linear, contentious, and stubbornly hard to control by managers; ambitious, in acknowledging that change in culture is possible, and that the quality of higher education is vital to the life chances of the learners it serves, and that it all depends on whether institutions of higher learning have the institutional will and wisdom to seek it, and pursue it The pieces discussed in this chapter offer a realistic guide of the obstacles to come as well as a solid foundation of trust in the fact that the ride, with dedication, nurturing and purpose that is inclusive, will be one worthwhile taking.

REFERENCES

Al-Fraihat, D., Joy, M., Masa'deh, R., & Sinclair, J. (2022). Evaluating e-learning systems success: An empirical study. *Computers in Human Behavior, 102*, 67–86. DOI: 10.1016/j.chb.2019.08.004

Bates, A. W. (2022). *Teaching in a digital age: Guidelines for designing teaching and learning* (3rd ed.). Tony Bates Associates Ltd.

Bolman, L. G., & Deal, T. E. (2022). *Reframing organizations: Artistry, choice, and leadership* (7th ed.). Jossey-Bass.

Bond, M., Buntins, K., Bedenlier, S., Zawacki-Richter, O., & Kerres, M. (2021). Mapping research in student engagement and educational technology in higher education: A systematic evidence map. *International Journal of Educational Technology in Higher Education, 17*(1), 1–30.

Brown, M., Nic Giolla Mhichil, M., Beirne, E., & Mac Lochlainn, C. (2022). The global micro-credential landscape: Charting a new credential ecology for lifelong learning. *Journal of Learning for Development, 8*(2), 228–254. DOI: 10.56059/jl4d.v8i2.525

Calderon, A. J., & Webber, K. L. (2021). Institutional research in the twenty-first century: Expanding roles and new directions. *New Directions for Institutional Research, 183*, 7–19.

Dollinger, M., Lodge, J., & Coates, H. (2023). Co-creation in higher education: Towards a conceptual model. *Journal of Marketing for Higher Education, 28*(2), 210–231. DOI: 10.1080/08841241.2018.1466756

Edmondson, A. C., & Bransby, D. P. (2023). Psychological safety comes of age: Observed themes in an established literature. *Annual Review of Organizational Psychology and Organizational Behavior, 10*(1), 55–78. DOI: 10.1146/annurev-orgpsych-120920-055217

Fullan, M., & Quinn, J. (2021). *The challenge and the opportunity of digital transformation*. Corwin Press.

Hallinger, P., & Chatpinyakoop, C. (2021). A bibliometric review of research on higher education for sustainable development, 1998–2018. *Sustainability (Basel), 11*(8), 2401. DOI: 10.3390/su11082401

Hiatt, J. M. (2022). *ADKAR: A model for change in business, government and our community* (Rev. ed.). Prosci Learning Center Publications.

Hodges, C., Moore, S., Lockee, B., Trust, T., & Bond, A. (2022). The difference between emergency remote teaching and online learning. *EDUCAUSE Review, 27*, 1–12.

Howell, R. (2022). Digital leadership in UK higher education: Competencies, contexts, and challenges. *Journal of Higher Education Policy and Management, 44*(3), 277–295.

Jisc. (2023). Digital experience insights survey 2023: Findings from students in UK higher education. Jisc.

Jones, M., Antonczak, L., & Sherring, P. (2021). Leading digital transformation in universities: A distributed leadership approach. *Journal of Higher Education Policy and Management, 43*(5), 495–510.

Kezar, A., & Holcombe, E. (2021). *Shared leadership in higher education: Important lessons from research and practice.* American Council on Education.

Kitchin, R. (2022). Thinking critically about and researching algorithms. *Information Communication and Society, 20*(1), 14–29. DOI: 10.1080/1369118X.2016.1154087

Kotter, J. P. (2021). Leading change (25th anniversary ed.). Harvard Business Review Press.

Liang, X., Kidwai, M. D., & Zhang, M. (2021). How AI is changing the work of knowledge workers. *MIT Sloan Management Review, 62*(2), 1–4.

Marinoni, G., van't Land, H., & Jensen, T. (2021). *The impact of COVID-19 on higher education around the world.* International Association of Universities.

Mwamba, J. N., Mulenga, I. M., & Muwanga-Zake, J. W. F. (2023). Digital transformation in African higher education: Lessons from consortium-driven innovation. *International Journal of Educational Development in Africa, 8*(1), 1–18.

Noesgaard, S. S., & Nielsen, J. A. (2021). The messy reality of digital transformation in public organizations: Two case studies of enterprise system implementation. *Government Information Quarterly, 38*(2), 101–558.

O'Reilly, C. A., & Tushman, M. L. (2021). *Lead and disrupt: How to solve the innovator's dilemma* (2nd ed.). Business Books. DOI: 10.1515/9781503629639

Orben, A., Przybylski, A. K., Blakemore, S.-J., & Kievit, R. A. (2022). Windows of developmental sensitivity to social media. *Nature Communications, 13*(1), 1649. DOI: 10.1038/s41467-022-29296-3 PMID: 35347142

Picciano, A. G. (2022). Theories and frameworks for online education: Seeking an integrated model. *Online Learning : The Official Journal of the Online Learning Consortium*, *21*(3), 166–190.

Prinsloo, P., & Slade, S. (2021). Student vulnerability, agency and learning analytics: An exploration. *Journal of Learning Analytics*, *4*(1), 159–182.

Queiros, A., Costa, P., & Pacheco, L. (2022). Stakeholder communication in digital transformation: Evidence from a Portuguese polytechnic. *Procedia Computer Science*, *196*, 785–793.

Rapanta, C., Botturi, L., Goodyear, P., Guardia, L., & Koole, M. (2021). Online university teaching during and after the COVID-19 crisis: Refocusing teacher presence and learning activity. *Postdigital Science and Education*, *2*(3), 923–945. DOI: 10.1007/s42438-020-00155-y PMID: 40477148

Redecker, C. (2021). *European framework for the digital competence of educators: DigCompEdu*. Publications Office of the European Union.

Sá, M. J., & Serpa, S. (2021). The COVID-19 pandemic as an opportunity to foster the sustainable development of teaching in higher education. *Sustainability (Basel)*, *12*(20), 8525. DOI: 10.3390/su12208525

Scanlon, E., Sharples, M., Fenton-O'Creevy, M., Fleck, J., Cooban, C., Ferguson, R., Cross, S., & Aczel, J. (2021). *Beyond prototypes: Enabling innovation in technology-enhanced learning*. Technology Enhanced Learning Research Programme, London Knowledge Lab.

Scheffel, M., Drachsler, H., Stoyanov, S., & Specht, M. (2022). Quality indicators for learning analytics. *Journal of Educational Technology & Society*, *17*(4), 117–132.

Schein, E. H., & Schein, P. A. (2021). *Organizational culture and leadership* (5th ed.). Wiley.

Selwyn, N. (2022). *Is technology good for education?* (2nd ed.). Polity Press.

Taddeo, M., McCutcheon, T., & Floridi, L. (2021). Trusting artificial intelligence in cybersecurity is a double-edged sword. *Nature Machine Intelligence*, *1*(12), 557–560. DOI: 10.1038/s42256-019-0109-1

Veletsianos, G., & Kimmons, R. (2021). Assumptions and challenges of open scholarship. *International Review of Research in Open and Distance Learning*, *13*(4), 166–189. DOI: 10.19173/irrodl.v13i4.1313

Vial, G. (2021). Understanding digital transformation: A review and a research agenda. *The Journal of Strategic Information Systems*, *28*(2), 118–144. DOI: 10.1016/j.jsis.2019.01.003

Zawacki-Richter, O., Marín, V. I., Bond, M., & Gouverneur, F. (2022). Systematic review of research on artificial intelligence applications in higher education — Where are the educators? *International Journal of Educational Technology in Higher Education*, *16*(1), 1–27. PMID: 35013716

Zhu, M., & Anagnostopoulos, D. (2021). Faculty response to top-down change initiatives in higher education. *The Journal of Higher Education*, *92*(4), 628–655.

Chapter 11
Capability Reconfiguration, AI-Enabled HR, and the Political Economy of Academic Performance:
Framework for Maturity in Postdigital Universities

Ashraf Alam
http://orcid.org/0000-0001-6178-1187
Department of Education, National Institute of Technology Calicut, Kozhikode, India

ABSTRACT

This chapter conceptualizes postdigital university maturity as governed capability reconfiguration, not platform accumulation. It synthesizes Dynamic Capabilities Theory, socio-technical systems, institutional logics, and the Job Demands-Resources Model to show that transformation stabilizes only when roles, decision rights, incentives, and protected time are redesigned into repeatable routines for inclusive digital pedagogy, integrity-by-design assessment, and coordinated student success. It reframes AI-enabled HR and talent analytics as legitimacy-critical decision architectures requiring construct validity, bias controls, proportional interpretability, contestability, and meaningful human control to avert Goodhart effects, surveillance drift, and burnout-driven capability loss. The outcome is an integrative maturity architecture linking workforce capability pathways to educational value, trust capital, and institutional sustainability.

DOI: 10.4018/979-8-3373-8959-2.ch011

1. INTRODUCTION

1.1 Purpose and Scope in Postdigital University Ecologies

This chapter develops a conceptual-theoretical architecture for understanding how postdigital universities can convert digital infrastructures into durable academic quality, ethical governance, and workforce sustainability through *capability reconfiguration* and strategically designed talent systems. The postdigital condition is treated as a structural reality in which platforms, data pipelines, automation, and hybrid presence reorganize epistemic practices, assessment regimes, advising logistics, scholarly collaboration, and institutional accountability. The analytical focus is not technology adoption, but the institutional mechanics that determine whether digital transformation produces coherent pedagogic value, credible research performance, and legitimate decision-making. The chapter therefore formalizes talent management as a capability-production system comprising role architecture, workload calculus, professional learning ecologies, incentive compatibility, and values-aligned analytics governance. It is written for interdisciplinary audiences who operate across policy, governance, workforce development, and learning technology, using a shared vocabulary of *dynamic capability*, *socio-technical alignment*, and *public-interest legitimacy* to keep the argument globally portable.

1.2 Core Problem Statement and the Strategy-Capability-Practice Disjunction

A recurring institutional failure is the treatment of digital transformation as a procurement-and-implementation sequence, while talent management remains confined to appraisal routines, compliance reporting, and administrivia. This structural split produces a strategy-capability-practice disjunction in which digital systems intensify coordination load, accelerate response expectations, and shift invisible labor onto faculty and third-space staff without redesigning roles, decision rights, or time entitlements. In such conditions, universities often experience predictable dysfunctions including fragmented digital pedagogy, inconsistent assessment integrity, uneven distribution of redesign effort, and superficial conformity to platform workflows. The political economy of academic performance amplifies these pathologies because audit rationalities, ranking incentives, and metric power can weaponize dashboards into surveillance infrastructures, triggering *Goodhart effects*, defensive performativity, and mission drift away from educational value. The chapter treats these outcomes as systemic, not incidental, requiring institutional design responses that integrate fairness, trust, and capability stewardship.

1.3 Central Constructs, Conceptual Boundaries, and Contextual Contingencies

The chapter operationalizes a compact construct system comprising *digital transformation*, *digital maturity*, *institutional capability*, *capability reconfiguration*, *talent architecture*, *AI-enabled HR*, *people analytics*, *academic performance regimes*, *student engagement value chains*, *trust capital*, and wellbeing sustainability. Digital maturity is defined as reliable, repeatable capability to deliver high-integrity teaching, credible evaluation, and risk-aware governance under datafied constraints, rather than a display of platform modernity (Budhwar et al., 2023; Al-Mughairi & Bhaskar, 2025; Eftimov & Kitanovikj, 2023). Capability reconfiguration denotes deliberate redistribution of specialized expertise, recalibration of workload models, redesign of academic roles, and revision of decision rights to reduce coordination friction and protect pedagogic quality. Boundary conditions are treated as causal constraints, including public versus private governance, resource gradients, regulatory and accreditation pressures, disciplinary epistemic cultures, unionization environments, and socio-digital inequities involving contract precarity, caregiving load, disability access, language marginalization, and differential access to protected learning time. These contingencies determine feasibility, legitimacy, and sustainability, and they shape the chapter's globally adaptable design logic.

1.4 Guiding Questions and Conceptual Contribution

The chapter is organized around five guiding questions that discipline the argument into testable propositions and implementable governance implications. First, how can universities theorize talent management as strategic capability formation, rather than a support-function utility. Second, which theory-combinations best explain transformation outcomes when role redesign, institutional logics, and sociotechnical constraints collide. Third, how can *AI-enabled HR* be governed so that decision support improves accuracy and coherence while preserving *procedural justice*, transparency, contestability, academic freedom, and duty-of-care. Fourth, what integrative model connects faculty capability trajectories to student engagement, assessment integrity, and institutional performance while treating burnout as a preventable governance failure, not an acceptable operating norm. Fifth, how do quantified performance regimes reshape behavior, ethics, and autonomy under datafication, and which institutional safeguards prevent metric substitution. The chapter contributes a maturity architecture centered on capability governance, a role-systems lens for academic work design, and a values-aligned analytics framework that constrains algorithmic overreach.

1.5 Architecture and Sectional Logic of the Argument

The chapter proceeds as a cumulative architecture in which each section adds an analytic layer while preserving narrative continuity and conceptual parsimony. Section 2 builds the theoretical foundation by integrating *Dynamic Capabilities Theory*, *Socio-Technical Systems Theory*, *Institutional Theory* and *institutional logics*, professional jurisdiction and boundary work, motivation and wellbeing models including *Self-Determination Theory* and the *Job Demands-Resources Model*, and AI governance constructs such as *algorithmic accountability* and *meaningful human control*. Table 1 in Section 2 consolidates these lenses into an explanatory scaffold for maturity-oriented governance. Section 3 formalizes an education-centered digital maturity and talent architecture with capability layers, role families, and misalignment diagnostics, consolidated in Table 2. Section 4 develops faculty capability formation as an ecosystem shaped by identity, incentives, equity constraints, and institutional scaffolding, operationalized through Table 3. Section 5 derives the talent-to-learning value chain for engagement, belonging, and integrity, anchored by Table 4. Section 6 governs AI-driven HR and analytics through legitimacy, risk, and sustainability, consolidated in Table 5, before Section 7 synthesizes implications and forward directions.

2. THEORETICAL FOUNDATIONS FOR INTEGRATING TALENT MANAGEMENT AND DIGITAL TRANSFORMATION IN HEIS

2.1 Digital Transformation as Institutional Reconfiguration

Digital transformation in higher education is best conceptualized as institutional reconfiguration across infrastructures, routines, governance, and value-creation logics, rather than as a bounded technology adoption event. The analytic distinction among *digitization*, *digitalization*, and *digital transformation* is consequential because it separates data conversion from process redesign, and separates process redesign from the deeper recalibration of authority, accountability, and academic work architecture (Fenwick et al., 2024; Rangel-de Lazaro & Duart, 2023; Thangaraju & Palani, 2024; Zhou et al., 2023). In postdigital universities, platforms operate as participation-infrastructures that reshape temporal rhythms, epistemic visibility, and evaluation granularity, thereby altering what is legible, auditable, and rewardable inside academic performance regimes. A rigorous transformation frame therefore foregrounds coordination costs, workflow friction, and institutional path dependence, treating change as a complex adaptive system with feedback loops, emergent resistance, and capability-debt dynamics. This orientation anticipates why maturity cannot be inferred from platform modernity alone, a claim structurally reinforced by the lens map consolidated in Table 1.

2.2 Talent Management as Strategic Capability Formation in University Work Systems

Talent management becomes strategically meaningful when it is theorized as capability formation, not as a compliance pipeline for recruitment, appraisal, and payroll rationalization. In universities, capability is a composite of epistemic production, pedagogic design, relational labor, ethical judgment, and governance participation, each of which is instantiated through role bundles, decision rights, and time entitlements rather than through individual attributes alone (Abdelwahab et al., 2023; Mwita & Kitole, 2025; Raman et al., 2024). A capability-centric lens integrates *strategic human resource management* with *AMO theory* and institutional design, insisting that ability-building is sterile without motivation-preserving incentives and opportunity structures that supply protected time, design support, and legitimate authority to act on learning signals. This reframing also treats third-space professionals as structural capability multipliers, since boundary-spanning translation across IT, pedagogy, assessment integrity, accessibility, and data governance determines whether transformation becomes coherent practice or fragmented improvisation. Theoretical coherence for these claims is elaborated through the multi-lens scaffold in Table 1, which ties talent architecture to maturity governance.

2.3 Theories that Jointly Explain Talent-Driven Postdigital Transformation

An integrative theory-stack is required because postdigital transformation is simultaneously strategic, socio-technical, institutional, psychosocial, and juridical in its constraint structure. *Dynamic Capabilities Theory* explains sensing, seizing, and reconfiguring under turbulence, while *socio-technical systems* and *sociomateriality* specify co-optimization between people, process, and platforms, including how tools configure attention, tempo, and accountability surfaces (Nguyen & Park, 2022; Baki et al., 2023; Sekli et al., 2024). *Institutional logics* and professional jurisdiction frameworks clarify why legitimacy, autonomy, and boundary work shape adoption, and why policy and ranking pressures can catalyze superficial compliance. Motivation and wellbeing constructs such as *Self-Determination Theory* and the *Job Demands-Resources Model* specify the micro-foundations of engagement, burnout, and trust. Algorithmic governance, measurement theory, and *procedural justice* supply the normative and epistemic guardrails for AI-enabled HR and performance analytics, as summarized in Table 1.

Table 1. Theoretical lenses for capability-centric postdigital university maturity governance

Theoretical Lens Bundle	Ontological Premise for University Systems	Mechanism for Academic Work Reconfiguration	Talent-Architecture Design Implication	Maturity-Governance Signal for Institutional Reliability
Dynamic Capability and Strategic HRM	Universities operate as adaptive capability-portfolios under volatility, where advantage derives from reconfigurable routines and allocative agility	Sensing-seizing-reconfiguring cycles translate environmental signals into redesigned roles, reskilled trajectories, and reallocated time-entitlements	Build capability pathways, role ladders, and resource-backed learning compacts that convert strategy into routinized competence	Evidence of fast-cycle learning, coherent resource redeployment, and stable performance under turbulence
Socio-Technical and Sociomaterial Alignment	Technologies are not neutral tools, they are mediators that co-produce practices, norms, and evaluative visibility	Co-optimization reduces workflow friction by redesigning handoffs, interfaces, and accountability surfaces around real tasks	Institutionalize co-design studios, boundary-spanner roles, and interoperable support services that reduce coordination load	Declining coordination costs, fewer workarounds, improved service-level predictability, and higher adoption integrity
Institutional Logics and Professional Jurisdiction	Universities are legitimacy-driven fields where professional autonomy and audit rationalities coexist in structural tension	Boundary work governs what counts as valid performance, who has decision rights, and which metrics acquire coercive power	Align evaluation regimes with professional standards, safeguard autonomy, and formalize jurisdiction for third-space integrators	Lower compliance theater, higher perceived legitimacy, fewer metric-gaming pathologies, and stronger collegial trust
Motivation, Work Design, and Wellbeing Sustainability	Human agency is resource-bounded, performance collapses when cognitive and emotional resources are chronically depleted	Autonomy-competence-relatedness dynamics and demands-resources balance determine adoption quality and burnout risk	Create protected time, workload equity models, and recognition systems that reward invisible labor and care work	Reduced burnout indicators, stable retention, higher discretionary effort, and durable pedagogic quality
Algorithmic Governance and Measurement Epistemics	Datafied decision systems are political instruments, validity and contestability determine legitimacy	Construct alignment, bias control, and procedural fairness reduce Goodhart effects and automation bias in HR decisions	Embed model risk ownership, auditability, appeals, and purpose limitation for AI-enabled HR and analytics	Transparent decision trails, contestable outcomes, fewer proxy distortions, and higher trust in governance

Table 1 operationalizes a pragmatic epistemology for maturity design by linking theory to mechanisms, then to talent architecture, then to governance observables, enabling institutions to diagnose capability gaps without collapsing educational value into simplistic proxies. The matrix also clarifies why AI-enabled HR is not a technical add-on but a high-stakes legitimacy device that can either stabilize fairness and decision quality or intensify audit power, depending on whether *algorithmic accountability*, *construct validity*, and *meaningful human control* are treated as non-negotiable governance primitives rather than optional ethical ornaments.

2.4 Conceptual Propositions and Integrative Claims for Capability-Centric Maturity

A capability-centric maturity thesis yields propositions that are actionable without becoming checklist reductionism. First, maturity gains are predominantly constrained by role architecture, workload calculus, and governance legitimacy, not by platform breadth or vendor sophistication, because capabilities reside in repeatable routines that survive staff turnover and policy churn (Alnaqbi et al., 2024; Mahmoud et al., 2025; Aguinis et al., 2024). Second, capability formation accelerates when learning is embedded in work design through protected time, co-design infrastructures, and incentive compatibility, rather than through episodic training disconnected from performance systems. Third, AI-enabled HR improves coherence only when the decision architecture enforces interpretability proportionate to stakes, bias controls aligned to equity constraints, and contestability through appeal pathways, thereby mitigating automation bias and proxy discrimination. Fourth, analytics regimes must be validity-governed to prevent *Goodhart effects*, where targets displace educational value and induce gaming equilibria. These propositions are not rhetorical, they are mechanism claims that can be audited through the governance signals specified in Table 1.

2.5 Education-Centered Value Model for Digital Talent Transformation

An education-centered value model is required to prevent maturity discourse from collapsing into performative auditability or marketized rank competition. Educational value is defined as the joint production of learning quality, inclusion, integrity, belonging, employability, and psychosocial wellbeing, treated as an institutional outcome generated through capability ecosystems rather than as an individual deficit to be remediated (Olan et al., 2024; Bodea et al., 2024; Abulail et al., 2025). This model introduces *capability justice* as a design constraint, insisting that access to training time, support expertise, and recognition must be equitably distributed across contract types, caregiving realities, disability access needs, language ecologies, and disciplinary workload asymmetries. It also frames trust capital as a strategic asset, since legitimacy collapses when performance governance becomes surveillance-heavy, procedurally opaque, or dismissive of professional autonomy. In operational terms, Table 1 implies that sustainable maturity requires a coupled governance stack, where validity, fairness, and workload sustainability are co-optimized so that transformation increases institutional capacity rather than extracting it.

3. CONCEPTUAL MODEL OF DIGITAL MATURITY AND TALENT ARCHITECTURE IN HEIS

3.1 Digital Maturity Models and Education-Centric Capability Lens

Digital maturity in higher education is best theorized as staged, evidence-bearing capability development across pedagogic quality, integrity infrastructures, data stewardship, and institutional culture, rather than as an inventory of platforms or a proxy for IT spend. A capability lens distinguishes infrastructural readiness from performative reliability, emphasizing whether the institution can repeatedly produce coherent learning experiences, defensible assessment judgments, and timely student support under variable constraints (Halid et al., 2024; Bhardwaj et al., 2023; Tuffaha & Perello-Marin, 2023). The most consequential failure pattern is the maturity-trap in which systems scale faster than human competence, governance legitimacy, and workload calculus, generating capability-debt that surfaces as workaround ecologies, brittle compliance, and reputational risk. Building on the theoretical mechanisms consolidated in Table 1, this section treats maturity as a cybernetic property of feedback loops, decision rights, and adaptive routines. The domain-to-role mapping in Table 2 prefigures how maturity domains must be co-designed with talent architecture to prevent metric substitution and coordination overload.

3.2 Institutional Capability Architecture for Postdigital Universities

A postdigital university functions as a stratified capability stack in which foundational infrastructure enables operational digitization, which in turn conditions academic delivery, analytic sensemaking, and governance legitimacy. Foundational layers include identity governance, cybersecurity, interoperability, and accessibility instrumentation, while operational layers include workflow digitization, service management, and data pipelines that reduce transaction friction. Academic layers comprise learning design competence, assessment architecture, feedback systems, and mentoring infrastructures, while analytic layers comprise learning analytics literacy, workforce analytics, and quality assurance epistemics grounded in construct validity. Governance layers supply procurement ethics, auditability, accountability, and risk ownership, and cultural layers supply psychological safety, collegial trust, and innovation orientation that stabilize adoption integrity (O'Brien et al., 2025; Jaboob et al., 2025; Alam & Mohanty, 2024). This architecture is best interpreted through *complex adaptive systems* logic, *resilience engineering*, and *control theory* analogies in which sensing, interpretation, and corrective action must remain proportionate and legitimacy-preserving. Table 2 operationalizes these layers by specifying the role-and-skill assemblages required for each maturity domain.

3.3 Talent Architecture as Role Systems

Talent architecture is an institutional design object, not a catalog of individual competencies, because roles encode task bundles, accountability surfaces, decision rights, and recognition logics that determine whether capabilities become repeatable routines. In postdigital universities, role systems must internalize pedagogic design, integrity-by-design assessment, student success orchestration, accessibility governance, and analytics interpretation as distributed responsibilities across faculty and third-space professionals, rather than as residual labor absorbed by individual goodwill (Dogru et al., 2024; Dutta & Mishra, 2025; Aini et al., 2024). A role-systems model requires explicit jurisdictional boundaries, escalation paths, and workload credits that prevent hidden labor and coordination overload, while preserving professional autonomy and epistemic diversity. The mapping in Table 2 specifies maturity domains as governance targets and translates them into capability signals, role assemblages, and failure modes, thereby rendering maturity actionable without degenerating into proxy-driven auditability. Table 2 also anticipates how *AMO theory* and *procedural justice* must be embedded in role design to sustain motivation and legitimacy.

Table 2. Digital maturity domains mapped to talent architecture essentials

Maturity Domain	Capability Signal Constellation	Required Role-and-Skill Assemblage	Governance Guardrails and Decision Rights	Typical Dysfunction If Misaligned
Pedagogic Design Fidelity	Coherent constructive alignment, accessibility compliance, feedback cadence stability, and learning experience consistency across modalities	*TPACK* fluency, learning-design partnering, assessment literacy, inclusive design competence, and facilitation craftsmanship across hybrid settings	Protected redesign time, peer review of course artifacts, template governance with local autonomy, and clear ownership for learning-quality standards	Tool-centric substitution, fragmented course navigation, inequitable participation, and high variance in student experience across sections
Assessment Integrity Architecture	Authentic task design, defensible standards, low misconduct incentives, and auditable judgment trails without punitive surveillance	Integrity-by-design assessment architects, rubric engineering capability, validity reasoning, and moderation competence with discipline-specific epistemics	Separation of supportive analytics from punitive enforcement, appeals pathways, transparent standards, and shared accountability for integrity governance	Adversarial compliance, over-proctoring normalization, false accusations, credibility erosion, and gaming behavior under metric pressure
Student Success Orchestration	Early support responsiveness, advising throughput reliability, belonging signals, and coordinated referral workflows across units	Mentoring role formalization, case management competence, culturally responsive advising, and cross-functional coordination literacy	Explicit decision rights for escalation, data minimization, consent discipline, and service-level norms that protect dignity and agency	Siloed interventions, alert fatigue, delayed support, inequitable outcomes, and student distrust of institutional monitoring
Analytics and Data Stewardship	Construct-valid metrics, interpretability proportional to stakes, reproducible pipelines, and controlled access with purpose limitation	Data stewards, model risk owners, analytics translators, and faculty analytics literacy for pedagogic judgment under uncertainty	Auditability, contestability, model documentation, access governance, and governance committees with stakeholder representation	Dashboard theater, proxy distortion, automation bias, opaque scoring, and legitimacy crises driven by unexplained decisions

continued on following page

Table 2. Continued

Maturity Domain	Capability Signal Constellation	Required Role-and-Skill Assemblage	Governance Guardrails and Decision Rights	Typical Dysfunction If Misaligned
Workforce Capability and Wellbeing Sustainability	Stable retention, manageable workload distributions, reduced burnout precursors, and sustained discretionary effort for quality improvement	Work design specialists, workload equity monitors, professional learning ecosystem builders, and psychologically safe leadership competence	Workload calculus reform, time entitlements, recognition of invisible labor, psychosocial safety norms, and transparent redistribution rules	Chronic exhaustion, capability attrition, compliance-only adoption, rising absenteeism, and quality decay masked by activity metrics
Governance and Procurement Legitimacy	Interoperability assurance, vendor lock-in minimization, ethical procurement discipline, and traceable accountability across decisions	Governance professionals, procurement risk analysts, legal-ethical stewards, and boundary spanners linking policy, pedagogy, and IT	Clear ownership of decision stakes, procurement transparency, exit strategies, and policy coherence across integrity, privacy, and evaluation	Fragmented governance, shadow systems, vendor dependency, inconsistent policy enforcement, and reputational damage under scrutiny

Table 2 functions as a translational instrument that converts abstract maturity discourse into institutionally governable design variables, namely capability signals, role assemblages, decision rights, and predictable dysfunctions. The model is intentionally anti-reductionist because it anchors analytics in measurement epistemics, protects integrity through legitimacy-preserving architectures, and treats wellbeing sustainability as a hard constraint on long-run performance capacity. When interpreted through the mechanisms in Table 1, the table clarifies why maturity is not achieved by scaling platforms, but by reconfiguring roles, incentives, and governance in ways that reduce coordination costs, preserve professional autonomy, and stabilize trust. The matrix also foregrounds that jurisdictional clarity and workload entitlements are not managerial luxuries, they are structural conditions for high-fidelity pedagogic design and defensible assessment judgments.

3.4 Role Redesign and Work Decomposition in Digital Transformation

Role redesign is the operational core of capability reconfiguration because digital transformation decomposes academic labor into modular tasks that must be recomposed into reliable workflows. In hybrid teaching systems, content production, facilitation, assessment design, feedback loops, mentoring, analytics interpretation, and integrity governance become partially separable modules with distinct cognitive demands, temporal rhythms, and quality risks (Porkodi & Cedro, 2025; Madanchian, 2024; Kong et al., 2024). Without explicit recomposition, coordination overhead increases through transaction frictions, duplicated effort, and ambiguity about accountability surfaces, a pattern consistent with *transaction cost economics* and coordination theory. Responsible augmentation with AI intensifies the need for design discipline because automation can accelerate output while degrading epistemic quality, fairness, and authenticity if task boundaries and review protocols remain unspecified. Role redesign therefore requires decision-right matrices, escalation routes, and workload accounting that recognizes design time, emotional labor, and coordination labor, not only contact hours and publication outputs. Table 2 provides the domain-specific blueprint for aligning role systems with maturity outcomes and avoiding invisible labor externalities.

3.5 Institutional Logics, Misalignment Risk, and Capability Legitimacy Dynamics

Maturity programs fail when institutional logics collide without a legitimacy-preserving settlement, particularly when managerial efficiency imperatives and audit rationalities attempt to dominate professional autonomy norms and disciplinary epistemic standards. Under such collisions, performance systems become gameable arenas, where *Goodhart effects*, principal-agent distortions, and reputational signaling incentives incentivize metric maximization rather than educational value creation (Pandey et al., 2023; Walczak & Cellary, 2023; Odugbesan et al., 2023). Capability legitimacy becomes the pivotal mediating construct because adoption quality depends on whether academic communities perceive role redesign, analytics governance, and evaluation criteria as procedurally fair, epistemically credible, and autonomy-respecting. When legitimacy collapses, predictable equilibria emerge including superficial compliance, shadow workarounds, risk aversion, and exit from institutional citizenship roles, which erodes the very routines that maturity requires. The governance signals and dysfunction pathways in Table 2 make these risks diagnostically explicit, while Table 1 supplies the theoretical mechanisms that explain why trust capital, justice perceptions, and workload sustainability are not peripheral ethics concerns, but core determinants of institutional reliability.

4. FACULTY CAPABILITY FORMATION AND DIGITAL COMPETENCY ECOSYSTEMS

4.1 Faculty Digital Competence as Multidimensional Professional Capability

Faculty capability in postdigital universities must be conceptualized as a multidimensional professional phenotype rather than a narrow toolkit of platform operation. Digital competence includes epistemic craftsmanship for disciplinary knowledge production, pedagogic design judgment for coherent learning architectures, and assessment-validity reasoning for defensible evaluative decisions under hybrid constraints (Alam & Mohanty, 2023; Wang & Pashmforoosh, 2024; Cambra-Fierro et al., 2025). It also includes accessibility and inclusion competence grounded in *Universal Design for Learning*, relational presence competence anchored in *Community of Inquiry* constructs, and ethical discernment for privacy, dignity, and data minimization across learning and HR analytics. Capability is therefore a role-embedded, time-entitled, institutionally scaffolded system property, not an individual trait, and its maturation depends on whether work design protects attention, reduces coordination load, and legitimizes redesign labor (Tzirides et al., 2024; Maimela & Mbonde, 2025; Apata et al., 2025). As signposted in Table 2, maturity domains require differentiated role-families, and Table 3 translates those role demands into competency domains with concrete institutional scaffolds that render capability formation repeatable, auditable, and sustainable.

4.2 Theoretical Frameworks for Capability Acceptance, Identity Congruence, and Practice Stabilization

Faculty capability uptake is governed by intersecting learning, motivation, implementation, and identity dynamics, making single-theory explanations structurally inadequate. *Andragogy* and adult learning logics imply that relevance, agency, and situated application determine transfer, while *Transformative Learning Theory* clarifies why deep adoption often requires epistemic reframing about authority, assessment, and student agency. Integrative pedagogy frameworks such as *TPACK* and constructive alignment anchor capability in coherent design rather than tool enthusiasm, while learning-science constructs, including cognitive load regulation, retrieval practice, and feedback timing, specify micro-mechanisms for learning efficacy in digital modalities (Kambur & Yildirim, 2023; Palos-Sánchez et al., 2022; Al-Zahrani & Alasmari, 2025). Adoption trajectories are further shaped by *Diffusion of Innovations* and implementation science constructs that distinguish fidelity from adaptive scaling, and by sensemaking dynamics that mediate whether transformation narratives are interpreted as professional enrichment or managerial encroachment. Table 3 consolidates these theoretical anchors into an ecosystem grammar that links competency domains to institutional scaffolding, thereby converting abstract theory into governable capability pathways.

4.3 Capability Ecosystems and Institutional Scaffolding for Professional Learning

Capability formation becomes durable only when universities design an ecosystem that converts episodic training into routinized practice through structured scaffolding, protected time, and boundary-spanning expertise. Effective ecosystems braid teaching and learning centers, instructional design partnerships, library and open-knowledge functions, accessibility services, assessment integrity stewardship, and data governance roles into a coherent capability supply chain that reduces cognitive burden and coordination friction (Klimova & Pikhart, 2025; Li et al., 2024; Qahtani & Alsmairat, 2023). This ecosystem must be engineered as a socio-technical service architecture with clear service-level expectations, consultative pathways, and artifact-based peer review that stabilizes quality across departments and contract types. The competency-to-scaffold mapping in Table 3 functions as an institutional design blueprint for building capability memory through templates, playbooks, and reusable learning objects, while preserving disciplinary epistemics and professional autonomy.

Table 3. Faculty capability ecosystem domains and institutional scaffolding safeguards

Competency Domain	Theoretical Anchor Constructs	Capability Formation Mechanism	Institutional Scaffolding Architecture	Risks and Governance Safeguards
Inclusive Learning Design Capability	*Universal Design for Learning*, accessibility-by-design, culturally responsive pedagogy	Translating learner variability into modular learning pathways, multimodal representation, and barrier-reducing participation structures	Accessibility specialists embedded in course design studios, validated template libraries, and assistive-technology readiness checks	Tokenistic compliance, accommodation delays, hidden exclusion, safeguarded through accessibility QA gates and escalation protocols
Assessment Integrity Engineering	validity reasoning, integrity-by-design, consequential evaluation governance	Replacing surveillance dependence with authentic task design, calibrated rubrics, moderation routines, and defensible judgment trails	Assessment design clinics, discipline-calibrated rubric banks, moderation calendars, and integrity governance councils	Over-proctoring normalization, false accusation risk, metric gaming, safeguarded through proportionality rules and contestability pathways
Hybrid Facilitation and Relational Presence	*Community of Inquiry*, social presence, dialogic pedagogy	Building interactional density through structured dialogue, presence cues, and psychologically safe participation norms	Faculty facilitation labs, peer observation protocols, studio-based rehearsal, and classroom analytics with minimality constraints	Attention fragmentation, participation inequities, performative engagement, safeguarded through inclusive facilitation standards and workload credits
Feedback Craftsmanship and Learning Analytics Judgment	formative assessment cycles, feedback literacy, measurement epistemics	Converting learning signals into timely, action-guiding feedback while resisting proxy substitution and automation bias	Feedback policy standards, annotated exemplar banks, analytics translators, and protected marking time allocations	Dashboard theater, automation bias, late feedback, safeguarded through construct alignment reviews and decision-right clarification

continued on following page

Table 3. Continued

Competency Domain	Theoretical Anchor Constructs	Capability Formation Mechanism	Institutional Scaffolding Architecture	Risks and Governance Safeguards
Data Ethics, Privacy, and Dignity Stewardship	purpose limitation, data minimization, *procedural justice*	Governing data flows with consent discipline, bounded use-cases, and transparent explanation proportional to decision stakes	Data stewards, model risk owners, audit logs, and redress mechanisms integrated into HR and learning analytics workflows	Function creep, surveillance distrust, inequitable impact, safeguarded through audits, appeals, and separation of supportive versus punitive uses
Professional Identity Resilience and Capability Citizenship	*Self-Determination Theory*, psychological safety, identity congruence	Sustaining autonomy, competence growth, and collegial relatedness to convert change into professional ownership	Communities of practice, mentoring ladders, recognition for capability stewardship, and psychologically safe leadership routines	Burnout, cynical compliance, exit from institutional citizenship, safeguarded through workload equity models and recognition reform

Table 3 operationalizes capability formation as a governance-ready system by linking competency domains to theoretical anchors, mechanistic pathways, and institutional scaffolds that can be resourced, monitored, and iteratively improved without collapsing into reductive metric regimes. The matrix also clarifies how risks emerge from predictable socio-technical failure modes, including compliance theater, proxy distortion, and surveillance distrust, and it specifies safeguards that preserve legitimacy through *construct validity*, *procedural justice*, and bounded decision architectures. When interpreted alongside Table 2, the table illustrates that maturity is achieved when ecosystems reduce coordination load, stabilize pedagogic quality, and protect inclusive access to capability resources, thereby preventing capability-debt accumulation and ensuring repeatable performance under heterogeneous constraints.

4.4 Incentives, Appraisal Ecologies, and Recognition Regimes as Capability Accelerators

Capability ecosystems fail when incentive structures reward visible outputs while devaluing redesign labor, mentoring intensity, accessibility work, and third-space coordination, thereby producing misaligned rational-choice equilibria and institutionalized underinvestment in quality. A capability-accelerating appraisal ecology must therefore integrate incentive compatibility with legitimacy, ensuring that evaluation regimes recognize artifact quality, pedagogic coherence, and integrity-by-design contributions, not merely activity counts or superficial engagement proxies (Arowosegbe et al., 2024; Yusuf et al., 2024; Shahzad et al., 2025). Motivation architectures derived from *Self-Determination Theory* imply that autonomy-preserving participation, competence-signaling feedback, and relatedness through collegial peer ecologies raise adoption fidelity, while the *Job Demands-Resources Model* implies that capability will degrade when resources, time entitlements, and psychosocial safety are not co-optimized. Recognition systems should internalize invisible labor through workload calculus reform, career pathway differentiation, and stewardship credits for capability citizenship, thereby preventing adverse selection where high-capability faculty exit or disengage (Zhang, 2024; Alam & Mohanty, 2022; Azeem et al., 2024). Table 3 provides the competency-level scaffolds that appraisal regimes must reward if institutions seek durable maturity rather than performative compliance.

4.5 Equity, Inclusion, and Digital Divide Dynamics within Faculty Capability Formation

Equity is not an adjunct to capability formation, it is a structural constraint that determines whether maturity pathways are scalable across heterogeneous faculty populations and institutional geographies. Capability access is stratified by contract precarity, caregiving load, disability accommodation reliability, language and epistemic marginalization, and differential access to protected time, producing uneven adoption and predictable inequities in who bears redesign labor (Santana & Díaz-Fernández, 2023; Tariq, 2024; Özer et al., 2024). A justice-informed capability model therefore requires distributive fairness in resource allocation, procedural fairness in workload assignment, and interactional fairness in governance communication, thereby operationalizing *organizational justice* as an infrastructure of trust rather than a moral afterthought. Inclusion must also be interpreted socio-technically, since platforms can intensify surveillance anxiety, amplify bias through proxy metrics, and increase coordination demands that penalize faculty with constrained temporal bandwidth (Gong et al., 2022; Delcker et al., 2024; Moore & Lookadoo, 2024). Equity governance should therefore institutionalize capability entitlements, accessible professional learning formats, and bias-aware analytics boundaries, aligning with the safeguards specified in Table 3 and the maturity-domain role logic established in Table 2.

5. STUDENT ENGAGEMENT, DIGITAL PEDAGOGY, AND THE TALENT-TO-LEARNING VALUE CHAIN

5.1 Student Engagement as an Institutional Capability Output

Student engagement in postdigital higher education is a capability-produced outcome that emerges from course architecture, feedback logistics, advising workflows, and belonging ecologies, rather than a psychological trait located inside the learner. Engagement must be treated as a multidimensional construct comprising behavioral participation, cognitive investment, affective attachment, and agentic contribution, each contingent on how teaching labor is designed, supported, and recognized (Mabungela, 2023; Quy et al., 2023; Abu Orabi et al., 2024). When faculty capability ecosystems are weak, the institution unintentionally produces engagement volatility through incoherent navigation structures, delayed feedback, inconsistent assessment standards, and fragmented support pathways that amplify uncertainty and withdrawal. Building on the capability scaffolding logic articulated in Table 3, this section models engagement as a value-chain effect of role clarity, workload entitlements, and integrity-by-design assessment, with the intervention architecture in Table 4 specifying how talent mechanisms translate into pedagogic reconfiguration (Kooli & Abadli, 2022; Chaudhry et al., 2023; Goswami et al., 2023). Engagement governance must resist proxy substitution, since clickstream visibility is not isomorphic with learning, and metric overreach can induce performativity, distrust, and participation suppression.

5.2 Theoretical Lenses Linking Talent Architecture to Engagement and Learning Value

A defensible talent-to-learning value chain requires a theory-stack that simultaneously captures motivation, interaction quality, assessment epistemics, and socio-technical mediation. *Self-Determination Theory* specifies autonomy-supportive pedagogic climates as the micro-foundation of durable engagement, while expectancy-value and self-efficacy constructs explain why effort is contingent on perceived attainability and consequential relevance (Xiao et al., 2025; Kumar & Raman, 2022; Alam, 2023c). *Community of Inquiry* constructs clarify how teaching presence, cognitive presence, and social presence become designable properties of hybrid courses when facilitation is resourced as a role, not treated as residual labor. Learning-science constructs, including cognitive load regulation, retrieval practice, spacing, and feedback efficacy, specify why engagement must be channeled into productive struggle rather than activity saturation (Agnihotri et al., 2024; Al-Jaghoub et al., 2025; Malik et al., 2022). Psychometric and assessment constructs, including *consequential validity* and integrity-by-design architectures, explain why authentic tasks and transparent standards reduce misconduct incentives and protect trust. Table 4 consolidates these constructs into intervention pathways that prevent engagement governance from degenerating into surveillance pedagogy and proxy-driven coercion.

5.3 The Capability-to-Pedagogy Pathway as a Governable Value Chain

The capability-to-pedagogy pathway becomes governable when universities treat talent interventions as engineered mechanisms that transform work design into observable learning conditions, rather than as inspirational rhetoric or episodic training. Protected redesign time converts latent pedagogic intent into coherent course architecture, co-design partnerships convert disciplinary expertise into accessible learning sequences, and integrity-oriented assessment engineering converts evaluation from surveillance dependence into authenticity and trust (Aydın et al., 2025; Segbenya et al., 2023; Prikshat et al., 2025). Analytics literacy converts signals into judgment only when decision rights and response capacity exist, and mentoring architectures convert institutional care into belonging and persistence through reliable relational access. These mechanisms are not interchangeable, they are functionally coupled to workload calculus, role jurisdiction, and accountability surfaces, which is why Table 4 specifies intervention archetypes alongside theoretical anchors, pedagogic effects, engagement mechanisms, and equity safeguards (Dong et al., 2026; Benouachane, 2024; Jangbahadur et al., 2025). The table also operationalizes construct alignment by making explicit how interventions reduce coordination load, stabilize feedback cadence, and protect dignity, thereby producing engagement that is epistemically meaningful rather than performatively visible.

Table 4. Talent interventions linking pedagogy, engagement, equity, and integrity mechanisms

Talent Intervention Archetype	Theoretical Construct Anchor	Pedagogic Reconfiguration Effect	Engagement Value-Chain Mechanism	Equity and Ethics Safeguard
Protected Redesign Time and Workload Credits	*Job Demands-Resources Model* and capability stewardship logic	Converts improvisational teaching into coherent learning architecture, constructive alignment, and accessible sequencing	Improves predictability of learning routines, reduces cognitive overload, and increases student trust in course coherence	Transparent workload calculus, distributive fairness checks, and recognition of invisible design labor
Co-Design Studios with Instructional Designers and Librarians	*Socio-Technical Systems Theory* and boundary-spanning integration	Produces interoperable course ecosystems, artifact-based quality assurance, and inclusive learning objects	Strengthens teaching presence and navigational clarity, increasing sustained participation and persistence	Accessibility-by-design gates, culturally responsive review, and local autonomy safeguards within shared standards
Integrity-by-Design Assessment Engineering	*Consequential Validity* and authenticity-oriented evaluation governance	Shifts evaluation from surveillance toward authentic tasks, calibrated rubrics, and defensible judgment trails	Reduces misconduct incentives, stabilizes fairness perceptions, and increases agentic engagement with meaningful tasks	Procedural justice routines, contestability pathways, and proportionality norms that avoid punitive overreach
Analytics Literacy with Decision Rights and Response Capacity	measurement epistemics and bounded rationality discipline	Enables interpretation of learning signals, targeted feedback, and timely instructional adaptation	Converts early signals into supportive action, reducing attrition risk and enhancing self-regulated learning	Purpose limitation, data minimization, and separation of supportive analytics from disciplinary enforcement
Mentoring and Belonging Infrastructure with Role Formalization	belongingness constructs and *Self-Determination Theory* relatedness pathway	Institutionalizes relational access, advising continuity, and psychologically safe learning climates	Increases persistence through social integration, perceived care, and reduced help-seeking friction	Equity monitoring for access, protection from stigma, and culturally safe escalation routes for complex needs
Feedback Policy Standards and Service-Level Norms	formative assessment cycles and feedback literacy constructs	Stabilizes feedback cadence, clarifies performance standards, and reduces ambiguity-induced anxiety	Enhances competence perceptions, increases effort persistence, and improves calibration of study strategies	Workload entitlements for marking time, bias-aware moderation routines, and safeguards against automation bias

Table 4 translates capability interventions into a disciplined causal grammar by coupling theoretical constructs with pedagogic reconfiguration effects and engagement mechanisms, enabling institutions to design, resource, and govern engagement without reverting to simplistic activity proxies. The matrix also clarifies that equity and ethics are not post hoc constraints, they are endogenous to performance reliability because procedural fairness, dignity protection, and workload realism preserve trust capital and reduce adversarial compliance. When interpreted alongside Table 3, the table shows that engagement stabilizes when capability ecosystems supply protected time, boundary-spanning expertise, and feedback infrastructures that convert learning signals into supportive action rather than punitive scrutiny. This alignment prevents surveillance-driven engagement governance from eroding belonging, and it limits Goodhart dynamics by privileging artifact quality and decision integrity over platform activity counts.

5.4 Risks of Algorithmic Engagement Governance and Surveillance Pedagogy

Algorithmic engagement governance becomes hazardous when institutions conflate legibility with learning, thereby converting trace data into pseudo-epistemic certainty and treating students as objects of monitoring rather than co-producers of learning. Proxy metrics can misclassify engagement, amplify bias through differential visibility, and trigger automation bias in instructional and disciplinary decisions, especially when interpretability is weak and contestability is absent (Malin et al., 2024; Alam, 2023b; Farrelly & Baker, 2023). Over-instrumentation also reshapes pedagogic norms by incentivizing compliance behavior, discouraging intellectual risk-taking, and compressing autonomy through constant nudging, which undermines *Self-Determination Theory* pathways and erodes trust. Surveillance pedagogy is further intensified when early-alert systems become coupled to punitive action rather than supportive care, producing chilling effects and help-seeking suppression among marginalized learners (Al Shibly & Alghizzawi, 2024; Gryncewicz et al., 2023; Jatobá et al., 2023). The safeguards encoded in Table 4, including purpose limitation, separation of supportive and punitive uses, and procedural justice routines, are therefore governance essentials rather than ethical embellishments. Engagement systems must be designed as dignity-preserving support infrastructures, with minimality discipline and explicit decision-right boundaries.

5.5 Bridging Theory to Institutional Design for High-Fidelity Digital Pedagogy

Bridging theory to institutional design requires translating constructs into governance primitives, role charters, and resource-backed routines that can survive leadership turnover and policy turbulence. Institutions should operationalize engagement as a value-chain outcome by embedding co-design studios, integrity-by-design assessment clinics, mentoring role formalization, and feedback service-level norms into the standard operating architecture, thereby converting exceptional practice into baseline reliability (Hamzah et al., 2025; Bhat, 2023; Faheem et al., 2024). Quality assurance should privilege artifact-based evidence, including alignment coherence, rubric defensibility, accessibility conformance, and feedback timeliness, interpreted through measurement epistemics rather than through activity proxies. Workload calculus must be recalibrated so that redesign labor, mentoring intensity, and coordination overhead are recognized as core production inputs, consistent with the protected-time logic in Table 4. Analytics should function as bounded decision support with contestability, not as a disciplinary panopticon, with transparent communication that stabilizes trust capital. In this design logic, engagement becomes an emergent property of coherent capability governance, not a behavioral compliance target.

6. AI-DRIVEN HR, TALENT ANALYTICS, GOVERNANCE, AND SUSTAINABILITY IN DIGITAL HEIS

6.1 AI-Enabled Talent Management as High-Stakes Socio-Ethical Governance

AI-enabled HR in higher education should be treated as a legitimacy-critical governance layer, not as a productivity add-on, because it shapes access to academic opportunity, career mobility, and institutional voice. In postdigital universities, AI commonly enters recruitment screening, competency inference, workload modeling, professional learning recommendations, retention risk scoring, and performance narrative augmentation, each of which can reconfigure power through differential visibility and proxy-based inference (Kaushal et al., 2023; Helmiatin et al., 2024; Malik et al., 2023). Because universities are public-interest knowledge institutions, the relevant design question is not whether automation is feasible, but whether decision architectures preserve *procedural justice*, dignity, academic freedom, and contestability under conditions of data asymmetry. This framing also requires non-delegable zones for consequential decisions, where *meaningful human control* is operationalized through accountable review, reason-giving, and appeal pathways (Prasad & De, 2024; Al-Hamad et al., 2023; Razia et al., 2023). The governance matrix in Table 5 is introduced here as an institutional instrument for aligning use-case scope, decision stakes, and safeguards with clear ownership.

6.2 Responsible Analytics and AI Governance through Multi-Framework Constraint Design

Responsible analytics in universities requires a constraint-based design paradigm that fuses measurement epistemics, risk governance, and normative legitimacy into a single operating logic. *Algorithmic accountability* demands traceability, documentation, and audit-ready decision trails, while fairness governance requires both outcome-focused parity checks and process-focused *procedural justice* routines that ensure consistent treatment, respectful explanation, and contestable outcomes (Mendy et al., 2025; Alam, 2023a; Tsiskaridze et al., 2023). Privacy governance must instantiate purpose limitation, data minimization, retention discipline, and role-based access control, so that supportive analytics cannot silently mutate into disciplinary surveillance through function creep. Human oversight must be engineered to counter automation bias through structured second-look review, calibration sessions, and escalation protocols that specify who can override models and under what evidentiary thresholds (Rabenu & Baruch, 2025; Sabil et al., 2023; Hannan & Liu, 2023). High-reliability governance adds incident reporting, near-miss learning, and drift monitoring, ensuring that model performance does not degrade silently under shifting populations and policy conditions. Table 5 operationalizes these constraints by mapping institutional controls to distinct HR use-cases and decision stakes.

6.3 Talent Analytics as Decision Architecture

Talent analytics becomes institutionally useful only when it is designed as a decision architecture with explicit constructs, validated indicators, and enforceable decision rights, rather than as a dashboard ecology that amplifies metric power without interpretive governance. Construct validity is central because universities routinely overcount what is visible, such as clicks, outputs, and throughput, while undercounting invisible labor, mentoring intensity, accessibility work, and coordination load, producing predictable *Goodhart effects* and adverse selection (Böhmer & Schinnenburg, 2023; Devi & Rroy, 2023; Nam & Bai, 2023). A maturity-grade analytics stack therefore requires data lineage, metric dictionaries, model registries, and proportional interpretability, meaning that explanation depth increases with decision stakes and potential harm. Risk controls must also include bias testing, adverse impact diagnostics, and contestability mechanisms so that individuals can challenge inferences derived from proxies (Saaida, 2023; Budhwar et al., 2022; Maghsoudi et al., 2024). Table 5 consolidates a governance-ready matrix that couples use-case categories with decision stakes, risks, controls, and accountable owners.

Table 5. Governance matrix for AI-driven HR decision integrity

Use-Case Category	Decision Stakes Profile	Dominant Risk Exposure	Required Control Stack	Accountable Institutional Owner
Recruitment and Shortlisting Support	High impact on access, diversity, and long-run capability composition across disciplines	Proxy discrimination, credentialism inflation, and opacity in screening thresholds	Model registry, bias and adverse impact testing, structured human review panels, and explanation that is applicant-legible	HR Head with Equal Opportunity Stewardship
Promotion and Tenure Decision Augmentation	Very high stakes affecting livelihood, academic freedom, and epistemic diversity	Metric substitution, gaming incentives, and disciplinary bias through publication proxy dominance	Construct-valid portfolios, peer moderation, decision traceability, appeal pathways, and prohibition of single-score determinism	Academic Affairs Head with Faculty Senate Oversight
Workload Allocation and Timetabling Analytics	High stakes for wellbeing, equity, and sustainable performance capacity	Hidden labor erasure, care-load inequity, and coordination overload through unrealistic assumptions	Transparent workload calculus, equity audits, protected time entitlements, grievance channels, and periodic recalibration cycles	Department Chair with Workload Equity Monitor
Professional Learning and Reskilling Recommendations	Medium stakes shaping capability trajectories and opportunity access	Over-personalization, surveillance creep, and inequitable access to time and learning resources	Purpose limitation, opt-in design, learning entitlements, accessibility assurance, and separation from performance discipline	Faculty Development Lead with Accessibility Steward

continued on following page

Table 5. Continued

Use-Case Category	Decision Stakes Profile	Dominant Risk Exposure	Required Control Stack	Accountable Institutional Owner
Retention Risk and Attrition Forecasting	Medium to high stakes affecting managerial interventions and workplace climate	Stigmatization, self-fulfilling labeling, and privacy erosion through sensitive inference	Minimality discipline, human-in-the-loop triage, confidential handling, supportive-only use boundaries, and audit logs	People Analytics Lead with Data Stewardship Officer
Performance Evaluation and Productivity Analytics	High stakes shaping incentives, identity, and institutional legitimacy	Performativity escalation, automation bias, and reputational harm through misclassification	Multi-source evidence triangulation, validity reviews, contestability, calibration forums, and strict separation of support versus sanction	Quality Assurance Head with Ethics Review Function

Table 5 enables governance by converting abstract ethical commitments into concrete institutional accountabilities, thereby reducing discretionary ambiguity that typically fuels distrust and compliance theater. The matrix also makes visible that different use-cases require different interpretability thresholds, control intensities, and ownership structures, which prevents the common error of applying uniform analytics rules to heterogeneous decision stakes. When coupled with the capability logic in Table 4, the table clarifies how supportive analytics can be bounded to enhance feedback, mentoring, and reskilling, while insulating academic freedom and dignity from surveillance drift. The framework therefore treats model governance, metric validity, and contestability as operational primitives that stabilize legitimacy under datafied performance regimes.

6.4 Wellbeing, Workload, and Digital Burnout as Sustainability-Critical Outcome Variables

Wellbeing sustainability is a hard constraint on institutional maturity because postdigital work intensifies cognitive load, coordination labor, and affective demands, thereby depleting the very human capital that maturity architectures presuppose. The *Job Demands-Resources Model* predicts predictable burnout trajectories when digital demands expand through always-on communication, continuous assessment cycles, and integrity policing, while resources remain static in staffing, protected time, and psychosocial safety (Nguyen et al., 2022; Fawaid et al., 2025; Gârdan et al., 2025). A governance-grade response requires workload measurement that recognizes redesign labor, mentoring intensity, accessibility compliance work, and coordination overhead as first-order production inputs, not as residual volunteerism. Digital humane governance then sets service-level norms for response expectations, establishes protected time entitlements, and funds third-space support to reduce friction and prevent capability-debt accumulation (Dugina et al., 2025; Ateeq et al., 2026; Alam, 2022). Talent analytics should be used to detect overload patterns and inequity gradients, but only within supportive boundaries defined by purpose limitation and contestability, consistent with the controls mapped in Table 5. Sustainability is achieved when performance expectations are structurally compatible with human resource regeneration.

6.5 Policy and Leadership for Institutional Sustainability under Legitimacy Constraints

Leadership for AI-enabled HR maturity is a governance practice of sensemaking, boundary-setting, and legitimacy maintenance, rather than a rhetorical exercise in digital optimism. Policy coherence must align recruitment, promotion, workload, integrity, and analytics governance so that faculty experience a stable institutional contract, where evaluation criteria are construct-valid, procedurally fair, and compatible with disciplinary epistemics (Slimi & Carballido, 2023; Wietrak et al., 2024; Nair et al., 2025). Participatory governance is operationally necessary because contested systems require shared ownership, stakeholder representation, and transparent decision rights, otherwise analytics becomes a unilateral control apparatus that triggers resistance, workaround ecologies, and exit from institutional citizenship. Procurement governance must enforce interoperability, audit clauses, data ownership discipline, and exit strategies, reducing vendor lock-in and ensuring that institutional values are not outsourced to opaque systems (Mahade et al., 2025; Etomes, 2024; Silveira, 2025). Global operating conditions also require cross-border data transfer discipline, multilingual fairness testing, and localization of support infrastructures so that capability access does not become geographically stratified. Table 5 provides the managerial substrate for these commitments by assigning accountable owners and minimum control stacks that can be audited without reducing education to metric spectacle.

7. CONCLUSION

7.1 Synthesis of Capability-Reconfiguration Thesis

This chapter has advanced a capability-reconfiguration thesis in which postdigital university maturity is theorized as a governed, role-embedded, legitimacy-dependent capacity to produce reliable educational value under datafied constraints, rather than as a function of platform modernity or procurement velocity. The conceptual spine integrates *Dynamic Capabilities Theory*, *socio-technical alignment*, *institutional logics*, and justice-grounded governance to show that transformation success depends on how institutions redesign roles, redistribute decision rights, and resource capability ecosystems with protected time, boundary-spanning expertise, and artifact-based quality assurance. Across Sections 2 through 6, the argument has treated measurement as an epistemic problem, analytics as a political instrument, and wellbeing as a sustainability constraint, thereby rejecting proxy-driven performance regimes that induce *Goodhart effects*, compliance theater, and capability-debt accumulation. The maturity construct is therefore stabilized by governance primitives, including construct validity, contestability, proportional interpretability, and *meaningful human control*, which collectively protect academic freedom, dignity, and trust capital while enabling coherent transformation.

7.2 High-Resolution Conceptual Takeaways for Cross-Sector Readerships

For academic and policy audiences, the framework clarifies that institutional performance in postdigital conditions is a system-level emergent property produced by coupled infrastructures, incentives, and legitimacy mechanisms, making simplistic modernization narratives analytically indefensible and operationally risky. For workforce development professionals and HR leaders, the chapter reframes talent management as capability formation, requiring role-systems design, workload calculus reform, and recognition regimes that internalize invisible labor, mentoring intensity, and third-space coordination as core production inputs. For digital learning technologists and analytics practitioners, the argument positions learning and workforce analytics as bounded decision support that must be validity-governed, bias-aware, and procedurally fair, with strict separation between supportive functions and punitive enforcement to prevent surveillance drift. For governance actors, including senior leadership and quality assurance units, the chapter establishes that trust is a strategic asset, and that participatory governance, transparent decision rights, and appeal pathways are not ethical ornamentation, but reliability engineering for complex institutions. These takeaways collectively specify a globally portable maturity logic that can be localized without diluting its normative constraints.

7.3 Forward-Looking Conceptual Directions and Maturity Pathway Horizons

Future conceptual development should prioritize the institutionalization of hybrid career pathways that legitimate teaching-intensive excellence, learning-design stewardship, and analytics translation as first-class academic contributions rather than peripheral service labor. A second direction concerns legitimacy dynamics under analytics-driven governance, where contestability design, explanation proportionality, and harm-sensitive oversight must evolve into standard operating norms to prevent algorithmic management from eroding autonomy and epistemic diversity. A third direction involves equity-centered capability justice, requiring entitlements for protected time, accessible professional learning, and bias-aware evaluation architectures so that capability accumulation does not become stratified by contract type, caregiving load, disability access, language marginalization, or geographic infrastructure disparities. Finally, the long-run institutional consequences of digital burnout demand a shift from resilience rhetoric to structural workload engineering, treating psychosocial safety, coordination load reduction, and regeneration capacity as hard constraints on performance, innovation, and ethical integrity. In these horizons, maturity is best understood as the sustained capacity to govern transformation without extracting the human and civic resources upon which universities fundamentally depend.

REFERENCES

Abdelwahab, H. R., Rauf, A., & Chen, D. (2023). Business students' perceptions of Dutch higher educational institutions in preparing them for artificial intelligence work environments. *Industry and Higher Education, 37*(1), 22–34. DOI: 10.1177/09504222221087614

Abu Orabi, T., Alahewat, A. M. M., Abualfalayeh, G., & Samara, H. H. (2024). The interdisciplinary nature of AI and human resource management: A bibliometric analysis. *Human Systems Management, 43*(6), 845–871. DOI: 10.3233/HSM-240054

Abulail, R. N., Badran, O. N., Shkoukani, M. A., & Omeish, F. (2025). Exploring the factors influencing AI adoption intentions in higher education: An integrated model of DOI, TOE, and TAM. *Computers, 14*(6), 230. DOI: 10.3390/computers14060230

Agnihotri, A., Grover, V., Balusamy, B., Gite, S., Arockiam, D., & Shankar, A. (2024, June). Utilizing the potential of AI to Revolutionize talent management in contemporary organizations. In *IET Conference Proceedings CP881* (Vol. 2024, No. 7, pp. 1-11). Stevenage, UK: The Institution of Engineering and Technology. DOI: 10.1049/icp.2024.2519

Aguinis, H., Beltran, J. R., & Cope, A. (2024). How to use generative AI as a human resource management assistant. *Organizational Dynamics, 53*(1), 101029. DOI: 10.1016/j.orgdyn.2024.101029

Aini, Q., Rusilowati, U., Asfi, M., Sunarya, P. A., Putra, S. N. W., & Zahra, A. R. A. (2024, August). Assessing the influence of artificial intelligence on human resource management practices. In *2024 3rd International Conference on Creative Communication and Innovative Technology (ICCIT)* (pp. 1-6). IEEE. DOI: 10.1109/ICCIT62134.2024.10701158

Al-Hamad, N., James, O. O., Afolabi, J. O. A., Olatoye, F. O., & Eboigbe, E. O. (2023). Innovative HR practices in higher education for global competitiveness. *Education Sustainability & Society, 7*(1), 21–30. DOI: 10.26480/ess.01.2024.21.30

Al-Jaghoub, S., Al-Qora'n, L. F., Al-Odat, A. M., & Alheet, A. F. (2025). Educators' perceptions on artificial intelligence in higher education: Insights from the Jordanian higher education. *International Journal of Information and Education Technology (IJIET), 15*(4), 716–731. DOI: 10.18178/ijiet.2025.15.4.2278

Al-Mughairi, H., & Bhaskar, P. (2025). Exploring the factors affecting the adoption AI techniques in higher education: Insights from teachers' perspectives on ChatGPT. *Journal of Research in Innovative Teaching & Learning, 18*(2), 232–247. DOI: 10.1108/JRIT-09-2023-0129

Al Shibly, M. S., & Alghizzawi, M. (2024, April). The impact of using AI in human resources management-a comparison approach. In *International Conference on Business and Technology* (pp. 1-10). Cham: Springer Nature Switzerland. DOI: 10.1007/978-3-031-67444-0_1

Al-Zahrani, A. M., & Alasmari, T. M. (2025). A comprehensive analysis of AI adoption, implementation strategies, and challenges in higher education across the Middle East and North Africa (MENA) region. *Education and Information Technologies, 30*(8), 11339–11389. DOI: 10.1007/s10639-024-13300-y

Alam, A. (2022). Impact of university's human resources practices on professors' occupational performance: empirical evidence from India's higher education sector. In *Inclusive businesses in developing economies: Converging people, profit, and corporate citizenship* (pp. 107–131). Springer International Publishing. DOI: 10.1007/978-3-031-12217-0_6

Alam, A. (2023a). Media multitasking with M-learning technology in real-time classroom learning: Analysing the dynamics in formal educational settings for the future of E-learning in India. In *2023 2nd International Conference on Smart Technologies and Systems for Next Generation Computing (ICSTSN)* (pp. 1-6). IEEE.

Alam, A. (2023b). The secret sauce of student success: Cracking the code by navigating the path to personalized learning with educational data mining. In *2023 2nd International Conference on Smart Technologies and Systems for Next Generation Computing (ICSTSN)* (pp. 1-8). IEEE.

Alam, A. (2023c). Intelligence unleashed: An argument for AI-enabled learning ecologies with real world examples of today and a peek into the future. In *International Conference on Innovations in Computer Science, Electronics & Electrical Engineering*-2022 (Vol. 2717, No. 1, p. 030001). AIP Publishing LLC. DOI: 10.1063/5.0129803

Alam, A., & Mohanty, A. (2022, December). Facial analytics or virtual avatars: competencies and design considerations for student-teacher interaction in AI-powered online education for effective classroom engagement. In *International Conference on Communication, Networks and Computing* (pp. 252-265). Cham: Springer Nature Switzerland.

Alam, A., & Mohanty, A. (2023, January). Learning on the move: a pedagogical framework for state-of-the-art mobile learning. In *International Conference on Data Management, Analytics & Innovation* (pp. 735-748). Singapore: Springer Nature Singapore. DOI: 10.1007/978-981-99-1414-2_52

Alam, A., & Mohanty, A. (2024). Integrated constructive robotics in education (ICRE) model: A paradigmatic framework for transformative learning in educational ecosystem. *Cogent Education, 11*(1), 2324487. DOI: 10.1080/2331186X.2024.2324487

Alnaqbi, E. J. A. A., Mohd-Shamsudin, F., & Alshurideh, M. T. (2024). Green HRM practices, green commitment, and green innovative work behavior in UAE higher education institutes. *Uncertain Supply Chain Management, 12*(2), 723–736. DOI: 10.5267/j.uscm.2024.1.013

Apata, O. E., Ajose, S. T., Apata, B. O., Olaitan, G. I., Oyewole, P. O., Ogunwale, O. M., & Feyijimi, T. (2025). Artificial intelligence in higher education: A systematic review of contributions to SDG 4 (quality education) and SDG 10 (reduced inequality). *International Journal of Educational Management*, •••, 1–18.

Arowosegbe, A., Alqahtani, J. S., & Oyelade, T. (2024, October). Perception of generative AI use in UK higher education. [). Frontiers Media SA.]. *Frontiers in Education, 9*, 1463208. DOI: 10.3389/feduc.2024.1463208

Ateeq, A., Siddiqui, S. A., Verma, A., Alnimer, R., Ateeq, R. A., & Almuraqab, N. A. S. (2026). AI in Higher Education HR: Assessing Adoption and Acceptance Trends in Administrative Practices. In *Strategic Decision-Making in Dynamic Business Environments: Systems and Control Perspectives* (pp. 965–987). Springer Nature Switzerland. DOI: 10.1007/978-3-032-07220-7_84

Aydın, Ö., Karaarslan, E., & Narin, N. G. (2025). Artificial intelligence, vr, ar and metaverse technologies for human resources management. *International Journal of Management Information Systems and Computer Science, 9*(2), 77–94. DOI: 10.33461/uybisbbd.1681947

Azeem, M. M., Febriyanto, U., Nurhadi, F. A., & Halid, H. (2024). Unlocking the Values of Artificial Intelligence (AI) in Human Resource Management (HRM) in Enhancing Employee Retention. *Global Business and Management Research, 16*(2).

Baki, N. U., Rasdi, R. M., Krauss, S. E., & Omar, M. K. (2023). Integrating artificial intelligence in human resource functions: Challenges and opportunities. *International Journal of Academic Research in Business & Social Sciences, 13*(8), 1262–1277.

Benouachane, H. (2024). AI in higher education: Balancing pedagogical benefits and ethical challenges. *Educational AI Review, 2*(5), 302–322.

Bhardwaj, B., Sharma, D., & Dhiman, M. C. (Eds.). (2023). *AI and emotional intelligence for modern business management*. IGI Global. DOI: 10.4018/979-8-3693-0418-1

Bhat, J. (2023). Automating Higher Education Administrative Processes with AI-Powered Workflows. *International Journal of Emerging Trends in Computer Science and Information Technology*, *4*(4), 147–157. DOI: 10.63282/3050-9246.IJETCSIT-V4I4P116

Bodea, C. N., Paparic, M., Mogos, R. I., & Dascalu, M. I. (2024). Artificial intelligence adoption in the workplace and its impact on the upskilling and reskilling strategies. *Amfiteatru Economic*, *26*(65), 126–144. DOI: 10.24818/EA/2024/65/126

Böhmer, N., & Schinnenburg, H. (2023). Critical exploration of AI-driven HRM to build up organizational capabilities. *Employee Relations*, *45*(5), 1057–1082. DOI: 10.1108/ER-04-2022-0202

Budhwar, P., Chowdhury, S., Wood, G., Aguinis, H., Bamber, G. J., Beltran, J. R., Boselie, P., Lee Cooke, F., Decker, S., DeNisi, A., Dey, P. K., Guest, D., Knoblich, A. J., Malik, A., Paauwe, J., Papagiannidis, S., Patel, C., Pereira, V., Ren, S., & Varma, A. (2023). Human resource management in the age of generative artificial intelligence: Perspectives and research directions on ChatGPT. *Human Resource Management Journal*, *33*(3), 606–659. DOI: 10.1111/1748-8583.12524

Budhwar, P., Malik, A., De Silva, M. T., & Thevisuthan, P. (2022). Artificial intelligence–challenges and opportunities for international HRM: A review and research agenda. *International Journal of Human Resource Management*, *33*(6), 1065–1097. DOI: 10.1080/09585192.2022.2035161

Cambra-Fierro, J. J., Blasco, M. F., López-Pérez, M. E. E., & Trifu, A. (2025). ChatGPT adoption and its influence on faculty well-being: An empirical research in higher education. *Education and Information Technologies*, *30*(2), 1517–1538. DOI: 10.1007/s10639-024-12871-0

Chaudhry, I. S., Sarwary, S. A. M., El Refae, G. A., & Chabchoub, H. (2023). Time to revisit existing student's performance evaluation approach in higher education sector in a new era of ChatGPT—A case study. *Cogent Education*, *10*(1), 2210461. DOI: 10.1080/2331186X.2023.2210461

Delcker, J., Heil, J., Ifenthaler, D., Seufert, S., & Spirgi, L. (2024). First-year students AI-competence as a predictor for intended and de facto use of AI-tools for supporting learning processes in higher education. *International Journal of Educational Technology in Higher Education*, *21*(1), 18. DOI: 10.1186/s41239-024-00452-7

Devi, D., & Rroy, A. D. (2023). Role of artificial intelligence (ai) in sustainable education of higher education institutions in Guwahati City: Teacher's perception. *International Management Review*, *19*, 111–116.

Dogru, T., Line, N., Hanks, L., Acikgoz, F., Abbott, J. A., Bakir, S., Berbekova, A., Bilgihan, A., Iskender, A., Kizildag, M., Lee, M., Lee, W., McGinley, S., Mody, M., Onder, I., Ozdemir, O., & Suess, C. (2024). The implications of generative artificial intelligence in academic research and higher education in tourism and hospitality. *Tourism Economics, 30*(5), 1083–1094. DOI: 10.1177/13548166231204065

Dong, S., Chuangprakhon, S., Liu, Q., & Guangguo, W. (2026). Mapping Research on Music Education Faculty Structure in Higher Education (1980–2025): A Bibliometric Analysis. *SAGE Open, 16*(1), 21582440261425921. DOI: 10.1177/21582440261425921

Dugina, T. A., Nefedova, N. N., Dybina, O. V., & Oshkina, A. A. (2025). Responsible HRM Based on AI as a Factor in Decreasing the Divide Between the University Education Market and the Labour Market. In *Bridging the Gap Between the Higher Education and Labor Markets: Relevance of the Fourth Industrial Revolution* (pp. 101–108). Springer Nature Singapore. DOI: 10.1007/978-981-96-1933-7_12

Dutta, D., & Mishra, S. K. (2025). Artificial intelligence-based virtual assistant and employee engagement: An empirical investigation. *Personnel Review, 54*(3), 913–934. DOI: 10.1108/PR-03-2023-0263

Eftimov, L., & Kitanovikj, B. (2023). Unlocking the Path to AI Adoption: Antecedents to Behavioral Intentions in Utilizing AI for Effective Job (Re) Design. *Journal of HRM, 26*(2), 123–134. DOI: 10.46287/OTTP6295

Etomes, S. E. (2024). Artificial Intelligence and Human Resource Management in Higher Education Institutions in Cameroon. In *HRM, Artificial Intelligence and the Future of Work: Insights from the Global South* (pp. 229–246). Springer Nature Switzerland. DOI: 10.1007/978-3-031-62369-1_12

Faheem, M. A., Anwer, S., Rayhan, Z., Ullah, M. A., Paudel, R., Ahmed, M. F., & Khan, H. (2024). AI-driven innovation in HRM and its impact on business management: An in-depth study of technology advancement and strategic implementation. *Nanotechnology Perceptions, 20*(S13), 1174–1193. DOI: 10.62441/nano-ntp.vi.2599

Farrelly, T., & Baker, N. (2023). Generative artificial intelligence: Implications and considerations for higher education practice. *Education Sciences, 13*(11), 1109. DOI: 10.3390/educsci13111109

Fawaid, A., Baharun, H., Hamzah, M., Munawwaroh, I., & Putri, D. F. (2025, March). AI-based career management to improve the quality of decision making in higher education. In *2025 IEEE Integrated STEM Education Conference (ISEC)* (pp. 1-8). IEEE. DOI: 10.1109/ISEC64801.2025.11147274

Fenwick, A., Molnar, G., & Frangos, P. (2024). The critical role of HRM in AI-driven digital transformation: A paradigm shift to enable firms to move from AI implementation to human-centric adoption. *Discover Artificial Intelligence*, *4*(1), 34. DOI: 10.1007/s44163-024-00125-4

Gârdan, I. P., Manu, M. B., Gârdan, D. A., Negoi ă, L. D. L., Pa tiu, C. A., Ghi ă, E., & Zaharia, A. (2025, February). Adopting AI in education: Optimizing human resource management considering teacher perceptions. [). Frontiers Media SA.]. *Frontiers in Education*, *10*, 1488147. DOI: 10.3389/feduc.2025.1488147

Gong, Y., Zhao, M., Wang, Q., & Lv, Z. (2022). Design and interactive performance of human resource management system based on artificial intelligence. *PLoS One*, *17*(1), e0262398. DOI: 10.1371/journal.pone.0262398

Goswami, M., Jain, S., Alam, T., Deifalla, A. F., Ragab, A. E., & Khargotra, R. (2023). Exploring the antecedents of AI adoption for effective HRM practices in the Indian pharmaceutical sector. *Frontiers in Pharmacology*, *14*, 1215706. DOI: 10.3389/fphar.2023.1215706

Gryncewicz, W., Zygała, R., & Pilch, A. (2023). AI in HRM: Case study analysis. Preliminary research. *Procedia Computer Science*, *225*, 2351–2360. DOI: 10.1016/j.procs.2023.10.226

Halid, H., Ravesangar, K., Mahadzir, S. L., & Halim, S. N. A. (2024). Artificial intelligence (AI) in human resource management (HRM). In *Building the future with human resource management* (pp. 37–70). Springer International Publishing. DOI: 10.1007/978-3-031-52811-8_2

Hamzah, H. A., Abu Seman, M. S., & Ahmed, M. (2025). The impact of artificial intelligence in enhancing online learning platform effectiveness in higher education. *Information Development*, *41*(3), 794–810. DOI: 10.1177/02666669251315842

Hannan, E., & Liu, S. (2023). AI: New source of competitiveness in higher education. *Competitiveness Review*, *33*(2), 265–279. DOI: 10.1108/CR-03-2021-0045

Helmiatin, H., Hidayat, A., & Kahar, M. R. (2024). Investigating the adoption of AI in higher education: A study of public universities in Indonesia. *Cogent Education*, *11*(1), 2380175. DOI: 10.1080/2331186X.2024.2380175

Jaboob, M., Hazaimeh, M., & Al-Ansi, A. M. (2025). Integration of generative AI techniques and applications in student behavior and cognitive achievement in Arab higher education. *International Journal of Human-Computer Interaction*, *41*(1), 353–366. DOI: 10.1080/10447318.2023.2300016

Jangbahadur, U., Ahlawat, S., Rozera, P., & Gupta, N. (2025, January). The effect of AI-enabled HRM dimensions on employee engagement and sustainable organisational performance: fusion skills as a moderator. In *Evidence-Based HRM: A Global Forum for Empirical Scholarship* (Vol. 13, No. 1, pp. 85-107). Emerald Publishing Limited. DOI: 10.1108/EBHRM-02-2023-0038

Jatobá, M. N., Ferreira, J. J., Fernandes, P. O., & Teixeira, J. P. (2023). Intelligent human resources for the adoption of artificial intelligence: A systematic literature review. *Journal of Organizational Change Management, 36*(7), 1099–1124. DOI: 10.1108/JOCM-03-2022-0075

Kambur, E., & Yildirim, T. (2023). From traditional to smart human resources management. *International Journal of Manpower*, *44*(3), 422–452. DOI: 10.1108/IJM-10-2021-0622

Kaushal, N., Kaurav, R. P. S., Sivathanu, B., & Kaushik, N. (2023). Artificial intelligence and HRM: Identifying future research Agenda using systematic literature review and bibliometric analysis. *Management Review Quarterly*, *73*(2), 455–493. DOI: 10.1007/s11301-021-00249-2

Klimova, B., & Pikhart, M. (2025). Exploring the effects of artificial intelligence on student and academic well-being in higher education: A mini-review. *Frontiers in Psychology*, *16*, 1498132. DOI: 10.3389/fpsyg.2025.1498132

Kong, H., Jiang, X., Zhou, X., Baum, T., Li, J., & Yu, J. (2024). Influence of artificial intelligence (AI) perception on career resilience and informal learning. *Tourism Review*, *79*(1), 219–233. DOI: 10.1108/TR-10-2022-0521

Kooli, C., & Abadli, R. (2022). Could education quality audit enhance human resources management processes of the higher education institutions? *Vision (Basel)*, *26*(4), 482–490. DOI: 10.1177/09722629211005599

Kumar, V. R., & Raman, R. (2022, March). Student Perceptions on Artificial Intelligence (AI) in higher education. In *2022 IEEE integrated STEM education conference (ISEC)* (pp. 450-454). IEEE.

Li, Y., Deng, Y., Peng, B., He, Y., Luo, Y., & Liu, Q. (2024). Generative Artificial Intelligence in Chinese Higher Education: Chinese Undergraduates' Use, Perception, and Attitudes. *Frontiers in Educational Research*, *7*(4).

Mabungela, M. (2023). Artificial Intelligence (AI) and Automation in the World of Work: A Threat to Employees? *Research in Social Sciences and Technology*, *8*(4), 135–146. DOI: 10.46303/ressat.2023.37

Madanchian, M. (2024). From recruitment to retention: AI tools for human resource decision-making. *Applied Sciences (Basel, Switzerland), 14*(24), 11750. DOI: 10.3390/app142411750

Maghsoudi, M., Shahri, M. K., Kermani, M. A. M. A., & Khanizad, R. (2024). Mapping the landscape of AI-driven human resource management: A social network analysis of research collaboration. *IEEE Access : Practical Innovations, Open Solutions, 13*, 3090–3114. DOI: 10.1109/ACCESS.2024.3523437

Mahade, A., Elmahi, A., Alomari, K. M., & Abdalla, A. A. (2025). Leveraging AI-driven insights to enhance sustainable human resource management performance: moderated mediation model: evidence from UAE higher education. *Discover Sustainability, 6*(1), 267. DOI: 10.1007/s43621-025-01114-y

Mahmoud, M. M. H., Ali, A. A., Alrifae, A. A., Eitah, R. A., & AlZubi, M. M. (2025). The impact of digital HRM system and digital transformation on HR efficiency with organizational agility as a moderator. *Discover Sustainability, 6*(1), 1038. DOI: 10.1007/s43621-025-01713-9

Maimela, C., & Mbonde, P. (2025). Artificial intelligence in South African universities: Curriculum transformation and decolonisation—aid or obstacle? *Frontiers in Sociology, 10*, 1543471. DOI: 10.3389/fsoc.2025.1543471

Malik, A., Budhwar, P., & Kazmi, B. A. (2023). Artificial intelligence (AI)-assisted HRM: Towards an extended strategic framework. *Human Resource Management Review, 33*(1), 100940. DOI: 10.1016/j.hrmr.2022.100940

Malik, A., Nguyen, T. M., & Budhwar, P. (2022). Towards a conceptual model of AI-mediated knowledge sharing exchange of HRM practices: Antecedents and consequences. *IEEE Transactions on Engineering Management, 71*, 13083–13095. DOI: 10.1109/TEM.2022.3163117

Malin, C. D., Fleiß, J., Seeber, I., Kubicek, B., Kupfer, C., & Thalmann, S. (2024). The application of AI in digital HRM–an experiment on human decision-making in personnel selection. *Business Process Management Journal, 30*(8), 284–312. DOI: 10.1108/BPMJ-11-2023-0884

Mendy, J., Jain, A., & Thomas, A. (2025). Artificial intelligence in the workplace–challenges, opportunities and HRM framework: A critical review and research agenda for change. *Journal of Managerial Psychology, 40*(5), 517–538.

Moore, S., & Lookadoo, K. (2024). Communicating clear guidance: Advice for generative AI policy development in higher education. *Business and Professional Communication Quarterly, 87*(4), 610–629. DOI: 10.1177/23294906241254786

Mwita, K. M., & Kitole, F. A. (2025). Potential benefits and challenges of artificial intelligence in human resource management in public institutions. *Discover Global Society, 3*(1), 35. DOI: 10.1007/s44282-025-00175-8

Nair, S., Banka, K., & Pandya, A. (2025). Humanizing AI in Higher Education: Rethinking HR, Ethics, and Skill Development for University Employees in the SDG Era. *INTI Journal, 2025*(5).

Nam, B. H., & Bai, Q. (2023). ChatGPT and its ethical implications for STEM research and higher education: A media discourse analysis. *International Journal of STEM Education, 10*(1), 66. DOI: 10.1186/s40594-023-00452-5

Nguyen, D. P., Phan, L. T., Ho, H. X., & Le, A. N. H. (2022). Human resource management practices in higher education: A literature review using co-word analysis. *International Journal of Management Education, 16*(1), 40–61.

Nguyen, L. A., & Park, M. (2022). Artificial intelligence in staffing. *Vision (Basel)*, •••, 09722629221096803.

O'Brien, C., Li, Z., Adotey, P. B., & Yohuno, G. (2025). Mapping a decade of digital transformation in HRM: Trends, implications, and future research directions. *Current Psychology, 44*(14), 13234–13253. DOI: 10.1007/s12144-025-08064-8

Odugbesan, J. A., Aghazadeh, S., Al Qaralleh, R. E., & Sogeke, O. S. (2023). Green talent management and employees' innovative work behavior: The roles of artificial intelligence and transformational leadership. *Journal of Knowledge Management, 27*(3), 696–716. DOI: 10.1108/JKM-08-2021-0601

Olan, F., Nyuur, R. B., & Arakpogun, E. O. (2024). AI: A knowledge sharing tool for improving employees' performance. *Journal of Decision Systems, 33*(4), 700–720. DOI: 10.1080/12460125.2023.2263687

Özer, M., Perc, M., & Suna, H. E. (2024). Artificial intelligence bias and the amplification of inequalities in the labor market. *Journal of Economy Culture and Society*, (69), 159–168.

Palos-Sánchez, P. R., Baena-Luna, P., Badicu, A., & Infante-Moro, J. C. (2022). Artificial intelligence and human resources management: A bibliometric analysis. *Applied Artificial Intelligence, 36*(1), 2145631. DOI: 10.1080/08839514.2022.2145631

Pandey, A., Balusamy, B., & Chilamkurti, N. (Eds.). (2023). *Disruptive artificial intelligence and sustainable human resource management: Impacts and innovations-The future of HR*. CRC Press. DOI: 10.1201/9781032622743

Porkodi, S., & Cedro, T. L. (2025). The ethical role of generative artificial intelligence in modern HR decision-making: A systematic literature review. *European Journal of Business and Management Research, 10*(1), 44–55. DOI: 10.24018/ejbmr.2025.10.1.2535

Prasad, K. D. V., & De, T. (2024). Generative AI as a catalyst for HRM practices: Mediating effects of trust. *Humanities & Social Sciences Communications, 11*(1), 1–16. DOI: 10.1057/s41599-024-03842-4

Prikshat, V., Kumar, S., Patel, P., & Varma, A. (2025). Impact of organisational facilitators and perceived HR effectiveness on acceptance of AI-augmented HRM: An integrated TAM and TPB perspective. *Personnel Review, 54*(3), 879–912. DOI: 10.1108/PR-04-2023-0303

Qahtani, E. H. A., & Alsmairat, M. A. (2023). Assisting artificial intelligence adoption drivers in human resources management: a mediation model. *Acta logistica, 10*(1), 141-150.

Quy, V. K., Thanh, B. T., Chehri, A., Linh, D. M., & Tuan, D. A. (2023). AI and digital transformation in higher education: Vision and approach of a specific university in Vietnam. *Sustainability (Basel), 15*(14), 11093. DOI: 10.3390/su151411093

Rabenu, E., & Baruch, Y. (2025). Cyborging HRM theory: From evolution to revolution–the challenges and trajectories of AI for the future role of HRM. *Personnel Review, 54*(1), 174–198. DOI: 10.1108/PR-02-2024-0111

Raman, R., Venugopalan, M., & Kamal, A. (2024). Evaluating human resources management literacy: A performance analysis of ChatGPT and bard. *Heliyon, 10*(5), e27026. DOI: 10.1016/j.heliyon.2024.e27026

Rangel-de Lazaro, G., & Duart, J. M. (2023). You can handle, you can teach it: Systematic review on the use of extended reality and artificial intelligence technologies for online higher education. *Sustainability (Basel), 15*(4), 3507. DOI: 10.3390/su15043507

Razia, B., Awwad, B., & Taqi, N. (2023). The relationship between artificial intelligence (AI) and its aspects in higher education. *Development and Learning in Organizations, 37*(3), 21–23. DOI: 10.1108/DLO-04-2022-0074

Saaida, M. B. (2023). AI-Driven transformations in higher education: Opportunities and challenges. *International journal of educational research and studies, 5*(1), 29-36.

Sabil, S., Bangkara, B. A., Mogea, T., Niswan, E., & Timotius, E. (2023). Identification of HRM improvement strategy using artificial intelligence in modern economic development. *International Journal of Professional Business Review: Int. J. Prof. Bus. Rev.*, *8*(6), 10.

Santana, M., & Díaz-Fernández, M. (2023). Competencies for the artificial intelligence age: Visualisation of the state of the art and future perspectives. *Review of Managerial Science*, *17*(6), 1971–2004. DOI: 10.1007/s11846-022-00613-w

Segbenya, M., Bervell, B., Frimpong-Manso, E., Otoo, I. C., Andzie, T. A., & Achina, S. (2023). Artificial intelligence in higher education: Modelling the antecedents of artificial intelligence usage and effects on 21st century employability skills among postgraduate students in Ghana. *Computers and Education: Artificial Intelligence*, *5*, 100188. DOI: 10.1016/j.caeai.2023.100188

Sekli, G. M., Godo, A., & Véliz, J. C. (2024). Generative AI Solutions for Faculty and Students: A Review of Literature and Roadmap for Future Research. *Journal of Information Technology Education*, *23*, 14. DOI: 10.28945/5304

Shahzad, M. F., Xu, S., & Zahid, H. (2025). Exploring the impact of generative AI-based technologies on learning performance through self-efficacy, fairness & ethics, creativity, and trust in higher education. *Education and Information Technologies*, *30*(3), 3691–3716. DOI: 10.1007/s10639-024-12949-9

Silveira, P. P.Pallavi Priya Silveira. (2025). Transforming Global Education through AI: Addressing Cross-Cultural Competencies and HRM Challenges in the Digital Age. *Journal of Integrative Education Studies*, *1*(1), 20–29. DOI: 10.64229/6na0be71

Slimi, Z., & Carballido, B. V. (2023). Navigating the Ethical Challenges of Artificial Intelligence in Higher Education: An Analysis of Seven Global AI Ethics Policies. *TEM journal*, *12*(2).

Tariq, M. U. (Ed.). (2024). *AI-driven learning and engagement in higher education*. IGI Global. DOI: 10.4018/979-8-3693-4074-5

Thangaraju, K., & Palani, P. (2024). Integrating Sustainability into Ai-Driven HRM Practices: Examining Employee Engagement and Organizational Performance in the IT Industry. *Pakistan Journal of Life and Social Sciences*, *22*(2). Advance online publication. DOI: 10.57239/PJLSS-2024-22.2.001008

Tsiskaridze, R., Reinhold, K., & Jarvis, M. (2023). Innovating HRM recruitment: A comprehensive review of AI deployment. *Marketing i menedžment innovacij*, *14*(4), 239-254.

Tuffaha, M., & Perello-Marin, M. R. (2023). Artificial intelligence definition, applications and adoption in human resource management: A systematic literature review. *International Journal of Business Innovation and Research*, *32*(3), 293–322. DOI: 10.1504/IJBIR.2023.134887

Tzirides, A. O. O., Zapata, G., Kastania, N. P., Saini, A. K., Castro, V., Ismael, S. A., You, Y., Santos, T. A., Searsmith, D., O'Brien, C., Cope, B., & Kalantzis, M. (2024). Combining human and artificial intelligence for enhanced AI literacy in higher education. *Computers and Education Open*, *6*, 100184. DOI: 10.1016/j.caeo.2024.100184

Walczak, K., & Cellary, W. (2023). Challenges for higher education in the era of widespread access to Generative AI. *Economics and Business Review*, *9*(2), 71–100. DOI: 10.18559/ebr.2023.2.743

Wang, J., & Pashmforoosh, R. (2024). A new framework for ethical artificial intelligence: Keeping HRD in the loop. *Human Resource Development International*, *27*(3), 428–451. DOI: 10.1080/13678868.2024.2346492

Wietrak, E., Berger, R., & Czakert, J. P. (2024). Integrating AI in people management: A practical exercise for higher education. In *ICERI2024 Proceedings* (pp. 9345-9352). IATED. DOI: 10.21125/iceri.2024.2364

Xiao, Q., Yan, J., & Bamber, G. J. (2025). How does AI-enabled HR analytics influence employee resilience: Job crafting as a mediator and HRM system strength as a moderator. *Personnel Review*, *54*(3), 824–843. DOI: 10.1108/PR-03-2023-0198

Yusuf, A., Pervin, N., & Román-González, M. (2024). Generative AI and the future of higher education: A threat to academic integrity or reformation? Evidence from multicultural perspectives. *International Journal of Educational Technology in Higher Education*, *21*(1), 21. DOI: 10.1186/s41239-024-00453-6

Zhang, H. (2024). Exploring the impact of AI on human resource management: A case study of organizational adaptation and employee dynamics. *IEEE Transactions on Engineering Management*, *71*, 14991–15004. DOI: 10.1109/TEM.2024.3457520

Zhou, Y., Wang, L., & Chen, W. (2023). The dark side of AI-enabled HRM on employees based on AI algorithmic features. *Journal of Organizational Change Management*, *36*(7), 1222–1241. DOI: 10.1108/JOCM-10-2022-0308

Chapter 12
From Concept to Reality: Deploying AI and Big Data Solutions in Talent Acquisition

Amrik Singh
http://orcid.org/0000-0003-3598-8787
Lovely Professional University, India.

ABSTRACT

Artificial Intelligence (AI) and Big Data will bring about a transformation in talent acquisition and provide unprecedented efficiencies and ratings of candidates as well as the possibility of eliminating human biases. Nevertheless, these technologies are not only as valuable as their conceptual power, but also the effective use in the new ecosystem of organizational recruitment. The chapter deals with the essential aspect of the theory to practice shift and discusses the practical aspects, strategic approaches and pitfalls faced in introducing AI and Big Data solutions in talent acquisition. It explores such critical points as the preparation of data infrastructure, the ethical creation of AI to be fair and transparent, the management of organizational change and the creation of human resources professionals, and the seamless integration of the AI tools with the already existing Applicant Tracking Systems (ATS). This chapter offers a roadmap to HR leaders and talent acquisition specialists looking to go beyond first pilots and strategically integrate AI and Big Data.

INTRODUCTION

The introduction of Artificial Intelligence (AI) and Big Data to talent acquisition is a paradigm change in the way companies recruit, appeal and keep talent. These instruments can bring impressive opportunities to simplify the processes, improve decision-making, and make human resource management more efficient in the age

DOI: 10.4018/979-8-3373-8959-2.ch012

of technological innovations. Artificial intelligence and Big Data implementation with its practical use in talent acquisition, outlining the best practices, challenges, and future trends.

Landscape of Talent Acquisition

The talent acquisition sphere is experiencing a drastic and ongoing change due to a combination of technological change, demographic shift in the workforce, and the expectations of the candidates. TA is no longer a strictly administrative role, but it has grown quickly to become a strategic business requirement that requires agility, foresight, and a clear sense of human capital dynamics. Artificial Intelligence (AI) and the widespread adoption of Big Data are the most notable driving force in this change and have radically altered each retention and customized interaction with the candidate. In this ever-competitive global market, especially the rapidly growing economies such as India where skills shortages are a key factor despite the fact that job markets are booming, organizations are forced to use advanced analytics to identify essential skills, reduce unconscious bias, and build an authentic employer brand that will make a splash amidst the growing automation. The procurement of talent has turned into a digital priority and no longer follows the age-old practice of human resource acquisition, which presupposed manual screening and personal networking.

AI application in Talent Acquisition

AI brings the elements of efficiency and automation to the recruitment process, which will overcome the inefficiencies and bias associated with traditional methods. Artificial Intelligence (AI) is rapidly becoming more than a buzzword to an essential strategic instrument of talent acquisition, fundamentally transforming the way organizations identify, attract, assess, and onboard talent. Its purpose is multifactorial, and it mainly aims at the enhancement of human capacity, efficiency, and data-driven decision-making. The AI-driven applications have been able to automate unimportant and time-intensive activities, including screening and processing of resumes, which could instantly filter through thousands of applications and select the most promising candidates based on alignment of skills and experience, thus significantly saving time to hire and workload on the recruiter. In addition to the automation process, AI is also adept at predictive analytics, highlighting how a company can use historical data to predict the success of its candidates, likely future attrition, and impending skills gaps to facilitate proactive planning of its workforce. By implementing chatbots as conversational AI, 24/7 1:1 and personalized interactions with candidates and offering support can be achieved and positively impact the overall candidate experience, as well as the turnover rates. More importantly, in a way that is ethically created and followed, AI can be used as an extremely potent tool to reduce the impact of unconsciousness by sorting by objective factors only and thus leading to more diversity and inclusion in the recruitment process (Tambe et al., 2019). In dynamic markets such as India, where large-scale hiring is a common practice, the ability of AI to scale operations without affecting quality and consistency is a redefining one, which is why recruiters can switch their administrative workload to strategic activity, relationship-building, and people-oriented aspects of talent acquisition.

Big Data in the field of Recruitment:

The real capability of AI in talent acquisition is discharged by its symbiotic partnership with Big Data. Big Data is the fuel, which gives the AI algorithms the enormous, heterogeneous, and rapidly growing amount of data on which to learn, discover patterns, and make informed predictions (Raghavan et al., 2020). In absence of a sound Big Data plan - including effective gathering, careful cleaning, careful integration of heterogenous sources (ATS, HRIS, third-party platforms), strict regulation AI models would be not intelligent enough to work. On the contrary, AI will offer an analytical engine to extract actionable information out of this vast amount of data, which could be unfeasible to process by the human brain. This unification is especially crucial in such markets as India, where heavy data volumes and a constantly changing talent environment are the order of the day, and the combination of the scale and depth of AI analytics and the breadth of Big Data allows organizations to take smarter, faster, and more fair hiring decisions, which eventually results in a major competitive advantage.

Table 1. Major challenges in traditional talent acquisition and AI–big data solutions

Traditional Talent Acquisition Challenge	Impact on Organizations	AI and Big Data Solution	Expected Outcome
Long Time-to-Hire (TTH)	Delayed hiring, reduced productivity, increased workload	AI-powered resume screening, automated interview scheduling, predictive candidate matching	Reduced hiring time and faster recruitment cycles
High Cost-per-Hire (CPH)	Increased recruitment expenditure on agencies, job portals, and manual processes	Recruitment process automation, optimized job advertising, AI-assisted sourcing	Lower recruitment costs and improved ROI
Poor Quality of Hire	Mismatch between candidate skills and job requirements, higher turnover	Predictive analytics, AI-based candidate assessment, competency matching	Improved employee performance and retention
Poor Candidate Experience	Candidate dissatisfaction, higher application abandonment, weak employer brand	AI chatbots, automated communication, personalized candidate engagement	Enhanced candidate satisfaction and employer reputation
Hiring Bias	Reduced workforce diversity and potential legal risks	Ethical AI algorithms, bias detection, transparent decision-making	Fairer and more inclusive recruitment process
Weak Candidate Sourcing	Limited access to qualified and passive candidates	Big Data analytics, AI-enabled talent sourcing, social media mining	Broader talent pool and higher-quality applicants
Lack of Workforce Forecasting	Reactive hiring and skill shortages	Predictive workforce analytics and labor market intelligence	Proactive workforce planning and strategic hiring

Sources: Author elaboration

Modern talent acquisition requires organizations to begin with a thorough self-appraisal to identify systemic inefficiencies and weaknesses within their recruitment processes before implementing improvement strategies. One of the most significant challenges is the long time-to-hire (TTH), where delays in filling critical positions reduce organizational productivity, increase workload for existing employees, and result in missed business opportunities. These delays are often caused by inefficient candidate sourcing, manual resume screening, and scheduling bottlenecks. Another pressing issue is the high cost-per-hire (CPH), as organizations frequently incur substantial expenses on third-party recruitment agencies, job portals, assessment tools, and recruiter time. Artificial intelligence (AI) can help optimize recruitment advertising, automate repetitive tasks, and reduce dependence on expensive external resources. Organizations also struggle with the poor quality of hire (QoH), where subjective evaluations, unconscious biases, and inconsistent hiring practices lead to selecting candidates who underperform, fail to align with organizational culture, or leave the organization prematurely. In addition, a poor candidate experience, characterized by lengthy application procedures, delayed communication, and inadequate feedback, often discourages applicants, damages employer branding, and shrinks the available talent pool. Pervasive hiring bias remains another critical concern, as human decision-making can be influenced by implicit prejudices related to gender, ethnicity, age, or socioeconomic background, thereby limiting workforce diversity and exposing organizations to legal and reputational risks. Furthermore, many organizations experience weak sourcing and candidate engagement, relying heavily on traditional job boards that often produce a limited or unsuitable applicant pool while struggling to identify and attract qualified passive candidates. Finally, the absence of predictive workforce insights restricts strategic talent planning, as conventional HR analytics primarily focus on historical data rather than forecasting future talent requirements, identifying emerging skill gaps, or predicting employee attrition. Addressing these interconnected challenges through data-driven recruitment strategies and AI-enabled technologies can significantly improve hiring efficiency, candidate quality, workforce diversity, and overall organizational performance.

LITERATURE REVIEW

Current Talent Acquisition (TA) is a complex and ever-evolving field, and is distant by far to the transactional recruiting of the former times. It is currently working at the junction of the business strategy, technology, and human experience, due to stiff competition over capable professionals and especially in emergent economies such as India. Among the significant current trends in TA, one should note a drastic change in the skills-based hiring approach as exhibited by often inappropriate focus on demonstrable competencies and potential and a lack of false prioritization of traditional academic credentials.

AI and Big Data Use Cases

The AI and Big Data in talent acquisition are opening up a host of new applications, which are bringing the traditional manual processes to smart, data-driven processes. Intelligent candidate sourcing and matching is one of the main uses, in which AI algorithms examine and match large datasets created by internal ATS, external professional networks, and the open web and apply them to identify the most suitable candidates, even passive ones, based on skills, experience, and cultural fit. This greatly enlarges the talent pool past the regular candidates. Resume screening and parsing also uses natural language processing (NLP) to find the main information in the resume quickly and rank the applicants and significantly decrease the administrative load on the recruiters. Moreover, predictive analytics uses past data on hiring and performance behaviors to determine the chances of a candidate succeeding in a position, the chances of new employees leaving the job, and even possible future skills shortages, which can be used to plan in advance on a strategic basis.

Table 2. AI and big data applications across the talent acquisition process

Recruitment Stage	AI/Big Data Technology	Primary Application	Organizational Benefits
Talent Sourcing	Machine Learning, Big Data Analytics	Identification of active and passive candidates from multiple platforms	Expanded talent pool and better sourcing efficiency
Resume Screening	Natural Language Processing (NLP)	Automated parsing, ranking, and filtering of resumes	Reduced recruiter workload and faster screening
Candidate Assessment	Predictive Analytics, Classification Models	Evaluation of candidate suitability and future job performance	Improved hiring accuracy and quality of hire
Candidate Engagement	AI Chatbots and Virtual Assistants	24/7 communication, query resolution, interview scheduling	Better candidate experience and higher engagement
Diversity & Inclusion	Ethical AI and Bias Detection Tools	Identification and mitigation of unconscious hiring bias	More equitable and diverse hiring decisions
Workforce Planning	Predictive Analytics and Forecasting Models	Forecasting talent demand, attrition, and skill gaps	Improved strategic workforce planning
Recruitment Decision Support	Business Intelligence Dashboards	Real-time recruitment analytics and KPI monitoring	Data-driven decision-making and continuous process improvement

Sources: Author elaboration

Chatbots and virtual assistants powered by AI improve the experience of candidates and help them feel special by offering personalized services 24/7, answering their questions, and automatically arranging interviews. Importantly, there is an emergence of bias detection and mitigation tools, which are based on AI that audit job descriptions and the overall candidate evaluation processes to identify unconscious biases, enhancing hiring processes by making them fair and diverse, which is especially relevant in a diverse and competitive talent market such as India. Having outlined the pain points, the next solution would be to map them to particular AI and Big Data abilities.

Global Scholarship/ Industry Viewpoints

The use of Artificial Intelligence (AI) and Big Data in talent recruitment has attracted a significant amount of scholarly and business interest across the world, transforming classic recruitment paradigms into data-driven and predictive and automated platforms. Critical review of international literature on the topic shows that there are still debates and substantial progress regarding the ethical, strategic, and organizational values of such technologies. Researchers including Upadhyay and Khandelwal (2018) and Chamorro-Premuzic et al. (2017) point out that AI can be used to transform the recruitment process into enhancing accuracy, efficiency, and objectivity by applying predictive analytics, natural language processing, and algorithmic screening to recruitment processes. The use of Big Data applications enables an organization to examine large numbers of candidates, determine predictors of performance, and match talent strategies to business objectives. Industry reports by Deloitte and Global talent trends of LinkedIn also further emphasize that the most successful companies are using AI tools: chatbots, automated resume screening, machine learning algorithms to personalize the engagement of candidates and to lower their time-to-hire metrics. In relative terms, though, regional studies point at AI-based recruitment being maturity and ethically governed differently in different contexts. In more developed economies like the U.S., U.K., and Singapore, studies are dedicated to maximizing the algorithmic fairness and explainability, which means that AI systems should adhere to the diversity and inclusion objectives (Raghavan et al., 2020). Conversely, the literature on emerging economies such as India, Brazil, and South Africa identifies limitations of infrastructures, privacy of data, and digital illiteracy among HR professionals as some of the greatest impediments to successful implementation of AI. The European Union laws, especially the suggested AI Act, have also given rise to the debate of accountability and transparency in algorithmic hiring a subject not so widely discussed in Asian and African literature (Floridi & Cowls, 2019). Comparative analysis, therefore, points to the fact that, even though developed economies are actively moving towards the ethical optimization, the developing areas continue to struggle with the underlying digital preparedness and data regulation issues. The experience of smaller companies and state-run organizations demonstrates that implementing such systems is not accepted without opposition because of its high cost and non-confidence in algorithmic decision-making and the possibility of losing a job because of HR employees. Such a departure between the corporate and smaller firms underscores a structural issue with the scalability of AI-based recruitment solutions. In addition to this, although it is a welcome change that AI can reduce human bias, empirical research continues to refute this notion by reporting that biased datasets can be propagated by the issue of human bias that is still not sufficiently addressed in both research and regulation. There are research gaps that remain unaddressed regarding long-term organizational effects of AI-based recruitment, including, in particular, its impact on employee retention rates, employee satisfaction, and cultural fit. The majority of existing research concentrates on such efficiency indicators as the time spent on hiring lessened or the expenses saved without properly examining the humanistic aspect of AI impact on the candidate experience and psychological security. Moreover, data science, behavioral psychology, and human resource management have not yet been cross-disciplinarily integrated. The limited number of comparative longitudinal studies that focus on the sustainability of AI-based talent acquisition in varied cultural and industrial settings also exist.

RESEARCH GAPS

Although there have been large academic and industrial activity on the topic of AI and Big Data in talent acquisition, various gaps in the research remain. First, most of the literature that has been conducted tends to focus on technological efficiency including automation, predictive analytics, and cost-reduction, but not the long-term human and organizational results. When it comes to the effects of AI-based recruitment on employee retention, engagement, and cultural assimilation, there is a lack of knowledge regarding the relationship between the two processes (Kim et al., 2025). This limits the comprehension of the strategic value of AI since it is concentrated on operational performance as opposed to holistic human resource performance. Second, the issue of ethicality and fairness have not been adequately addressed particularly in the various global contexts. The majority of the works on algorithmic bias are based in developed economies and concentrate on compliance and transparency models. Nevertheless, there has been little empirical research in the emerging markets that have low quality of data, limited digital infrastructure, and weak regulatory frameworks on how AI systems can cause or alleviate social inequalities in the hiring process. Limited but critical comparative cross-cultural studies which analyze these differences are rare to come by but are necessary in the creation of internationally applicable models of governance.

DISCUSSION AND INTERPRETATION

The increased adoption of Artificial Intelligence (AI) and Big Data in the recruitment process has raised much concern globally regarding the protection of data, the accountability of the algorithm, and the ethical governance.

Global Regulatory and Ethical Systems

With organizations becoming more and more automated to hire predictive analytics and resume screening algorithms, as well as chatbots, the necessity to match these systems with effective legal and ethical frameworks becomes especially acute. The general trend of AI regulation in recruitment is influenced by major regulatory regimes, including the General Data Protection Regulation (GDPR) of the European Union, the Consumer Privacy Act (CCPA) of California, and the Digital Personal Data Protection (DPDP) Act of 2023 of India, all of which focus on the rights of the data, transparency, and fairness. GDPR (Europe): Can Candidates be certain of their rights and even more Algorithms? The GDPR is one of the most extensive systems of data protection in the world, which has a direct impact on AI applications in the recruitment process. Candidate data are regarded as personal data, with the GDPR permitting the individuals to have their rights regarding the processing, storage, and collection of their information. Article 22, which stipulates the right to access personal data, the right to an explanation, and the informed consent, enables candidates to emphasize the fully automated decision-making systems. In the case of recruitment artificial intelligence, it implies that algorithms to screen or rate candidates have to offer clear-cut rationales and be subject to human control. HR teams working in the EU are forced to assure the legitimate data processing, reduce the amount of data gathered to the amount needed to make hiring choices, and follow the principles of privacy by design. Failure to comply may also lead to heavy fines, forcing organizations to embrace ethical audit and algorithmic transparency systems.

CCPA (California):

California Consumer Privacy Act (CCPA) is designed to provide the same protections to job applicants and employees in California, and it is aimed at consumer control over personal data. The candidates have a right to be informed about the collection of their personal data, correct it, or delete it and decline sharing it with third parties. In the case of AI-based recruitment systems, compliance means having a well-defined policy on data disclosure, ensuring that applicants agree to analytics-based tests, and giving them an option to confirm or delete their data. The vendors of AI should also guarantee that the sensitive personal information is not unintentionally discriminated or used by automated decision tools.

DPDP Act (India, 2023):

Legal Data Processing and International Movement of Data

In the context of recruitment, it highlights the lawfulity of data processing, limitation of purpose and data collection on the basis of consent. Organisations that have applied AI in the hiring process should specify the role of data gathering and ensure that it is used in that situation only. The Act also governs the cross-border data transfer by obligating organizations to have sufficient protection of data they share with foreign AI vendors. Indian HR departments are thus required to use greater measures in securing data, ensuring that they are transparent with future employees in relation to the use of AI in decision-making, and adhere to the rules of the country they are operating in as well as their partners.

Procedural compliance implications on AI Vendors and HR Teams

In the case of AI solution providers, such frameworks require making ethical and legal compliance a part of system design by using anonymization, data minimization and explainability of algorithms. Vendors should also undertake bias audit, model interpretability and keep compliance documentation, which the clients can review. On their part, the HR departments need to be data custodians - keeping track of AI tools, ensuring fairness validity, and designing systems of redressal of grievances by the candidates. Interdepartmental cooperation of legal, IT and HR functions is necessary in order to preserve compliance and trust. Essentially, global regulatory systems are not only restrictive but also facilitative to responsible innovations. They lead organizations in the path of creating open, responsible, and fair AI systems so that the efficiency of technology in the recruitment process does not sacrifice ethical integrity and human dignity.

Cross-Industry and Cross-Cultural Comparisons

The further insight into the deployment of AI and Big Data in talent acquisition needs an integrative perspective that will compare industries and cultures. The use and consequences of these technologies vary widely, depending on the sectors which include technology, hospitality and the public sector as the priority, operational framework, and ethical supervisory mechanisms are different. As an example, Google, IBM, and Microsoft are the first in the technology sector to incorporate AI-based talent analytics. Their recruitment processes use machine learning to forecast candidate performance, screening, and unconscious bias. Technological expertise, rich data infrastructure, and special AI ethics boards make the pace of adoption even faster, with the standard of fairness and transparency taken into consideration. The example of Google in Responsible AI framework incorporates algorithmic audits and human control to ensure no discriminatory results of hiring are achieved. However, this is not the case in the hospitality industry, which is more risk-averse, as exemplified by international chains such as Marriott International. Although Marriott is applying AI-based functionality in resume parsing, chatbots in handling candidates and workforce analytics in productivity, the company is cautiously approaching this adoption because it does not want to lose the human element in service-focused societies. In this case, the ethical management focuses on empathy, cultural fit, and guest-centered values and does not rely on pure algorithmic optimization. The Singapore Civil Service is a unique example of a hybrid model in the public sector. Data analytics is applied in governmental recruitment to improve meritocracy and inclusivity, but is limited by high transparency and accountability criteria. The Public Service Division of Singapore has invested in explainable AI tools that correspond with the Smart Nation initiative of the country to ensure that the process of automation is in line with the principles of fairness and national development. In contrast to commercial enterprises whose activities are guided by profit motives, the trust, equity, and adherence to administrative ethics within the public institutions are more important- although this leads to slower adoption but an improved system of governance. A comparison of these industries indicates a trade-off between speed of innovation and the depth of ethical consideration: the technology industry is more innovative but has been criticized due to being biased and lacking transparency, whereas hospitality and government organizations are characterized by human control, inclusivity, and ethical standards. The AI acceptance and implementation in the recruitment process is also influenced by cultural diversity. In the collectivist societies like India, China, and Japan, the hiring practices tend to focus on group harmony and loyalty, and social fit. These AI systems are generally modified to assess collaboration and cultural fit, which is a manifestation of the larger societal values. To take one example, Japanese companies that implement AI-based recruitment tools tend to combine a test of compatibility and long-term commitment in a team instead of focusing on personal performance (Floridi & Cowls, 2019). On the other hand, in individualist cultures like the United States, the United Kingdom or Australia, meritocracy, innovation and self-efficacy take priority in the recruitment technologies. In this case, AI is created to recognize high-performing people basing on psychometric analytics and performance prediction algorithms, which are consistent with the principles of autonomy and competition. It is also possible that due to cross-cultural differences, candidates will not trust AI decision-making. Studies have showing that applicants of collectivist societies have more trust in institutional authority and mediation of technologies so long as it is consistent with the group norms.

SETTING SPECIFIC, ATTAINABLE GOALS AND KPIS

The implementation of AI and Big Data solutions in talent acquisition is a matter of success, and it is critical to set clear and quantifiable goals and Key Performance Indicators (KPI). Lack of set goals will also lead to poor performance of even sophisticated AI equipment or misdirected orientation towards the organizational needs. When SMART framework is used Specific, Measurable, Achievable, Relevant, and Time-bound organizations can establish the exact benchmarks to follow during implementation and assessment. This form of structured approach makes AI interventions purpose-oriented, outcome-driven, and improvements-oriented. As an example, in the application of the resume screening a typical goal is to be more efficient without compromising the quality of the candidate. An example of a SMART goal would be to cut down on average recruiters spending time on initial resume screening by 40 percent in six months on positions with high volume of more than 100 applications. The corresponding KPIs would be the mean screening time in each of the roles, the number of candidates qualified in an hour, and recruiter satisfaction scores associated with the screening activities. These indicators do not only measure the operational efficiency but also human aspects since technology should complement HR departments instead of overwhelming them. With a candidate experience chatbot, the set goals change to enhance interaction and minimize the turnover during the recruiting process. An organization may have an example of improving its level of candidate satisfaction by 15 percent and cutting the drop-off rates by 10 percent in an application stage within a period of nine months. The KPIs that will be utilized in this application are the level of satisfaction with the candidate survey, the application completion rate, and the rate at which the chatbot manages to resolve candidate queries. Connecting AI performance to the results, which are candidate-dependent, will allow recruiters to make sure that automation will improve the overall experience instead of just simplifying internal procedures. The other important use case is predictive attrition modeling where the aim is to retention high-potential employees proactively. A SMART goal can be to make a five percent higher retention of new employees during their first year with the help of AI-assisted interventions. Some of the KPIs in this case might be new hires 6- and 12-months retention rate and the accuracy of the attrition prediction model. These signs offer a twofold viewpoint, assessing the foretelling power of the algorithm, and the efficiency of the intervention managed by people with the help of AI information. All these aims are supported by a solid data base, the key foundation of

AI implementation. This data base building is achieved by strategic data gathering, thorough cleaning, careful integration across the platforms and stringent security measures to ensure confidentiality of information about the candidates and employees. An in-depth data approach starts by compiling all the useful internal and external data sources, including Applicant Tracking Systems (ATS), Human Resource Information Systems (HRIS), Learning Management Systems (LMS), and publicly accessible data on the labor market. After being collected, data should be organized and authenticated to be accurate, complete and consistent. Further, the combination of disparate data sets allows deeper insights which can be used to form predictive models to correlate candidate behavior, performance indicators and organization results. Along with the necessary professional privacy controls, the continuous data quality audits will guarantee the ethical performance and high reliability of operations. To conclude, to ensure that AI deployments meet the organization goals, it is critical to set clear SMART objectives and KPIs. Combined with an effective data base and strategic collection, cleaning, and integration engines, this solution is a quantifiable and responsible framework that converts AI-powered efforts in talent acquisition into effective, evidence-based practices.

Internal and External Data Sources

In the modern era of data-based human resource management organizations are highly dependent on a mix of internal and external sources of data to make sound decisions about talent issues. The most common and accessible data sources are usually internal data, as this source of data is created using the internal systems and processes of the organization. Such streams of data provide in-depth knowledge about the behavioural trends, performance, the level of employee engagement as well as the health of the organisation in general. One of the most vital internal databases is the Applicant Tracking System (ATS), which keeps comprehensive records about all candidates that have been engaging with the company in the course of the recruitment process. This would contain profiles, resumes, application history, interview notes, offer details and reasons of rejection. The use of ATS data assists companies in determining the bottlenecks in the recruitment process, as well as the preference of candidates and the provision of hiring solutions in the long-run. On the same note, the Human Resources Information System (HRIS) or the Human Capital Management (HCM) systems are a holistic database that holds employee demographic data, employment experience, salary, performance appraisals, internal mobility, and training history. With this type of systems, the HR professionals can be able to determine workforce trends, retention risk and also align talents strategies with organizational objectives. The Learning Management System (LMS) is another valuable source of internal information because it is also used to trace the training completion, certification, and skill advancement of employees. LMS platforms data can be utilized to determine the gaps in skills and create specific learning interventions that can result in upskilling and career advancement. Learning data are closely related to the insights that are based on the Performance Management Systems that record individual and team performance indicators, goal advancement, and feedback interactions. This information is used to measure productivity, identify the best performers, and develop data-driven performance improvement strategies by the organizations. The Onboarding Platforms also reveal important information, particularly on the level of engagement of the new hires, the completion of the onboarding activities, and the prompt feedback. These indicators are instrumental to the enhancement of the onboarding process and the minimization of initial attrition. Further, Employee Surveys and Exit Interviews provide qualitative and quantitative data that captures employee sentiment, satisfaction rates and departure reasons and provides a first hand glimpse of the organizational culture and experience of employees. Conversely, the External Data Sources expand the analytical spectrum due to the market and industry-level point of view. The sources allow the HR departments to benchmark their practices, remain competitive, and foresee external factors that may affect talent supply. The main sources of information about the profile of candidates, trends within the industry, salary rates, and competitiveness in the recruitment process are Job Boards and Professional Networking Sites like LinkedIn, indeed, and Glassdoor. These websites allow recruiters to increase the pool of talent and track the job ads of competitors. Moreover, Social Media Platforms are a great source of professional information and industry discussions which, with sound ethics, are useful and publicly available, and demonstrate developing skill patterns and talent attitudes. Government workforce statistics or industry reports further put workforce dynamics such as unemployment rates, shortages of skills and migration patterns into perspective. This macro level knowledge assists organizations in aligning the recruitment and workforce planning approaches with the market reality. Economic Indicators like the GDP growth, inflation, or consumer confidence also determine hiring trends because it indicates times of growth or shrinkage in the job market. Finally, Competitor Data, which is derived as a result of public reporting, company websites, or corporate publications, provides information about how competitors procure and retain talent, the compensation scheme, and the growth patterns in the organizations. The combination of internal and external data sources is the basis of the contemporary talent analytics. Where internal data offers an opportunity to have the level of insight into the current human capital, external data places these insights within the contexts of wider market forces. An optimum mix between the two is the ability to make sure that the organizations are not only able to effectively manage their current workforce but also keep up and competitive in the changing global labor market.

AI/ML Models for Talent Acquisition

Choosing the right AI/ML models for specific talent acquisition challenges is a critical decision that directly impacts the success and ethical integrity of the deployment. It requires a deep understanding of the problem being solved, the nature and quality of available data, and the desired output. For tasks like automated resume screening and candidate matching, classification models such as Logistic Regression, Support Vector Machines, or Gradient Boosting Machines are often effective, trained on historical data of successful hires to predict "fit" for new applicants. When dealing with unstructured text data from resumes, job descriptions, or social media, Natural Language Processing (NLP) techniques, often utilizing large language models (LLMs) or sophisticated word embeddings like BERT, are essential for accurate parsing, sentiment analysis, and extracting relevant skills. For predictive analytics concerning employee attrition or future workforce needs, regression models or time-series forecasting models (like ARIMA or Prophet) come into play, identifying patterns in historical HR data to forecast future trends. Meanwhile, unsupervised learning algorithms like K-Means clustering can be invaluable for segmenting candidate pools or identifying emerging skill clusters.

Strategic Insights for AI-Enabled Talent Acquisition

Talent acquisition is a sensitive subject that requires the optimal selection of AI/ML models to address particular talent acquisition challenges that directly determine the success and ethical correctness of the deployed application. It presupposes a profound knowledge of the issue under solution, the character and the quality of the available data, and the intended result. In applications such as automated resume screening and matching candidates, logistic regression-based, support vector machines-based or gradient boosting machine classification models can provide good performance, based on past data of successful applicants to forecast fit to new applicants. Natural Language Processing (NLP), which typically uses big language models (LLMs) or more advanced word embeddings such as BERT, is critical to successfully process unstructured text data (resumes, job descriptions, and social media) in order to achieve accurate parsing, sentiment analysis, and extracting the skills as desired. Regression or time-series forecasting models (such as ARIMA or Prophet) would be used to predictive analytics to employee turnover, or workforce requirements in the future, based on trends in past HR data. At the same time, unsupervised learning algorithms such as the K-Means clustering could prove invaluable to grouping candidate pools or identifying new skill clusters.

Intelligence on AI-based talent acquisition

AI and Big Data implementation in talent acquisition can be seen as a ground-breaking opportunity to streamline recruitment, improve candidate experience and allow making data-based decisions. The key to this change lies in the judicious and unjudged use of supervised and unsupervised learning methods. Supervised learning enables organizations to use past labeled data to forecast categorical and continuous forecasts. Logistic Regression, Support Vector Machines, Decision Trees, Random Forests, Gradient Boosting and Neural Networks classification algorithms can be used to predict hires versus non-hires, high-potential internal candidates, and predict new hire attrition. Equally, regression models, such as Linear, Ridge and Lasso Regression, can give actionable information regarding time-to-fill jobs, salary prediction and recruitment expenses that can enable the HR departments to plan and allocate resources effectively. Unsupervised learning is an enhancement to these abilities as it reveals the hidden patterns of the unlabeled data. The clustering algorithms such as K-Means, hierarchical clustering, and DBSCAN provide the possibility to divide the candidate pools into smaller segments based on skills, experience, or other characteristics that would be important, and dimensionality reduction algorithms such as PCA and t-SNE allow visualization and the preparation of models. The mentioned techniques, besides aiding strategic workforce planning, optimize the targeted sourcing and learning development activities. Moreover, AI is enhanced to cover a wider range of functions via Natural Language Processing (NLP) and recommendation systems that allow us to process resumes, recommend jobs, perform sentiment analysis and tailored candidate outreach. New computer vision applications that are ethically sensitive provide potential to verify an identity and perform a structured video interview analysis, which underlines how extensive AI potential is in recruitment. The effectiveness of such AI solutions is inevitably associated with a powerful technology stack and data infrastructure. The flexibility to handle the structured and unstructured recruitment data is available in programming languages like Python and R, in relational databases, and in NoSQL databases. To supplement this infrastructure, BI and visualization systems (Tableau, Power BI, Qlik Sense) guarantee that the insights are understandable, practical, and available to the HR stakeholders. Strict training and validation procedures are necessary to optimize the model. Data division into training, validation, and test sets is done correctly to allow an unbiased assessment, and hyperparameter optimization, cross-validation, and predictive performance measures (accuracy, precision, recall, F1-score, MAE, RMSE, R2) are used to optimize predictive results. These technical processes should be accompanied by continuous bias detection and ethical review since the necessity of fairness and accountability cannot be overestimated. Another vital point is a smooth connection with the current HR technology such as ATS,

HRIS, video platforms, and job boards. Human-AI partnership can be achieved by an API-first framework, automated data pipelines, and a friendly user interface/ user experience, as AI can enhance, not make recruiter workflows more complex.

Recruiter Roles and Dimensions of Sustainability

The incorporation of Artificial Intelligence (AI) and Big Data into the recruitment is not only changing the way organizations find and contact talent, but also how recruiters establish their professional identities. Recruiters must learn to interpret the logic of algorithms, screen AI-based suggestions, and make sure that robots are going to adhere to the rules of fairness, transparency, and inclusion. This change can be viewed as an essential break with transactional hiring, in favor of data-driven decision-making, in which human judgment is part of the technological accuracy. The recruiter of tomorrow will have to have hybrid skills: the analytical skills required to read predictive analytics, ethical skills to challenge bias in algorithms and emotional skills to stay emphatic in their work with candidates. Socially, AI can be used to conduct a more equalized recruitment process by eliminating unconscious bias and increasing the pool of diverse candidates. However, the potential can be achieved only under the condition of training algorithms on inclusive data and monitoring them to achieve fairness. Sustainable AI hiring is thus the act of designing systems that can promote diversity, accessibility, and equality as well as expedite efficiency. In ethics and governance, sustainability involves coming up with structures that guarantee inter-candidate, inter-recruiter, and inter-organization trust in the long run. This involves the introduction of transparency to automated decision-making, feedback to the rejected applicants, and the human touch in the digital world. Ethical sustainability is also the ability to keep data on candidates confidential, avoid manipulating algorithms, and avoiding the urge to conduct intrusive surveillance-related analytics. This vision would transform recruiters into data custodians of digital fairness charged with the duty of maintaining humanity in a data-driven system. Aligning data intelligence with ethical and sustainable approaches, organizations would have an opportunity to establish recruitment ecosystems that are efficient, intelligent, fair, transparent, and socially responsible at the same time, which would not only lead to the efficient and intelligent recruitment ecosystem but also to the fair, transparent, and socially responsible one, keeping technological progress highly consistent with the human values and long-term well-being of organizations.

CHALLENGES AND IMPLICATIONS

The most advanced AI and Big Data systems will not provide the value to the organization without proper implementation, especially to the most human recruiters and hiring managers themselves. This would require an active change management and stakeholder management strategy. One of them is the issue of dealings with the perception of the black box and distrust of AI, which can be an internal struggle with fear of job loss, or biased results. The organizations will need to directly spend much on transparency, how AI models work, their limitations, and most importantly, there is the need to state that AI is an augmentation tool, but not a substitution to human judgment. As an example, in the active job market in India, where it is important to pay much attention to the human relationship and cultural peculiarities, it is crucial to make the AI improve, instead of weaken, the interaction between people. That will necessitate thorough training and upskilling of recruiters so that they can perceive and interpret AI-generated insights, use automated solutions successfully and dedicate their energies to strategic and empathetic candidate interaction. Moreover, early and regular feedback between the end-users and the AI development team enables the continuous refinement and fosters the feeling of ownership, as the solutions will develop to better fit the real-world needs and overcome the initial resistance, resulting in successful adoption of the technologies in organizations. Technology is not a skill that would guarantee success. The most significant factors that can determine the success of AI and Big Data implementation in TA are the human and organizational ones.

AI-driven Recruitment candidate trust and experience

The one of the most urgent issues of implementing AI and the solutions based on the Big Data in the sphere of recruitment is the establishment and the preservation of the trust between the candidates and their automated order. As the process of hiring candidates becomes increasingly reliant on algorithms, there is an overall lack of confidence among the applicants in the fairness, empathy, and transparency of AI systems. Research has revealed that although the candidates like the functionality and the convenience of AI-based recruitment sites, they are worried about whether algorithms have the ability to see the potential in people beyond statistics and search words. The fear of algorithmic bias, loss of personal approach, and the unpredictability of the decision-making cause emotional disconnectivity, and candidates are not sure whether automated results are justified and fair. To give an example, the rejection of applicants without a clear description, as well as the use of AI chatbots instead of direct man-to-man communication at the stage of initial conversation during the recruitment process, makes the recruitment process feel impersonal to both the organization and the candidates, lowering the organizational image and reducing interest in the recruitment process. Applicants are becoming insistent on the use of AI in hiring. Research indicates that more than six out of ten applicants use hybrid evaluation models when using AI screening with human interaction. This choice is a more general craving in favor of technological efficiency, as well as, emotional reassurance. In order to overcome this trust gap, the organizations need to be transparent enough that they explain how the AI tools work, what data is being collected and how it is analyzed and what is the final decision. Transparency demystifies the process as well as expresses respect of candidate autonomy. As soon as candidates realize that AI can be viewed as an aid tool and not an alternative to a human decision, their confidence in the system is increased remarkably. In time and constructive feedback is also important in dispelling the perception of bias and strengthening an organization in the fairness and accountability. The collaboration of AI and human in recruitment interviews is the key to enhancing the experience of the candidates. Training HR professionals to act responsibly when interpreting AI outputs and empathetically approach the candidates is also important instead of setting up interviewers with AI. Other companies like Unilever and Hilton have effectively deployed blended models of recruitment with AI at the first stage of screening and video analytics but human recruiters complete hiring with final interviews, which ensures scalability and human touch. Finally, with everything mentioned, to defeat the dilemma of AI-based recruitment, one must take a middle ground one that incorporates both the precision of algorithms and human sensitivity.

THE FUTURE TRAJECTORY

The future of AI and Big Data in talent acquisition leads to more advanced, combined and ethically-nuanced applications that have a profound redefinition of the role of a recruiter and the process of a candidate. We are quickly transitioning to AI-assisted automation as AI-augmented human intelligence, where algorithms are used as co-pilots, performing data-intensive tasks, such as advanced candidate matching, predictive analytics of skills longevity, and even simulating team dynamics, so that recruiters are free to spend time developing strategies to build relationships, cultural testing, and empathetic interaction. Generative AI will transform the content-making process, whether it is creating a personalized job description and contact email or creating convincing interview simulations. It is not only the technological progress that will determine the future of AI and Big Data in talent acquisition, but the way organizations are able to navigate the ethics, sustainability, and human adaptability critically. With the process of automation transforming the recruitment landscapes, the job description of the recruiters is no longer those administrative coordinators, but strategic data interpreters and AI ethicists. Recruiters in this new paradigm cannot conduct interviews or go through resumes because their role is to act as curators of algorithmic judgment based on AI-generated insights, confirm model fairness, and make sure their decisions are in line with organizational values. The future recruiter must be able to seamlessly combine digital literacy and ethical sensibility, quantitative analytics with qualitative intuition. The change requires new skills: knowledge of laws on privacy of data, auditing of the work of algorithms and discussing artificial intelligence-based decisions with applicants. Since predictive analytics are bound to be increasingly relied upon by organizations in their matters of talent forecasting, the human factor will be transformed into making sure that these forecasts are fairly, intelligibly, and consistent to the principles of human rights. The ethical dimension of AI in recruitment also suggests that the reduction of bias and diversity should be a sustainable direction instead of a mandatory requirement.

Fairness Aware Algorithms

The future systems should thus incorporate fairness aware algorithms, ongoing bias detection and different data representation to facilitate inclusive hiring. The environmental aspect of sustainability is also the maximization of data processing efficiency and reduction of the carbon footprint of big data AI computations. Socially speaking, the firms will be forced to redefine AI as an empowerment tool that will enable access to underrepresented groups and increase access to people with disabilities and create more jobs regardless of geography. Nevertheless, the technologies which were supposed to be fair and efficient also present a great threat in terms of ethics and security when used improperly. The development of deepfake tests as simulated interviews by AI poses a threat to authenticity in online interviews, and the challenge of algorithmic manipulation of job seekers with the help of AI tools to cheat automated interviewing systems puts the validity of hiring data at risk. In addition, the increased adoption of analytics systems based on surveillance, including face detection or speech emotion recognition, is blurring the distinction between evaluation and encroachment. Without proper governing, such practices could easily destroy the trust, violate the privacy and legitimize the practice of intrusive monitoring in the name of efficiency. Thus, the recruitment ecosystems in the future will require robust ethical governance systems and intersectoral partnerships with the view to responsible AI creation and implementation. Organizations should become foresight-driven and governance-oriented toward the realization of the AI potential in a responsible manner. The future of the AI-informed recruitment process can be reduced to a single phrase: it is not about the capabilities of the machine to substitute the human factor, but about rethinking the very meaning of being a human in the world of data. The future path requires the ability to be consciously innovative as technological advanced, yet ethical awareness, sustainability, and compassion. It is the only way that AI in talent acquisition can become more than a means of efficiency into a means of fairness, inclusion, and integrity over time with the organization.

CONCLUSION

The implementation of AI and Big Data solutions in talent acquisition is not an imaginary idea of the future, but a current strategic necessity. The organizations that manage to navigate through such transformation will open the door to new efficiencies and greatly improve the candidate experience as well as, most importantly, the quality and diversity of their hires will improve significantly. The path to reality has its complications and requires careful consideration of the quality of data, the careful choice of models, the performance of strong technical implementation, and, probably, a deep belief in ethical AI and change management strategy. It entails developing a culture of data-driven insights and empowering its individuals with smart tools. It is the future of talent acquisition, which is intelligent, data-driven, and intrinsically human-enhanced.

REFERENCES

Chamorro-Premuzic, T., Akhtar, R., & Winsborough, D. (2017). The datafication of talent: How technology shapes talent management decisions. *Journal of Organizational Effectiveness: People and Performance*, *4*(1), 70–81.

Floridi, L., & Cowls, J. (2019). A unified framework of five principles for AI in society. *Harvard Data Science Review*. Advance online publication. DOI: 10.1162/99608f92.8cd550d1

Kim, E., Balloli, V., Karimian, B., Bondi-Kelly, E., & Fish, B. (2025, October). RelAItionship Building: Analyzing Recruitment Strategies for Participatory AI. In *Proceedings of the AAAI/ACM Conference on AI, Ethics, and Society* (Vol. 8, No. 2, pp. 1426-1439). DOI: 10.1609/aies.v8i2.36643

Raghavan, M., Barocas, S., Kleinberg, J., & Levy, D. (2020). Mitigating bias in algorithmic hiring: Evaluating claims and practices. *Proceedings of the ACM Conference on Fairness, Accountability, and Transparency*. https://doi.org/DOI: 10.1145/3351095.3372828

Tambe, P., Cappelli, P., & Yakubovich, V. (2019). Artificial intelligence in human resources management: Challenges and a path forward. *California Management Review*, *61*(4), 15–42. DOI: 10.1177/0008125619867910

Upadhyay, A. K., & Khandelwal, K. (2018). Applying artificial intelligence: Implications for recruitment. *Strategic HR Review*, *17*(5), 255–258. DOI: 10.1108/SHR-07-2018-0051

KEY TERMS AND DEFINITIONS

Applicant Tracking System (ATS): An Applicant Tracking System (ATS) is a digital recruitment platform that stores, organizes, and manages candidate information throughout the hiring process. Modern ATS platforms integrate AI capabilities for automated resume screening, candidate ranking, and workflow management.

Artificial Intelligence (AI): Artificial Intelligence refers to computer systems capable of performing tasks that normally require human intelligence, such as resume screening, candidate matching, predictive analysis, and decision support in recruitment. AI improves hiring speed, accuracy, and efficiency by automating repetitive recruitment activities.

Big Data: Big Data refers to extremely large and diverse datasets generated from sources such as Applicant Tracking Systems (ATS), HR Information Systems (HRIS), social media, job portals, and labor market databases. These datasets enable organizations to identify recruitment trends, predict workforce needs, and make evidence-based hiring decisions.

Candidate Experience: Candidate experience encompasses every interaction an applicant has with an organization during the recruitment process. AI-powered communication, personalized engagement, timely feedback, and transparent hiring practices improve candidate satisfaction and strengthen employer branding.

Ethical AI: Ethical AI refers to the development and deployment of AI systems that are transparent, fair, accountable, and free from discriminatory bias. Ethical AI ensures compliance with privacy regulations while promoting diversity, inclusion, and responsible recruitment practices.

Machine Learning (ML): Machine Learning is a subset of AI in which algorithms learn patterns from historical data to improve predictions without explicit programming. In recruitment, ML models are used for candidate matching, performance prediction, attrition forecasting, and workforce analytics.

Natural Language Processing (NLP): Natural Language Processing is a branch of AI that enables computers to understand, interpret, and process human language. In talent acquisition, NLP is widely used for resume parsing, skill extraction, job description analysis, chatbot interactions, and semantic candidate matching.

Predictive Analytics: Predictive analytics involves using historical recruitment and employee data with statistical and machine learning techniques to forecast hiring outcomes, employee performance, attrition risk, and future workforce requirements. It supports proactive talent management decisions.

Talent Acquisition: Talent acquisition is a strategic approach to identifying, attracting, recruiting, selecting, and retaining qualified employees. Unlike traditional recruitment, it focuses on long-term workforce planning, employer branding, and aligning talent strategies with organizational objectives.

Workforce Analytics: Workforce analytics is the systematic analysis of employee and recruitment data to support strategic human resource decisions. By combining AI and Big Data, organizations can monitor recruitment performance, identify skill gaps, forecast talent demand, and optimize workforce planning for long-term organizational success.

Compilation of References

Abdelwahab, H. R., Rauf, A., & Chen, D. (2023). Business students' perceptions of Dutch higher educational institutions in preparing them for artificial intelligence work environments. *Industry and Higher Education*, *37*(1), 22–34. DOI: 10.1177/09504222221087614

Abhari, K. (2025). Employee participation in digital transformation: From digitalization sentiment to transformation predisposition. *Information & Management*, *62*(8), 104212. Advance online publication. DOI: 10.1016/j.im.2025.104212

Abiwu, L., & Martins, I. (2022). Talent development as a source of sustainable competitive advantage for higher education institutions during the COVID-19 pandemic. *SA Journal of Human Resource Management*, *20*, a1777. DOI: 10.4102/sajhrm.v20i0.1777

Abu Orabi, T., Alahewat, A. M. M., Abualfalayeh, G., & Samara, H. H. (2024). The interdisciplinary nature of AI and human resource management: A bibliometric analysis. *Human Systems Management*, *43*(6), 845–871. DOI: 10.3233/HSM-240054

Abulail, R. N., Badran, O. N., Shkoukani, M. A., & Omeish, F. (2025). Exploring the factors influencing AI adoption intentions in higher education: An integrated model of DOI, TOE, and TAM. *Computers*, *14*(6), 230. DOI: 10.3390/computers14060230

Adamakis, M., & Rachiotis, T. (2025). Artificial Intelligence in Higher Education: A State-of-the-Art Overview of Pedagogical Integrity, Artificial Intelligence Literacy, and Policy Integration. *Encyclopedia*, *5*(4), 180. DOI: 10.3390/encyclopedia5040180

Afifa, U. K. (2026). Integrated Islamic School Management: Leaders' Policies and Stakeholders' Responses. *Social Criticism of Islamic Studies*, *1*(1), 41–55.

Aftimos, S., & Diab-Bahman, R. (2025). AI-driven talent management: Transforming workforce strategies in the digital age. In M. Lowe & Y. Luximon (Eds.), *creativity, innovation, and entrepreneurship. AHFE international conference* (AHFE Open Access, Vol. 166, pp. 29–58). AHFE International. https://doi.org/DOI: 10.54941/ahfe1006110

Aftimos, S., & Diab-Bahman, R. (2026, June). "To AI or Not to AI?"—When Synergies Collide. In *Proceedings* (Vol. 142, No. 1, p. 8). MDPI.

Aftimos, S., & Al Saeed, F. (2023). Cultural diversity: Profiling done right! In *Global Citizenship and Its Impact on Multiculturalism in the Workplace* (pp. 113–128). IGI Global Scientific Publishing. DOI: 10.4018/978-1-6684-5436-7.ch005

Aftimos, S., & Khafash, M. (2026). Embedding talent management in the digital transformation of universities in Kuwait. In *Organizational change, innovation, and consumer behavior in the digital economy* (pp. 29–58). IGI Global Scientific Publishing. DOI: 10.4018/979-8-2600-1453-0.ch002

Aghion, P., Boustan, L., Hoxby, C., & Vandenbussche, J. (2009). The Causal Impact of Education on Economic Growth: Evidence from U.S. *Brookings Papers on Economic Activity*, *1*(1), 1–73.

Agnihotri, A., Grover, V., Balusamy, B., Gite, S., Arockiam, D., & Shankar, A. (2024, June). Utilizing the potential of AI to Revolutionize talent management in contemporary organizations. In *IET Conference Proceedings CP881* (Vol. 2024, No. 7, pp. 1-11). Stevenage, UK: The Institution of Engineering and Technology. DOI: 10.1049/icp.2024.2519

Aguinis, H., Beltran, J. R., & Cope, A. (2024). How to use generative AI as a human resource management assistant. *Organizational Dynamics*, *53*(1), 101029. DOI: 10.1016/j.orgdyn.2024.101029

Agustina, R., Kamdi, W., Hadi, S., Muladi, S., & Nurhadi, D. (2020). Influence of the principal's digital leadership on the reflective practices of vocational teachers mediated by trust, self-efficacy, and work engagement. *International Journal of Learning. Teaching and Educational Research*, *19*(11), 24–40. DOI: 10.26803/ijlter.19.11.2

Ahmad, R., Mehmood, S. T., & Ijaz, S. (2023). Digital literacy competencies: A study of distance learners of Higher Education Regulatory Authority Khyber Pakhtunkhwa. *Pakistan Journal of Distance & Online Learning*, *9*(1). https://eric.ed.gov/?id=EJ1401028

Ahsan, M. J. (2025). Cultivating a culture of learning: The role of leadership in fostering lifelong development. *The Learning Organization*, *32*(2), 282–306. DOI: 10.1108/TLO-03-2024-0099

Aini, Q., Rusilowati, U., Asfi, M., Sunarya, P. A., Putra, S. N. W., & Zahra, A. R. A. (2024, August). Assessing the influence of artificial intelligence on human resource management practices. In *2024 3rd International Conference on Creative Communication and Innovative Technology (ICCIT)* (pp. 1-6). IEEE. DOI: 10.1109/ICCIT62134.2024.10701158

Al Hashimi, A. S. A., Azmin, A. A., & Junoh, M. Z. M. (2021). Talent management in higher education: A critical review. *International Journal of Education. Psychology and Counseling*, *6*(44), 155–166.

Al Shibly, M. S., & Alghizzawi, M. (2024, April). The impact of using AI in human resources management-a comparison approach. In *International Conference on Business and Technology* (pp. 1-10). Cham: Springer Nature Switzerland. DOI: 10.1007/978-3-031-67444-0_1

Alam, A. (2023a). Media multitasking with M-learning technology in real-time classroom learning: Analysing the dynamics in formal educational settings for the future of E-learning in India. In *2023 2nd International Conference on Smart Technologies and Systems for Next Generation Computing (ICSTSN)* (pp. 1-6). IEEE.

Alam, A. (2023b). The secret sauce of student success: Cracking the code by navigating the path to personalized learning with educational data mining. In *2023 2nd International Conference on Smart Technologies and Systems for Next Generation Computing (ICSTSN)* (pp. 1-8). IEEE.

Alam, A., & Mohanty, A. (2022, December). Facial analytics or virtual avatars: competencies and design considerations for student-teacher interaction in AI-powered online education for effective classroom engagement. In *International Conference on Communication, Networks and Computing* (pp. 252-265). Cham: Springer Nature Switzerland.

Alam, A., & Mohanty, A. (2023, January). Learning on the move: a pedagogical framework for state-of-the-art mobile learning. In *International Conference on Data Management, Analytics & Innovation* (pp. 735-748). Singapore: Springer Nature Singapore. DOI: 10.1007/978-981-99-1414-2_52

Alam, A. (2022). Impact of university's human resources practices on professors' occupational performance: empirical evidence from India's higher education sector. In *Inclusive businesses in developing economies: Converging people, profit, and corporate citizenship* (pp. 107–131). Springer International Publishing. DOI: 10.1007/978-3-031-12217-0_6

Alam, A. (2023c). Intelligence unleashed: An argument for AI-enabled learning ecologies with real world examples of today and a peek into the future. In *International Conference on Innovations in Computer Science, Electronics & Electrical Engineering*-2022 (Vol. 2717, No. 1, p. 030001). AIP Publishing LLC. DOI: 10.1063/5.0129803

Alam, A., & Mohanty, A. (2024). Integrated constructive robotics in education (ICRE) model: A paradigmatic framework for transformative learning in educational ecosystem. *Cogent Education, 11*(1), 2324487. DOI: 10.1080/2331186X.2024.2324487

Albrecht, S., Bakker, A., Gruman, J., Macey, W., & Saks, A. (2018). Employee engagement in the digital age. *Human Resource Management Review, 28*(3), 227–238.

Alenezi, F. (2025). The use of digital libraries and its relationship to digital competence and AI literacy among students of the College of Basic Education in Kuwait. *Education for Information*. Advance online publication. DOI: 10.3233/EFI-240078

Al-Fraihat, D., Joy, M., Masa'deh, R., & Sinclair, J. (2022). Evaluating e-learning systems success: An empirical study. *Computers in Human Behavior, 102*, 67–86. DOI: 10.1016/j.chb.2019.08.004

Al-Hamad, N., James, O. O., Afolabi, J. O. A., Olatoye, F. O., & Eboigbe, E. O. (2023). Innovative HR practices in higher education for global competitiveness. *Education Sustainability & Society, 7*(1), 21–30. DOI: 10.26480/ess.01.2024.21.30

Alhogail, A., & Mirza, A. (2011). Implementing a virtual learning environment (VLE) in a higher education institution: A change management approach. *Journal of Theoretical and Applied Information Technology, 31*, 42–52.

Al-Jaghoub, S., Al-Qora'n, L. F., Al-Odat, A. M., & Alheet, A. F. (2025). Educators' perceptions on artificial intelligence in higher education: Insights from the Jordanian higher education. *International Journal of Information and Education Technology (IJIET), 15*(4), 716–731. DOI: 10.18178/ijiet.2025.15.4.2278

Allui, A., & Sahni, J. (2016). Strategic human resource management in higher education institutions. Empirical evidence from Saudi Arabia. *Procedia: Social and Behavioral Sciences, 235*, 361–371. DOI: 10.1016/j.sbspro.2016.11.044

Al-Mughairi, H., & Bhaskar, P. (2025). Exploring the factors affecting the adoption AI techniques in higher education: Insights from teachers' perspectives on ChatGPT. *Journal of Research in Innovative Teaching & Learning, 18*(2), 232–247. DOI: 10.1108/JRIT-09-2023-0129

Alnaqbi, E. J. A. A., Mohd-Shamsudin, F., & Alshurideh, M. T. (2024). Green HRM practices, green commitment, and green innovative work behavior in UAE higher education institutes. *Uncertain Supply Chain Management, 12*(2), 723–736. DOI: 10.5267/j.uscm.2024.1.013

Al-Rashidi, F., Diab-Bahman, R., & Al-Enzi, A. (2021). The impact of socio-economic factors on human capital investments. *International Journal of Entrepreneurship, 25*, 1–14.

Alshehab, A., Alfozan, T., Gaderrab, H., Alahmad, M., & Alkandari, A. (2022). Identifying significant elements of the digital transformation of organization in Kuwait. *Indonesian Journal of Electrical Engineering and Computer Science,* 26(1), 318–325. https://doi.org/. i1.pp318-325DOI: 10.11591/ijeecs.v26

Alvarez, L. (2023). Liderazgo digital: El nuevo estilo para gerenciar. *Revista Científica Internacional, 6*(1), 61–72. DOI: 10.46734/revcientifica.v6i1.64

Al-Zahrani, A. M., & Alasmari, T. M. (2025). A comprehensive analysis of AI adoption, implementation strategies, and challenges in higher education across the Middle East and North Africa (MENA) region. *Education and Information Technologies, 30*(8), 11339–11389. DOI: 10.1007/s10639-024-13300-y

Apata, O. E., Ajose, S. T., Apata, B. O., Olaitan, G. I., Oyewole, P. O., Ogunwale, O. M., & Feyijimi, T. (2025). Artificial intelligence in higher education: A systematic review of contributions to SDG 4 (quality education) and SDG 10 (reduced inequality). *International Journal of Educational Management,* •••, 1–18.

Armstrong, M., & Taylor, S. (2023). *Armstrong's handbook of human resource management practice: A guide to the theory and practice of people management.* Kogan Page Publishers.

Arowosegbe, A., Alqahtani, J. S., & Oyelade, T. (2024, October). Perception of generative AI use in UK higher education. [). Frontiers Media SA.]. *Frontiers in Education, 9*, 1463208. DOI: 10.3389/feduc.2024.1463208

Ashraf, M. A. (2019). Influences of working conditions and faculty retention on quality education in private universities in Bangladesh. An analysis using SEM. *International Journal of Educational Management, 33*(1), 149–165. DOI: 10.1108/IJEM-03-2018-0121

Association of College and Research Libraries (ACRL). (2015). *Framework for information literacy for higher education*. American Library Association. https://www.ala.org/acrl/standards/ilframework

Ateeq, A., Siddiqui, S. A., Verma, A., Alnimer, R., Ateeq, R. A., & Almuraqab, N. A. S. (2026). AI in Higher Education HR: Assessing Adoption and Acceptance Trends in Administrative Practices. In *Strategic Decision-Making in Dynamic Business Environments: Systems and Control Perspectives* (pp. 965–987). Springer Nature Switzerland. DOI: 10.1007/978-3-032-07220-7_84

Attaran, M., Attaran, S., & Kirkland, D. (2019). The need for digital workplace: Increasing workforce productivity in the information age. [IJEIS]. *International Journal of Enterprise Information Systems*, *15*(1), 1–23. DOI: 10.4018/IJEIS.2019010101

Attewell, P. (1990). What is Skill? *Work and Occupations*, *17*(4), 422–448. DOI: 10.1177/0730888490017004003

Avolio, B., Sosik, J., Kahai, S., & Baker, B. (2014). E-leadership: Re-examining transformations in leadership source and transmisión. *The Leadership Quarterly*, *25*(1), 105–131. DOI: 10.1016/j.leaqua.2013.11.003

Aydın, Ö., Karaarslan, E., & Narin, N. G. (2025). Artificial intelligence, vr, ar and metaverse technologies for human resources management. *International Journal of Management Information Systems and Computer Science*, *9*(2), 77–94. DOI: 10.33461/uybisbbd.1681947

Aytar, O., & Arslan, R. (2024). Future-shaping themes. Digital age foresight in Turkish university strategic plans. *Strategic Management*, *29*(4), 70–81. DOI: 10.5937/StraMan2300062A

Azeem, M. M., Febriyanto, U., Nurhadi, F. A., & Halid, H. (2024). Unlocking the Values of Artificial Intelligence (AI) in Human Resource Management (HRM) in Enhancing Employee Retention. *Global Business and Management Research*, *16*(2).

Azuwandri, A. (2026). The Role Of Digital HR In Improving Indonesian Human Resource Competence In The Era Of Industry 4.0 Transformation. *Focus of Human Resource Management Journal*, *1*(1), 31–36.

Backhaus, K., & Tikoo, S. (2004). Conceptualizing and researching employer branding. *Career Development International*, *9*(5), 501–517. DOI: 10.1108/13620430410550754

Bai, C., Dallasega, P., Orzes, G., & Sarkis, J. (2020). Industry 4.0 technologies assessment: A sustainability perspective. *International Journal of Production Economics*, *229*, 107776. DOI: 10.1016/j.ijpe.2020.107776

Baki, N. U., Rasdi, R. M., Krauss, S. E., & Omar, M. K. (2023). Integrating artificial intelligence in human resource functions: Challenges and opportunities. *International Journal of Academic Research in Business & Social Sciences*, *13*(8), 1262–1277.

Barney, J. (1991). Firm resources and sustained competitive advantage. *Journal of Management*, *17*(1), 99–120. DOI: 10.1177/014920639101700108

Barocas, S., & Selbst, A. D. (2016). Big data's disparate impact. *California Law Review*, *104*(3), 671–732.

Barro, R. (1996). *Determinants of Economic Growth: A Cross-Country Empirical Study* (5698). https://doi.org/DOI: 10.3386/w5698

Basilotta-Gómez-Pablos, V., Matarranz, M., Casado-Aranda, L.-A., & Otto, A. (2022). Teachers' digital competencies in higher education: A systematic literature review. *International Journal of Educational Technology in Higher Education*, *19*(1), 8. DOI: 10.1186/s41239-021-00312-8

Bates, A. W. (2022). *Teaching in a digital age: Guidelines for designing teaching and learning* (3rd ed.). Tony Bates Associates Ltd., https://pressbooks.bccampus.ca/teachinginadigitalagev3m/

Becher, T., & Trowler, P. (2001). *Academic tribes and territories* (2nd ed.). McGraw-Hill/Open University Press.

Becker, G. S. (1964). *Human Capital: A Theoretical and Empirical Analysis, with Special Reference to Education*. University of Chicago Press.

Benavides, L. M. C., Tamayo Arias, J. A., Arango Serna, M. D., Branch Bedoya, J. W., & Burgos, D. (2020). Digital transformation in higher education institutions: A systematic literature review. *Sensors (Basel)*, *20*(11), 3291. DOI: 10.3390/s20113291 PMID: 32526998

Benouachane, H. (2024). AI in higher education: Balancing pedagogical benefits and ethical challenges. *Educational AI Review*, *2*(5), 302–322.

Benson, T. A., Cohen, A. L., & Buskist, W. (2005). Rapport: Its relation to student attitudes and behaviors toward teachers and classes. *Teaching of Psychology*, *32*(4), 237–239.

Bharadwaj, A., Sawy, E., Pavlou, A., & Venkatraman, N. (2013). Digital business strategy: Toward a next generation of insights. *Management Information Systems Quarterly*, *37*(2), 471–482. DOI: 10.25300/MISQ/2013/37:2.3

Bhardwaj, B., Sharma, D., & Dhiman, M. C. (Eds.). (2023). *AI and emotional intelligence for modern business management*. IGI Global. DOI: 10.4018/979-8-3693-0418-1

Bhaskar, P., Khan, M., & Bhaskar, P. (2026). Establishing an AI Ethics Governance Committee in Higher Education: A Theoretical Framework. In Kalafat Çat, A., Yetgin, M., & Sarker, J. (Eds.), *Navigating Modern Digital Communication Ethics and Law* (pp. 105–124). IGI Global Scientific Publishing., DOI: 10.4018/979-8-3373-1702-1.ch004

Bhat, J. (2023). Automating Higher Education Administrative Processes with AI-Powered Workflows. *International Journal of Emerging Trends in Computer Science and Information Technology*, *4*(4), 147–157. DOI: 10.63282/3050-9246.IJETCSIT-V4I4P116

Biondi, L., & Russo, S. (2022). Integrating strategic planning and performance management in universities. A multiple case-study analysis. *The Journal of Management and Governance*, *26*(2), 417–448. DOI: 10.1007/s10997-022-09628-7

Bisri, A., Putri, A., & Rosmansyah, Y. (2023). A systematic literature review on digital transformation in higher education. Revealing key success factors. *International Journal of Emerging Technologies in Learning*, *18*(14), 164–187. DOI: 10.3991/ijet.v18i14.40201

Blankesteijn, M. L., & Ghorbani, A. (2025). Embracing the digital horizon: Future scenarios for the Dutch higher education system. *Futures*, *174*, 103702. Advance online publication. DOI: 10.1016/j.futures.2025.103702

Blei, D. M., Ng, A. Y., & Jordan, M. I. (2003). Latent dirichlet allocation. *Journal of Machine Learning Research*, *3*(Jan), 993–1022.

Bodea, C. N., Paparic, M., Mogos, R. I., & Dascalu, M. I. (2024). Artificial intelligence adoption in the workplace and its impact on the upskilling and reskilling strategies. *Amfiteatru Economic*, *26*(65), 126–144. DOI: 10.24818/EA/2024/65/126

Böhmer, N., & Schinnenburg, H. (2023). Critical exploration of AI-driven HRM to build up organizational capabilities. *Employee Relations*, *45*(5), 1057–1082. DOI: 10.1108/ER-04-2022-0202

Bolander, P., Werr, A., & Asplund, K. (2017). The practice of talent management: A framework and typology. *Personnel Review*, *46*(8), 1523–1551. DOI: 10.1108/PR-02-2016-0037

Bolman, L. G., & Deal, T. E. (2022). *Reframing organizations: Artistry, choice, and leadership* (7th ed.). Jossey-Bass.

Bond, M., Buntins, K., Bedenlier, S., Zawacki-Richter, O., & Kerres, M. (2021). Mapping research in student engagement and educational technology in higher education: A systematic evidence map. *International Journal of Educational Technology in Higher Education*, *17*(1), 1–30.

Bond, M., Marín, V. I., Dolch, C., Bedenlier, S., & Zawacki-Richter, O. (2018). Digital transformation in German higher education. Student and teacher perceptions and usage of digital media. *International Journal of Educational Technology in Higher Education*, *15*(1), 48. DOI: 10.1186/s41239-018-0130-1

Bone, M., Ehlinger, E. G., & Stephany, F. (2025). Skills or degree? The rise of skill-based hiring for AI and green jobs. *Technological Forecasting and Social Change*, *214*, 124042. DOI: 10.1016/j.techfore.2025.124042

Boone, C. G., Pickett, S. T. A., Bammer, G., Bawa, K., Dunne, J. A., Gordon, I. J., Hart, D., Hellmann, J., Miller, A., New, M., Ometto, J. P., Taylor, K., Wendorf, G., Agrawal, A., Bertsch, P., Campbell, C., Dodd, P., Janetos, A., & Mallee, H. (2020). Preparing interdisciplinary leadership for a sustainable future. *Sustainability Science*, *15*(6), 1723–1733. DOI: 10.1007/s11625-020-00823-9 PMID: 32837574

Börner, K., Contractor, N., Falk-Krzesinski, H. J., Fiore, S. M., Hall, K. L., Keyton, J., Spring, B., Stokols, D., Trochim, W., & Uzzi, B. (2010). A multi-level systems perspective for the science of team science. *Science Translational Medicine*, *2*(49), 49cm24. Advance online publication. DOI: 10.1126/scitranslmed.3001399 PMID: 20844283

Börner, K., Scrivner, O., Gallant, M., Ma, S., Liu, X., Chewning, K., Wu, L., & Evans, J. A. (2018). Skill discrepancies between research, education, and jobs reveal the critical need to supply soft skills for the data economy. *Proceedings of the National Academy of Sciences of the United States of America*, *115*(50), 12630–12637. DOI: 10.1073/pnas.1804247115 PMID: 30530667

Bostrom, N., & Yudkowsky, E. (2014). The Ethics of Artificial Intelligence. In Frankish, K., & Ramsey, W. M. (Eds.), *The Cambridge Handbook of Artificial Intelligence* (pp. 316–334). Cambridge University Press., DOI: 10.1017/CBO9781139046855.020

Bowen, G. A. (2009). Document analysis as a qualitative research method. *Qualitative Research Journal*, *9*(2), 27–40. DOI: 10.3316/QRJ0902027

Boyer, E. L. (1990). *Scholarship reconsidered: Priorities of the professoriate*. Carnegie Foundation for the Advancement of Teaching.

Bradley, A. P. (2016). Talent management for universities. *Australian Universities' Review. The*, *58*(1), 13–19.

Brady, S. S., Brubaker, L., Fok, C. S., Gahagan, S., Lewis, C. E., Lewis, J., Lowder, J. L., Nodora, J., Stapleton, A., Palmer, M. H., Mueller, E., Fitzgerald, C. M., Hardacker, C. T., Hebert-Beirne, J., Lavender, M., Shoham, D. A., Burgio, K., Markland, A., McGwin, G., & Constantine, M.Prevention of Lower Urinary Tract Symptoms (PLUS) Research Consortium. (2020). Development of conceptual models to guide public health research, practice, and policy: Synthesizing traditional and contemporary paradigms. *Health Promotion Practice*, *21*(4), 510–524. DOI: 10.1177/1524839919890869 PMID: 31910039

Bresciani, S., Ferraris, A., Romano, M., & Santoro, G. (2021). *Building a digital transformation strategy, digital transformation management for agile organizations: A compass to sail the digital world.* Emerald Publishing Limited., DOI: 10.1108/978-1- 80043-171-32021100

Brøgger, K., Moscovitz, H., Robertson, S. L., & Lee, J. J. (2025). *World Yearbook of Education 2026: The Shifting Geopolitics of Higher Education: Knowledge, Power, Protest.* Taylor & Francis., DOI: 10.4324/9781003442264

Brown, M., Nic Giolla Mhichil, M., Beirne, E., & Mac Lochlainn, C. (2022). The global micro-credential landscape: Charting a new credential ecology for lifelong learning. *Journal of Learning for Development*, *8*(2), 228–254. DOI: 10.56059/jl4d.v8i2.525

Budhwar, P., Chowdhury, S., Wood, G., Aguinis, H., Bamber, G. J., Beltran, J. R., Boselie, P., Lee Cooke, F., Decker, S., DeNisi, A., Dey, P. K., Guest, D., Knoblich, A. J., Malik, A., Paauwe, J., Papagiannidis, S., Patel, C., Pereira, V., Ren, S., & Varma, A. (2023). Human resource management in the age of generative artificial intelligence: Perspectives and research directions on ChatGPT. *Human Resource Management Journal*, *33*(3), 606–659. DOI: 10.1111/1748-8583.12524

Budhwar, P., Malik, A., De Silva, M. T., & Thevisuthan, P. (2022). Artificial intelligence–challenges and opportunities for international HRM: A review and research agenda. *International Journal of Human Resource Management*, *33*(6), 1065–1097. DOI: 10.1080/09585192.2022.2035161

Bughin, J., Deakin, J., & O'Beirne, B. (2019). Digital transformation: Improving the odds of success. *The McKinsey Quarterly*, *22*, 1–5.

Bygstad, B., Øvrelid, E., Ludvigsen, S., & Dæhlen, M. (2022). From dual digitalization to digital learning space: Exploring the digital transformation of higher education. *Computers & Education*, *182*, 104463. DOI: 10.1016/j.compedu.2022.104463

Cabero-Almenara, J., Gutiérrez-Castillo, J. J., Guillén-Gámez, F. D., & Gaete-Bravo, A. F. (2022). Digital competence of higher education students as a predictor of academic success. *Technology. Knowledge and Learning*, *28*(2), 683–702. DOI: 10.1007/s10758-022-09624-8

Calderon, A. J., & Webber, K. L. (2021). Institutional research in the twenty-first century: Expanding roles and new directions. *New Directions for Institutional Research*, *183*, 7–19.

Cambra-Fierro, J. J., Blasco, M. F., López-Pérez, M. E. E., & Trifu, A. (2025). ChatGPT adoption and its influence on faculty well-being: An empirical research in higher education. *Education and Information Technologies*, *30*(2), 1517–1538. DOI: 10.1007/s10639-024-12871-0

Cann, O. (2016). *$100 trillion by 2025: The digital dividend for society and business.* World Economic Forum. https://www.weforum.org/press/2016/01/100-trillionby-2025-the-digital-dividend-for-society-and-business/

Cappelli, P., & Keller, J. R. (2014). Talent management: Conceptual approaches and practical challenges. *Annual Review of Organizational Psychology and Organizational Behavior*, *1*(1), 305–331. DOI: 10.1146/annurev-orgpsych-031413-091314

Carmo, J. E. S., Lacerda, D. P., Klingenberg, C. O., & Piran, F. A. S. (2025). Digital transformation in the management of higher education institutions. *Sustainable Futures : An Applied Journal of Technology, Environment and Society*, *9*, 100692. DOI: 10.1016/j.sftr.2025.100692

Carretero, S., Vuorikari, R., & Punie, Y. (2017). *DigComp 2.1: The digital competence framework for citizens with eight proficiency levels and examples of use.* Publications Office of the European Union., DOI: 10.2760/38842

Castañeda, L., & Selwyn, N. (2018). More than tools? Making sense of the ongoing digitizations of higher education. *International Journal of Educational Technology in Higher Education*, *15*(1), 22. DOI: 10.1186/s41239-018-0109-y

Chamorro-Premuzic, T., Akhtar, R., & Winsborough, D. (2017). The datafication of talent: How technology shapes talent management decisions. *Journal of Organizational Effectiveness: People and Performance*, *4*(1), 70–81.

Chan, C. K. Y., & Colloton, T. (2024). *Generative AI in Higher Education: The ChatGPT Effect* (1st ed.). Routledge., DOI: 10.4324/9781003459026

Charles, T. (2025). AI in professional development for English language teachers. In Ali, M., Fazal, S., & Ayyaz, S. (Eds.), *AI applications for English language learning* (pp. 73–92). IGI Global., DOI: 10.4018/979-8-3693-9077-1.ch004

Charles, T., & Papadaki, M. (2025). Ethical leadership in technology integration and digital education. In Soles, B., & Meyerott, T. (Eds.), *Diverse leadership perspectives in education: From K-12 to higher education* (pp. 437–454). IGI Global Scientific Publishing., DOI: 10.4018/979-8-3693-6115-3.ch016

Chaudhry, I. S., Sarwary, S. A. M., El Refae, G. A., & Chabchoub, H. (2023). Time to revisit existing student's performance evaluation approach in higher education sector in a new era of ChatGPT—A case study. *Cogent Education*, *10*(1), 2210461. DOI: 10.1080/2331186X.2023.2210461

Cheng, Z., Jin, X., & Kwak, W. J. (2025). Using the new positive aspect of digital leadership to improve organizational sustainability: Testing moderated mediation model. *Acta Psychologica*, *255*, 104963. DOI: 10.1016/j.actpsy.2025.104963

Chiu, T. K. F., Ahmad, Z., Ismail, M., & Sanusi, I. T. (2024). What are artificial intelligence literacy and competency? A comprehensive framework to support them. *Computers and Education Open*, *6*, 100171. Advance online publication. DOI: 10.1016/j.caeo.2024.100171

Chong, L. Y. Q., Lim, T. S., & Nipo, D. T. (2026). Human resource analytics adoption and its impact on talent management and operational performance: Evidence from Malaysian firms. *Journal of Modelling in Management*, *21*(4), 1–20. DOI: 10.1108/JM2-06-2025-0307

Chui, M., Manyika, J., Miremadi, M., Henke, N., Chung, R., Nel, P., & Malhotra, S. (2018). *Notes from the AI frontier: Insights from hundreds of use cases*. M. G. Institute. https://www.mckinsey.com/featured-insights/artificial-intelligence/notes-from-the-ai-frontier-applications-and-value-of-deep-learning

Clark, C., Cluver, M., Fishman, T., & Kunkel, D. (2025). *2025 higher education trends*. https://www.deloitte.com/us/en/insights/industry/articles-on-higher-education/2025-us-higher-education-trends.html

Cohen, J. (2013). *Statistical power analysis for the behavioral sciences*. Routledge. DOI: 10.4324/9780203771587

Collings, D. G., Vaiman, V., & Scullion, H. (2022). Talent management: A decade of developments.

Collings, D. G., & Mellahi, K. (2009). Strategic talent management: A review and research agenda. *Human Resource Management Review*, *19*(4), 304–313. DOI: 10.1016/j.hrmr.2009.04.001

Commonfund Institute. (2025). *2025 Higher Education Price Index (HEPI) Report*. https://www.commonfund.org/research-center/press-releases/2025-higher-education-price-index-hepi-report-released

Cortellazzo, L., Bruni, E., & Zampieri, R. (2019). The role of leadership in a digitalized world: A review. *Frontiers in Psychology*, *10*, 1938. DOI: 10.3389/fpsyg.2019.01938

Cosgrove, J., & Cachia, R. (2025). *DigComp 3.0: European Digital Competence Framework* (5th ed.). Publications Office of the European Union., DOI: 10.2760/0001149

Cotter, J. J., O'Brien, F., & Kelly, É. V. (2026). Integrating Knowledge Management, Project Management, and Human Resource Management for Organisational Resilience in the Construction Industry. *Buildings (Basel, Switzerland)*, *16*(3), 511. DOI: 10.3390/buildings16030511

Csernoch, M. (2025). Lean digital education to resolve the paradox of the illusion of digital prosperity. *Journal of Innovation & Knowledge*, *10*(1), 100676. DOI: 10.1016/j.jik.2025.100676

Dahlen, S. P., & Hanson, K. (2023). In their words: Student reflections on information-seeking behaviors. *Journal of Academic Librarianship*, *49*(4), 102713. DOI: 10.1016/j.acalib.2023.102713

Dahlstrom, E., Brooks, D. C., & Bichsel, J. (2014). *The current ecosystem of learning management systems in higher education: Student, faculty, and IT perspectives*. EDUCAUSE Center for Analysis and Research.

de Wit, H., Altbach, P., & Glass, C. (2025). Global Higher Education Transformation: The 2025 International Crisis. *International Higher Education*, (123), 1–2. DOI: 10.6017/895b9e0d.789fabbc

Decramer, A., Smolders, C., & Vanderstraeten, A. (2013). Employee performance management culture and system features in higher education. Relationship with employee performance management satisfaction. *International Journal of Human Resource Management*, *24*(2), 352–371. DOI: 10.1080/09585192.2012.680602

Delcker, J., Heil, J., Ifenthaler, D., Seufert, S., & Spirgi, L. (2024). First-year students AI-competence as a predictor for intended and de facto use of AI-tools for supporting learning processes in higher education. *International Journal of Educational Technology in Higher Education*, *21*(1), 18. DOI: 10.1186/s41239-024-00452-7

Devi, D., & Rroy, A. D. (2023). Role of artificial intelligence (ai) in sustainable education of higher education institutions in Guwahati City: Teacher's perception. *International Management Review*, *19*, 111–116.

Diab-Bahman, R. (2024). *Sustainable business in the Arab region: Corporate social responsibility vs culture*. Emerald Publishing Limited. DOI: 10.1108/9781835493267

Diab-Bahman, R., & Al-Enzi, A. (2021). The emotional impact of COVID-19 on undergrads: Hybrid open access. *Clinical Schizophrenia & Related Psychoses*, *15*(2). Advance online publication. 10.71/CSRP.RBAE.170521

Diab-Bahman, R., Al-Enzi, A., Sharafeddine, W., & Aftimos, S. (2022). The effect of attendance on student performance: Implications of using virtual learning on overall performance. *Journal of Applied Research in Higher Education*, *14*(3), 1175–1192. DOI: 10.1108/JARHE-04-2021-0135

Diab-Bahman, R., & Bahman, T. A. (2022). Forensic accounting and corporate governance. In *Handbook of research on the significance of forensic accounting techniques in corporate governance* (pp. 150–166). IGI Global Scientific Publishing. DOI: 10.4018/978-1-7998-8754-6.ch008

Díaz-García, V., Montero-Navarro, A., Rodríguez-Sánchez, J. L., & Gallego-Losada, R. (2022). Digitalization and digital transformation in higher education: A bibliometric analysis. *Frontiers in Psychology*, *13*, 1081595. DOI: 10.3389/fpsyg.2022.1081595 PMID: 36533011

DiMaggio, P., & Powell, W. (1983). The iron cage revisited: Institutional isomorphism and collective rationality in organizational fields. *American Sociological Review*, *48*(2), 147–160. DOI: 10.2307/2095101

Dittes, S., Richter, S., Richter, A., & Smolnik, S. (2019). Toward the workplace of the future: How organizations can facilitate digital work. *Business Horizons*, *62*(5), 649–661. DOI: 10.1016/j.bushor.2019.05.004

Dogan, M., & Arslan, H. (2026). Empowering Academics in the Digital Age: Navigating the Transformation of Higher Education. *European Journal of Education*, *61*(1), e70420. DOI: 10.1111/ejed.70420

Dogru, T., Line, N., Hanks, L., Acikgoz, F., Abbott, J. A., Bakir, S., Berbekova, A., Bilgihan, A., Iskender, A., Kizildag, M., Lee, M., Lee, W., McGinley, S., Mody, M., Onder, I., Ozdemir, O., & Suess, C. (2024). The implications of generative artificial intelligence in academic research and higher education in tourism and hospitality. *Tourism Economics*, *30*(5), 1083–1094. DOI: 10.1177/13548166231204065

Dollinger, M., Lodge, J., & Coates, H. (2023). Co-creation in higher education: Towards a conceptual model. *Journal of Marketing for Higher Education*, *28*(2), 210–231. DOI: 10.1080/08841241.2018.1466756

Dong, S., Chuangprakhon, S., Liu, Q., & Guangguo, W. (2026). Mapping Research on Music Education Faculty Structure in Higher Education (1980–2025): A Bibliometric Analysis. *SAGE Open*, *16*(1), 21582440261425921. DOI: 10.1177/21582440261425921

Draganac, D., Jović, D., & Novak, A. (2022). Digital competencies in selected European countries among university and high-school students: Programming is lagging behind. Business Systems Research: International journal of the Society for Advancing Innovation and Research in Economy, 13(2), 135-154. DOI: 10.2478/bsrj-2022-0019

Dugina, T. A., Nefedova, N. N., Dybina, O. V., & Oshkina, A. A. (2025). Responsible HRM Based on AI as a Factor in Decreasing the Divide Between the University Education Market and the Labour Market. In *Bridging the Gap Between the Higher Education and Labor Markets: Relevance of the Fourth Industrial Revolution* (pp. 101–108). Springer Nature Singapore. DOI: 10.1007/978-981-96-1933-7_12

Dunn, O. J. (1961). Multiple comparisons among means. *Journal of the American Statistical Association*, *56*(293), 52–64. DOI: 10.1080/01621459.1961.10482090

Dutta, D., & Mishra, S. K. (2025). Artificial intelligence-based virtual assistant and employee engagement: An empirical investigation. *Personnel Review*, *54*(3), 913–934. DOI: 10.1108/PR-03-2023-0263

Eckhardt, J., Ciuchta, M., & Carpenter, M. (2018). Open innovation, information, and entrepreneurship within platform ecosystems. *Strategic Entrepreneurship Journal*, *12*(3), 369–391. DOI: 10.1002/sej.1298

Edmondson, A. C., & Bransby, D. P. (2023). Psychological safety comes of age: Observed themes in an established literature. *Annual Review of Organizational Psychology and Organizational Behavior*, *10*(1), 55–78. DOI: 10.1146/annurev-orgpsych-120920-055217

Eftimov, L., & Kitanovikj, B. (2023). Unlocking the Path to AI Adoption: Antecedents to Behavioral Intentions in Utilizing AI for Effective Job (Re) Design. *Journal of HRM*, *26*(2), 123–134. DOI: 10.46287/OTTP6295

El Garem, R. A. (2026). HR digital transformation: Enhancing human resource management through technology. *Future Business Journal*, *12*(1), 5. DOI: 10.1186/s43093-025-00703-7

Elhussein, G., Leopold, T., Silva, A., & Zahidi, S. (2023). *Defining education 4.0: A taxonomy for the future of learning*. https://www3.weforum.org/docs/WEF_Defining_Education_4.0_2023.pdf

Emery, F. E., & Trist, E. L. (1960). Socio-Technical Systems. In Churchman, C. W., & Verhulst, M. (Eds.), *Management Sciences: Models and Techniques* (Vol. 2, pp. 83–97).

Escamilla-Mejía, M. G., Alfaro-Ponce, B., Aali-Bujari, A., & Hernández-Veleros, Z. S. (2025). Differentiated Impact of Higher Education by Gender, Age, and Income Level on Economic Growth: Evidence for OECD Countries. *Multidisciplinary Journal of Educational Research, 15*(1), 72–90. DOI: 10.17583/remie.15206

Eshima, S., Imai, K., & Sasaki, T. (2024). Keyword-assisted topic models. *American Journal of Political Science*, *68*(2), 730–750. DOI: 10.1111/ajps.12779

Espina-Romero, L. (2023). Collaboration and interdisciplinarity in scientific research: Fostering synergy to address current challenges. *IPSA Scientia. Revista Científica Multidisciplinaria*, *8*(2), 8–9. DOI: 10.25214/27114406.1627

Espina-Romero, L., & Guerrero-Alcedo, J. (2022). Fields Touched by Digitalization: Analysis of Scientific Activity in Scopus. *Sustainability (Basel)*, *14*(21), 14425. DOI: 10.3390/su142114425

Etomes, S. E. (2024). Artificial Intelligence and Human Resource Management in Higher Education Institutions in Cameroon. In *HRM, Artificial Intelligence and the Future of Work: Insights from the Global South* (pp. 229–246). Springer Nature Switzerland. DOI: 10.1007/978-3-031-62369-1_12

Etzkowitz, H., & Leydesdorff, L. (2000). The dynamics of innovation: From national systems and 'mode 2' to a triple helix of university-industry-government relations. *Research Policy*, *29*(2), 109–123. DOI: 10.1016/S0048-7333(99)00055-4

European Commission High-Level Expert Group on Artificial Intelligence. (2019). *Ethics guidelines for trustworthy AI*. European Commission.

European Data Protection Board. (2018). *Guidelines on automated individual decision-making and profiling for the purposes of Regulation 2016/679*. EDPB.

Fahad, S., Khan, I. U., Bibi, A., & Sarwar, A. (2026). The Impact of Multi-Dimensional Engagement on Talent Retention and Organizational Performance: The Mediating Role of Employee Engagement in the Nursing Workforce. *Journal of Political Stability Archive*, *4*(1), 208–226. DOI: 10.63468/jpsa.4.1.12

Faheem, M. A., Anwer, S., Rayhan, Z., Ullah, M. A., Paudel, R., Ahmed, M. F., & Khan, H. (2024). AI-driven innovation in HRM and its impact on business management: An in-depth study of technology advancement and strategic implementation. *Nanotechnology Perceptions, 20*(S13), 1174–1193. DOI: 10.62441/nano-ntp.vi.2599

Farias-Gaytan, S., Aguaded, I., & Ramírez-Montoya, M.-S. (2023). Digital transformation and digital literacy in the context of complexity within higher education institutions: A systematic literature review. *Humanities & Social Sciences Communications, 10*(1), 386. DOI: 10.1057/s41599-023-01875-9

Farrelly, T., & Baker, N. (2023). Generative artificial intelligence: Implications and considerations for higher education practice. *Education Sciences, 13*(11), 1109. DOI: 10.3390/educsci13111109

Fawaid, A., Baharun, H., Hamzah, M., Munawwaroh, I., & Putri, D. F. (2025, March). AI-based career management to improve the quality of decision making in higher education. In *2025 IEEE Integrated STEM Education Conference (ISEC)* (pp. 1-8). IEEE. DOI: 10.1109/ISEC64801.2025.11147274

Fennelly, O., Grogan, L., Reed, A., & Hardiker, N. (2022). Use of standardized terminologies in clinical practice: A scoping review. *International Journal of Medical Informatics, 149*, 104431. DOI: 10.1016/j.ijmedinf.2021.104431

Fenwick, A., Molnar, G., & Frangos, P. (2024). The critical role of HRM in AI-driven digital transformation: A paradigm shift to enable firms to move from AI implementation to human-centric adoption. *Discover Artificial Intelligence, 4*(1), 34. DOI: 10.1007/s44163-024-00125-4

Fernández-Batanero, J. M., Román-Graván, P., Montenegro-Rueda, M., López-Meneses, E., & Fernández-Cerero, J. (2021). Digital teaching competence in higher education: A systematic review. *Education Sciences, 11*(11), 689. DOI: 10.3390/educsci11110689

Floridi, L., & Cowls, J. (2019). A unified framework of five principles for AI in society. *Harvard Data Science Review*. Advance online publication. DOI: 10.1162/99608f92.8cd550d1

Freitas, A., & Paredes, J. (2018). Understanding the faculty perspectives influencing their innovative practices in MOOCs/SPOCs: A case study. *International Journal of Educational Technology in Higher Education, 15*(1), 5. DOI: 10.1186/s41239-017-0086-6

Fullan, M., & Quinn, J. (2021). *The challenge and the opportunity of digital transformation*. Corwin Press.

Fuller, J. B., & Raman, M. (2017). *Dismissed by degrees: How degree inflation is undermining US competitiveness and hurting America's middle class. Published by Accenture, Grads of Life*. Harvard Business School.

Gandy, R., Harrison, P., & Gold, J. (2018). Talent management in higher education: Is turnover relevant? *European Journal of Training and Development*, *42*(9), 597–610. DOI: 10.1108/EJTD-11-2017-0099

Gârdan, I. P., Manu, M. B., Gârdan, D. A., Negoi ă, L. D. L., Pa tiu, C. A., Ghi ă, E., & Zaharia, A. (2025, February). Adopting AI in education: Optimizing human resource management considering teacher perceptions. [). Frontiers Media SA.]. *Frontiers in Education*, *10*, 1488147. DOI: 10.3389/feduc.2025.1488147

Georgopoulou, M. S., Troussas, C., Krouska, A., & Sgouropoulou, C. (2025). Digital literacy in higher education: Examining university students' competence in online information practices. *Computers*, *14*(12), 528. DOI: 10.3390/computers14120528

Gerli, F., Bonesso, S., & Pizzi, C. (2015). Boundaryless career and career success: The impact of emotional and social competencies. *Frontiers in Psychology*, *6*, 1304. Advance online publication. DOI: 10.3389/fpsyg.2015.01304 PMID: 26388809

Getenet, S., Cantle, R., Redmond, P., & Albion, P. (2024). Students' digital technology attitude, literacy and self-efficacy and their effect on online learning engagement. *International Journal of Educational Technology in Higher Education*, *21*(1), 3. Advance online publication. DOI: 10.1186/s41239-023-00437-y

Gkrimpizi, T., Peristeras, V., & Magnisalis, I. (2023). Classification of barriers to digital transformation in higher education institutions. Systematic literature review. *Education Sciences*, *13*(7), 746. DOI: 10.3390/educsci13070746

Gkrimpizi, T., Peristeras, V., & Magnisalis, I. (2024). Defining the meaning and scope of digital transformation in higher education institutions. *Administrative Sciences*, *14*(3), 48. DOI: 10.3390/admsci14030048

Glazier, R. A. (2016). Building rapport to improve retention and success in online classes. *Journal of Political Science Education*, *12*(4), 437–456. DOI: 10.1080/15512169.2016.1155994

Gledson, B., Zulu, S. L., Saad, A. M., & Ponton, H. (2024). Digital leadership framework to support firm-level digital transformations for Construction 4.0. *Construction Innovation*, *24*(1), 341–364. DOI: 10.1108/CI-12-2022-0328

Gong, Y., Zhao, M., Wang, Q., & Lv, Z. (2022). Design and interactive performance of human resource management system based on artificial intelligence. *PLoS One*, *17*(1), e0262398. DOI: 10.1371/journal.pone.0262398

Goswami, M., Jain, S., Alam, T., Deifalla, A. F., Ragab, A. E., & Khargotra, R. (2023). Exploring the antecedents of AI adoption for effective HRM practices in the Indian pharmaceutical sector. *Frontiers in Pharmacology*, *14*, 1215706. DOI: 10.3389/fphar.2023.1215706

Grawe, N. D. (2018). *Demographics and the demand for higher education*. JHU Press.

Grimm, A., Steegh, A., Çolakoğlu, J., Kubsch, M., & Neumann, K. (2023). Positioning responsible learning analytics in the context of STEM identity development with a focus on under-served students. *Frontiers in Education*, *7*, 1082748. DOI: 10.3389/feduc.2022.1082748

Gruman, J. A., & Saks, A. M. (2018). Performance management and employee engagement. *Human Resource Management Review*, *28*(2), 155–168. DOI: 10.1016/j.hrmr.2017.11.007

Gryncewicz, W., Zygała, R., & Pilch, A. (2023). AI in HRM: Case study analysis. Preliminary research. *Procedia Computer Science*, *225*, 2351–2360. DOI: 10.1016/j.procs.2023.10.226

Halid, H., Ravesangar, K., Mahadzir, S. L., & Halim, S. N. A. (2024). Artificial intelligence (AI) in human resource management (HRM). In *Building the future with human resource management* (pp. 37–70). Springer International Publishing. DOI: 10.1007/978-3-031-52811-8_2

Hallinger, P., & Chatpinyakoop, C. (2021). A bibliometric review of research on higher education for sustainable development, 1998–2018. *Sustainability (Basel)*, *11*(8), 2401. DOI: 10.3390/su11082401

Hamzah, H. A., Abu Seman, M. S., & Ahmed, M. (2025). The impact of artificial intelligence in enhancing online learning platform effectiveness in higher education. *Information Development*, *41*(3), 794–810. DOI: 10.1177/02666669251315842

Hanelt, A., Bohnsack, R., Marz, D., & Antunes Marante, C. (2021). A systematic review of the literature on digital transformation: Insights and implications for strategy and organizational change. *Journal of Management Studies*, *58*(5), 1159–1197. DOI: 10.1111/joms.12639

Hannan, E., & Liu, S. (2023). AI: New source of competitiveness in higher education. *Competitiveness Review*, *33*(2), 265–279. DOI: 10.1108/CR-03-2021-0045

Hannan, S. A. (2023). Development of digital transformation in higher education institutions. *Journal of Computer Science & Computational Mathematics*, *13*(01), 1–8. DOI: 10.20967/jcscm.2023.01.001

Haque, S. M. S., Shaha, S., & Sharmin, S. (2024). Future-proofing the workforce: Training and development in the digital age. *European Journal of Human Resource Management Studies*, *7*(2). Advance online publication. DOI: 10.46827/ejhrms.v7i2.1637

Harris, A., Jones, M., & Baba, S. (2013). Distributed leadership and digital collaborative learning. *British Journal of Educational Technology*, *44*(6), 926–939. DOI: 10.1111/bjet.12107

Hase, S., & Davis, L. (1999). *From competence to capability: The implications for human resource development and management* Association of Management and International Association of Management 17th Annual Conference, San Diego, CA.

Hashemi Petrudi, S. H., Ghomi, H., & Mazaheriasad, M. (2022). An integrated fuzzy Delphi and Best Worst Method for performance measurement in higher education. *Decision Analytics Journal*, *4*, 100121. DOI: 10.1016/j.dajour.2022.100121

Helmiatin, H., Hidayat, A., & Kahar, M. R. (2024). Investigating the adoption of AI in higher education: A study of public universities in Indonesia. *Cogent Education*, *11*(1), 2380175. DOI: 10.1080/2331186X.2024.2380175

Hiatt, J. M. (2022). *ADKAR: A model for change in business, government and our community* (Rev. ed.). Prosci Learning Center Publications.

Higgs, M., & Dulewicz, V. (2016). *Leading with emotional intelligence*. Palgrave Macmillan. DOI: 10.1007/978-3-319-32637-5

Hodges, C., Moore, S., Lockee, B., Trust, T., & Bond, A. (2022). The difference between emergency remote teaching and online learning. *EDUCAUSE Review*, *27*, 1–12.

Holmes, W., Bialik, M., & Fadel, C. (2019). *Artificial Intelligence in Education: Promises and Implications for Teaching and Learning*. Center for Curriculum Redesign.

Holon, I. Q. (2024). *Higher Education Digital Capability (HEDC) Framework*. https://www.holoniq.com/higher-education-digital-capability-framework

Hossain, M. Z., & Rafat, S. O. G. (2026). Artificial Intelligence-Driven Talent Management in Higher Education: Ethical, Strategic, and Socio-Technical Perspectives. *Journal of Artificial Intelligence and Technological Development*, *48*(1), 33–44. DOI: 10.59324/jaitd.2026.2(2).03

Howaniec, H., Karyy, O., & Pawliczek, A. (2022). The role of universities in shaping talents—The case of the Czech Republic, Poland, and Ukraine. *Sustainability (Basel), 14*(9), 5476. DOI: 10.3390/su14095476

Howell, R. (2022). Digital leadership in UK higher education: Competencies, contexts, and challenges. *Journal of Higher Education Policy and Management, 44*(3), 277–295.

Huang, Z., Sulaiman, N., Yunus, M. M., & Li, X. (2026). Analysis of Blended Learning in Higher Education Based on CiteSpace (2001-2024). *Electronic Journal of e-Learning, 24*(1), 138–161. DOI: 10.34190/ejel.24.1.4290

Hussain, S. M., & Shoukat, L. (2026). Administrative Dysfunction in Pakistan Higher Education: A Qualitative Exploration of Institutional Sclerosis, Democratic Deficits, and Post-Colonial Persistence. *Social Science Review Archives, 4*(1), 977–993. DOI: 10.70670/sra.v4i1.1616

IIE. (2025). *Open Doors 2025: Report on International Educational Exchange*. https://opendoorsdata.org/wp-content/uploads/2025/11/OpenDoors25_PresentationPDF.pdf

Jabareen, Y. (2009). Building a conceptual framework: Philosophy, definitions, and procedure. *International Journal of Qualitative Methods, 8*(4), 49–62. DOI: 10.1177/160940690900800406

Jaboob, M., Hazaimeh, M., & Al-Ansi, A. M. (2025). Integration of generative AI techniques and applications in student behavior and cognitive achievement in Arab higher education. *International Journal of Human-Computer Interaction, 41*(1), 353–366. DOI: 10.1080/10447318.2023.2300016

James, J., Malkin, T., & Nusche, D. (2025). *Trends Shaping Education 2025*. OECD Publishing., DOI: 10.1787/6ae408c1-

Jangbahadur, U., Ahlawat, S., Rozera, P., & Gupta, N. (2025, January). The effect of AI-enabled HRM dimensions on employee engagement and sustainable organisational performance: fusion skills as a moderator. In *Evidence-Based HRM: A Global Forum for Empirical Scholarship* (Vol. 13, No. 1, pp. 85-107). Emerald Publishing Limited. DOI: 10.1108/EBHRM-02-2023-0038

Jani, A., Muduli, A., & Kishore, K. (2023). Human resource transformation in India: Examining the role digital human resource technology and human resource role. *The International Journal of Organizational Analysis, 31*(4), 959–972. DOI: 10.1108/IJOA-08-2021-2886

Jasim, T. A., Khairy, H. A., Fayyad, S., & Al-Romeedy, B. S. (2024). Digital leadership and creative performance in tourism and hotel enterprises: Leveraging strategic agility and organizational learning culture. *Geo Journal of Tourism and Geosites, 54*(2 supplement), 872–884. DOI: 10.30892/gtg.542spl11-1262

Jatobá, M. N., Ferreira, J. J., Fernandes, P. O., & Teixeira, J. P. (2023). Intelligent human resources for the adoption of artificial intelligence: A systematic literature review. *Journal of Organizational Change Management, 36*(7), 1099–1124. DOI: 10.1108/JOCM-03-2022-0075

Jayashree, P., El Barachi, M., & Hamza, F. (2022). Practice of sustainability leadership: A multi-stakeholder inclusive framework. *Sustainability (Basel), 14*(10), 6346. DOI: 10.3390/su14106346

Jing, M. (2025). Higher education digital academic leadership: Understanding leadership roles in digital transformation. *Education Sciences, 15*(5), 606. DOI: 10.3390/educsci15050606

Jisc. (2020). *University of Edinburgh: Building digital capability*. https://digitalcapability.jisc.ac.uk/case-studies/university-edinburgh/

Jisc. (2022). *Building digital capabilities framework: The six elements defined*. https://digitalcapability.jisc.ac.uk/what-is-digital-capability/individual-digital-capabilities/

Jisc. (2023). Digital experience insights survey 2023: Findings from students in UK higher education. Jisc.

Johnston, B., MacNeill, S., & Smyth, K. (2019). *Conceptualising the digital university: The intersection of policy, pedagogy and practice*. Springer.

Joint Research Centre. European Commission. (2025). *Digital Competence Framework for Citizens (DigComp)*. Publications Office of the European Union. https://joint-research-centre.ec.europa.eu/digcomp_en

Jones, M., Antonczak, L., & Sherring, P. (2021). Leading digital transformation in universities: A distributed leadership approach. *Journal of Higher Education Policy and Management, 43*(5), 495–510.

Jones, P., & Wynn, M. (2021). The leading digital technology companies and their approach to sustainable development. *Sustainability (Basel), 13*(12), 6612. DOI: 10.3390/su13126612

Kambur, E., & Yildirim, T. (2023). From traditional to smart human resources management. *International Journal of Manpower, 44*(3), 422–452. DOI: 10.1108/IJM-10-2021-0622

Kamela, M. (2024). Cut the CRAAP: Replacing vertical evaluation with lateral reading. *New Directions for Teaching and Learning*, *2024*(178), 71–80. DOI: 10.1002/tl.20608

Kane, G. (2019). The technology fallacy: People are the real key to digital transformation. *Research Technology Management*, *62*(6), 44–49. DOI: 10.1080/08956308.2019.1661079

Kaputa, V., Loučanová, E., & Tejerina-Gaite, F. A. (2022). Digital transformation in higher education institutions as a driver of social oriented innovations. In *Social innovation in higher education: Landscape, practices, and opportunities* (pp. 61–85). Springer International Publishing. DOI: 10.1007/978-3-030-84044-0_4

Karakaş, A., Kıngır, S., & Öztel, A. (2016). Evaluation of university employees' work behaviours performance via entropy-based TOPSIS methods. *Electronic Journal of Social Sciences*, *15*(58), 1046–1058. DOI: 10.17755/esosder.67295

Kasmia, N. B., & M'hamed, H. (2023). Digitalization of higher education: Impacts on management practices and institutional developement. A literature review. *Conhecimento & Diversidade*, *15*(39), 56–82. DOI: 10.18316/rcd.v15i39.11135

Kaushal, N., Kaurav, R. P. S., Sivathanu, B., & Kaushik, N. (2023). Artificial intelligence and HRM: Identifying future research Agenda using systematic literature review and bibliometric analysis. *Management Review Quarterly*, *73*(2), 455–493. DOI: 10.1007/s11301-021-00249-2

Kayanja, W., Kyambade, M., & Kiggundu, T. (2025). Exploring digital transformation in higher education setting: Theshift to fully automated and paperless systems. *Cogent Education*, *12*(1), 2489800. DOI: 10.1080/2331186X.2025.2489800

Kelley, S. (2022). Employee perceptions of the effective adoption of AI principles. *Journal of Business Ethics*, *178*(4), 871–893. DOI: 10.1007/s10551-022-05051-y PMID: 35818389

Keskin, S., Çinar, M., & Demir, Ö. (2022). A quantitative content analysis of Turkish state universities' official websites in terms of their preparedness and actions during emergency distance education in the early phase of the COVID-19 pandemic period. *Education and Information Technologies*, *27*(1), 493–523. DOI: 10.1007/s10639-021-10744-4 PMID: 34667430

Kezar, A., & Holcombe, E. (2021). *Shared leadership in higher education: Important lessons from research and practice*. American Council on Education.

Khan, G. F., Bhatt, A. S., Siddiqui, M. H., & Mishra, M. (2026). Impact of Strategic Leadership Styles and Leadership Support on Employee Engagement in Indian Higher Education. *International Review of Management and Marketing*, *16*(2), 253–262. DOI: 10.32479/irmm.21493

Khan, M., Zubair, S., & Malik, A. (2022). Digital leadership and its influence on organizational success: A case study in the private sector. *Journal of Organization and Management*, *36*(4), 46–59.

Kharchenko, A., Nalyvaiko, O., Kreydun, N., Sheiko, A., Ptushka, A., Khatuntseva, S., Zotova, L., & Kharkiv, N. K. (2024). Digital technologies as a factor in transforming university learning. *Revista Romaneasca Pentru Educatie Multidimensionala*, *16*(4), 97–126. DOI: 10.18662/rrem/16.4/909

Khuntia, J., Saldanha, T., Mithas, S., & Sambamurthy, V. (2018). Information technology and sustainability: Evidence from an emerging economy. *Production and Operations Management*, *27*(4), 756–773. DOI: 10.1111/poms.12822

Khushk, A., Zhiying, L., Yi, X., & Aman, N. (2026). AI-driven HR transformation in Chinese automotive industry: Strategies and implications. *Business Process Management Journal*, *32*(1), 30–50. DOI: 10.1108/BPMJ-11-2023-0915

Kim, E., Balloli, V., Karimian, B., Bondi-Kelly, E., & Fish, B. (2025, October). RelAItionship Building: Analyzing Recruitment Strategies for Participatory AI. In *Proceedings of the AAAI/ACM Conference on AI, Ethics, and Society* (Vol. 8, No. 2, pp. 1426-1439). DOI: 10.1609/aies.v8i2.36643

Kitchin, R. (2022). Thinking critically about and researching algorithms. *Information Communication and Society*, *20*(1), 14–29. DOI: 10.1080/1369118X.2016.1154087

Klimova, B., & Pikhart, M. (2025). Exploring the effects of artificial intelligence on student and academic well-being in higher education: A mini-review. *Frontiers in Psychology*, *16*, 1498132. DOI: 10.3389/fpsyg.2025.1498132

Kong, H., Jiang, X., Zhou, X., Baum, T., Li, J., & Yu, J. (2024). Influence of artificial intelligence (AI) perception on career resilience and informal learning. *Tourism Review*, *79*(1), 219–233. DOI: 10.1108/TR-10-2022-0521

Kooli, C., & Abadli, R. (2022). Could education quality audit enhance human resources management processes of the higher education institutions? *Vision (Basel)*, *26*(4), 482–490. DOI: 10.1177/09722629211005599

Kornita, S. E., & Tampubolon, D. (2026). Bridging Skill Gaps in the Palm Oil Workforce: A Mixed-Methods Training Needs Assessment of Plantation Workers in Kampar Regency, Indonesia. *Journal of Cultural Analysis and Social Change*, 1400-1408.

Koseda, E., Cohen, I. K., McIntosh, B., & Cooper, J. (2024). Internationalisation and digital transformation in higher education: The impact of Education 4.0 on teaching, learning and assessment. *Active Learning in Higher Education.*

Kotter, J. P. (2021). Leading change (25th anniversary ed.). Harvard Business Review Press.

Kruskal, W. H., & Wallis, W. A. (1952). Use of ranks in one-criterion variance analysis. *Journal of the American Statistical Association*, *47*(260), 583–621. DOI: 10.1080/01621459.1952.10483441

Kuhlthau, C. C. (2004). Seeking meaning: A process approach to library and information services. *Information Research*, *9*(3).

Kuluşaklı, E. (2024). Distance learners' basic digital competence in higher education. *Yükseköğretim ve Bilim Dergisi*, *14*(2), 358–365. DOI: 10.5961/higheredusci.1455479

Kumar, M., Najeeb, A., Rajora, H., & Rani, P. (2026). Privacy in the Digital Workplace: Reforming Data Protection Law for Monitoring and HRIS. In *Legal Frameworks of Human Resource Management Reform* (pp. 37-54). IGI Global Scientific Publishing.

Kumar, V. R., & Raman, R. (2022, March). Student Perceptions on Artificial Intelligence (AI) in higher education. In *2022 IEEE integrated STEM education conference (ISEC)* (pp. 450-454). IEEE.

Kuzu, Ö. H. (2020). Digital transformation in higher education. A case study on strategic plans. *Higher Education in Russia*, *29*(3), 9–23. DOI: 10.31992/0869-3617-2019-29-3-9-23

Kyambade, M., Namuddu, R., Mugambwa, J., & Namatovu, A. (2024). I can't express myself at work: Encouraging socially responsible leadership and psychological safety in higher education setting. *Cogent Education*, *11*(1), 2373560. DOI: 10.1080/2331186X.2024.2373560

Lammers, W. J., & Gillaspy, J. A. (2013). A brief measure of student–instructor rapport predicts student outcomes. *Teaching of Psychology*, *40*(4), 314–317.

Lam, T. (2026). The importance of ethics, governance and leadership in meeting the artificial intelligence challenge in higher education: A critical review. *Cogent Education*, *13*(1), 2636441. Advance online publication. DOI: 10.1080/2331186X.2026.2636441

Leeder, C., & Shah, C. (2016). Practicing critical evaluation of online sources improves student search behavior. *Journal of Academic Librarianship*, *42*(4), 459–468. DOI: 10.1016/j.acalib.2016.04.001

Lei, J., Hall, J. A., Wang, Q., & Alenezi, M. (2023). Digital learning and digital institutions in higher education. *Education Sciences*, *13*(1), 88. DOI: 10.3390/educsci13010088

Leikuma-Rimicane, L., Baloran, E. T., Ceballos, R. F., & Medina, M. N. D. (2022). The role of higher education in shaping global talent competitiveness and talent growth. *International Journal of Information and Education Technology (IJIET)*, *12*(11), 1211–1220. DOI: 10.18178/ijiet.2022.12.11.1741

Liang, X., Kidwai, M. D., & Zhang, M. (2021). How AI is changing the work of knowledge workers. *MIT Sloan Management Review*, *62*(2), 1–4.

Li, Y., Deng, Y., Peng, B., He, Y., Luo, Y., & Liu, Q. (2024). Generative Artificial Intelligence in Chinese Higher Education: Chinese Undergraduates' Use, Perception, and Attitudes. *Frontiers in Educational Research*, *7*(4).

Loidl, V. (2026). Designing Human-Centered Organizations: Practical Insights and Future Research Opportunities. *Journal of Organizational Behavior Review*, *8*(1), 100–126.

Lucas, R. E.Jr. (1988). On the mechanics of economic development. *Journal of Monetary Economics*, *22*(1), 3–42. DOI: 10.1016/0304-3932(88)90168-7

Lund, B. D., Warren, S. J., & Teel, Z. A. (2026). Measuring university students' satisfaction with traditional search engines and generative AI tools as information sources. *arXiv preprint* arXiv:2601.00493. https://arxiv.org/abs/2601.00493 [Preprint; under review]

Mabungela, M. (2023). Artificial Intelligence (AI) and Automation in the World of Work: A Threat to Employees? *Research in Social Sciences and Technology*, *8*(4), 135–146. DOI: 10.46303/ressat.2023.37

Madanchian, M., & Taherdoost, H. (2025). The Digital Leader's Toolkit: Essential Skills and Competencies, Tech-Driven Leadership. In M., Madanchian & H. Taherdoost (Eds.), *Strategies to Maximize Business Potential with Emerging Technologies*, (pp. 21-43). https://doi.org/DOI: 10.1108/978-1-83708-046-520251002

Madanchian, M. (2024). From recruitment to retention: AI tools for human resource decision-making. *Applied Sciences (Basel, Switzerland)*, *14*(24), 11750. DOI: 10.3390/app142411750

Madgavkar, A., Canal Noguer, M., Bradley, C., White, O., Smit, S., & Radigan, T. (2025). *Dependency and Depopulation? Confronting the Consequences of a New Demographic Reality*. M. G. Institute. https://www.mckinsey.com/~/media/mckinsey/mckinsey%20global%20institute/our%20research/dependency%20and%20depopulation%20confronting%20the%20consequences%20of%20a%20new%20demographic%20reality/dependency-and-depopulation-confronting-the-consequences-of-a-new-demographic-reality.pdf

Maghsoudi, M., Shahri, M. K., Kermani, M. A. M. A., & Khanizad, R. (2024). Mapping the landscape of AI-driven human resource management: A social network analysis of research collaboration. *IEEE Access : Practical Innovations, Open Solutions*, *13*, 3090–3114. DOI: 10.1109/ACCESS.2024.3523437

Mahade, A., Elmahi, A., Alomari, K. M., & Abdalla, A. A. (2025). Leveraging AI-driven insights to enhance sustainable human resource management performance: moderated mediation model: evidence from UAE higher education. *Discover Sustainability*, *6*(1), 267. DOI: 10.1007/s43621-025-01114-y

Maharani, H., Amaliah, I., & Nurhayati, N. (2026). Resilience of Alpha Generation: Digital Resiliency, Organizational Culture, and Talent Management. *International Journal of Science. Technology & Management*, *7*(1), 90–97.

Mahmoud, M. M. H., Ali, A. A., Alrifae, A. A., Eitah, R. A., & AlZubi, M. M. (2025). The impact of digital HRM system and digital transformation on HR efficiency with organizational agility as a moderator. *Discover Sustainability*, *6*(1), 1038. DOI: 10.1007/s43621-025-01713-9

Maier, M. (2014). *DirichletReg: Dirichlet Regression for Compositional Data in R*. https://doi.org/DOI: 10.57938/ad3142d3-2fcd-4c37-aec6-8e0bd7d077e1

Maimela, C., & Mbonde, P. (2025). Artificial intelligence in South African universities: Curriculum transformation and decolonisation—aid or obstacle? *Frontiers in Sociology*, *10*, 1543471. DOI: 10.3389/fsoc.2025.1543471

Malik, A., Budhwar, P., & Kazmi, B. A. (2023). Artificial intelligence (AI)-assisted HRM: Towards an extended strategic framework. *Human Resource Management Review*, *33*(1), 100940. DOI: 10.1016/j.hrmr.2022.100940

Malik, A., Nguyen, T. M., & Budhwar, P. (2022). Towards a conceptual model of AI-mediated knowledge sharing exchange of HRM practices: Antecedents and consequences. *IEEE Transactions on Engineering Management*, *71*, 13083–13095. DOI: 10.1109/TEM.2022.3163117

Malin, C. D., Fleiß, J., Seeber, I., Kubicek, B., Kupfer, C., & Thalmann, S. (2024). The application of AI in digital HRM–an experiment on human decision-making in personnel selection. *Business Process Management Journal*, *30*(8), 284–312. DOI: 10.1108/BPMJ-11-2023-0884

Mamoun, A., & Mousa, M. (2018). Business model innovation as strategic process: A case study of China's most innovative firms. *Global Business and Management Research*, *10*(2), 1–18.

Manetti, A., Lara-Navarra, P., & Sánchez-Navarro, J. (2022a). Design process for the generation of future education scenarios. *Comunicar*, *73*(73), 33–44. DOI: 10.3916/C73-2022-03

Marin, L. (2021). The Digital University. In *On the Possibility of a Digital University: Thinking and Mediatic Displacement at the University* (pp. 57–77). Springer International Publishing. https://doi.org/DOI: 10.1007/978-3-030-65976-9_4

Marinoni, G., van't Land, H., & Jensen, T. (2021). *The impact of COVID-19 on higher education around the world*. International Association of Universities.

Markova S. V. Alieva A. B. Dadova M. Kh.. (2026). The impact of integration of artificial intelligence and ESG principles on the development of the innovation economy in education. ekonomika i upravlenie problemy resheniya. 2/5(167):84-94 DOI: 10.36871/ek.up.p.r.2026.02.05.011

Marks, A., Al-Ali, M., Atassi, R., Abualkishik, A. Z., & Rezgui, Y. (2020). Digital transformation in higher education. A framework for maturity assessment. *International Journal of Advanced Computer Science and Applications*, *11*(12), 504–513. DOI: 10.14569/IJACSA.2020.0111261

Marler, J. H., & Boudreau, J. W. (2017). An evidence-based review of HR analytics. *International Journal of Human Resource Management*, *28*(1), 3–26. DOI: 10.1080/09585192.2016.1244699

Martínez-Peláez, R., Ochoa-Brust, A., Rivera, S., Félix, V. G., Ostos, R., Brito, H., Félix, R. A., & Mena, L. J. (2023). Role of digital transformation for achieving sustainability: Mediated role of stakeholders, key capabilities, and technology. *Sustainability (Basel)*, *15*(14), 11221. DOI: 10.3390/su151411221

Matsunaga, M. (2024). The role of digital literacy in leadership. In *Employee uncertainty over digital transformation: Mechanisms and solutions* (pp. 139–188). Springer Nature Singapore. DOI: 10.1007/978-981-99-8409-1_4

Mayer, S., Abou Refaie, R., & Uebernickel, F. (2026). The challenges and opportunities of hybrid education with location asynchrony: Implications for education policy. *Policy Futures in Education*, *24*(1), 82–104. DOI: 10.1177/14782103231224507

McDonnell, A., Collings, D. G., Mellahi, K., & Schuler, R. (2017). Talent management: A systematic review and future prospects. *European Journal of International Management*, *11*(1), 86–128. DOI: 10.1504/EJIM.2017.081253

Mejías-Acosta, A., D'Armas Regnault, M., Vargas-Cano, E., Cárdenas-Cobo, J., & Vidal-Silva, C. (2024). Assessment of digital competencies in higher education students: Development and validation of a measurement scale. *Frontiers in Education*, *9*, 1497376. Advance online publication. DOI: 10.3389/feduc.2024.1497376

Mendy, J., Jain, A., & Thomas, A. (2025). Artificial intelligence in the workplace–challenges, opportunities and HRM framework: A critical review and research agenda for change. *Journal of Managerial Psychology*, *40*(5), 517–538.

Meyer, J. W., & Rowan, B. (1977). Institutionalized organizations: Formal structure as myth and ceremony. *AJS; American Journal of Sociology*, *83*(2), 340–363. DOI: 10.1086/226550

Miao, F., & Holmes, W. (2023). *Guidance for generative AI in education and research*. https://www.unesco.org/en/articles/guidance-generative-ai-education-and-research

Miao, F., & Holmes, W. (2023). *Guidance for generative AI in education and research*. UNESCO. https://www.unesco.org/en/articles/guidance-generative-ai-education-and-research

Miao, F., & Cukurova, M. (2024). *AI competency framework for teachers*. UNESCO., DOI: 10.54675/ZJTE2084

Mihardjo, L., Sasmoko, S., Alamsjah, F., & Elidjen, E. (2019). Digital leadership impacts on developing dynamic capability and strategic alliance based on market orientation. *Polish Journal of Management Studies*, *19*(2), 285–297. DOI: 10.17512/pjms.2019.19.2.24

Mintzberg, H., & Waters, J. A. (1985). Of strategies, deliberate and emergent. *Strategic Management Journal*, *6*(3), 257–272. DOI: 10.1002/smj.4250060306

Mishra, L., Gupta, T., & Shree, A. (2020). Online teaching-learning in higher education during lockdown. *International Journal of Educational Research Open*, *1*, 100012. DOI: 10.1016/j.ijedro.2020.100012 PMID: 35059663

Mishra, P., & Koehler, M. J. (2006). Technological pedagogical content knowledge: A framework for teacher knowledge. *Teachers College Record*, *108*(6), 1017–1054. DOI: 10.1111/j.1467-9620.2006.00684.x

Modi, R. K., & Garg, R. (2025). The Role of Artificial Intelligence in Transforming Higher Education: Opportunities and Challenges. *Exploresearch*, *02*(02), 59–65. DOI: 10.62823/ExRe/2025/02/02.53

Moghtadaie, L., & Taji, M. (2016). Study of the performance of faculty members according to talent management approach in higher education. *Educational Research Review*, *11*(8), 781–790.

Mohamed Hashim, M. A., Tlemsani, I., & Matthews, R. (2022). Higher education strategy in digital transformation. *Education and Information Technologies*, *27*(3), 3171–3195. DOI: 10.1007/s10639-021-10739-1 PMID: 34539217

Monitor, I. C. E. F. (2025). *New analysis forecasts international student mobility through 2030: Regulated Regionalism*. https://monitor.icef.com/2025/07/new-analysis-forecasts-international-student-mobility-through-2030/

Moore, S., & Lookadoo, K. (2024). Communicating clear guidance: Advice for generative AI policy development in higher education. *Business and Professional Communication Quarterly*, *87*(4), 610–629. DOI: 10.1177/23294906241254786

Muchsam, Y., Maulana, M. A., Cegunawan, C., & Yuda, M. S. (2026). Digital Industry: Talent Mapping and Triple Helix Partnerships for Strengthening Services Exports. *The Eastasouth Management and Business*, *4*(02), 511–522. DOI: 10.58812/esmb.v4i02.852

Muda, F. P. (2026). Implementation of the balanced scorecard in higher education performance management: A comparative study between Indonesia and international cases. *Klabat Journal of Management*, *7*(1), 1–22. DOI: 10.60090/kjm.v7i1.1333.1-22

Muilenburg, L. Y., & Berge, Z. L. (2005). Student barriers to online learning. *Distance Education*, *26*(1), 29–48. DOI: 10.1080/01587910500081269

Murphy, E., & Rodríguez-Manzanares, M. A. (2012). Rapport in distance education. *International Review of Research in Open and Distance Learning*, *13*(1), 167–190. DOI: 10.19173/irrodl.v13i1.1057

Musakuro, R. N. (2022). A framework development for talent management in the higher education sector. *SA Journal of Human Resource Management*, *20*, 1671. DOI: 10.4102/sajhrm.v20i0.1671

Mustafa, A., & Goh, M. (1996). Multi-criterion models for higher education administration. *Omega, 24*(2), 167–178. DOI: 10.1016/0305-0483(95)00053-4

Mwamba, J. N., Mulenga, I. M., & Muwanga-Zake, J. W. F. (2023). Digital transformation in African higher education: Lessons from consortium-driven innovation. *International Journal of Educational Development in Africa*, *8*(1), 1–18.

Mwita, K. M., & Kitole, F. A. (2025). Potential benefits and challenges of artificial intelligence in human resource management in public institutions. *Discover Global Society*, *3*(1), 35. DOI: 10.1007/s44282-025-00175-8

Naeem, M., Ozuem, W., Howell, K., & Ranfagni, S. (2023). A step-by-step process of thematic analysis to develop a conceptual model in qualitative research. *International Journal of Qualitative Methods*, *22*, 1–18. DOI: 10.1177/16094069231205789

Naidoo-Chetty, M., & du Plessis, M. (2021). Job demands and job resources of academics in higher education. *Frontiers in Psychology*, *12*, 631171. DOI: 10.3389/fpsyg.2021.631171 PMID: 34248738

Nair, S., Banka, K., & Pandya, A. (2025). Humanizing AI in Higher Education: Rethinking HR, Ethics, and Skill Development for University Employees in the SDG Era. *INTI Journal, 2025*(5).

Nair, S., Banka, K., & Pandya, A. (2025). *Humanizing AI in Higher Education: Rethinking HR, Ethics, and Skill Development for University Employees in the SDG Era*. INTI Journal., DOI: 10.61453/INTIj.202560

Namatovu, A., & Kyambade, M. (2025). Leveraging AI in academia: University students' adoption of ChatGPT for writing coursework (take home) assignments through the lens of UTAUT2. *Cogent Education, 12*(1), 2485522. DOI: 10.1080/2331186X.2025.2485522

Nam, B. H., & Bai, Q. (2023). ChatGPT and its ethical implications for STEM research and higher education: A media discourse analysis. *International Journal of STEM Education, 10*(1), 66. DOI: 10.1186/s40594-023-00452-5

Naoum, R. F., Szakadáti, T., & Balogh, G. (2026). Artificial Intelligence (AI) in human resource management (HRM): a systematic review of its dual impact on diversity, equity, and inclusion (DEI). *Management Review Quarterly*, 1-72.

Naoum, R. F., Szakadáti, T., & Balogh, G. (2026). *Artificial intelligence (AI) in human resource management (HRM): A systematic review of its dual impact on diversity, equity, and inclusion (DEI)*. Management Review Quarterly., DOI: 10.1007/s11301-025-00580-y

National Student Clearinghouse. (2024). *Current term enrollment estimates: Fall 2024*. https://nscresearchcenter.org/current-term-enrollment-estimates/

Naufalin, L. R., Indrawati, C. D. S., Indriayu, M., & Noviani, L. (2026). Bridging Religiosity and Digital Competence: The Mediating Role of Digital Ethics in Higher Education. *Munaddhomah: Jurnal Manajemen Pendidikan Islam*, *7*(1), 92–108. DOI: 10.31538/munaddhomah.v7i1.2455

NCES. (2023). *Undergraduate enrollment (Condition of Education)*. https://nces.ed.gov/programs/coe/indicator/cha

Nguyen, D. P., Phan, L. T., Ho, H. X., & Le, A. N. H. (2022). Human resource management practices in higher education: A literature review using co-word analysis. *International Journal of Management Education*, *16*(1), 40–61.

Nguyen, L. A., & Park, M. (2022). Artificial intelligence in staffing. *Vision (Basel)*, •••, 09722629221096803.

Noesgaard, S. S., & Nielsen, J. A. (2021). The messy reality of digital transformation in public organizations: Two case studies of enterprise system implementation. *Government Information Quarterly*, *38*(2), 101–558.

Nurhas, I., Aditya, B. R., Jacob, D. W., & Pawlowski, J. M. (2021). Understanding the challenges of rapid digital transformation. The case of the COVID-19 pandemic in higher education. *Behaviour & Information Technology*, *42*(16), 2773–2789. DOI: 10.1080/0144929X.2021.1962977

Nyale, D., Karume, S., Kipkebut, A., & Mukudi, F. (2025). Digital skills landscape: A systematic review of current academic programs, industry demands, and the digital divide's impact on graduate competencies. *Industry and Higher Education*, *0*(0), 09504222251370105. DOI: 10.1177/09504222251370105

O'Brien, C., Li, Z., Adotey, P. B., & Yohuno, G. (2025). Mapping a decade of digital transformation in HRM: Trends, implications, and future research directions. *Current Psychology*, *44*(14), 13234–13253. DOI: 10.1007/s12144-025-08064-8

O'Callaghan, S., Calloway, L. J., Walker, J. P., Elson, R. J., Dwyer, C., & Boumediene, S. (2021). Digital literacy and accounting students: Implications for the profession. *Global Journal of Accounting and Finance*, *5*(1), 45–63. DOI: 10.47177/GJAF.05.01.2021.045

O'Reilly, C. A., & Tushman, M. L. (2021). *Lead and disrupt: How to solve the innovator's dilemma* (2nd ed.). Business Books. DOI: 10.1515/9781503629639

Odugbesan, J. A., Aghazadeh, S., Al Qaralleh, R. E., & Sogeke, O. S. (2023). Green talent management and employees' innovative work behavior: The roles of artificial intelligence and transformational leadership. *Journal of Knowledge Management, 27*(3), 696–716. DOI: 10.1108/JKM-08-2021-0601

OECD. (2018). *The future of education and skills 2030: The future we want.* https://www.oecd.org/content/dam/oecd/en/publications/reports/2018/06/the-future-of-education-and-skills_5424dd26/54ac7020-en.pdf

OECD. (2025a). *Education at a Glance 2025: OECD Indicators.* https://doi.org/ DOI: 10.1787/1c0d9c79-en

OECD. (2025b). *The Financial Sustainability of Higher Education: Insights from Policy in OECD Countries* (Vol. P). OECD Publishing., DOI: 10.1787/f544ccfe-

Ogogo, A. U., & Qureshi, A. (2026). Comparative Study On Talent Identification And Talent Retention: Nigeria As A Developing Country And The Western World. *INTERNATIONAL JOURNAL OF ADVANCES IN SIGNAL AND IMAGE SCIENCES*, 353-371.

Oksana, K. R. A. V. C. H. U. K. (2026). Human-centric digital leadership for HRM 5.0 ecosystem readiness. *ORA E INTELIGENTE I DEZVOLTARE REGIONALĂ, 10*(01), 55–85.

Olan, F., Nyuur, R. B., & Arakpogun, E. O. (2024). AI: A knowledge sharing tool for improving employees' performance. *Journal of Decision Systems, 33*(4), 700–720. DOI: 10.1080/12460125.2023.2263687

Onan, G. (2024). Digital Transformation and Digital Leadership in Higher Education Institutions: Insights from the Literature. *International Journal of New Approaches in Social Studies, 8*(2), 198–213. DOI: 10.38015/sbyy.1587587

Orben, A., Przybylski, A. K., Blakemore, S.-J., & Kievit, R. A. (2022). Windows of developmental sensitivity to social media. *Nature Communications, 13*(1), 1649. DOI: 10.1038/s41467-022-29296-3 PMID: 35347142

Organisation for Economic Co-operation and Development. (2019). *OECD AI principles*. OECD.

Özer, M., Perc, M., & Suna, H. E. (2024). Artificial intelligence bias and the amplification of inequalities in the labor market. *Journal of Economy Culture and Society*, (69), 159–168.

Palmer, C. L., Teffeau, L. C., & Pirmann, C. M. (2009). *Scholarly information practices in the online environment : themes from literature and implications for library service development*. 57.https://www.researchgate.net/publication/230800450_Scholarly_Information_Practices_in_the_Online_Environment_Themes_from_the_Literature_and_Implications_for_Library_Service_Development

Palos-Sánchez, P. R., Baena-Luna, P., Badicu, A., & Infante-Moro, J. C. (2022). Artificial intelligence and human resources management: A bibliometric analysis. *Applied Artificial Intelligence*, *36*(1), 2145631. DOI: 10.1080/08839514.2022.2145631

Pandey, A., Balusamy, B., & Chilamkurti, N. (Eds.). (2023). *Disruptive artificial intelligence and sustainable human resource management: Impacts and innovations-The future of HR*. CRC Press. DOI: 10.1201/9781032622743

Pang, H., Dong, S., Tan, P., Wang, H., & Li, J. (2025), From data to decisions: AI-Augmented geoscience and engineering in natural gas industry, Natural Gas Industry B, Volume 12, Issue 2, PP 101-109, ISSN 2352-8540, DOI: 10.1016/j.ngib.2025.04.001

Pathak, A., & Mishra, S. (2025). An Empirical Exploration of MOOC Effectiveness Towards Participants' Intention-Fulfilment and Learners' Satisfaction. Vision. *The Journal of Business Perspective*, *29*(1), 67–80. DOI: 10.1177/09722629211054170

Pathak, A., & Quttainah, M. A. (2026). Charting the Future: AI's Evolving Role in Human Capital Management. In Mehra, P., Olga Titovna, E., Agrawal, S., Kansra, P., & Stefanovic, M. (Eds.), *AI-Enabled Workforce Management for Hybrid Workplaces* (pp. 69–96). IGI Global Scientific Publishing., DOI: 10.4018/979-8-3373-5871-0.ch003

Peddi, S., & Manoharan, G. (2026). Ethical Guidelines for the thoughtful Implementation of AI in Higher Education. *EthAIca: Journal of Ethics. AI and Critical Analysis*, (5), 409.

Pelser, A. M. (2026). Human-Centric and Sustainable Digital Transformation: Are Higher Education Institutions Ready to Manage and Develop Talent in the Age of AI?. *Észak-magyarországi Stratégiai Füzetek, 22*(04), 20-28.

Pew Charitable Trusts. (2019). *Two Decades of Change in Federal and State Higher Education Funding*. https://www.pew.org/-/media/assets/2019/10/fedstatefundinghigheredu_chartbook_v1.pdf

Pew Charitable Trusts. (2025). *Higher Education's Uncertain Fiscal Future* https://www.pew.org/en/research-and-analysis/articles/2025/11/12/higher-educations-uncertain-fiscal-future

Pham, D. H. (2021). The professional development of academic staff in higher education institutions. *Journal of Teacher Education for Sustainability*, *23*(1), 115–131. DOI: 10.2478/jtes-2021-0009

Picciano, A. G. (2022). Theories and frameworks for online education: Seeking an integrated model. *Online Learning : The Official Journal of the Online Learning Consortium*, *21*(3), 166–190.

Piccoli, G., Ahmad, R., & Ives, B. (2001). Web-based virtual learning environments. *Management Information Systems Quarterly*, *25*(4), 401–426. DOI: 10.2307/3250989

Pittman, J., Anderson, J., Bentley, E., Clanton, C., Hammonds, L. S., McCoy, K. T., Otts, J. A., Riley, B. H., & Sturm, T. A. (2026). Gap analysis methodology for mapping baccalaureate and graduate nursing curricula to the AACN essentials: A step-wise approach. *Journal of Professional Nursing : Official Journal of the American Association of Colleges of Nursing*, *63*, 26–32. DOI: 10.1016/j.profnurs.2025.12.009 PMID: 41796558

Pongton, P., & Suntravuth, S. (2019). Communication satisfaction, employee, engagement, job satisfaction, and job performance in higher education institution. *ABAC Journal*, *39*(3), 90–110.

Porkodi, S., & Cedro, T. L. (2025). The ethical role of generative artificial intelligence in modern HR decision-making: A systematic literature review. *European Journal of Business and Management Research*, *10*(1), 44–55. DOI: 10.24018/ejbmr.2025.10.1.2535

Prasad, K. D. V., & De, T. (2024). Generative AI as a catalyst for HRM practices: Mediating effects of trust. *Humanities & Social Sciences Communications*, *11*(1), 1–16. DOI: 10.1057/s41599-024-03842-4

Prikshat, V., Kumar, S., Patel, P., & Varma, A. (2025). Impact of organisational facilitators and perceived HR effectiveness on acceptance of AI-augmented HRM: An integrated TAM and TPB perspective. *Personnel Review*, *54*(3), 879–912. DOI: 10.1108/PR-04-2023-0303

Prinsloo, P., & Slade, S. (2021). Student vulnerability, agency and learning analytics: An exploration. *Journal of Learning Analytics*, *4*(1), 159–182.

Probojakti, W., Utami, H. N., Prasetya, A., & Riza, M. F. (2025). Driving sustainable competitive advantage in banking: The role of transformational leadership and digital transformation in organizational agility and corporate resiliency. *Business Strategy and the Environment*, *34*(1), 670–689. DOI: 10.1002/bse.4005

Putranto, S. A. E. (2026). Human Resource Analytics and Data-Driven Decision Making: Implications for Talent Acquisition and Retention Strategies. [JUMPER]. *Journal Management & Economics Review*, *3*(8), 439–452.

Qahtani, E. H. A., & Alsmairat, M. A. (2023). Assisting artificial intelligence adoption drivers in human resources management: a mediation model. *Acta logistica, 10*(1), 141-150.

Queiros, A., Costa, P., & Pacheco, L. (2022). Stakeholder communication in digital transformation: Evidence from a Portuguese polytechnic. *Procedia Computer Science*, *196*, 785–793.

Quy, V. K., Thanh, B. T., Chehri, A., Linh, D. M., & Tuan, D. A. (2023). AI and digital transformation in higher education: Vision and approach of a specific university in Vietnam. *Sustainability (Basel)*, *15*(14), 11093. DOI: 10.3390/su151411093

Rabenu, E., & Baruch, Y. (2025). Cyborging HRM theory: From evolution to revolution–the challenges and trajectories of AI for the future role of HRM. *Personnel Review*, *54*(1), 174–198. DOI: 10.1108/PR-02-2024-0111

Raes, A., Detienne, L., Windey, I., & Depaepe, F. (2020). Hybrid learning environments. *Computers & Education*, *143*, 103682. Advance online publication. DOI: 10.1016/j.compedu.2019.103682

Raghavan, M., Barocas, S., Kleinberg, J., & Levy, D. (2020). Mitigating bias in algorithmic hiring: Evaluating claims and practices. *Proceedings of the ACM Conference on Fairness, Accountability, and Transparency*. https://doi.org/DOI: 10.1145/3351095.3372828

Ramaditya, M., Maarif, M. S., Affandi, J., & Sukmawati, A. (2022). Reinventing talent management. How to maximise performance in higher education. *Frontiers in Education*, *7*, 929697. DOI: 10.3389/feduc.2022.929697

Raman, R., Venugopalan, M., & Kamal, A. (2024). Evaluating human resources management literacy: A performance analysis of ChatGPT and bard. *Heliyon*, *10*(5), e27026. DOI: 10.1016/j.heliyon.2024.e27026

Ramírez-Montoya, M. S., McGreal, R. y Obiageli Agbu, J.-F. (2022). Horizontes digitales complejos en el futuro de la educación 4.0: luces desde las recomendaciones de UNESCO. *RIED-Revista Iberoamericana de Educación a Distancia, 25*(2), 09-21. https://doi.org/DOI: 10.5944/ried.25.2.33843

Ranga, M., & Etzkowitz, H. (2013). Triple Helix Systems: An Analytical Framework for Innovation Policy and Practice in the Knowledge Society. *Industry and Higher Education, 27*(4), 237-262. [REMOVED HYPERLINK FIELD]https://doi.org/DOI: 10.1016/j.caeo.2023.100151

Rangel-de Lazaro, G., & Duart, J. M. (2023). You can handle, you can teach it: Systematic review on the use of extended reality and artificial intelligence technologies for online higher education. *Sustainability (Basel), 15*(4), 3507. DOI: 10.3390/su15043507

Rapanta, C., Botturi, L., Goodyear, P., Guàrdia, L., & Koole, M. (2020). Online University Teaching During and After the Covid-19 Crisis: Refocusing Teacher Presence and Learning Activity. *Postdigital Science and Education, 2*(3), 923–945. DOI: 10.1007/s42438-020-00155-y PMID: 40477148

Razali, R., Arifin, M. A., Shafie, L. A., Azizan, F. L., & Ishak, M. A. M. (2024). Mapping the landscape of talent management research in higher education. A bibliometric analysis. *Cogent Business & Management, 11*(1), 229–300. DOI: 10.1080/23311975.2023.2298300

Razia, B., & Awwad, B. (2022). *A comprehensive review of blockchain technology and its related aspects in higher education* (pp. 553–571). Technologies, artificial intelligence and the future of learning post-COVID-19: The crucial role of international accreditation.

Razia, B., Awwad, B., & Taqui, N. (2022). The relationship between artificial intelligence (AI) and its aspects in higher education. *Development and Learning in Organizations, 37*(3), 21–23. DOI: 10.1108/DLO-04-2022-0074

Redecker, C. (2021). *European framework for the digital competence of educators: DigCompEdu*. Publications Office of the European Union.

Redecker, C., & Punie, Y. (2017). European framework for the digital competence of educators. *DigCompEdu*, (927973718X). Advance online publication. DOI: 10.2760/159770

Rincón-Rodríguez, I. C., Chaparro-Medina, J. E., Ortiz-Ortiz, E. G., Plata-Acosta, Y. I., Zarta-Botero, M., Crespo, J. E., & García-Lirios, C. (2025). Human talent management in higher education institutions. Facing challenges and taking advantage of opportunities in the 4.0 era. *Multidisciplinary Journal of Educational Research, 15*(3), 170–181. DOI: 10.17583/remie.16140

Robert, J., Muscanell, N., McCormack, M., Pelletier, K., Arnold, K., Arbino, N., Young, K., & Reeves, J. (2025). 2025 EDUCAUSE Horizon Report: teaching and learning edition. *Horizon Report.*

Robertson, J., Johnson, R. B., & McGhee, J. (2024). Significant challenges facing small institutions in America. *New Directions for Student Services, 2024*(188), 11–22. DOI: 10.1002/ss.20533

Robson, F., & Mavin, S. (2014). Evaluating training and development in UK universities. Staff perceptions. *European Journal of Training and Development, 38*(6), 553–569. DOI: 10.1108/EJTD-04-2013-0039

Rozi, A., Junengsih, J., Alam, S., Pawar, A., Sumarjo, W., & Sunarsi, D. (2026). Impact of HR Management on AI Implementation and Data Protection in Indonesian Manufacturing. [IJCITSM]. *International Journal of Cyber and IT Service Management, 6*(1), 51–64. DOI: 10.34306/ijcitsm.v6i1.226

Rudito, P., & Sinaga, M. F. (2017). *Digital mastery, Membangun kepemimpinan digital untuk memenangkan era disrupsi.* Gramedia Pustaka Utama.

Rüth, R., & Netzer, T. (2020). The key elements of cultural intelligence as a driver for digital leadership success. *Leadership, Educaton, Personality. An Interdisciplinary Journal, 2*(1), 3–8.

Saaida, M. B. (2023). AI-Driven transformations in higher education: Opportunities and challenges. *International journal of educational research and studies, 5*(1), 29-36.

Sabil, S., Bangkara, B. A., Mogea, T., Niswan, E., & Timotius, E. (2023). Identification of HRM improvement strategy using artificial intelligence in modern economic development. *International Journal of Professional Business Review: Int. J. Prof. Bus. Rev., 8*(6), 10.

Safi, M., Abdallah, F., Erturk, A., & Alkhayyat, R. (2024). Digital readiness of the workforce for successful digital transformation: Exploring new digital competencies. *Proceedings, 101*, 21. DOI: 10.3390/proceedings2024101021

Sahid, N. Z., & Ridzuan, N. B. (2025). Digital literacy skills and academic-library engagement among Generation Z students in Malaysian higher education. *International Journal of Research and Innovation in Social Science, 9*(10), 7643–7656. Advance online publication. DOI: 10.47772/IJRISS.2025.910000623

Sainger, G. (2025). Fostering a Sustainable Future: The Role of Digital Leadership in Cultivating an SDG-Oriented Organisational Culture. In Jasola, M., & Singh, N. (Eds.), *Digital Transformation Of Business World: A Managerial Perspective* (pp. 97–112). Emerald Insight., DOI: 10.1108/978-1-83662-046-420251007

Salama, R., & Hinton, T. (2023). Online higher education: Current landscape and future trends. *Journal of Further and Higher Education, 47*(7), 913–924. DOI: 10.1080/0309877X.2023.2200136

Sá, M. J., & Serpa, S. (2021). The COVID-19 pandemic as an opportunity to foster the sustainable development of teaching in higher education. *Sustainability (Basel), 12*(20), 8525. DOI: 10.3390/su12208525

Santana, M., & Díaz-Fernández, M. (2023). Competencies for the artificial intelligence age: Visualisation of the state of the art and future perspectives. *Review of Managerial Science, 17*(6), 1971–2004. DOI: 10.1007/s11846-022-00613-w

Saraih, E., Wong, S., Asimiran, S., & Khambari, M. (2022). Contemporary communication conduit among exemplar school principals in Malaysian schools. *Research and Practice in Technology Enhanced Learning, 17*(1), 4. Advance online publication. DOI: 10.1186/s41039-022-00179-x

Sarfraz, M., Ivascu, L., Abdullah, M., Ozturk, I., & Tariq, J. (2022). Exploring a Pathway to Sustainable Performance in Manufacturing Firms: The Interplay between Innovation Capabilities, Green Process and Product Innovations and Digital Leadership. *Sustainability (Basel), 14*(10), 5945. DOI: 10.3390/su14105945

Sattari-Ardabili, F., & Narimani, M. (2026). Hybrid education as a new paradigm in higher education. *Revista Mexicana de Investigación e Intervención Educativa, 5*(1), 51–57. DOI: 10.62697/rmiie.v5i1.272

Saxena, A., Ramaswamy, M., Beale, J., Marciniuk, D., & Smith, P. (2021). Striving for the United Nations (UN) sustainable development goals (SDGs): What will it take? *Discover Sustainability, 2*(1), 1–14. DOI: 10.1007/s43621-021-00029-8

Scanlon, E. (2018). Digital Scholarship: Identity, Interdisciplinarity, and Openness. *Frontiers in Digital Humanities, 5*, 3. Advance online publication. DOI: 10.3389/fdigh.2018.00003

Scanlon, E., Sharples, M., Fenton-O'Creevy, M., Fleck, J., Cooban, C., Ferguson, R., Cross, S., & Aczel, J. (2021). *Beyond prototypes: Enabling innovation in technology-enhanced learning*. Technology Enhanced Learning Research Programme, London Knowledge Lab.

Schaal, T., Tischendorf, T., Sydorenko, O., Karagulova, M., Chettykbayev, R., & Brauweiler, H.-C. (2025). Self-assessed vs. reported digital competence among health students in Germany, Sillat, L. H., Tammets, K., & Laanpere, M. (2021). Digital competence assessment methods in higher education: A systematic literature review. *Education Sciences, 11*(8), 402.

Schaap, L., Nijland, F., Cents-Boonstra, M., & Vanlommel, K. (2025). A framework supporting the innovative capacity of higher education institutions: An integrative literature review. *Sustainability (Basel)*, *17*(14), 6517. DOI: 10.3390/su17146517

Scheffel, M., Drachsler, H., Stoyanov, S., & Specht, M. (2022). Quality indicators for learning analytics. *Journal of Educational Technology & Society*, *17*(4), 117–132.

Schein, E. H., & Schein, P. A. (2021). *Organizational culture and leadership* (5th ed.). Wiley.

Schultz, T. W. (1961). Investment in Human Capital. *The American Economic Review*, *51*(1), 1–17. https://www.jstor.org/stable/1818907

Scullion, H., & Collings, D. G. (2011). *Global talent management*. Routledge. DOI: 10.4324/9780203865682

Seabolt, B., & Arends, B. (2000). *Remaining real in a virtual world.*

Segbenya, M., Bervell, B., Frimpong-Manso, E., Otoo, I. C., Andzie, T. A., & Achina, S. (2023). Artificial intelligence in higher education: Modelling the antecedents of artificial intelligence usage and effects on 21st century employability skills among postgraduate students in Ghana. *Computers and Education: Artificial Intelligence*, *5*, 100188. DOI: 10.1016/j.caeai.2023.100188

Sejdiu, N. P., & Sejdiu, S. (2025). The quiet transformation of higher education in the AI era. *Open Research Europe*, *5*, 249. DOI: 10.12688/openreseurope.20715.1 PMID: 40963694

Sekli, G. M., Godo, A., & Véliz, J. C. (2024). Generative AI Solutions for Faculty and Students: A Review of Literature and Roadmap for Future Research. *Journal of Information Technology Education*, *23*, 14. DOI: 10.28945/5304

Selwyn, N. (2022). *Is technology good for education?* (2nd ed.). Polity Press.

Shafiee, M., & Goodarzi, S. (2026). The role of employer branding in talent management: Analysis of key strategies and tools. *The International Journal of Organizational Analysis*, *34*(1), 99–114. DOI: 10.1108/IJOA-10-2024-4900

Shahzad, M. F., Xu, S., & Zahid, H. (2025). Exploring the impact of generative AI-based technologies on learning performance through self-efficacy, fairness & ethics, creativity, and trust in higher education. *Education and Information Technologies*, *30*(3), 3691–3716. DOI: 10.1007/s10639-024-12949-9

Shamseer, L., Moher, D., Clarke, M., Ghersi, D., Liberati, A., Petticrew, M., Shekelle, P., & Stewart, L. A.PRISMA-P Group. (2015). Preferred reporting items for systematic review and meta-analysis protocols (PRISMA-P) 2015: Elaboration and explanation. *BMJ (Clinical Research Ed.)*, *349*(jan02 1), g7647. DOI: 10.1136/bmj.g7647 PMID: 25555855

Sharafeddine, W., Diab-Bahman, R., & Al-Enzi, A. (2024). The impact of fasting on workplace productivity and well-being: A review of fasting in Ramadan. *International Journal of Productivity and Quality Management*, *41*(1), 32–48. DOI: 10.1504/IJPQM.2024.136191

SHEEO. (2024). *State higher education finance (SHEF): FY 2023*. State Higher Education Executive Officers Association.

SHEEO. (2025). *State Higher Education Finance: FY 2024*. https://shef.sheeo.org/wp-content/uploads/2025/05/SHEEO_SHEF_FY24_Report.pdf

Sheri, A. A., Nori, N. R., & Gupta, S. K. (2021). The role of strategic intelligence in enhancing effective talent management: A study on some academic institutions of Duhok Governorate. [AJNU]. *Academic Journal of Nawroz University*, *10*(2), 137–155. DOI: 10.25007/ajnu.v10n2a929

Shifa, S., Abbas, S. J., & Muhammad, K. K. (2026). HR Analytic as a Strategic Tool: Predicting Talent Retention and Performance. *The Critical Review of Social Sciences Studies*, *4*(1), 387–395. DOI: 10.59075/vhtstj93

Siemens, G. (2013). Learning analytics: The emergence of a discipline. *The American Behavioral Scientist*, *57*(10), 1380–1400. DOI: 10.1177/0002764213498851

Sillat, L. H., Tammets, K., & Laanpere, M. (2021). Digital competence assessment methods in higher education: A systematic literature review. *Education Sciences*, *11*(8), 402. DOI: 10.3390/educsci11080402

Silveira, P. P.Pallavi Priya Silveira. (2025). Transforming Global Education through AI: Addressing Cross-Cultural Competencies and HRM Challenges in the Digital Age. *Journal of Integrative Education Studies*, *1*(1), 20–29. DOI: 10.64229/6na0be71

Simon, H. A. (2013). *Administrative behavior* (4th ed.). Simon and Schuster.

Simovic, V., Safi, M., Bradić-Martinović, A., Sarhan, H., Bhagat, R., & Ivanovic, D. (2023). How competent are our students in digital entrepreneurship? *Proceedings*, *85*(1), 18. DOI: 10.3390/proceedings2023085018

Singun, A. J. (2025). Unveiling the barriers to digital transformation in higher education institutions: A systematic literature review. *Discover Education*, *4*(1), 37. Advance online publication. DOI: 10.1007/s44217-025-00430-9

Slimi, Z., & Carballido, B. V. (2023). Navigating the Ethical Challenges of Artificial Intelligence in Higher Education: An Analysis of Seven Global AI Ethics Policies. *TEM journal, 12*(2).

Slimi, Z., & Carballido, V. B. (2023). Navigating the Ethical Challenges of Artificial Intelligence in Higher Education: An Analysis of Seven Global AI Ethics Policies, TEM Journal. Volume 12, Issue 2, PP 590-602, ISSN 2217-8309, DOI: DOI: 10.18421/TEM122-02

Soergel, B., Kriegler, E., Weindl, I., Rauner, S., Dirnaichner, A., Ruhe, C., Hofmann, M., Bauer, N., Bertram, C., Bodirsky, B. L., Leimbach, M., Leininger, J., Levesque, A., Luderer, G., Pehl, M., Wingens, C., Baumstark, L., Beier, F., Dietrich, J. P., & Popp, A. (2021). A sustainable development pathway for climate action within the UN 2039 Agenda. *Nature Climate Change*, *11*(8), 656–664. DOI: 10.1038/s41558-021-01098-3

Soomro, K. A., Kale, U., Curtis, R., Akcaoglu, M., & Bernstein, M. (2020). Digital divide among higher education faculty. *International Journal of Educational Technology in Higher Education*, *17*(1), 21. DOI: 10.1186/s41239-020-00191-5 PMID: 41001069

Sosa, E., Salinas Ibañez, J., & de Benito, C. (2018). Factores que afectan la incorporación de Tecnologías Emergentes en el aula: Una mirada desde expertos (docentes) Iberoamericanos. *Revista Espacios*, *39*(2), 1–15.

Sun, D., Ba, S., Cha, Y., Yu, J., Chiang, F.-K., & Hai, M. D. Cher-Ping Lim (2026), Empowering university teachers in higher education: A generative AI-responsive competency framework, Computers and Education: Artificial Intelligence, Volume 10, 2026,100542, ISSN 2666-920X, DOI: 10.1016/j.caeai.2026.100542

Sun, T., & Yoon, M. (2025). The impact of digital transformation on faculty performance in higher education: The mediating role of digital self-efficacy and the moderating role of task-technology fit. *Frontiers in Psychology*, *16*, 1693375. DOI: 10.3389/fpsyg.2025.1693375 PMID: 41190117

Swailes, S. (2016). The cultural evolution of talent management: A memetic analysis. *Human Resource Development Review*, *15*(3), 340–358. DOI: 10.1177/1534484316664812

Szostak, M. (Ed.). (2025). *Organizations, Humanism and AI: An Aesthetics Approach* (1st ed.). Routledge., DOI: 10.4324/9781003662723

Taamneh, A. M., Taamneh, M., Alsaad, A., & Al-Okaily, M. (2022). Talent management and academic context: A comparative study of public and private universities. *EuroMed Journal of Business, 17*(4), 731–751. DOI: 10.1108/EMJB-08-2020-0088

Taddeo, M., McCutcheon, T., & Floridi, L. (2021). Trusting artificial intelligence in cybersecurity is a double-edged sword. *Nature Machine Intelligence, 1*(12), 557–560. DOI: 10.1038/s42256-019-0109-1

Tafesse, W., Aguilar, M. P., Sayed, S., & Tariq, U. (2024). Digital overload, coping mechanisms, and student engagement: An empirical investigation based on the S-O-R framework. *SAGE Open, 14*(1), 21582440241236087. Advance online publication. DOI: 10.1177/21582440241236087

Tambe, P., Cappelli, P., & Yakubovich, V. (2019). Artificial intelligence in human resources management: Challenges and a path forward. *California Management Review, 61*(4), 15–42. DOI: 10.1177/0008125619867910

Tang, J., Huang, P., & Yan, S. (2025). Digital transformation in higher education: Logical framework, practical dilemmas, and implementation approaches. *Frontiers in Psychology, 16*, 1565591. Advance online publication. DOI: 10.3389/fpsyg.2025.1565591 PMID: 41280162

Tanucan, J., Negrido, C., & Malaga, G. (2022). Digital Leadership of School Heads and Job Satisfaction of Teachers in the Philippines during the Pandemic. *International Journal of Learning. Teaching and Educational Research, 21*(10), 1–18. DOI: 10.26803/ijlter.21.10.1

Tapsir, S. H., Yusof, R., & Hashmi, A. (2026). Transformational leadership, Green HRM and top management commitment: Pathways to sustainability in Malaysian higher education. *Journal of Applied Research in Higher Education, 18*(2), 478–494. DOI: 10.1108/JARHE-09-2024-0493

Tariq, J., Shahab, H., & Zahoor, H. (2026). Talent Management in Organizational Landscape: A Systematic Review of Literature. *Policy Journal of Social Science Review, 4*(2), 351–369.

Tariq, M. U. (Ed.). (2024). *AI-driven learning and engagement in higher education*. IGI Global. DOI: 10.4018/979-8-3693-4074-5

Tathavadekar, V. P., & Mahankale, N. R. (2026). Digital HR for sustainable value chains: Bridging tech maturity and green talent in emerging economies. *Strategic HR Review, 25*(1), 28–34. DOI: 10.1108/SHR-07-2025-0067

Tebenko, V., Kutsai, N., Shashyna, M., Omelianenko, O., & Bakushevych, I. (2024). Digital transformation in business: The impact of technology on efficiency, innovation and competitiveness. *Economic Affairs*, *69*(Special Issue), 307–315. DOI: 10.46852/0424-2513.1.2024.32

Teker, S., Teker, D., & Basak TAVMAN, E. (2025). STRATEGIES FOR DIGITAL TRANSFORMATION OF UNIVERSITIES. *Http://Jtie.Upol.Cz/Doi/, 17*(1), 147–166. https://doi.org/DOI: <ALIGNMENT.qj></ALIGNMENT>10.5507/Jtie.2025.005.Html

Tenberga, I., & Daniela, L. (2024). Artificial intelligence literacy competencies for teachers through self-assessment tools. *Sustainability (Basel)*, *16*(23), 10386. DOI: 10.3390/su162310386

Thangaraju, K., & Palani, P. (2024). Integrating Sustainability into Ai-Driven HRM Practices: Examining Employee Engagement and Organizational Performance in the IT Industry. *Pakistan Journal of Life and Social Sciences*, *22*(2). Advance online publication. DOI: 10.57239/PJLSS-2024-22.2.001008

Thomas, S., Nair, D. S., Joseph, J., Srampical, S. G., & Cleetus, R. S. (2026). Examining the sustainable integration of artificial intelligence in human resource digitalization in the context of Industry 4.0. *European Public & Social Innovation Review*, *11*, 1–14. DOI: 10.31637/epsir-2026-2044

Tsiskaridze, R., Reinhold, K., & Jarvis, M. (2023). Innovating HRM recruitment: A comprehensive review of AI deployment. *Marketing i menedžment innovacij, 14*(4), 239-254.

Tuffaha, M., & Perello-Marin, M. R. (2023). Artificial intelligence definition, applications and adoption in human resource management: A systematic literature review. *International Journal of Business Innovation and Research*, *32*(3), 293–322. DOI: 10.1504/IJBIR.2023.134887

Tursunbayeva, A., Fernandez, V., Gallardo-Gallardo, E., & Moschera, L. (2025). Artificial intelligence and digital data in recruitment: Exploring business and engineering candidates' perceptions of organizational attractiveness. *European Management Journal*. Advance online publication. DOI: 10.1016/j.emj.2025.03.002

Tursunbayeva, A., Pagliari, C., Di Lauro, S., & Antonelli, G. (2022). The ethics of people analytics: Risks, opportunities and recommendations. *Personnel Review*, *51*(3), 900–921. DOI: 10.1108/PR-12-2019-0680

Tzirides, A. O., Zapata, G., Kastania, N. P., Saini, A. K., Castro, V., Ismael, S. A., You, Y., Santos, T. A. D., Searsmith, D., O'Brien, C., Cope, B., & Kalantzis, M. (2024). Combining human and artificial intelligence for enhanced AI literacy in higher education. *Computers and Education Open*, *6*, 100184. Advance online publication. DOI: 10.1016/j.caeo.2024.100184

UCL. (n.d.). *ABC Learning Design @ UCL*. Retrieved June 30, 2026, from https://blogs.ucl.ac.uk/abc-ld/

UNESCO. (2021). *Recommendation on the ethics of artificial intelligence*. UNESCO.

UNESCO. (2025). *UIS Data Browser: Global flow of tertiary-level students*. https://uis.unesco.org/en/uis-student-flow

United Nations. (2018). *Sustainable Development Goals*. United Nations.

United Nations. (2024). *The sustainable development goals report 2024*. United Nations. Retrieved September 4, 2024, from https://www.un.org/sustainabledevelopment/ progress-report

Upadhyay, A. K., & Khandelwal, K. (2018). Applying artificial intelligence: Implications for recruitment. *Strategic HR Review*, *17*(5), 255–258. DOI: 10.1108/SHR-07-2018-0051

Urenda, S. D. R., Yparrea, N. G., Moreira, E. L., Uicab, M. C., & Grez, A. G. (2022, September). Digital Competencies for Content Curation in the Open Education Framework. In *2022 XII International Conference on Virtual Campus (JICV)* (pp. 1-4). IEEE. DOI: 10.1109/JICV56113.2022.9934776

Valencia, M. (2005). El capital humano, otro activo de su empresa. *Entramado*, 1 (2), 20 – 33. https://www.redalyc.org/pdf/2654/265420471004.pdf

Varma, R. R., Umesh, I. M., Nagesh, Y. N., & Kumara Swamy, K. S. (2021). Digital transformation in higher education institutions-an overview. *International Journal of Applied Engineering Research: IJAER*, *16*(4), 278–282.

Veletsianos, G., & Kimmons, R. (2021). Assumptions and challenges of open scholarship. *International Review of Research in Open and Distance Learning*, *13*(4), 166–189. DOI: 10.19173/irrodl.v13i4.1313

Venkatesh, V., Morris, M. G., Davis, G. B., & Davis, F. D. (2003). User acceptance of information technology: Toward a unified view. *Management Information Systems Quarterly*, *27*(3), 425–478. DOI: 10.2307/30036540

Vial, G. (2019). Understanding digital transformation: A review and a research agenda. *The Journal of Strategic Information Systems*, *28*(2), 118–144. DOI: 10.1016/j.jsis.2019.01.003

Vignieri, V., & Santoni, R. (2026). Open innovation in the public sector: Managing knowledge assets for public value creation through dynamic performance management. *International Journal of Public Sector Management*, •••, 1–28. DOI: 10.1108/IJPSM-03-2025-0103

Wahyuningtyas, R. (2015). An integrated talent management system: Challenges for competitive advantage. *International Business Management*, *9*(4), 384–390.

Walczak, K., & Cellary, W. (2023). Challenges for higher education in the era of widespread access to Generative AI. *Economics and Business Review*, *9*(2), 71–100. DOI: 10.18559/ebr.2023.2.743

Walker, A., & White, G. (2013). *Technology-enhanced language learning*. Oxford University Press.

Wang, J., & Pashmforoosh, R. (2024). A new framework for ethical artificial intelligence: Keeping HRD in the loop. *Human Resource Development International*, *27*(3), 428–451. DOI: 10.1080/13678868.2024.2346492

Wang, Q., Ma, Z., Zhang, G., & Miao, Q. (2025). Digital transformation driving educational reforms in higher education: A paradigm shift in teaching and learning. *SAGE Open*, *15*(1), 254–272. Advance online publication. DOI: 10.1177/25902547251395880

Wang, T., Lin, X., & Sheng, F. (2022). Digital leadership and exploratory innovation: From the dual perspectives of strategic orientation and organizational culture. *Frontiers in Psychology*, *13*, 902693. DOI: 10.3389/fpsyg.2022.902693

Watson, D., Webb, R., Cook, S., & Grant, K. (2025). Does the internet lead to surface searching and a deficiency of discovery in student learning? *Education and Information Technologies*, *30*(14), 19853–19878. DOI: 10.1007/s10639-025-13498-5

WEF. (2023). *The future of jobs report*. https://www.weforum.org/publications/the-future-of-jobs-report-2023/

Wengler, S., Hildmann, G., & Vossebein, U. (2021). Digital transformation in sales as an evolving process. *Journal of Business and Industrial Marketing*, *36*(4), 599–614. DOI: 10.1108/JBIM-03-2020-0124

Wentzel, K. R. (2009). Students' relationships with teachers. In the *Handbook of motivation at school.*

Westerman, G., Bonnet, D., & McAfee, A. (2014). *Leading digital: Turning technology into business transformation.* Harvard Business Press.

Wietrak, E., Berger, R., & Czakert, J. P. (2024). Integrating AI in people management: A practical exercise for higher education. In *ICERI2024 Proceedings* (pp. 9345-9352). IATED. DOI: 10.21125/iceri.2024.2364

Wilson, J. H., & Ryan, R. G. (2013). Professor–student rapport scale: Six items predict student outcomes. *Teaching of Psychology*, *40*(2), 130–133. DOI: 10.1177/0098628312475033

Wilson, J. H., Ryan, R. G., & Pugh, J. L. (2010). Professor–student rapport scale. *Teaching of Psychology*, *37*(4), 246–251. DOI: 10.1080/00986283.2010.510976

Wright, P. M., & McMahan, G. C. (1992). Theoretical perspectives for strategic human resource management. *Journal of Management*, *18*(2), 295–320. DOI: 10.1177/014920639201800205

Wu, C., Zang, H., & Carroll, J. M. (2024). AI Governance in Higher Education: Case Studies of Guidance at Big Ten Universities. Arxiv, Computer Science. https://doi.org//arXiv.2409.02017DOI: 10.48550

Wu, C., Zhang, H., & Carroll, J. M. (2024). AI governance in higher education: Case studies of guidance at Big Ten universities. *Future Internet*, *16*(10), 354. DOI: 10.3390/fi16100354

Xiao, Q., Yan, J., & Bamber, G. J. (2025). How does AI-enabled HR analytics influence employee resilience: Job crafting as a mediator and HRM system strength as a moderator. *Personnel Review*, *54*(3), 824–843. DOI: 10.1108/PR-03-2023-0198

Yadav, M., Dewasiri, N. J., & Aquino Jr, P. G. (2026). The Legal Challenges and Opportunities of Using AI in HR Functions. *Legal Frameworks of Human Resource Management Reform*, 55-88.

Young, C., Perović, N., Havemann, L., & Shackleford-Cesare, K. (Eds.). (2026). *ABC Learning Design: Active, blended, connected and beyond.* UCL Press. https://uclpress.co.uk/book/abc-learning-design/

Young, K., Küçük, Z. D., Delahunty, T., Dempsey, M., & Maglaperidze, N. (2026). Evaluating the impact of a digital competency-based placement model on STEM pre-service teachers' digital competence and teaching experiences. *Teaching and Teacher Education*, *175*, 105466. DOI: 10.1016/j.tate.2026.105466

Yusuf, A., Pervin, N., & Román-González, M. (2024). Generative AI and the future of higher education: A threat to academic integrity or reformation? Evidence from multicultural perspectives. *International Journal of Educational Technology in Higher Education*, *21*(1), 21. DOI: 10.1186/s41239-024-00453-6

Zabalawi, I., Kordahji, H., & Aftimos, S. (2024). Digital transformation in universities: Strategic framework, implementation tools, and leadership. In *Higher education in the Arab world: Digital transformation* (pp. 145–210). Springer Nature Switzerland. DOI: 10.1007/978-3-031-70779-7_8

Zawacki-Richter, O., Marín, V. I., Bond, M., & Gouverneur, F. (2022). Systematic review of research on artificial intelligence applications in higher education—Where are the educators? *International Journal of Educational Technology in Higher Education*, *16*(1), 1–27. PMID: 35013716

Zeike, S., Bradbury, K., Lindert, L., & Pfaff, H. (2019). Digital leadership skills and associations with psychological well-being. *International Journal of Environmental Research and Public Health*, *16*(14), 2628. Advance online publication. DOI: 10.3390/ijerph16142628

Zhang, C. (2026). Digital Empowerment in Design: A Literature Review of Design Ecosystem Service Platforms. *Review of Economic Assessment*, *5*(1), 24–58. DOI: 10.58567/rea05010002

Zhang, H. (2024). Exploring the impact of AI on human resource management: A case study of organizational adaptation and employee dynamics. *IEEE Transactions on Engineering Management*, *71*, 14991–15004. DOI: 10.1109/TEM.2024.3457520

Zhang, Y., & Liu, C. (2023). Online teaching quality evaluation. Entropy TOPSIS and grouped regression model. *International Journal of Emerging Technologies in Learning*, *18*(16), 36–49. DOI: 10.3991/ijet.v18i16.41353

Zhao, Y., Pinto Llorente, A. M., & Sánchez Gómez, M. C. (2021). Digital competence in higher education research: A systematic literature review. *Computers & Education*, *168*, 104212. Advance online publication. DOI: 10.1016/j.compedu.2021.104212 PMID: 36568577

Zhao, Y., Sánchez Gómez, M. C., Pinto Llorente, A. M., & Zhao, L. (2021). Digital competence in higher education: Students' perception and personal factors. *Sustainability (Basel)*, *13*(21), 12184. DOI: 10.3390/su132112184

Zhou, Y., Wang, L., & Chen, W. (2023). The dark side of AI-enabled HRM on employees based on AI algorithmic features. *Journal of Organizational Change Management*, *36*(7), 1222–1241. DOI: 10.1108/JOCM-10-2022-0308

Zhukabayeva, T., Baumuratova, D., Zholshiyeva, L., Karabay, A., & Abdrakhmanov, K. (2025). Digital Transformation in Higher Education: Toward a National Model of Digital University in Kazakhstan Through Global and Local Comparison. *Sustainability 2025, Vol. 17, Page 11132, 17*(24), 11132. https://doi.org/DOI: 10.3390/su172411132

Zhu, M., & Anagnostopoulos, D. (2021). Faculty response to top-down change initiatives in higher education. *The Journal of Higher Education, 92*(4), 628–655.

Živković, Ž., & Panić, M. (2020). Development of science and education in theWestern Balkan countries: Competitiveness with the EU. *Scientometrics, 124*(3), 2319–2339. DOI: 10.1007/s11192-020-03554-x

Živković, Z., & Panić, M. (2024). PhD studies in transition conditions – the basis for educational system and economic development: A case study Serbia. *Serbian Journal of Management, 19*(2), 339–355. DOI: 10.5937/sjm19-53172

Zuboff, S. (2019). *The age of surveillance capitalism: The fight for a human future at the new frontier of power*. Profile Books.

Zulu, S. L., Saad, A. M., Ajayi, S. O., Dulaimi, M., & Unuigbe, M. (2023). Digital leadership enactment in the construction industry: Barriers undermining effective transformation. *Engineering, Construction, and Architectural Management, 31*(10), 3493–3514. DOI: 10.1108/ECAM-05-2022-0491

About the Contributors

Sapheya Aftimos is an assistant professor at the Australian University in Kuwait, College of Business. She holds a Doctorate in Business Administration from Aston University (UK), where her research explored talent management practices in higher education institutions. Her academic interests include human resource management, digital transformation, and higher education development. Dr. Aftimos has contributed to book chapters, journal publications, and conferences, with a focus on embedding strategic talent management within digital transformation frameworks. She is also actively involved in curriculum development, research committees, and initiatives that enhance student engagement and well-being.

***

A.K. Subramani is a distinguished academic with a PhD in Business Administration from Manonmaniam Sundaranar University, Tirunelveli, India. With 20 years of teaching experience, he has made significant contributions to the field of human resource management and organisational behaviour. He has an impressive publication record with more than 100 articles in international journals, including three papers in the ABDC-A category, eight in the ABDC-B category, three in the ABDC-C category, 60 in Scopus-indexed journals, and thirteen in Web of Science journals. He has served as a resource person for various training workshops on SPSS and AMOS software packages.

Joji Abey working as Chairperson of Business Management Department, Kingdom University, Bahrain. To her credit she published more than 75 articles in International Peer Reviewed Journals.

Matt Aftimos is a Tech Lead and Staff Software Engineer with over seven years of experience designing and building scalable software systems, with a focus on backend development, APIs, and data-driven platforms. His work includes the application of artificial intelligence and machine learning techniques to enhance system performance, search relevance, and decision-making capabilities. He has 5 years of teaching experience, supporting students in developing technical skills and applying theoretical concepts in practical, real-world contexts. His interests include software architecture, artificial intelligence, and the intersection of data systems and intelligent applications.

Sara Al Shihab holds an MA from the University of Liverpool in the United Kingdom and a BA from Kuwait University in Kuwait. She is a Senior Instructor at the Australian University of Kuwait. She has published in the areas of Communicative Language Teaching (CLT) and the attitudes and motivations of language learners. Her research interests include educational pedagogies, with a particular focus on educational psychology, digital methods in language teaching and learning, and the use of generative AI and large language models (LLMs) to enhance student learning.

Ashraf Alam is currently serving as an Assistant Professor in the Department of Education at NIT Calicut, Kerala, India. He has been recognised among the World's Top 2% Scientists by Stanford University and Elsevier. His academic contributions include more than 85 Scopus-indexed publications and over 100 conference presentations delivered at national and international academic forums. His work has appeared in reputed research publication platforms including Elsevier, Springer, Taylor & Francis, CRC Press, Routledge, Atlantis Press, Springer Nature, Palgrave Macmillan, and IEEE. He earned his Ph.D. from IIT Kharagpur, where his research engaged with foundational concerns in educational policy, curriculum design, educational technology, philosophy of education, innovation in education, educational administration, governance, and pedagogical transformation. His work is grounded in a transdisciplinary orientation that draws from educational sciences, digital pedagogy, curriculum theory, learning analytics, sustainability education, instructional design, artificial intelligence, ethics of technology, and socio-technical studies. Dr. Ashraf's scholarship strives to interrogate and expand the boundaries of educational thought by examining the epistemological, ethical, and social dimensions of digital and post-digital pedagogies. His work critically engages with the changing nature of knowledge production, learner agency, pedagogical mediation, and institutional transformation in technologically saturated educational environments. He is particularly invested in advancing inclusive digital learning, gamified instructional strategies, AI-mediated educational ecosystems, and ethically governed technology integration in education. His research agenda is animated by the pursuit of design-oriented, ethically attuned, and contextually responsive frameworks that can support meaningful educational reform. Through his work, he seeks to contribute to the development of pedagogical models that are not only technologically innovative but also socially just, epistemically inclusive, developmentally sensitive, and aligned with the broader goals of sustainable and human-centred education.

Bodour H. AlShakhss was born on August 22, 1987, into a loving and educated family. Her upbringing in a nurturing environment instilled in her a strong appreciation for knowledge, curiosity, and the pursuit of academic excellence. Dr. AlShakhss pursued her passion for information studies, eventually earning her position as an Assistant Professor in the Australian University of Kuwait after pursuing her doctrate degree in Information Studies at Simmons University in Boston. Her academic journey reflects a commitment to advancing research and contributing to the field of information science. Throughout her career, Dr. AlShakhss has actively participated in numerous conferences, sharing her insights and engaging with fellow scholars. She has been an integral member of various university committees, contributing to institutional development and academic governance. Beyond the university setting, she has also taken part in non-organizational events, demonstrating her dedication to community engagement and knowledge dissemination. Dr. AlShakhss's research interests are diverse and impactful. She is particularly passionate about: Information seeking behavior Marketing and its intersections with information studies Family business-related materials Information search methodologies Her work in these areas highlights her interdisciplinary approach and her commitment to exploring how information shapes decision-making, business practices, and human behavior.

Edgar O. Cardoso, PhD is Professor - Researcher since 2009 on Division of Postgraduate Studies and Research of the Superior School of Commerce and Administration (ESCA) of the National Polytechnic Institute (IPN), Mexico City. In his position conducts research projects focused on the management and development of education in educational programs at senior level. He is currently the coordinator of the Doctoral Program in Administrative Sciences He teaches courses Methodological Seminar I, II, III and Statistics for Educational Research to Master's and Research Seminars I, II and III as well as Research Visits I, II, III and IV to PhD level. Dr. Cardoso earned his doctorate at the IPN. He has a master of science in management and development of education in the ESCA-IPN. His research includes evaluation of educational programs and executive education. He belongs to the National System of Researchers with the level II distinction in the SECIHTI of Mexico. He has directed several research projects in the area of educational management. He has conducted thesis addresses at the master's and doctoral level in the educational area. ORCID: https://orcid.org/0000-0001-7588 -9439 e-mail: eoce@hotmail.com; ecardosoe@ipn.mx

Tendai Charles is an Assistant Professor of Education at the British University in Dubai. He holds an MSc in Data Analytics & Social Statistics from the University of Manchester and a PhD in Education from the University of York. He is an accredited researcher with the Office for National Statistics and is a Fellow of the Royal Statistical Society. He is a post-positivist researcher who specialises in evidence-based education and uses computational statistics for secondary data analyses.

D.Bhuvanendran, Assistant Professor of Management, Nallamuthu Gounder Mahalingam College, Pollachi. To his credit she published more than 15 articles in International Journals.

Najwan Fares is a Senior Lecturer in Biological Sciences at Fatima College of Health Sciences (UAE) and is pursuing a PhD in Education at the British University in Dubai.

K.Kumuthadevi working as Dean, School of Commerce at KPR College of Arts Science and Research, Coimbatore

Majdi Anwar Quttainah earned his Ph.D. degree in Management from Rensselaer Polytechnic Institute, Lally School of Management & Technology (USA); MBA degree with merits from the Business School & Entrepreneurship at Newcastle University (UK), and bachelor's degree in International Business from the American International University in London (UK). Dr. Quttainah is an associate professor of management in the College of Business Administration at Kuwait University. His research and teaching interests are corporate governance and strategies, entrepreneurship & small businesses, and organizational development. In addition, as a recognition of his research, he was awarded the Best Young Researcher academic year 2016/2017 Kuwait University. He is an active scholar, presently working as senior editor of FIIB Business Review (Scopus, WoS, Published by the Sage Publishing). His research won several recognition and awards including the Best Paper Award at the 76th Annual Meeting of the Academy of Management Anaheim, CA, the Best Paper Award at the AGBA's 12th Annual World Congress, Kuantan City (State of Pahang), Malaysia, and the Best Paper Award of the Gorontalo International Conference of Project Management (ICPM) - Gorontalo/Indonesia. Also, at the home country level the best paper award for the Kuwait Economic Researcher Award by the Central Bank of Kuwait; May 2019 and 2022.

R. Velmurugan is presently working as a Professor in the Department of Commerce at Karpagam Academy of Higher Education, Coimbatore. He began his career as a Project Fellow under a UGC-sponsored Major Research Project at

NGM College, Pollachi. He has 19 years of teaching experience and 15 years of research experience. To his credit, he has successfully supervised 25 Ph.D. scholars and 5 M.Phil. scholars. At present, two scholars have submitted their theses, and six Ph.D. scholars are pursuing their research under his guidance. He has published 168 research articles in various international journals, of which 137 are in Scopus-indexed journals, 15 in Web of Science journals, and 76 in edited volumes. He has also participated in and presented 27 papers in international seminars/conferences and 154 papers in national seminars/conferences. He has served as an external examiner for numerous M.Phil. and Ph.D. viva voce examinations. He has been a Vice-Chancellor's nominee for Doctoral Committee meetings at Bharathiar University, Coimbatore, and Periyar University, Salem. He has also served as Chairperson at various national-level conferences. Furthermore, he has contributed as an expert in Syllabus Scrutiny Committees, Question Paper Scrutiny Committees, and Boards of Studies at several reputed colleges. In recognition of his meritorious contributions, he has received awards such as Best Paper Presenter, Best Research Supervisor, and Best Faculty Award from various research foundations and councils. He has also served as a resource person for 27 guest lectures, 30 workshops, and 10 faculty development programmes.

Richard Rutter is Associate Professor in the College of Business at the Australian University in Kuwait and Visiting Research Fellow of Norwich Business School at the University of East Anglia in the United Kingdom. Richard's primary research interests include data analytics, digital marketing, marketing innovation and technology, and consumer behaviour. His work is published in the Journal of Business Research, Internet Research, International Journal of Tourism Research, Place Branding and Public Diplomacy, and Journal of Political Marketing amongst others.

Ahmet Bahadır Şimşek received his Ph.D. in 2019 from the Hacettepe University Department of Business Administration. He has been working as a lecturer/researcher at the Faculty of Health Sciences at Gumushane University since 2019. He gives lectures within the scope of operations research and conducts thesis consultancy in various undergraduate and graduate programs such as Health Management, Disaster Management and Business Administration. His research interest focuses on mathematical modeling applications in managerial decision-making and includes interdisciplinary collaboration.

Aybala Şimşek is an industrial engineer. Her PhD education is ongoing and she is also working as a researcher at Burdur Mehmet Akif Ersoy University. Her research interests are Optimisation, Operations Research, Multi-Criteria Decision Making, and Ergonomics and Human Factors Management.

Tuğçe Şimşek is an academic researcher and lecturer at Gümüşhane University, Department of Human Resources Management. She has demonstrated her commitment to scientific pursuits by completing her doctoral studies in the field of Management and Organization. Her research interests span a wide range of areas, including organizational behavior, human resources management, management and organization studies. Dr. Şimşek has also produced studies covering crisis management and leadership types. With her academic contributions, she has focused intensely on various aspects of management and human resources and shed light on the complexities of these fields. Dr. Şimşek is known for her efforts to combine her knowledge and experiences in various fields by adopting an interdisciplinary approach in her studies. Dr. Şimşek's work reflects her passion for advancing our understanding of management practices and their impact on organizations.

Amrik Singh is working as Professor and HOD in the School of Hotel Management and Tourism at Lovely Professional University, Punjab, India. He obtained his Ph.D. degree in Hotel Management from Kurukshetra University, Haryana, India. He has published 115 Scopus-indexed publications. He has published 12 patents, and 01 patent has been granted in the inter-disciplinary domain. Dr. Amrik Singh participated and acted as a resource person in various national and international conferences, seminars, research workshops, and industry talks. He has published 20 books with IGI Global Publication, Emerald Publication, Bentham Publication, Nova Publication etc., on trending areas such as Food waste, Artificial Intelligence, Mountain Tourism, Virtual tourism, Healthcare Tourism, Guest behavior in tourism and hospitality. His area of research interest are Accommodation management, sustainability, Green practices, Human Resource Management in Hospitality, Artificial Intelligence, AR VR in hospitality, Hotel pricing, Employee Disability, Work life balance, women empowerment etc. He is currently guiding 8 Ph.D. scholars, and 5 Ph.D. scholars have been awarded Ph.D.

Nevena Veselinović, PhD, is a Research Associate at the Institute for Information Technologies, University of Kragujevac, and the Institute of Economic Sciences, Belgrade. Her research expertise includes digital economics, econometric modelling, and empirical quantitative analysis. She is particularly interested in the economic effects of digital transformation, innovation, and applies advanced econometric techniques to address contemporary research and policy challenges.

Index

A

B

C

D

E

G

H

I

L

O

P

R

S

T

U